MAYA FEATURE CREATURE CREATIONS

MAYA FEATURE CREATURE CREATIONS

Todd Palamar

FIREWALL MEDIA
(An Imprint of Laxmi Publications Pvt.Ltd.)
An ISO 9001:2015 Company
BENGALURU • CHENNAI • GUWAHATI • HYDERABAD
KOCHI • KOLKATA • LUCKNOW • RANCHI
NEW DELHI

MAYA FEATURE CREATURE CREATIONS

Printed and bound in India
First Edition : 2008, *Reprint* :2012, 2014, 2018, 2020, 2024; *Edition* : 2026
FMA-2750-659- MAYA FEATURE CREAT CREAT
ISBN: 81-7008-353-2
Price: ₹ 659.00

PUBLISHED IN INDIA BY

FIREWALL MEDIA
(An Imprint of Laxmi Publications Pvt.Ltd.)
An ISO 9001:2015 Company
113, GOLDEN HOUSE, GURUDWARA ROAD, DARYAGANJ,
NEW DELHI - 110002, INDIA

Corporate Office : B-33, Sector-5, Noida,
Gautambuddha Nagar (U.P.) - 201 301, INDIA
Telephone : +91-120-44 46 900
www.laxmipublications.com
info@laxmipublications.com

Branches

✆	Bengaluru	080-26 75 69 30
✆	Chennai	044-24 34 47 26
✆	Guwahati	0361-254 36 69
✆	Hyderabad	040-27 55 53 83
✆	Kochi	0484-405 13 03
✆	Kolkata	033-40 04 77 79
✆	Lucknow	0522-430 36 13
✆	Ranchi	0651-224 24 64

C—R/026/08
Printed at: Ajit Printer, Delhi.

Contents

Acknowledgments xiii

Preface xv

PART I IN THE BEGINNING... 1

CHAPTER 1 GETTING READY 3

On a Personal Note 4

What You Will Get out of It 5

What You Need to Know 5

TUTORIAL: Smooth Bind 6

Overview 15

Conclusion 17

CHAPTER 2 PRE-PRODUCTION 19

The Pre-Production Process 20

- Brainstorming 20
- Story 21
- Budget 22
- Assets 22

Get Organized and Stay That Way 22

Three-Ring Binders 23
CG Project Management 24
The Default Pose 31
Conclusion 32

CHAPTER 3 BIOLOGY 101: IMITATING LIFE 33
Finding Common Ground 34
Layers of Anatomy 35
Skin 36
The Skeleton 38
Muscles and Tendons 40
Fat 43
Connective Tissue 45
Conclusion 46

PART II REFERENCE MATERIAL 49

CHAPTER 4 DESIGN AND CONQUER 51
The Physical Design 52
Creating a Working Design 53
Maquettes 54
Clays 58
Tools 61
Armatures 67
TUTORIAL: Building the Armature 69
Working Environments 96
Conclusion 99

CHAPTER 5 SCULPTING 101

Beginning Your Sculpture 102
TUTORIAL: The "Build Up" Method 103
Tips and Tricks 109
TUTORIAL: Rubber Stamps 109
TUTORIAL: Biomechanical Vein 111
Sculpting 112
TUTORIAL: Sculpting 113
Finishing Touches 130
TUTORIAL: Repairs 132
Conclusion 133

CHAPTER 6 SCANNED DATA 135

Raw Data 136
Creating NURBS Patches 137
TUTORIAL: Live Surfaces 138
TUTORIAL: SubD to NURBS 147
Conclusion 151

PART III MODELING FOR FILM 153

CHAPTER 7 THE TOOLS 155

Polygons 157
Polygon UVs 161
NURBS Surfaces 165
NURBS UVs 168
Subdivision Surfaces 168
Subdivision Surface UVs 170
Conclusion 171

CHAPTER 8 THE POLYGON PROXY 173

The Base Model 174
TUTORIAL: Modeling the Polygon Proxy 175
The Base UVs 185
TUTORIAL: Roughing the UVs 186
Conclusion 189

CHAPTER 9 MODELING THE SKELETON 191

The Skeleton Model 192
TUTORIAL: The Arm 193
TUTORIAL: The Skull 198
Conclusion 205

CHAPTER 10 MODELING THE SKIN 207

The Skin 208
TUTORIAL: The Nose 209
TUTORIAL: The Eye 216
TUTORIAL: The Hand 222
Conclusion 231

PART IV TEXTURING FOR FILM 233

CHAPTER 11 RESOLUTIONS 235

UV Placement 236
TUTORIAL: Mapping UVs 237
Output Resolution 243
TUTORIAL: Determining Resolution 245
Conclusion 249

CHAPTER 12	**MAKE IT REAL**	**251**
	Color Maps	252
	TUTORIAL: The Color Map	252
	TUTORIAL: Paint FX	260
	TUTORIAL: Painting Out Seams	265
	Diffuse Maps	267
	TUTORIAL: Diffuse	268
	Specular Maps	269
	Bump Maps	271
	TUTORIAL: Bump Map	272
	Displacement Maps	275
	TUTORIAL: Displacement Height	276
	TUTORIAL: Multiple Displacement Maps	283
	Conclusion	284
PART V	**ANATOMICALLY CORRECT**	**285**
CHAPTER 13	**SKELETONS**	**287**
	Skeletal Motion	288
	Building an IK System	290
	TUTORIAL: IK Arm	292
	Supination and Pronation	297
	TUTORIAL: Pronation	298
	Connecting Bones	302
	TUTORIAL: Rigid-Body Bones	302
	Conclusion	303

CHAPTER 14 MUSCLES AND TENDONS 305

Muscle and Tendon Motion 306
Modeling Muscles and Tendons 307
TUTORIAL: Building Muscles 307
TUTORIAL: Building Tendons 312
Simulating Muscle Motion 316
TUTORIAL: Bicep Muscle 1 317
TUTORIAL: Bicep Muscle 2 318
TUTORIAL: Bicep Muscle 3 322
Simulating Tendon Motion 326
TUTORIAL: Hand Tendon 326
Conclusion 329

CHAPTER 15 THE DYNAMICS OF LIFE 331

The Skin 332
TUTORIAL: Making Skin 333
Deforming the Skin with Anatomy 338
TUTORIAL: Adding Anatomy 338
Wrinkles 341
TUTORIAL: Wrinkles 343
Conclusion 345

CHAPTER 16 FAT 347

Creating Fat Deposits 348
TUTORIAL: Fat Deposit 348
Conclusion 351

PART VI CONCLUSION 355

CHAPTER 17 WRAPPING IT UP 357

Troubleshooting 358

Future Endeavors 364

APPENDIX ABOUT THE CD-ROM 365

System Requirements 366

INDEX 367

ACKNOWLEDGMENTS

I wish to thank Ramahan Faulk, an exceptional character artist, for his contribution to the Fire Monster's anatomy. He served nine years in the United States Navy as a jet engine mechanic and trouble-shooter for various aircraft. During his career, he developed a passion for 3D animation and has been honing his skill in all areas of character development for film and games. I would like to thank him for his time and contributions to this book. More of his work can be seen at his Web site, *http://www.nocturnalartistry.com.*

I want to thank Frank Fieser, an instructor at Full Sail Center for the Recording Arts, for his unbelievable work on the cover art. Frank is a compositor and designer. More of his work can be seen at *http://www.ffieser.com.*

I also wish to thank Chris Chaney and Aaron Faircloth for all of their support and assistance.

PREFACE

When I was growing up, there were almost no learning re sources at my disposal. Trial and error is extremely frustrating. Around the age of seven, I saw an interview with Ray Harryhausen on the making of *Clash of the Titans.* That was the first "making of" I'd seen. He told of making foam puppets from sculptures and placing ball-and-socket joints inside to give them the ability to be positioned one frame at a time. I turned to my father and said, "Dad I need some ball-and-socket joints." Years passed. My thirst for knowledge grew exponentially. I watched every movie and read every article that implied "How they did it." I picked up tidbits of information, nothing more than buzzwords really. Until one day, I found a magazine called *Cinemagic* at a collector's shop. This magazine didn't just describe the entire process of creating a special effect in one paragraph; it actually had step-by-step instructions with photos. More important, it told how to do it on a shoestring budget and where to buy the materials. My twelve-year-old world exploded. I was officially making movies. I bought back issue after back issue, and couldn't wait for a new issue to arrive. Suddenly, they stopped coming. Not even a year after finding it, the magazine had been cancelled.

So my quest began again. I scoured libraries, bookstores, and the *TV Guide* for anything that would talk about how to create special effects. Most of them were on entirely different subjects, but shared the same materials that I heard were being used in the effects industry. However, nothing proved more valuable than my own experiments. Working in my garage at every hour of the day, sometimes in place of going to school, I made short stop-motion movies. Trying to make each movie bigger than the last grew to be incredibly expensive. I wasn't very good and made many mistakes over and over. I constantly destroyed my equipment and accidentally burned down my sets. The knowledge that I had acquired was, as they say, only half the battle. The other half was the actual application. I did not have any practical sense of style.

When you train under someone or work for someone in a trade, you learn at a gradual, ordered rate. Not having anyone to learn from except a magazine, I would take everything that I had read and try to apply it before mastering any one skill. I never took the time to refine what I had learned. I was my only judge and teacher. Although I was extremely critical of my work, it didn't matter. It looked bad, and I didn't know how to fix it. I needed training. So I found one of the few schools around that actually taught special effects, California Institute of the Arts, and applied. It didn't take long for them to reject me.

Well as luck would have it, before I graduated high school, heading into some uncertain future, I got a job working on a low-budget movie called *Vampire Trailer Park*. This was it; nothing was going to stop me now. I was in charge of all of the special effects. I was learning a tremendous amount about the industry and spending a lot of my own money on research and development. I ferreted out work on more low-budget movies, but followed the same pattern—learning about the industry by spending all my money.

I began to feel as if I were in school, except there wasn't a teacher. This was the college I did not attend; except it was a lot harder. I wasn't allowed to make mistakes. Things needed to be right the first time. My knowledge was growing, but at a slow rate. I still had to find out the answers myself. Even when things worked out, I wasn't sure if I was doing it the right way.

Those years were very difficult—struggling to find work and scavenging for knowledge, the whole time thinking that there must be a better way to learn this stuff. Why were there no books on the subjects that I wanted to learn? I needed in-depth discussions, which not only told how to do something, but also explained why and with what. I needed to walk away with an understanding, not just a memorized process. To this day I cannot answer this question. I can only guess that it is because the people creating those special effects are too busy, under non-disclosure contracts, or their techniques are dependent upon proprietary equipment and software. In today's world, we are inundated with information; knowledge is at our fingertips. We can learn anything from a new language to how to produce cold fusion. But when it comes down to learning how a special effect is generated, it is still a well-guarded secret. There are countless books that will show you all the basics you can stand, but most are nothing more than a reprint of the manual that comes with the software. What we really need is a publication, like the defunct *Cinemagic* magazine, which will walk us through the entire process of creating a special effect in a way that is feasible for most of us to do.

Now that I am older and wiser, I have come to grips with my self-taught ways and have learned that the majority of my practices were indeed the correct way of doing things. Knowing this has built up my confidence, and now things are much easier for me. Problems can be solved. I now know where to look for the answers to my questions and how to apply the results efficiently and effectively. It took me twenty-one years to get to this point.

I am writing this book to provide you with what I never had: a step-by-step instruction manual on how to solve problems, answer your questions, and give you the knowledge to make your visions come true. This book is filled with my own experiences and knowledge. It is up to you what to do with this information. The intent is for you to learn from my mistakes and benefit from my accomplishments.

PART

I

IN THE BEGINNING...

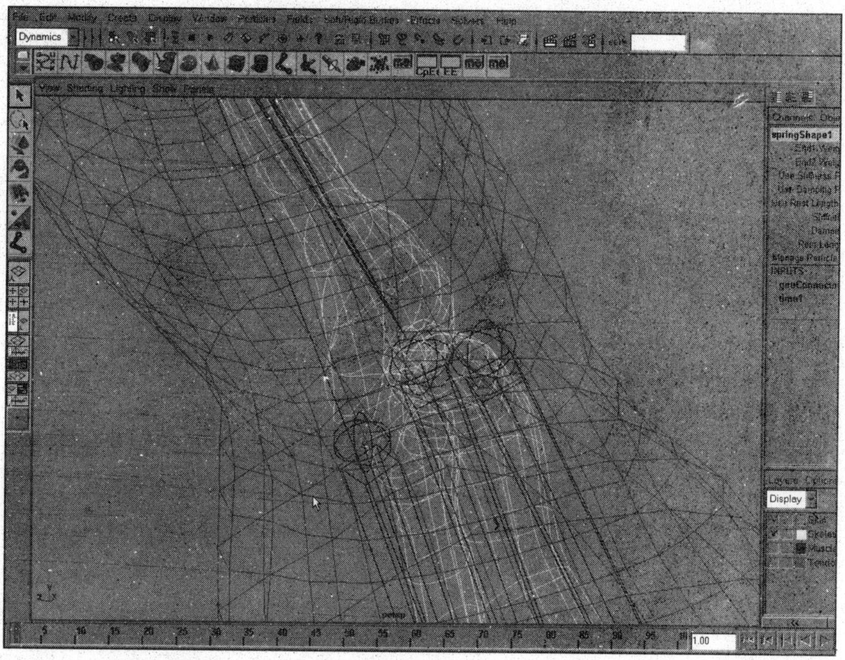

CHAPTER

1 GETTING READY

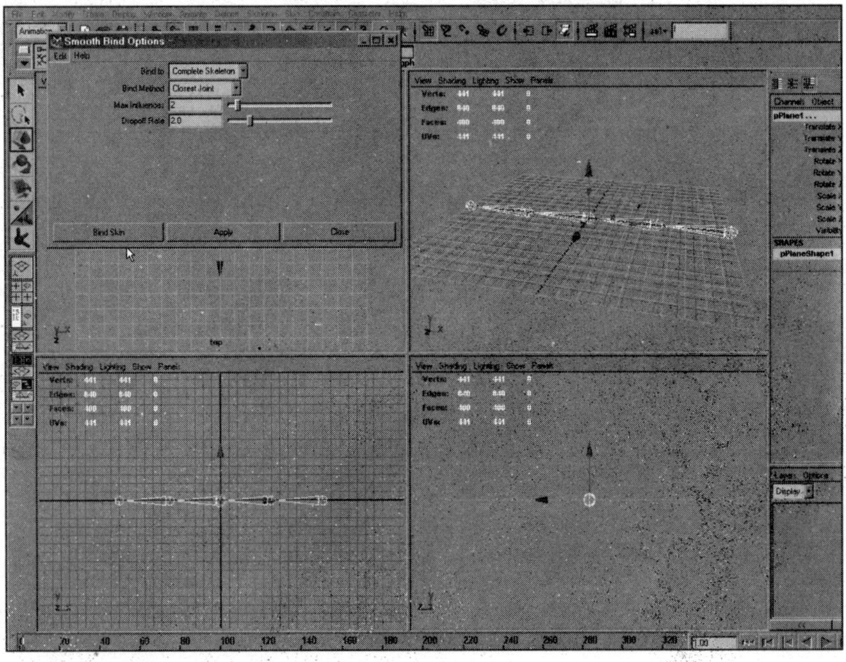

Preparing for what is to come is like answering the unanswerable. What do I need? Am I missing something? You rush out the door only to find out later that you are not ready. There is no denying it, all of us have been through it, and we will go through it again. It is impossible to know everything, let alone be prepared for it. However, the more we can learn, the better. It all boils down to the saying, "Knowing is half the battle." It affects us on a daily basis. Knowledge is power.

On a Personal Note

I can remember sitting down in the theater ready to watch *Jurassic Park* for the first time, thinking about my next stop-motion animation project. It was going to be great because I was going to use my Amiga 500 computer to polish certain scenes. After the movie ended, my would-be career as a stop-motion animator ended. At that point I realized the irony of *Jurassic Park.* It was proposed in the movie that the dinosaurs did not die out and become extinct. Instead they evolved and adapted to the growing changes. Whether it was meant to be, this was a powerful message I could not ignore. The next day I began teaching myself how to be a computer animator.

Jurassic Park inspired me to change my life. I hope this book may inspire some to adapt to the growing changes of this industry. Reexamine your skills and partake of new ones to achieve better results. It is easy to fall into an artistic slump, to become complacent with the work you are doing. With technology moving rapidly, we're starting to see a convergence of tools and industries. Games are becoming movies. Animators are becoming programmers. The gap between real-time and photo-realistic rendering is narrowing. Things once considered valuable only to animators are now as equally valuable to modelers. Take time to relearn what you have already learned and explore other tools disassociated with your discipline.

Another purpose for writing this book is that nothing excites me more than seeing a well-animated character. In the past few years, I think I have been excited twice. We are seeing the same animation over and over. The characters and creatures seem to be growing stiffer. Complicated animation sequences are cut due to budget constraints. Movies are being made with many boring, rigid creatures in place of a great, active one. Let's go back and refine what we have learned instead of rushing off to the next level. We seem to have forgotten that CG characters are actors, too. Let's allow them to act.

What You Will Get out of It

Upon completing this book, you will walk away with a character sculpted in clay and modeled with subdivision surfaces using Maya by Alias/Wavefront. At the heart of this book we will establish a method for building anatomy-based, photo-realistic computer-generated characters with physics-driven skin. The step-by-step instructions and explanations will provide you with a solid method that will yield incredible results. In addition, you will gain a powerful understanding of subdivision surfaces.

What You Need to Know

Before beginning this book you need to have a solid understanding of Maya. The book involves polygons, NURBS, subdivision surfaces, inverse kinematics, polygonal texturing, and in-depth dynamic simulations. A basic understanding and familiarity with the terms associated with these tools is required. In addition to a well-rounded comprehension of Maya, it is advised that you possess some traditional art skills, such as drawing or sculpting. Every aspect of building a creature for a film environment, from design to setting up a physics-driven skin, is covered in this book. And just so you know, learning these aspects can be quite time-consuming.

To appreciate physics-driven skin, it helps to understand today's methods of skinning characters. These methods bind vertices directly to joints or geometry, which prohibits the skinned surface from moving independently of any underlying geometry. It also locks the skinned vertices to specific objects, and this connection forces the skin to move exactly as the object influencing it. Whether it is a skeleton or an influencing piece of geometry, the results are the same.

Let's create a quick example of a smooth-bound object.

TUTORIAL

SMOOTH BIND

Step 1: From the Create pull-down menu, open the Plane settings from Polygon Primitives as shown in Figure 1.1. Change the divisions to 20 and 20.

Step 2: Switch to the Animation module. From the Skeleton pull-down menu select the Joint tool. Draw four joints in the side view the length of the plane as shown in Figure 1.2. You might need to change the joint display size depending on your default settings.

Step 3: Select the joint chain and plane. From the Skinning pull-down menu, open the Smooth Bind attributes. Change the number of joints to 2 and the distance to 2 as shown in Figure 1.3. Skin the plane to the joints.

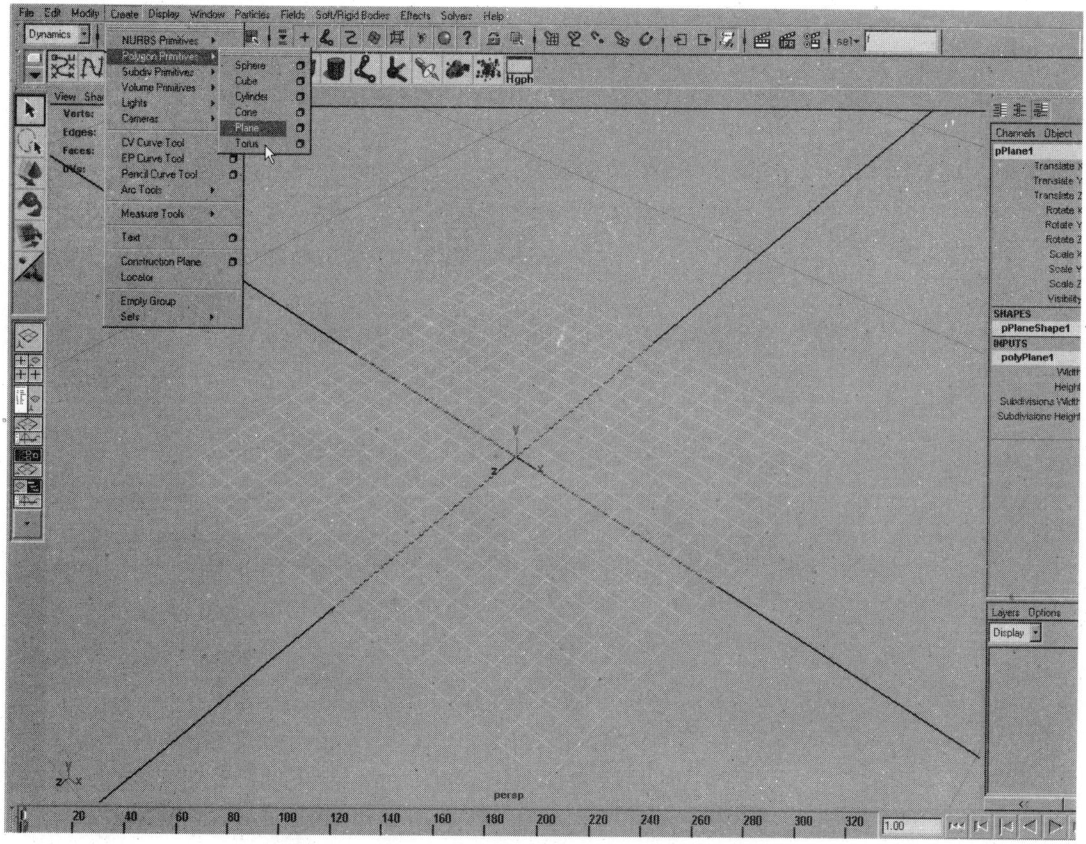

FIGURE 1.1 Create a plane with 20 divisions in the U and the V.

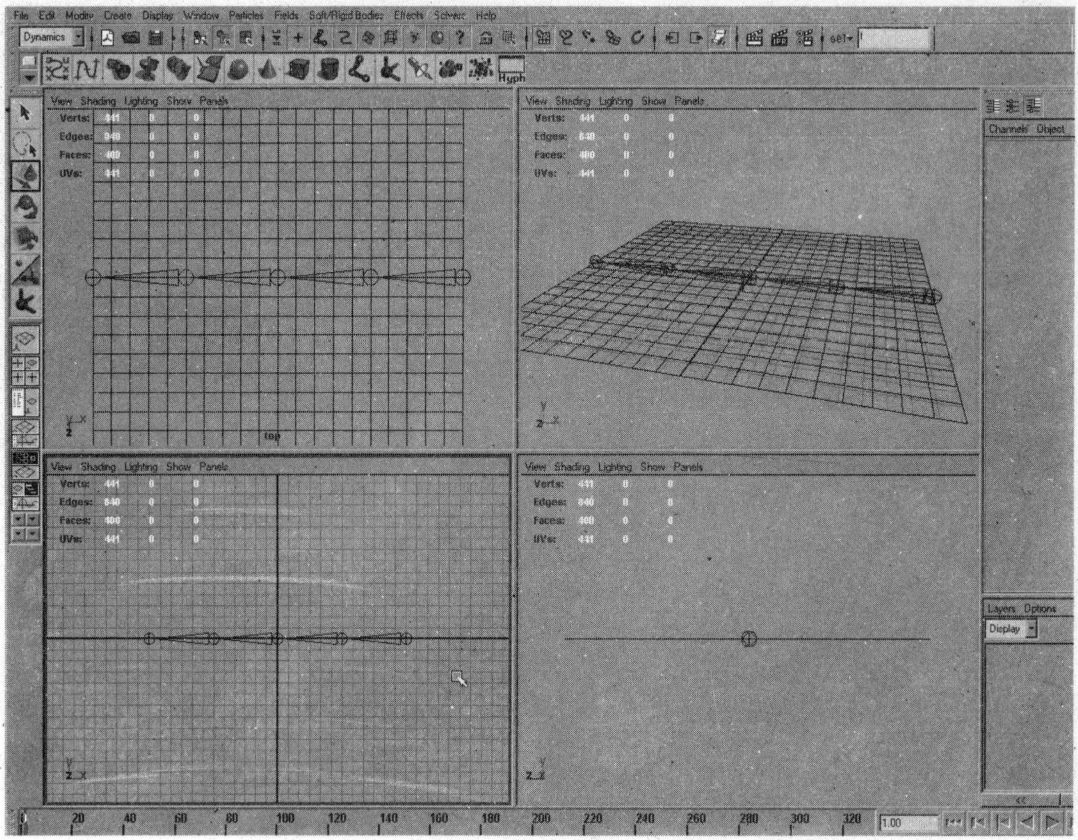

FIGURE 1.2 Draw four skeletal joints.

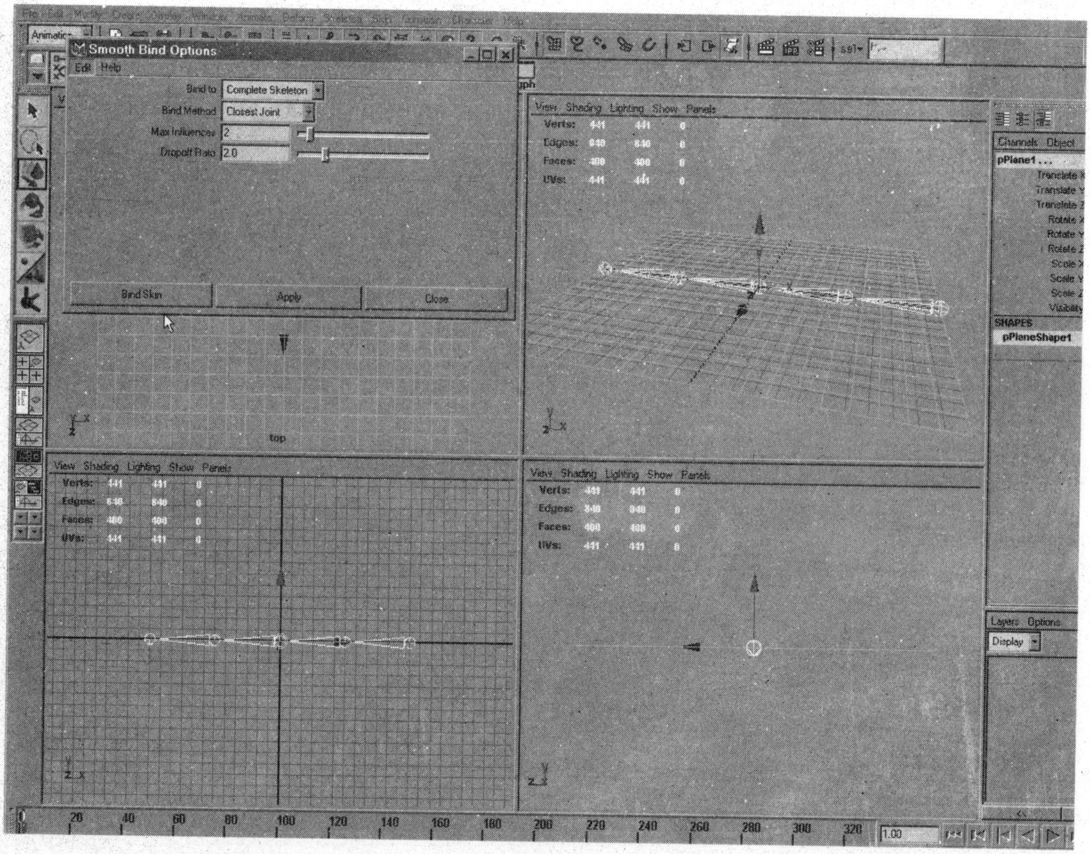

FIGURE 1.3 Change the smooth bind settings and skin the geometry.

Step 4: From the Create pull-down menu make a default cylinder from Polygon Primitives. Rotate the cylinder so it is parallel to the plane. Scale the cylinder to the length of the plane and change its circumference to roughly one-tenth of the plane. Position the cylinder slightly under the plane as shown in Figure 1.4.

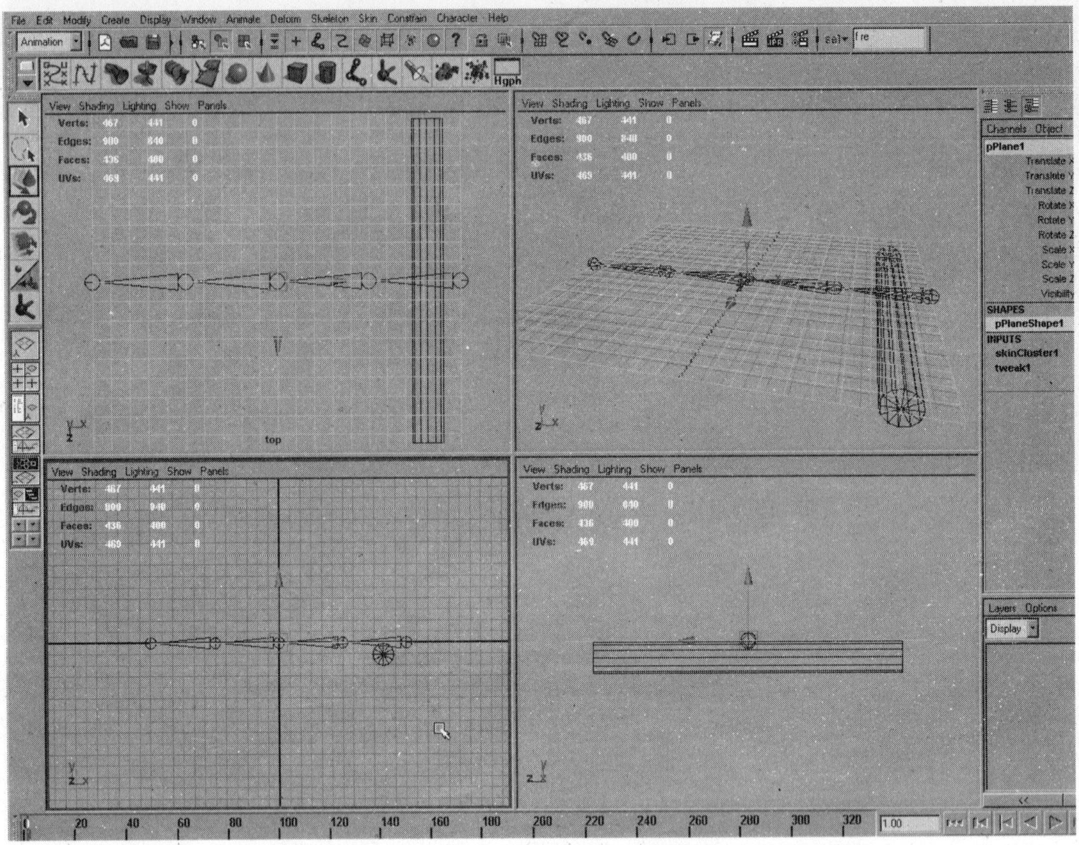

FIGURE 1.4 Create a cylinder and reshape it to fit under the plane.

Step 5: Select the cylinder and then the plane. From the Skin pull-down menu choose Edit Smooth Skin, Add Influence. Figure 1.5 shows the action.

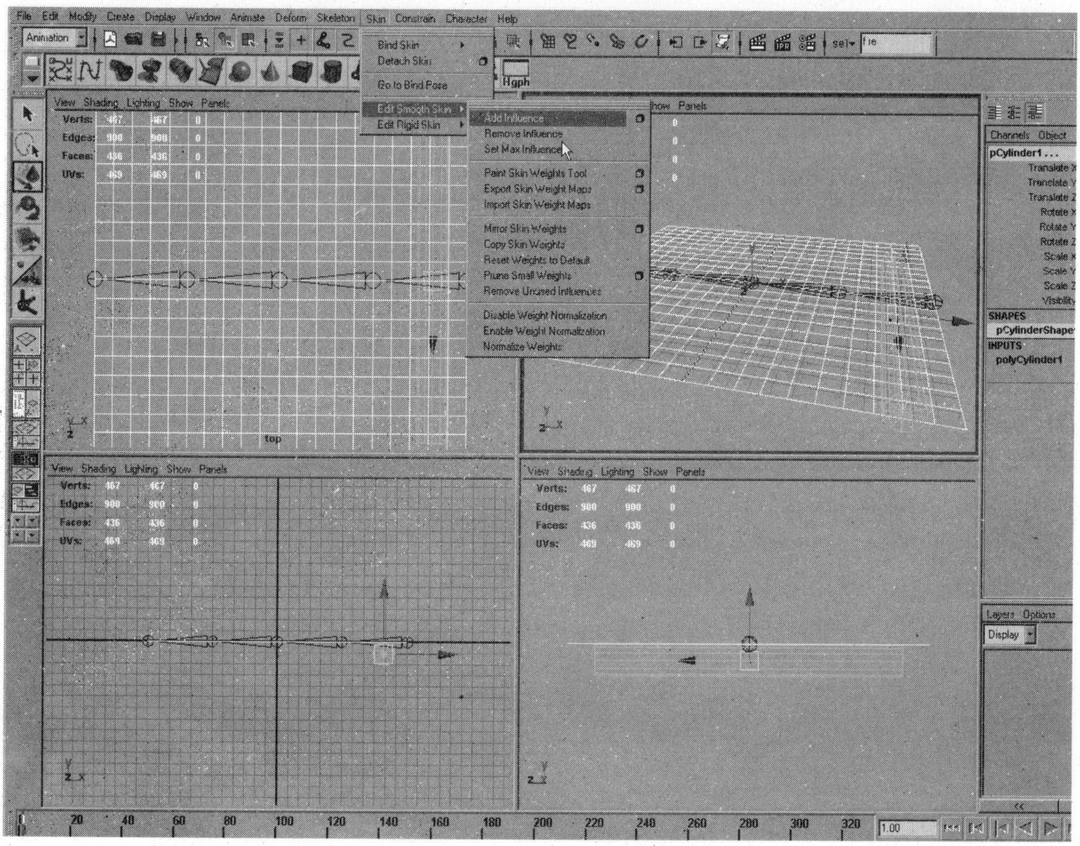

FIGURE 1.5 Make the cylinder an influence object of the plane.

Step 6: Select the cylinder and set a keyframe at frame 0. Move the time slider to frame 30. Translate the cylinder 2 units in the positive Y as shown in Figure 1.6. Set another keyframe for the cylinder.

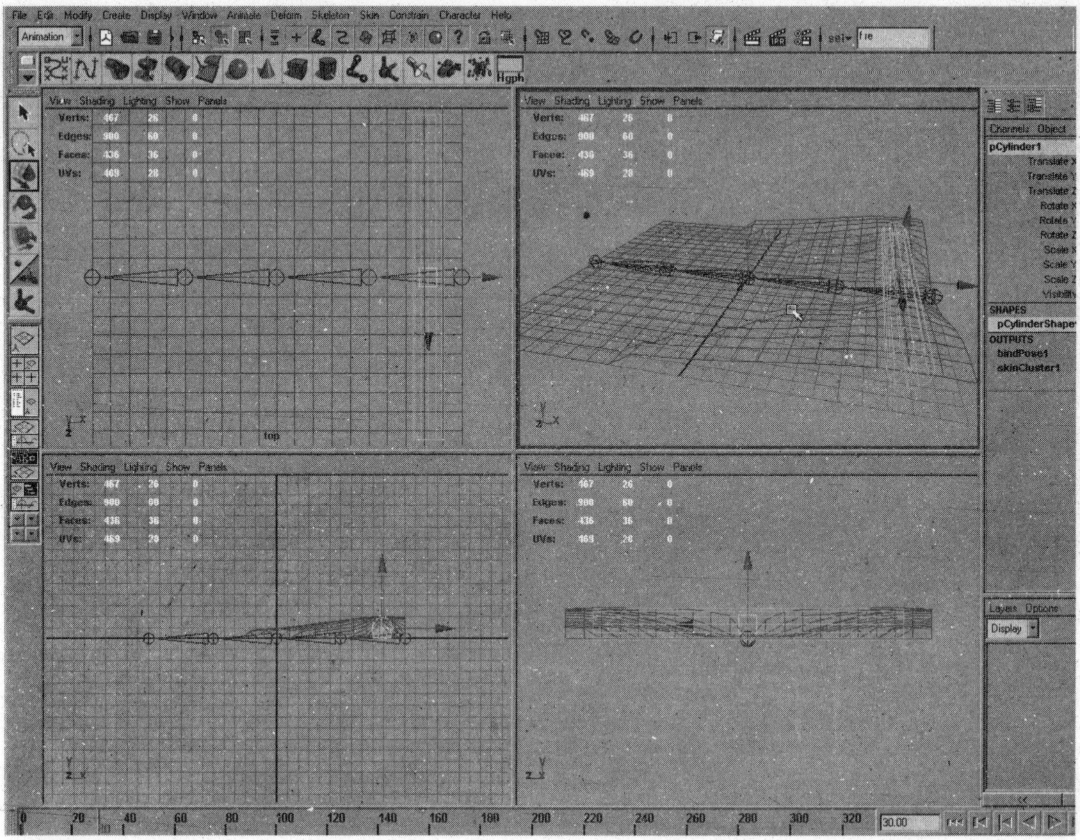

FIGURE 1.6 After setting a keyframe at frame 0, translate the cylinder in the Y and set another keyframe.

Step 7: Move the time slider to frame 90. Translate the cylinder in the negative X as shown in Figure 1.7. Set another keyframe.

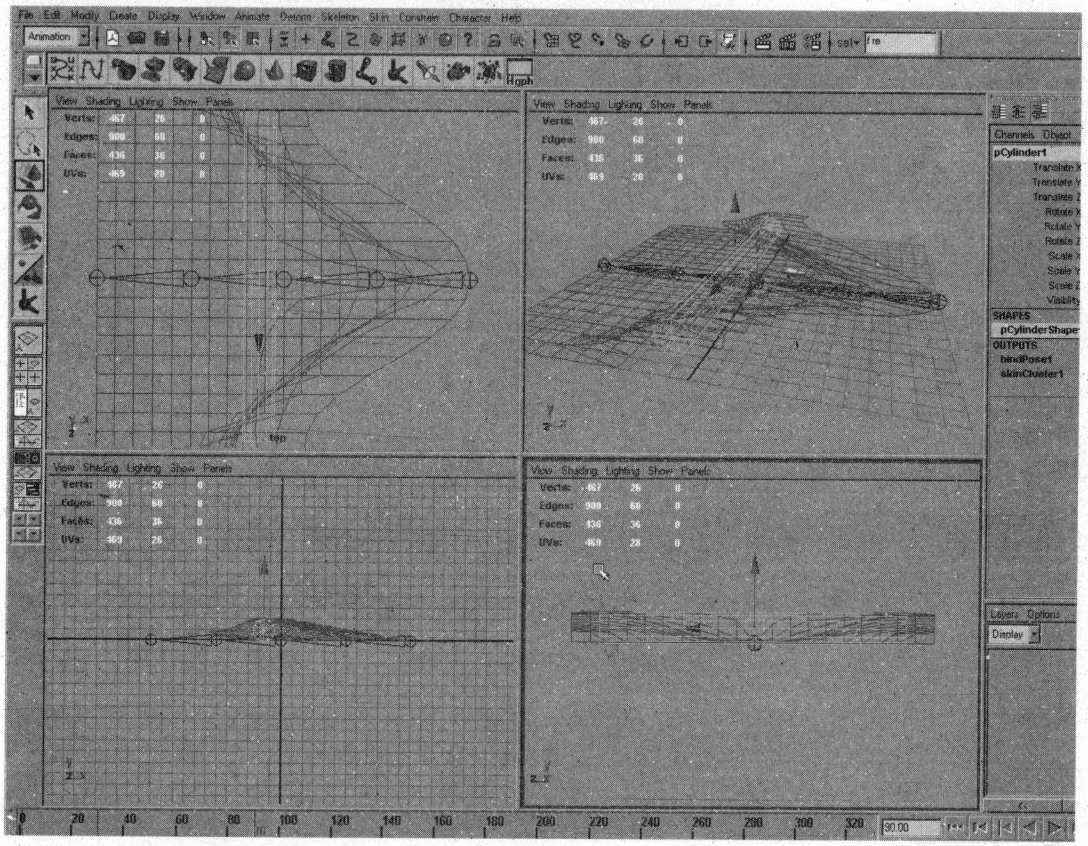

FIGURE 1.7 Translate the cylinder in the X and set another key at frame 90.

FIGURE 1.8 This is a single frame from the animation. Notice how the geometry pulls.

Step 8: Move the time slider to 0. Play back the result of the animation. Figure 1.8 shows the problem with binding.

ON THE CD

Located on the CD-ROM you will also find an animation demonstrating the above procedure. Open the Chapter 1 folder, and play the file named "Smooth Bind." Study your own hand and compare it to the results of the animation. Pretend the plane is the top of your hand and the cylinder a tendon underneath. Real skin does not react in this manner. The outcome is drastically different and unusable.

With a physics-driven skin, the binding procedure is merely a reference. The skin or surface geometry is allowed to move independently of the bind. Influencing objects such as muscle and bone are used to push surface geometry. The bind acts as a goal to which the skin returns. This also allows objects to move under the skin as shown in Figure 1.9.

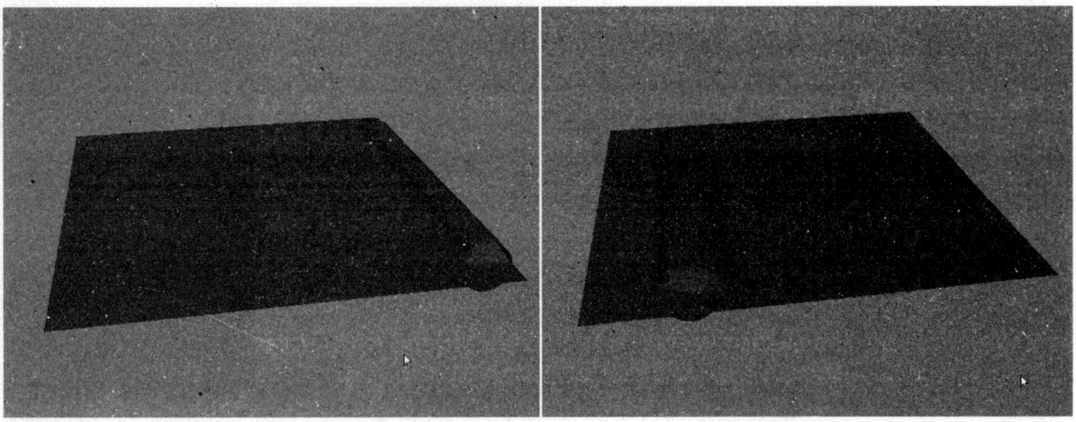

FIGURE 1.9 This is the first and last frame of animation using a physics-driven skin.

ON THE CD

Play the animation named "Physics Skin" in the Chapter 1 folder. This animation is an example of the physics-driven skin. Compare this animation to your hand and to the bound-skin example.

OVERVIEW

Building a computer-generated character is a lengthy process whether it is for film, television, or games. Technology has made incredible advances automating a lot of the steps; however, automation is expensive and out of reach for most individuals and small companies. The process described in this book is affor able and achievable. The following provides an overview of the steps used to build the film-quality creature described in this book.

Step 1: Draw a two-dimensional rough draft of the character.

Step 2: Build a three-dimensional physical model for reference. To accomplish this, we will sculpt a prototype in clay and build a poseable version using foam and rubber.

Step 3: Model the character using Maya.

Step 4: Apply color and texture maps to give the model a finished look.

Step 5: Build the internal anatomy of the creature in the computer.

Step 6: Establish a relationship between the anatomy and the model of the creature.

This book is designed to allow you to build your own character. The tutorials are used to introduce concepts, practices, and theories. Upon completing them, apply what you have learned to your own creations. Most of the tutorials have an associated Maya scene file that is already set up, enabling you to jump right in. Experiment with these scene files beyond the tutorial explanations until you have a strong grasp of the material introduced, and feel free to test new methods and improve upon the procedures. Take this knowledge and expand on it.

Expect a character to take months to complete. Each stage is time consuming and requires work and resources outside of the computer. The more homework and studying done, the better your creatures will turn out. Remember, building a character is a linear process, and each stage must be complete before moving on to the next. Take the time to get your best results.

CONCLUSION

Learning software packages has become an enormous undertaking. Many developers even offer certified training for their products because of the wide range of features they have included in the various versions of their products. As the packages get bigger so does the learning curve, and Maya is no exception. The amazing power of Maya is in its open architecture. This is not the ability to write your own plug-ins, albeit an awesome feature in itself. Instead it's the boundless interaction between tools. Virtually every tool and function can be layered on top of another, enabling you to get different results based upon the order. This allows you to perform complex operations without having to write proprietary scripts. This does not eliminate the need for scripting, but it does provide alternatives in some cases. Often special proprietary tools must be written to achieve the effect desired, but for most of us, this isn't an option. In general, artists stay away from code and scripting. However, as software becomes more robust, computers faster, and expectations greater, artists are turning to simpler integrated software languages to make models bigger, better, and faster. The knowledge and creation of these specialized tools is a tremendous asset to any artist's repertoire. Perhaps even more valuable, though, is a solid understanding of the tools at our disposal.

It can take years to fully grasp every function of a 3D package. The best approach is to start with a single aspect, such as modeling. Learn all the tools inside and out before moving on. When it comes to creating an animated character for film, we're now able to maximize the software's potential. The more we know about particular tools and features, the greater our characters become. The variety of tools discussed in this book was chosen for the practicality and the benefit of the project, not for the sake of demonstration. Each of these tools was considered carefully to achieve the quickest and best-looking results.

CHAPTER

2 PRE-PRODUCTION

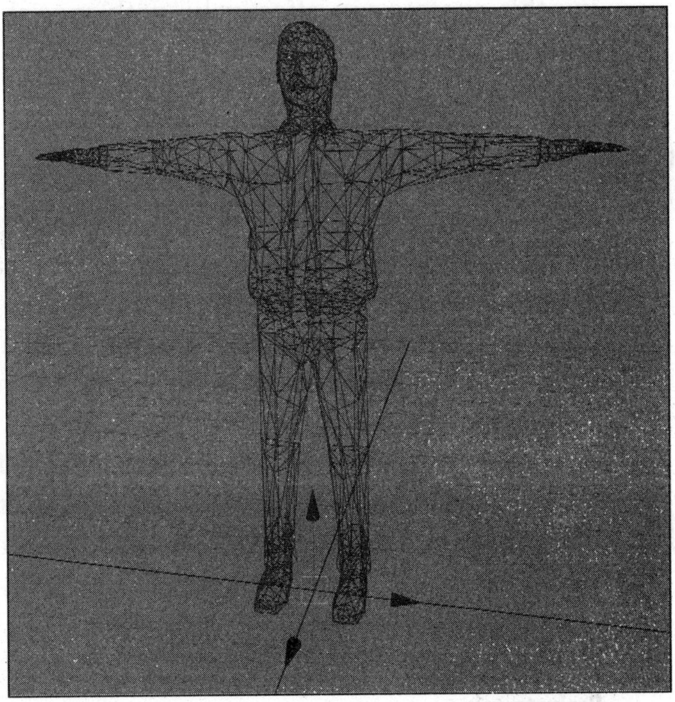

Planning is the most important step in any production. Too many movies come out with underdeveloped, shallow characters that feel rushed because of poor pre-production. A good rule of thumb to use is, for every week of production, plan on two weeks of pre-production.

Chapter 1 established the goal of creating a photo-realistic, film-quality model and discussed the steps needed to accomplish this. Everything prior to actually animating the creature is considered pre-production. In this chapter, we will look at ways of making this process run effectively, with special attention given to organization.

The Pre-Production Process

Pre-production begins the moment you conceive an idea. This complicated process can be simplified to four stages. The first stage is brainstorming; write down every thought, no matter how minute, to develop the story. A definite beginning, middle, and end are necessary in order to write the second stage, the story. Once these are done, the third stage, budget, can be addressed. Available resources are the most influencing factors in planning the budget. The last stage is creating assets where you execute portions of the budget to build models and sets. Each of these phases should be treated with equal importance. They all shape the outcome of the production.

Brainstorming

The first phase in any production is to decide what the production is about. What is the plot? Who are the characters? Where is it set? There are many different ways to come up with these ideas, and no one set formula works for everyone. For instance, ideas usually come to me in the form of a scene. Just one bit of action or dialogue is all that is needed for an idea for a whole movie to evolve.

From there, the plot begins to form and characters are born. Once the plot is cohesive, it is time to work on character development. Empowering the characters to move the story along is a challenging task and is often done in a backward process. Begin by visualizing them in action, then decide what their history is and how it will influence their decisions today.

Once you have a solid character, the ideas just seem to keep flowing. This is the time to grab a notepad and keep track of your ideas wherever you go. Keep paper and plenty of Post-it Notes handy; you never know when you will have another good idea. Even though some of the notes you take might seem irrelevant at the time, they might come into play in unexpected ways down the road.

Story

You can't develop a character without a story or a story without a character. Their development happens simultaneously through words, actions, and emotions. The character's features are used to help tell the past, present, and future.

The story phase is the time to decide whether it is based in reality or fantasy. This isn't referring specifically to a time or place but to the laws that govern the world. A reality-based production uses the properties of the real world. You must apply the laws of physics and principles of mathematics to control and influence the environment and characters. This doesn't mean there can't be flying dragons or aliens from another planet. It means that they will be affected by the same scientific truths we understand today. This is the science in science fiction; it is fiction based on real-world science. Fantasy-based stories impose the suspension of disbelief, or asking us to believe in something because we're told to. There are no facts to back it up; it is merely stated, or implied, as truth.

Out of the story phase come the script, screenplay, and storyboards. The script defines the dialog and emotions of the characters, the screenplay incorporates the action, and the storyboards illustrate the screenplay.

Budget

The budget is the business side of filmmaking, and just like any business, there are three influencing factors: cost, quality, and time. Each plays a vital role in the development of a story. They determine how the story will be told and if it will be told at all. Realistically, you can never have all three. In most cases, businesses are lucky to get two. Delivering the highest quality requires more money. If you don't have a lot of money, it will take more time. If you don't have a lot of time, you are going to have poor quality, but if you are willing to sacrifice more time for the same amount of money, you can improve the quality.

Time is the most important aspect. Creating film-quality CG characters is extremely time consuming. Budget your time well. Allow for errors and adequate research and development. Any shortcuts you make here will end up costing you in the long run.

Assets

With money, time, and resources locked down, it's time to start creating the elements needed to make the production. These assets include characters, props, environments, and special effects. When completed, you're ready to move into production and begin filming these elements.

GET ORGANIZED AND STAY THAT WAY

Organization is a state of mind; if you feel like you know where everything is, you're organized. The problem arises when someone else tries to work within the environment that you have created. When working with teams, it is critical to be truly organized and not just in your own mind.

It can be difficult, even painful, to arrange techniques, notes, and assets in a fashion that allows you and others to access the material easily, but it is essential to get your materials organized, so everything is clear when it is time to finalize the project. After finishing a job, you want nothing more than to put it behind you and never look back. This is why "housekeeping" must be a part of the production process. This entails sifting through your notes, computer directories, and software scene files to remove the things that didn't work out or are no longer necessary. When the housekeeping is done, the job is done. After doing this a couple of times, it will become part of your routine and make all of your tasks easier to manage.

The first half of housekeeping is to organize the paperwork. Even though most of the creation process is done on the computer, there is often a long paper trail. Whether you have notes to yourself, reminders, and major discoveries, or a journal of your progress, these pieces of paper add up and are important to keep for future reference.

The second half is to clean the computer. Starting with the highest directories, work your way down to the smallest scene file and move, delete, and rename as you go. It is important to preserve your work in an organized fashion for future projects or posterity.

Three-Ring Binders

Getting focused and organized from the start allows more time for creativity and idea development. To accommodate the paper monster, all of the information can be kept in a three-ring project binder. Each project should have its own binder to keep it organized throughout the entire process. The binders that have pockets and sleeves on the inside are really good for these purposes. This way CD-ROMs and floppies can be stored with the written materials. Numbered dividers between sections and a table of contents that are updated constantly keep everything in one place, in one format. For example, for a new story idea there would be numbered tabs for the Script, Screenplay, Notes, Conventions, Schedule, and Budget. The paperwork and notes for each of these components gets filed in the right section immediately, and the more important material might have sub tabs or highlighted pages. (See Figure 2.1.)

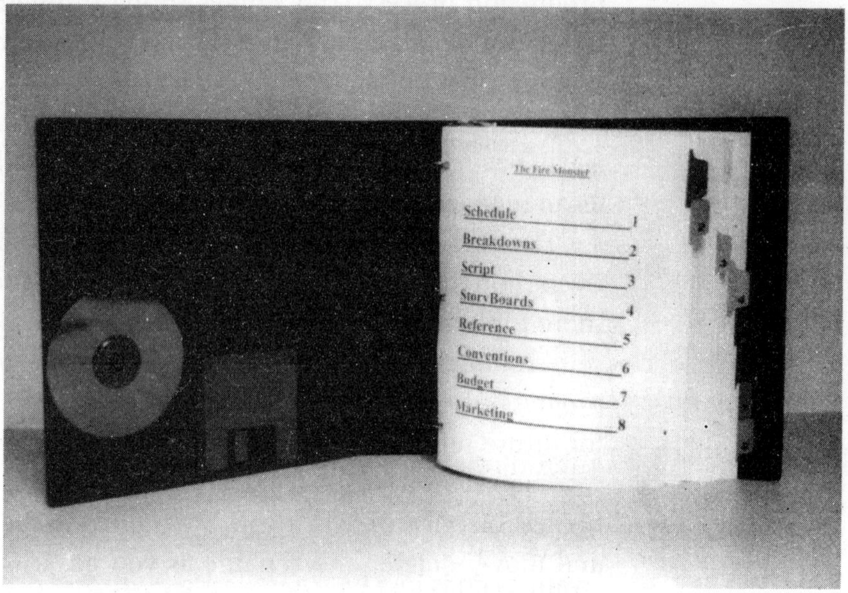

FIGURE 2.1 Organization of a three-ring binder with tabs.

To keep things as simplistic as possible, keep parallel folders or directories on the computer. Simply create a directory with the same name as the binder and include a directory for each item listed in the table of contents. This way the information is easy to find at all times for everyone involved. Once the directories have been established, the files or assets can be structured.

CG Project Management

One of the less-appreciated aspects of housekeeping is managing assets. Specifically, the elements built inside software packages. During the CG process, these elements are built in separate scene files, sometimes even in separate pieces of software. Whether you are supervising a team or a single artist, there are five areas that should always be established in advance to help bring all of the components together seamlessly.

Naming Conventions

The road to true organization is through proper naming. Naming conventions can effectively save hours, even days, on a project. Without them, files might be overwritten or deleted. Names reduce overall confusion and keep everyone on the team speaking the same language. Clear, well thought out names eliminate the need to open files to determine what they are. Conventions also minimize searching through large directories and remove any conflicts that the software could have with duplicate names.

At the beginning of every project, the entire team needs to establish rules for naming all assets including directories and renders. The same rule applies even if you are working alone. Simplicity is the key to any good naming convention. The last thing that you want to do is invent an abstract convention using terms that do not describe the file. The name should reflect exactly what is contained in it, which is relevant to the project. For instance, you wouldn't name a large palm tree "XValpha3." Although the letters and numbers may signify exactly what it is, through deciphering a code, it forces the artist to learn a new language. There is no good reason to do this. In addition, do not leave the software-assigned name to an object. This is an act of laziness and does not describe what the object is in accordance to the production.

Let's take a look at some rules to follow for proper naming. The following example involves applying rules to the model of a bear. It is one of eight bears modeled, ranging in type and color, so we need to be specific.

Name objects for what they are.

If you create a primitive sphere, the software will automatically name it "NurbsSphere1." Unless you are doing a tutorial on creating

CASE STUDY

After skinning a character inside Maya, I started to weight the vertices. Everything was working fine until I got to a section of the arm. Suddenly, the weights could not be altered. I backtracked to make sure the history was deleted before skinning, and checked to see that the Hold feature was off for all of my influences. None of this fixed the problem. Then I noticed it, two joints that were named the exact same thing. When this happens, the software doesn't know which object is really influencing the vertices, so it locks them both. The names given to nodes are the only names the software has to go by, so any misspellings or duplicates will confuse the user and the software. Be careful with your naming.

a NURBS sphere, this name is insufficient in describing what the object actually is. Name things for what they are and use only common terms vital to the classification of your data.

The necessary information about the bear is that it is brown in color and it is a grizzly. Therefore, a suitable name could be brown grizzly bear.

No spaces in names.

This can be a problem when crossing platforms from Windows to Unix, as Unix will not recognize names with spaces unless you force it to do so. This entails extra work; usually it is just a matter of another keystroke or two, but nevertheless, it's extra work. It also extends the name, however, without spaces it is more difficult to read: browngrizzlybear.

No special characters.

This rule is done for us most of the time. Special characters include symbols such as "@#$%&*/." Software has become smart enough to eliminate these characters automatically. The one exception to this rule is the use of the underscore "_": brown_grizzly_bear.

Use capital letters to separate words.

This is not necessary, but it can help in making your names easier to read and shorter. Instead of using the underscore to separate words, we can move them together and use a capital letter: "BrownGrizzlyBear." Capital letters can also be used to specify directories.

No names longer than twelve characters.

Your limit does not have to be twelve characters; the point is you have a limit. Making names that scroll off the screen doesn't help anyone. Some software still requires 8.3 formats. This states that you have eight characters in your name and a three-character extension such as tga or tif. In order to get the names down to a reasonable amount that can be read easily, we can omit vowels and double consonants: "BrwnGrzlyBr." This also prevents anyone on the team from inventing different abbreviations.

Place adjectives last.

This might seem awkward and harder to read, but it makes finding multiple files of the same type easier. For example, let's say that it is your first day on the job and you are told to texture map all of the trees. There are twenty different varieties of CG trees mixed in with bushes, plants, and flowers all in one model bank. Software is smart enough to sort files several different ways, but it can't separate them by description. You could waste valuable time sifting through this long list of models trying to decipher the trees from the bushes. However, if the adjectives were placed last and everything were properly named, you could list the models out alphabetically, and simply search for Tree or Tr: "BrBrwnGrzly."

This might seem like a lot of rules for keeping it simple, but they are basic enough not to cause confusion. The other advantage is that anyone new to the project can read these file names with little to no explanation. What's even better is it will preserve your assets for years to come.

Scale

What's the big deal? Why does it matter? Scale is monumentally important, for without it, our models are not photo-realistic. It is the one way we have to insure accuracy. When the scale is ignored, or incorrectly set, we have no way to gauge the precision of our work. This is a tremendous help when copying reference material. On a team project, where there are several modelers, if a scale is not set, you will end up with a wide range of sizes. A problem like this may seem trivial at first, but when you have a character in one scale and an environment in another, the problem grows exponentially. After your character is skinned, you cannot change its scale properly without having to redo expressions and some deformers. Even then your character may not scale uniformly due to the construction of its hierarchy. If you scale the environment, you will lose your lighting and camera setup. Scale is not an eight-hour conversation. It merely entails stating one unit is equal to another unit. Be cautious about making a scene too large. In virtual space, size really doesn't matter. However, all of your parameters will be a reflection of the scale, possibly exceeding attribute and tool limitations.

Build scenes at zero.

At the center of Cartesian space, our XYZ coordinates read zero. We build all of our models on top of the XZ-plane to keep them above our software grid, where the ground plane usually resides. Models should be built symmetrically in the Y-plane. This does not mean your model must be perfectly symmetrical down to the CV or vertex. What it means is that your models are symmetrically in pose and position so that they are well balanced. (See Figure 2.2.)

Delete unused elements.

This is part of the housekeeping process. Go through scene files at every development stage and remove anything not relevant to the scene. This may sound simple enough but can, in fact, be cumber-

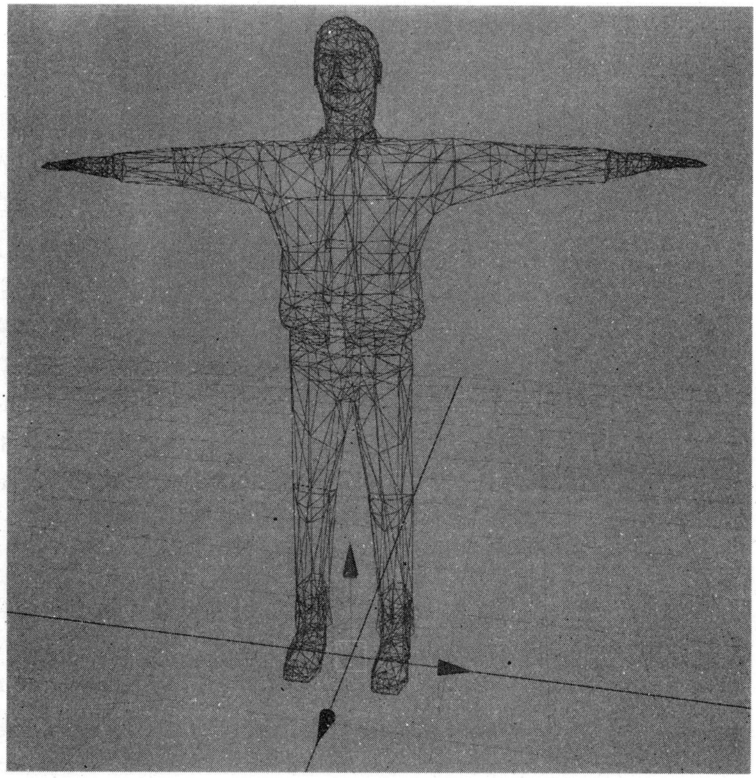

FIGURE 2.2 Model built at zero on top of the XZ-plane.

some. The modeling and texturing phases often require tools that generate locators, nodes, and curves. These elements can get lost if forgotten. They might lie buried in a hierarchy and show up only as "underworld" nodes. In order to keep our geometry clean, we must go back, find these elements, and delete them. If they are allowed to stay, they can prohibit your character from animating properly and significantly reduce playback speeds. The golden rule is, if you don't know why or what it is, delete it. Sometimes this might cause your model to explode. At that point, learn why it is there. CG artists are like ship captains; they must know every nook and cranny of their ship. If you don't know why something is there or what it does, find out!

CASE STUDY

A few years back, I was hired to work on a video game for the PlayStation. One of my first tasks was to fix and finish texture mapping several vehicles for the game. I say fix because they were having problems seeing the models of vehicles when they exported to the console. Basically, they were not showing up. So, I went through each of the models, checking to make sure all of the transforms were zeroed out and the models were located in the center of the world. I found a few discrepancies, but nothing too severe. I re-exported a model into the game engine, but again nothing was there. Or nothing was wrong. This was a little too weird.

I took it upon myself to export a different model that I had seen work before. The hope was if I could export a model that worked, I could compare it against the vehicle models and find where the error was. So, I exported a large piece of terrain. It showed up in the game engine without a hitch. I took the terrain and a vehicle and loaded them both into the 3D software. I found that the two objects were of a different scale. Not only were they proportionally incorrect, but also the standard in which they were measured was incorrect, i.e., meters to feet.

With this knowledge I went back to the game engine to look for my vehicle. I pulled the camera back to reveal my large chunk of terrain was actually sitting on the dashboard of the car. At this point I went to my supervisor and asked what scale we were using to build all of the models. The answer made everything clear; there was no scale. Every model up to this point had been haphazardly thrown together, and not just by one artist but several. This locked in the demise of the project. No communication had taken place between the programmers and artists to determine how large models should be built.

I knew the programmers must have a scale because it is in their nature to run the numbers. It's impossible to calculate distance traveled when you don't have any concept of what distance is. I got the scale, ran the numbers, and redid all of the vehicles. Not that big a deal, you say? Well, actual time spent from the point of receiving the problem to correcting all of the models was five days. Let alone the time somebody else spent trying to solve this problem before I got there. Five days to fix a problem that would have been prevented in five minutes if a scale had been established.

Use project directories.

Most software packages create project directories so they can automatically find and save necessary files to a scene. Effectively using these directories can be a big time-saver. Maya allows you to name these directories anything you want. This is important if you are moving models around or uprooting the project hierarchy. To keep your files mobile, it is necessary to use relative paths as opposed to absolute paths. These refer to the location of a file on your system or media (e.g., hard drive, CD-ROM, Zip disk).

Absolute paths—The location of a file based upon the root of a file system.

D:\maya\projects\default\sourceimages\

Relative paths—The location of a file based solely on its position within a project hierarchy.

sourceimages\

If you move files with absolute paths, you will have to reassign their locations inside Maya. Relative paths are used automatically if the data is in the current project directory.

THE DEFAULT POSE

The created physical posture of our creature is the default pose. Maya refers to this as the "bind pose." Basically the same, the bind pose refers to the position in which the creature was set up or skinned. Typically the shape is formed to expose any hidden areas, or what is commonly referred to in the sculpting world as undercuts. Creatures with a different amount of appendages or disproportionate torsos have different default poses. Ideally the posture of the creature should be one that allows optimal access to its topology through the creature's normal native movements. You want to avoid moving your creature into a pose in which it wouldn't ordinarily be. In human beings their legs should be slightly spread apart and arms out far enough to shape geometry underneath them. If you were to model a horse, you would not model its legs at right angles pushing out of the side of the horse. You would model it as the horse usually stands with its legs perpendicular to its body. This might make it challenging to get into certain areas, but it is easier than repairing damage done to the geometry by deviating from its natural form.

Conclusion

Trying to work within these parameters can sometimes be more daunting than the work itself. We become overburdened with tasks considered to be menial and spend more time trying to get out of it than we would have if we had just done the task in the first place. This little game we play is never more real than when it comes to the pre-production process. The sooner these techniques become second nature, the faster you get your work done. The real bonus is in the quality, performance, and versatility of everything you do.

Keep in mind this is a necessary part of the process. Without it, it is difficult, if not impossible, to bring your story to fruition. Understand in the beginning the amount of time required and plan accordingly. In the next chapter, we will learn the basics of human anatomy and how it plays a part in the development of any reality-based creature.

CHAPTER

3 BIOLOGY 101: IMITATING LIFE

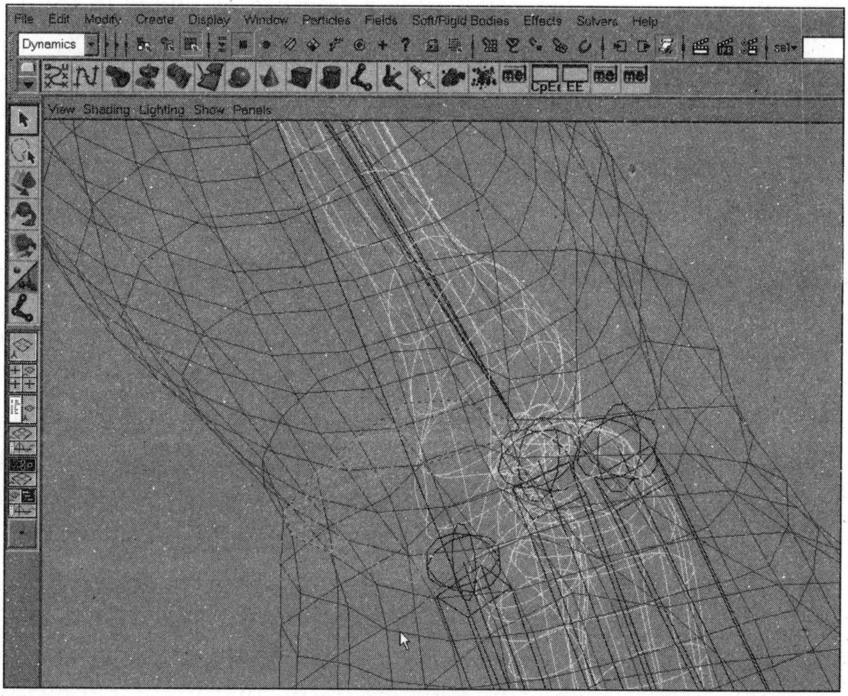

Powerful, versatile, and unique. The most incredible machine ever known is the driving force behind our creature. This machine is capable of processing and organizing large amounts of data at incredible speeds. Its memory limitations are undiscovered, and it is capable of creating any geometrical shape and can texture with an unlimited color palette. This machine has the ability to reproduce itself, yet we don't fully understand how it works. Its design has been improved for more than two million years. This machine is the human body.

In developing a creature, we need to think in terms of reality. Don't think of how to do something in CG—think about how it's done in the real world. The closer we come to imitating Mother Nature, the closer we come to photo-realism. The trick is to find tools that can produce these results.

Finding Common Ground

All life is created with unique features, serves a purpose, and works within its environment. When it comes to creating a character, as artists our goal is to supply that same uniqueness and purpose found in nature. Whether it is of this world or another, our creations were born somewhere. The environment they live in or came from influences their skin, muscle mass, coloring, hair, and everything about them. Instead of reaching for the unimaginable, we need only look in our own backyard.

The theory of evolution suggests all life originated from the same simplistic organism, that life has transformed from a single cell into a complex organism through a series of changes. Whether you believe it or not, it is easy to see how one could come up with the idea. Starting with a simplistic organism, you might recognize similarities between it and an organism with greater complexity. As life develops and becomes more intricate, it's easier to notice species that share external features, internal systems, and instincts. At the top of this elaborate web are Homo sapiens. From the basic composition of our cells, to the more elaborate ability to reproduce, we share a common thread with all life. Therefore, our own bodies can provide detailed information on how a fictitious organism might look and act. The goal is to create a creature that greatly differs from a human in appearance, but upon close inspection reveals the same internal composition. For instance, compare a human to an alligator. These two types of organisms look outwardly different. Examining their anatomies, however, we see that both possess muscles, bones, lungs, skin, etc. Although their appearance and individual anatomy are relevant, our primary concern is functionality. Do muscles expand and contract the same? Do their motions influence the skin? If we successfully make these simple comparisons, the human anatomy provides a superior source of reference. On the other hand, if we were building a creature resembling an amoeba, our comparisons would fail, and we'd be forced to find an alternate source of reference.

Layers of Anatomy

The human body is a marvel of design and function. The dynamics of our own anatomy provide us with a fount of inspiration and reference. Even though we are creating a fictional monster, it must look and act alive. Reference material does not exist for a character of this description, so our goal is to find real-world objects of similar qualities. We could choose an animal closely mimicking the product of our imagination. However, to develop our character, we need to look past the skin and examine the inner workings of existing life. But finding detailed anatomic descriptions and drawings of specific animals can be challenging. The human being, on the other hand, has been mapped and remapped. Studying its anatomy gives us new ideas and solutions to problems we have not yet considered. Luckily, reference material on human anatomy is easy to find and is literally inside us all. To accurately answer our questions and create a fictitious character, we must understand how anatomy works, then translate it to our character. We will, therefore, study human anatomy and learn how muscles, bones, tendons, and skin work together to move the way they do.

For the purpose of feasibly replicating a complex organism, it's necessary to break the anatomy down and identify our requirements. Our character needs to move in an anatomically correct way and its outer skin needs to deform realistically. There is no need to replicate any element not outwardly affecting our character's appearance, which will eliminate the majority of complex systems of the human body. We can identify elements of influence and place them into a layer of our own description.

The primary elements that define our layers and the names used to describe them are the skin, skeleton, muscle, and fat. Secondary elements to be grouped into their own layer and categorized as internal organs are the heart, lungs, and stomach. As we discuss the purpose and function of each layer, consider how these elements could be modified for a creature of your own design. Remember it's not solely for appearance, but how your creature sustains its own life and appears real.

The process of creating CG characters is moving closer to the process of cloning life. As computers become more powerful and audiences increasingly sophisticated, our challenge is clear: build a more-perfect beast. To accomplish this task, we must advance from the old methods of skinning vertex by vertex to the more realistic life-interpreting techniques by studying human anatomy. We can then make connections from the real world to the CG world. This process is no easy task and should not be considered for every character, but those sharing the screen in a prominent fashion must have an ordered level of existence to achieve believability alongside their real, living coactors.

Skin

The process of creating a CG character begins and ends with the skin layer. The geometry defining the looks and features of the creature is constructed first. This is done to achieve the look required and is usually established long before we think about its anatomy. With this preconceived vision, it is easy to see how muscle and bone fit inside.

Real-Life Skin

The skin encases all other layers. It's a strong, highly complex, unique surface that allows the body to interact with its world. A tough lattice of connecting tissue, the skin keeps out microscopic invaders, regulates heat loss, and limits penetration. It helps communicate emotion, age, and health. Skin works as a whole; indenting one area radiates outwardly, pulling the surrounding skin toward the influencing force. The harder the skin is pushed, the greater the affected area. When the force is removed, the skin springs back to its original position without leaving a lasting imprint. If you could pull on the skin hard enough, it would either reach its elastic limitations and tear or come off as one piece.

Skin can be grouped into three types: hairy, hairless, and delicate. Hairy skin covers a considerable part of the body. The hair can sense the environment without allowing it direct contact with the skin. It acts as an early warning system and aids in thermal protection. Thicker, hairless skin covers much less of the body and is reserved for areas such as the hands and feet. This skin is grooved to create a frictional surface, giving it the ability to grip opposing objects. Delicate skin, such as the lips, has no hair, is thinner than the hairy or hairless skin, and is more sensitive.

The skin is attached deeply to connective tissues around points of articulation. Skin creasing, skin lines, and wrinkles can be found all over the body and are more than just defining lines. Creasing helps the skin expand and contract and ease joint rotation.

Digital Skin

We will impose the elasticity of skin to our polygon surface and describe the connectivity of its tissues to the rest of the layers. Whether real or CG, the skin layer is an outer shell influenced by objects moving underneath it. These objects are not necessarily attached to the skin. Therefore the CG skin needs to keep its shape while other elements inside or outside of the body stretch and deform it.

To accomplish this in Maya we will use soft bodies. A soft-body object is a piece of geometry that has a particle assigned to each vertex. Dynamic forces can influence every particle moving associated vertices. Soft bodies create a duplicate of your original model that retains the original vertex positions of the model, allowing the particles to return to their original positions. This creates the effect of skin elasticity.

The Skeleton

When talking about skeletons for CG characters, it is very easy to get confused. In Maya, hierarchies of joints are called skeletons. For our purposes, the terms "skeleton" and "joint" refer to real-life skeletons, joints, and their modeled digital counterparts. Therefore, we label all Maya joints as IK, inverse kinematics, or FK, forward kinematics.

Real-Life Skeletons

The purpose of the skeleton is to provide shape and support to the body. Whether the body is in motion or idle, it's the skeleton that defines the appearance. The human skeleton is considered bilaterally symmetrical; from head to toe, one side is the same as the other side. The human skeleton exists on the inside of the body and is called an endoskeleton, but skeletons can also exist on the outside of the body as an exoskeleton. Most animals possess both types, providing a certain amount of protection and defense. An interesting part of the human skeleton is the teeth, by definition an exoskeleton. The teeth aid in consumption, communication, and defense. Creatures with more prominent exoskeletons, such as turtles or insects, rely on this outer shell for protection against predators. Usually, creatures with this outer defense lack the mobility or dexterity of organisms without it. In this way, nature creates a balance so that all life has an equal chance of survival.

Skeletons, simply put, are an organized collection of individual bones. They can be sorted by shape and size into groups of long, short, flat, and irregular. Bones basically work as levers acted upon by muscles and tendons. The longer the bone is, the greater the leverage, hence allowing for more speed and power. Long bones are usually found in limbs such as legs and arms and typically provide locomotion and broad movement. These bones are made up of a tubular shaft with expanding ends designed to support articulation. One example is the humerus bone of the arm and a smaller example would be the metacarpal bones in the hands. Bones classified as short bones occur in the wrist and the heel of the foot. Their appearances range from a wedge shape to a cube shape, and they are designed to handle pressure. Flat bones can be found in the cranium and the scapula (shoulder blade). All other bones not fitting into any of these three categories are considered irregular bones.

A bone's function, or the demand placed upon it, greatly influences the length and girth of a bone over time. This is true regardless of the demand. If a bone is not in use it will decrease in size, and with use it will increase in size, just like a muscle. Therefore, the stronger the organism, the bigger-boned it is.

The point at which two bones meet is a joint. These areas are usually surrounded by cartilage and fluid that allow for smooth motion and act as a shock absorber. Not all joints are capable of movement. For instance, where the ribs connect to vertebrae there is no movement. Articulated joints can be labeled based on their range of motion as uni-axial, bi-axial, or multi-axial. Each has an additional degree of freedom compared to the last.

Digital Skeletons

CG bones are polygon objects made into rigid bodies. Since the skin is a soft body, setting the bones as a rigid body allows for collision detection, thus deforming the skin or pushing the skin out. The geometry making up individual bones needs to be smooth and uniform; jagged points can slip through collision detection.

Underneath the digital skeleton lay FK and IK. Both of these elements need to be drawn from joint to joint ending at the point of articulation. Using a joint's range of motion, we can set limitations to the rotation values of the IK and FK. In addition, the thickness of individual bones should be honored and bones should not be allowed to penetrate one another. All of this helps prevent the character from moving illegally.

Muscles and Tendons

Muscles are the driving force behind all of life's motion. Without muscles, our skin would be like a floppy rubber suit. At first thought, you might want to build every muscle in order to have the perfect creature, however, this would be impractical and only increase render times without a noticeable difference in appearance. We need to keep in mind that CG muscles do not serve a practical purpose, only decoration. This might seem a bit contradictory, but muscles only need to influence the skin, not actually drive the skeleton. We need them to provide only the illusion of real muscle. If it doesn't directly influence the skin, it's not needed.

Real-Life Muscles and Tendons

A muscle is a group of fibers capable of contracting. There are three different muscle groups: cardiac, non-striating, and skeletal. Cardiac muscles are those of the heart; non-striated, or smooth, muscles are involuntary, working mostly on soft tissue and organs to accomplish bodily processes. Both are predominately deep muscles manifesting little to no visible changes in the surface of the skin. It is the superficial muscles, or skeletal muscles, that give the body definition.

Skeletal muscles form a vastly complex, interwoven mesh of fibrous tissues. So much so, it's hard to tell where one muscle ends and another begins. They lie next to and on top of internal organs in order to protect them. The skeletal muscles act upon bone to rotate it about its joint. Muscles connect directly to bone or to tendons. Tendons are slightly elastic, but don't produce any noticeable stretching in the skin. However, they are flexible, which enables them to wind around bony surfaces. Tendons bond with the belly of a muscle and extend across a joint to attach to another bone. The contracting muscle pulls the tendon, in turn rotating the bone.

Where the muscles or tendons connect to bone is extremely important. This directly affects the power and direction of the bone's motion. In order to have motion at a joint, we have two bones, one fixed and one mobile. The origin of the contracting muscle resides on the fixed bone. The attachment of the tendon on the mobile bone is key in determining the power and direction. All skeletal muscles can be classified as spurt, shunt, or spin based upon their attachments. Muscles display all three types of control, but one is always more prevalent.

In a spurt muscle, shown in Figure 3.1, the fixed attachment runs in series with the mobile attachment but is farther from the joint, enabling a powerful swing. These muscles are most effective at initiating and continuing slow movements.

Shunt muscles (Figure 3.2) are the opposite of spurt muscles and have their mobile attachment farther from the joint. The majority of the power delivered by a shunt muscle is exerted toward the joint to keep the joint from separating.

Spin muscles, shown in Figure 3.3, connect to bone in a spiral manner. These attachments are not in series with one another, causing the bone to spin or twist about its articulation.

The actions of individual muscles and groups of muscles work together to produce complex motion. An isolated bend at the elbow is not the action of one muscle but many working to stabilize, balance, lift, and return the bone to a resting position.

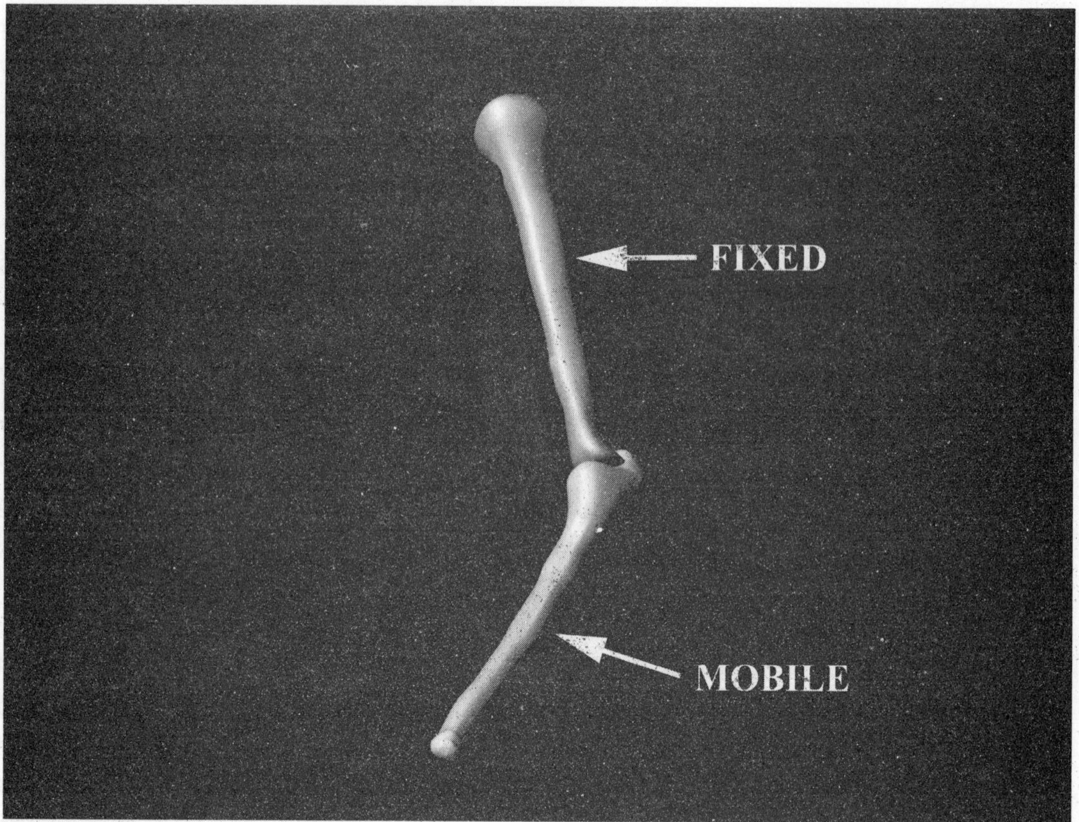

FIGURE 3.1 This is an example of a spurt muscle.

Digital Muscles and Tendons

Muscles and tendons range in size and shape and may connect to bone in two or more locations. These focal points are locked down while the rest of the object expands and contracts with a motion that is difficult to replicate. In order to accomplish this, Maya IK skeletons are employed. We will parent the root to one end of a bone and the effector, or IK handle, to another bone or tendon. The more accurate the CG muscle, the harder it is to animate.

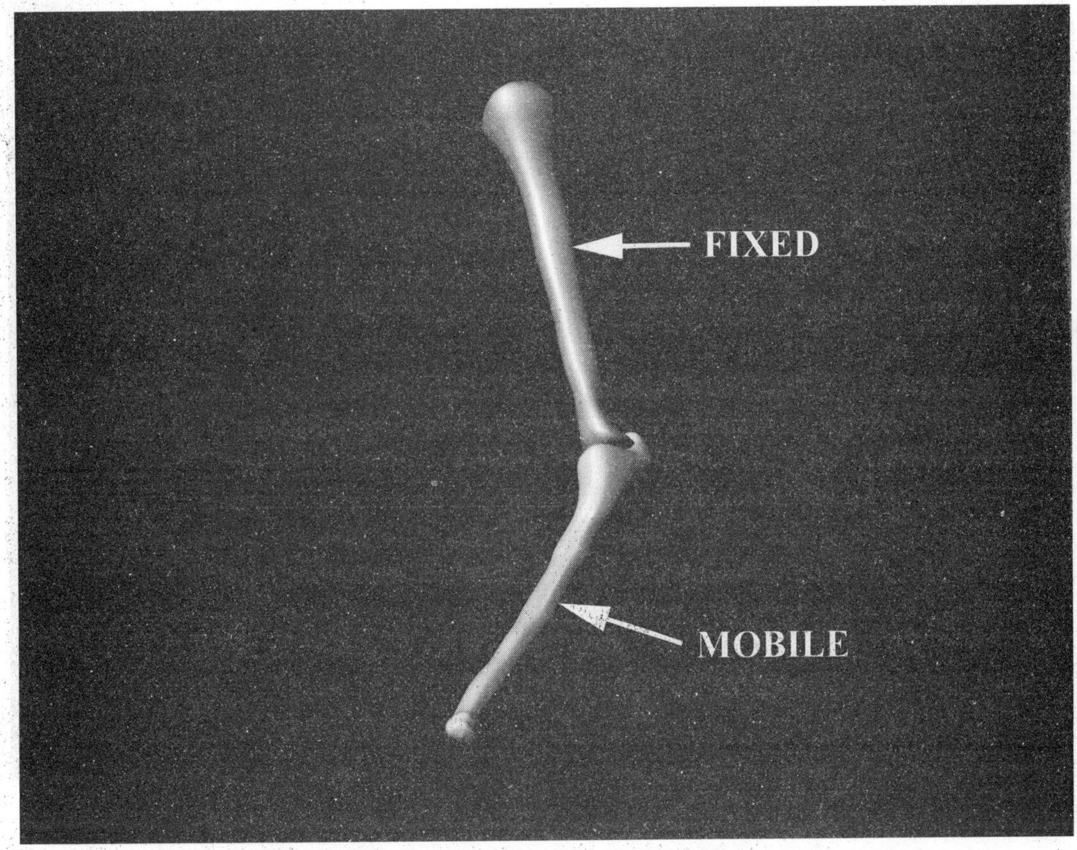

FIGURE 3.2 This is an example of a shunt muscle.

We could debate whether a muscle is a soft body or rigid body. In reality they would be considered soft bodies. However, for our simulation they are rigid bodies. This simplifies their interaction with the skin and makes for an easier setup with little to no sacrifice in quality.

Fat

Fat cells are located throughout the body. They are found acting as a cushion to surrounding organs, behind the eyeball, inside joints

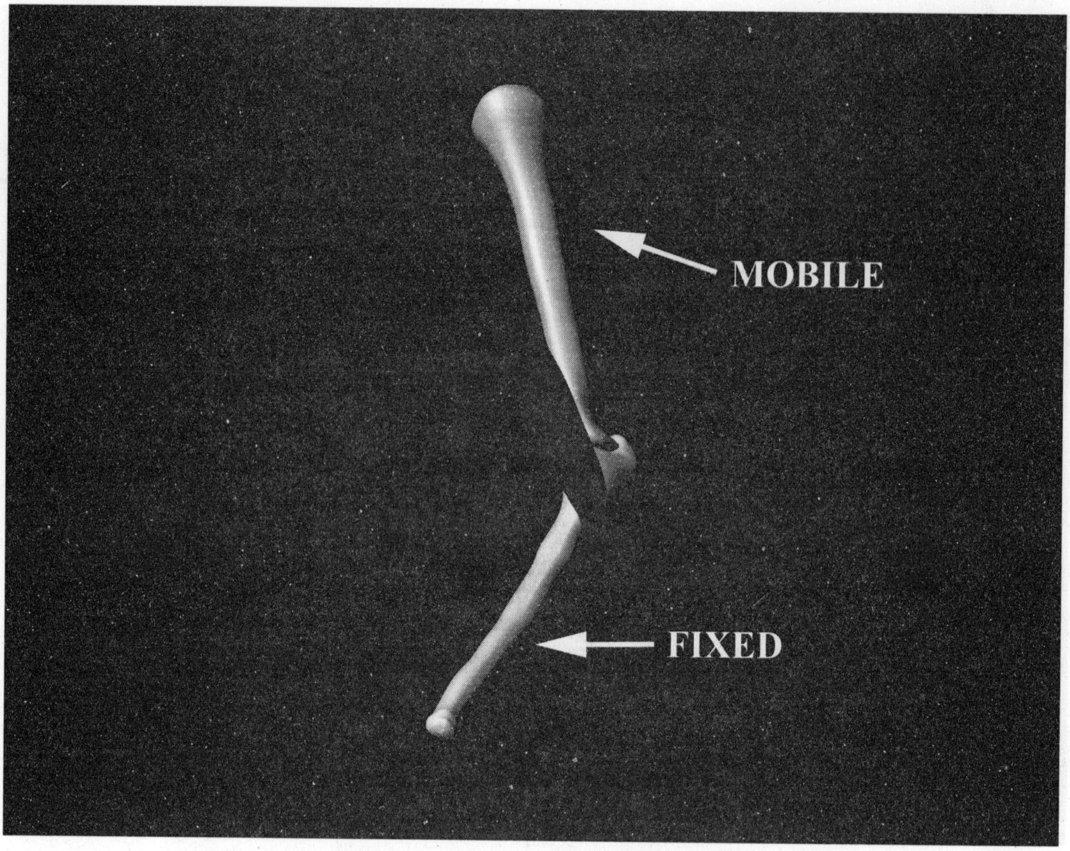

FIGURE 3.3 This is an example of a spin muscle.

and in the pads of hands and feet. Fat cells are more widely recognizable when they accumulate just under the skin. This subcutaneous fat can reveal age and gender. Females naturally have more fat cells than males and they are distributed more widely throughout the female body. A distinguishing factor is the increased abundance of fat in the breasts. In males, fat is more localized in the trunk, tapering off through the extremities. In both sexes fat increases during middle age, adding to the aforementioned areas. During the latter half of fetal and early infancy stages, fat builds in the body giving it a rounded, bulbous appearance. In elderly people fat diminishes, returning the body to one of its early fetal states of a significantly wrinkled appearance. The interesting correlation is we develop and deteriorate in the same manner.

Fat has many different functions. It is used for energy and thermal insulation. Organisms in colder climates, including humans, have a higher abundance of superficial fat to keep them warm. Furthermore, fat can act as a shock absorber and cushion. It clusters around internal organs and inside joints and is a protective subcutaneous layer for regions of the body.

The most distinctive visual trait of fat is its incompressibility. Instead of diminishing in size or collapsing like a sponge when pressure is applied to it, fat will divert the force, pushing other fat cells out of the way. This characteristic also causes "jiggle" between the cells as they bounce off of one another. When any type of force is applied, whether from gravity or direct pressure, fat works to retain its shape and volume.

Fat has properties similar to skin, but fat properties are more exemplified. We need only to make fat objects soft bodies and increase the amount of "jiggle." These simple pieces of geometry can then be placed into our CG body and applied as collision objects. Because the actions of fat and skin are close, we must be careful to not get carried away when placing fat. It should only be used in genetically predisposed areas or special characters. To cover the whole body in a layer of fat would be redundant, yielding unwanted results.

Connective Tissue

We need connective tissue to anchor our CG skin. This tissue can be described using springs that may be attached to vertices not under the control of a soft body. Therefore, we can affix a particle from a soft body to a vertex on a muscle or inside a joint, as shown in Figure 3.4, by running a spring from one particle to a vertex on any underlying layer. Like real skin, this will hold its place, generating wrinkles or folds.

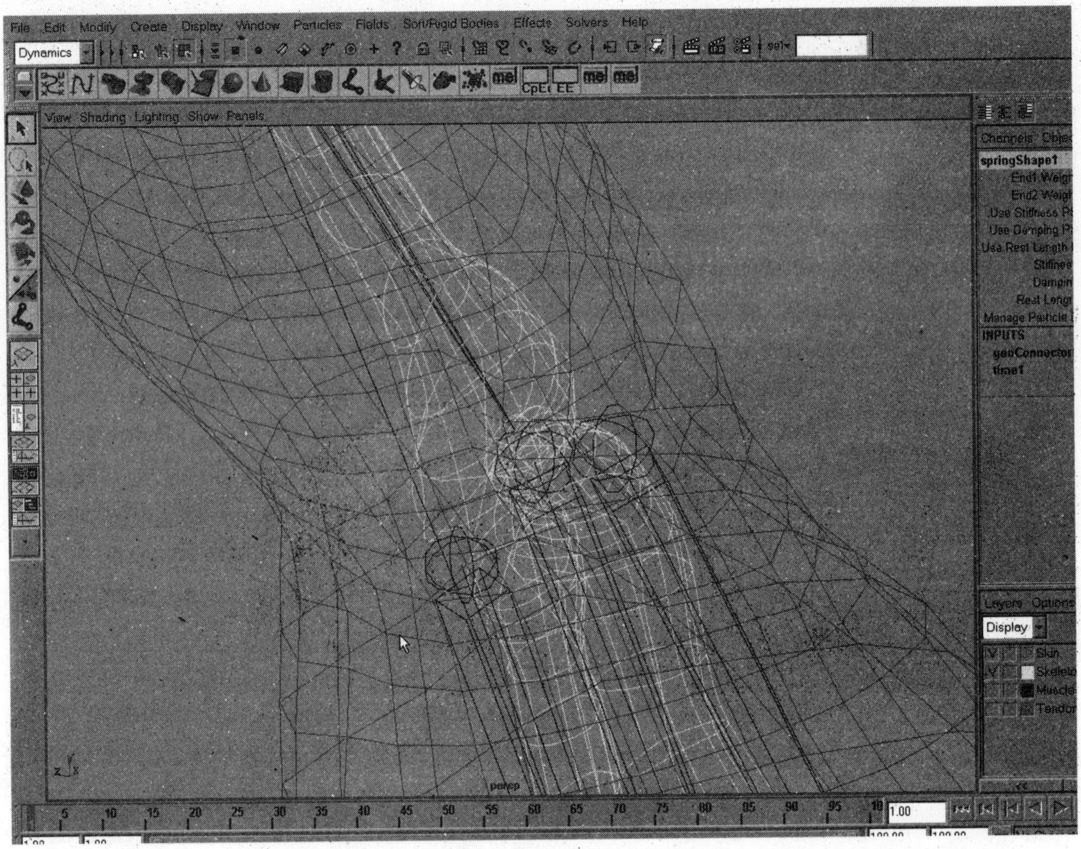

FIGURE 3.4 Springs are attached to the soft-body object and to a normal piece of geometry.

Conclusion

In the end, we will have a creature capable of deforming its own skin. This method will effectively bypass the normal skinning procedure of a rigid or smooth bind. In fact, it will save setup time and produce results unobtainable by normal skinning methods. This procedure will automate muscle and bone deformation, fat jiggle, skin wrinkling, skin shake, and impacts to the skin exterior. The pitfalls are in the extra models needed and increased render times. As technology grows, this becomes less of a problem. The up side is that once we build bone and muscles, they can be modified easily to work with other creatures regardless of their shape and size.

Perhaps the most intriguing aspect of this information is that we can use it not only to shape our creatures, but also to shape our stories. Having this much detail in our creations opens the door for certain limitations. If we describe our characters anatomically, our characters might not be able to do everything that we planned, thus forcing us to devise alternative actions that ultimately make for a more interesting and believable story.

PART

II

REFERENCE MATERIAL

CHAPTER

4 DESIGN AND CONQUER

In Chapter 3 we discussed the essence of human anatomy and its role in the development of photo-realistic computer-generated creatures. Skin, muscles, bones, tendons, and fat all contribute to the design of a character. With this information, Chapter 4 develops a creature and begins construction on reference material needed to complete it.

THE PHYSICAL DESIGN

It's not good enough to think you have a solid idea of what your character will look like. So many details still need to be worked out that it's impossible to refine a character in your head. The information needs to be extracted and recreated in the physical world many times. Creating a rough draft of your idea helps flesh out form and attitude. When modeling directly from your mind to CG, you never get a feel of the character or walk in its shoes. The ambition should be to share in the birth of your creature. This is your baby; raise it properly. Make sure it has everything needed to enter the world.

The following is a list of four attributes needed to define a character and help describe the character's attitude and disposition. These are generalities that could be applied to any living creature.

Age—All living things go through a metamorphosis from the time they are born to the time they die. Features become more distinct and there is an overall increase in size. Halfway through its life the reverse begins to happen. Definition becomes lost in sagging skin while deteriorating anatomy results in a diminishing size. Then there is a third metamorphosis, decomposition, taking place after they die.

Environment—The world in which our creature lives. This includes any natural occurrences such as the changing of seasons or monsoonal rains. Attributes that may influence our creature from the environment are temperature, atmosphere, coexisting life, terrain, evolution, and standing within the food chain.

Gender—The sex of a creature plays a vital role in determining attitude and form. Males and females generally differ anatomically in muscle mass and skeletal makeup. This is quite visible in outward appearances. An excellent example of this is the black widow spider. The female of the species is considerably larger than her male counterpart.

Occupation—This characteristic is probably the most fun. This would encompass what the creature does on a daily basis in order to sustain its life. Hunting for food, finding shelter, procreation, and recreation would all be attributes of occupation.

Creating a Working Design

The name of the creature designed in this book is the "Fire Monster." This beast lives in the earth, burrowing through the crust and ingesting molten lava. Based on that description alone, a lot can be determined about its appearance and behavior. Using the four attributes just outlined, a creature profile can be created.

Age—The beast is in its adolescence. Its species lives for a few hundred thousand years. In the early stages of its life, it may have defenses other than strength, agility, and experience to insure survival of the species, such as spikes or a hard outer shell.

Environment—The creature lives in the earth, surrounded by dirt, rock, and lava most of its life, infrequently seeing the light of day. Due to its earthly dwelling, its eyes might be small with limited vision.

Gender—The Fire Monster is a male. Gender will play an important role in his behavior. Due to his age and life span he will have a very long puberty stage. The creature is exploring new ground and testing the limits of his physical being. Physical changes are also derived from his gender, dictating muscle mass and overall size.

Occupation—The Fire Monster will sleep for thousands of years, waking only to eat by tunneling to lava pools for a meal and racing to an aquifer to quench his thirst.

From this information the creature's features begin to take shape. In order for the Fire Monster to move underground he must possess tools for digging. He should have sharp, durable nails and strong muscles. He must have thick skin and a body shape that would allow dirt and rocks to pass over him. His coloring could range greatly, but to fit his name and his diet, bright reds and oranges seem appropriate. Having a healthy diet of lava would also imply an elevated body temperature and the ability to withstand high temperatures.

The first step in the visualization of a character is to sketch or draw it out. There are several off-the-shelf 2D paint packages that make sketching a character easy. Scanning photographs of real-world objects, then cutting and pasting characteristics together, is a simple method for roughing out a design. Figure 4.1 shows a preliminary image of the Fire Monster's head. The importance of this image is to get an idea of skin texture, color, and head shape.

MAQUETTES

Two-dimensional images provide a limited amount of information in a three-dimensional world. Creating a maquette, or preliminary sculpture, leaves no questions unanswered. This prototype gives you the opportunity to make mistakes and test ideas. It's easier to modify clay than geometry. A version of your creature existing outside of the computer will not only help you visualize the result, but also will give a scale for the CG model. Many special effects houses, whether they are building traditional or computer-generated creatures, sculpt a prototype before building anything else. This helps

FIGURE 4.1 This is the rough draft of the Fire Monster's head, painted using a 2D paint package.

everyone involved in the production envision the size and scope of the creature. Furthermore, it provides excellent reference material for scanning or sharing between multiple companies or departments.

Sculpting a character does not mean that you build the Statue of Liberty. The intention is to establish proportion and form; fine detail is not entirely necessary. However, the closer you get to your vision, the easier it is to replicate in the computer. To demystify this art form, we will take a look at the materials and tools at our disposal. Once we establish a basic toolset, we can sculpt our creature.

The fascinating aspect about sculpting a character is that it parallels and complements its construction in the virtual 3D world. The entire process is a mirrored reflection of the CG process. To help you get comfortable with both procedures, here is a step-by-step explanation of the sculpting process and comparisons to the

CG world. Thinking in these terms helps tremendously if you are a traditional sculptor crossing over to CG or vise versa.

Step 1: Select a material with which to model. Clay is the easiest, cheapest, and most versatile material. (CG Equivalent: polygons, NURBS, and subdivision surfaces)
Step 2: Build an armature or skeleton on which to sculpt. This will provide the basic shape and give support to the clay. (CG Equivalent: joints, modeled bones, and IK skeleton)
Step 3: Add the first layer of clay, rough out the creature's exterior shape and symmetry. (CG Equivalent: any of the modeling tools such as loft, birail, or polygon extrude)
Step 4: Smooth the clay and add the first layer of detail. This includes defining features such as eyes, ears, nose, muscles, and overall contours. (CG Equivalent: adding and shaping geometry)
Step 5: Add the second layer of detail, shaping muscle definition, heavy wrinkles, and all other medium to large details. (CG Equivalent: any tool capable of pushing and pulling CVs or vertices)
Step 6: Add fine skin texture, small wrinkles, tiny bumps, and everything else. (CG Equivalent: adding bump maps and displacement maps)
Step 7: The clay sculpture is finished and left to dry. After it has completely dried out, it can be painted. (CG Equivalent: color maps and any mapping method that influences color)

The actual sculpting process is closest to modeling with subdivision surfaces. Start out with a base layer to flesh out a primitive design, subdividing that layer and each successive layer to gain an increasing amount of detail. Identifying these similarities keeps you thinking about modeling the creature in CG the entire time you're sculpting. This makes modeling with the computer easier and faster because you already know the tools and techniques needed to get the desired result.

The Fire Monster's first maquette was built in an action pose. The model was intended to work out the details not yet realized in 2D. The sculpture is shown in Figures 4.2 and 4.3.

The sculpture also provides some insight into the creature's attitude and behavior. It shows how he carries himself while standing and walking. This also helps to spark new ideas and get a taste of his personality. Some of the attributes described in the beginning of this chapter were incorporated into the sculpture, but several more still need to be added to support the character's actions and lifestyle. The first maquette will serve as reference material for

FIGURE 4.2 The finished sculpture of the Fire Monster as viewed from the front.

FIGURE 4.3 The finished sculpture of the Fire Monster as viewed from the side.

the second maquette, using it to identify design flaws and required additions. The top of his head, for instance, needs to be shaped more like a spade shovel to enable him to dig underground easily. His back needs to be altered to carry dirt from his head down to his tail, and some flexible spikes or quills need to be added to split the sand as he burrows.

CLAYS

There are three different types of clay suitable for creating a maquette, and they each have advantages and disadvantages. Choose the clay that best suits your needs based upon skill, time, and purpose. The following clays can be found at art, hobby, and craft supply shops and special effects suppliers.

Water Based—Also called air-dry or wet clay, this material, shown in Figure 4.4, begins to dry out as soon as the box is opened. Basically, this clay is a very fine powder mixed with water. This means a high amount of detail can be obtained due to the microscopic particles making this compound, but when the water evaporates, the clay becomes solid. It is ready to be used right out of the box and requires no warming or kneading. When the clay begins to dry out, you simply add water to return it to a malleable state. A disadvantage to this clay is that it shrinks when it dries. You can't actually notice your sculpture shrinking because it is a minimal amount. A problem arises, though, when you have a rigid armature inside your

FIGURE 4.4 This is an example of five pounds of air-dry clay.

sculpture because it might prevent the clay from shrinking, which can result in cracking.

Examples: Claystone, Boneware

Cost: low, prices range from $0.25 to $1.50 per pound

Oil Based—This type of clay, shown in Figure 4.5, is designed to never dry out. It is mixed with oils to keep it pliable and comes in different grades, ranging from soft to hard. The harder the clay, the easier it is to add fine detail. Due to the oils, it is temperature sensitive and becomes more manageable when warm, but beware of overheating, as it will cause the clay to internally liquefy. Do not touch liquefied clay. Since this clay doesn't dry out, it is necessary to make a mold of your finished sculpture. From that mold, make a rigid cast using other materials—as many times as needed.

Example: Roma Plastilinia

Cost: moderate, prices range from $2.00 to $4.00 per pound

FIGURE 4.5 This is an example of a one-pound block of oil-based clay.

Polymer—A compound similar to oil-based products, except you can bake it in a conventional oven, creating a solid, permanent form. This clay, shown in Figure 4.6, is very versatile and can be sanded, drilled, or carved after it dries. You can achieve a fair amount of detail with this clay, but it lacks the fine grain found in other clays.

Examples: Sculpey and Super Sculpey

Cost: high, prices range from $8.00 to $10.00 per pound

FIGURE 4.6 This is an example of polymer clay.

TOOLS

Sculpting tools can be used with all clay types. The only difference is the amount of pressure applied with the tool. There are many commercial tools available, but there are no limits to what you can use to sculpt. If it makes an impression, it's a suitable tool. Some of the best tools are those you find in your own kitchen. If you can't afford to purchase them, find something equivalent around the house.

Thin line—Provides intricate, sharp detail and clean removal. Can be found with single or double loops. (See Figure 4.7.)

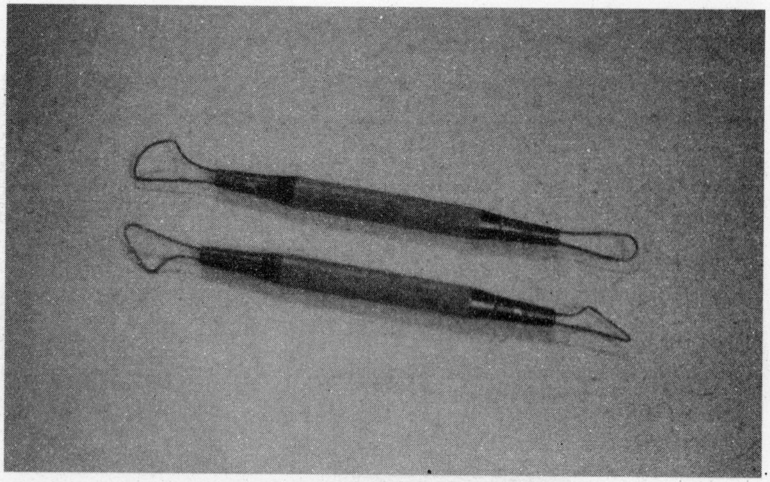

FIGURE 4.7 Examples of thin-line tools.

Sgraffito—Used to scratch or cut away clay. Excellent for fine detail, but produces sharp cuts. (See Figure 4.8.)

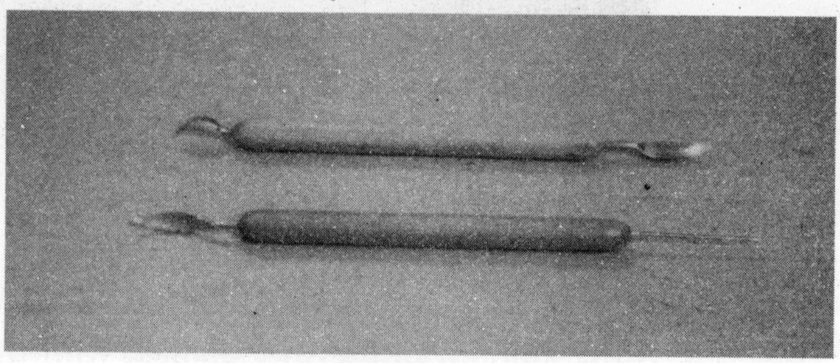

FIGURE 4.8 Examples of sgraffito tools.

Dental—Right out of the dentist's office, these stainless steel instruments are good for scraping and shaping clay. (See Figure 4.9.)

Modeling—These rubber, metal, plastic, or wood tools can give a full range of impressionable detail. Obtainable in a wide variety

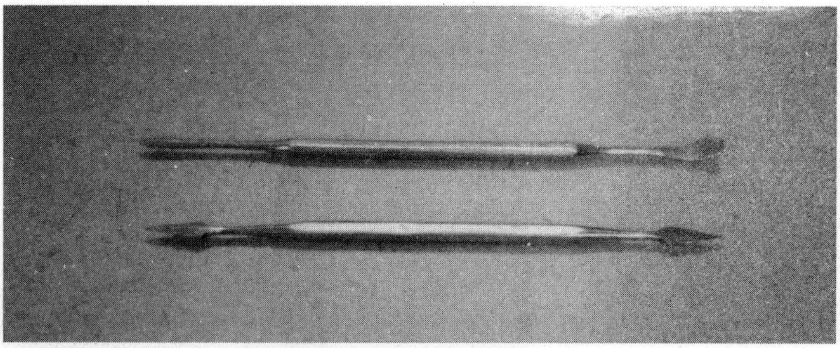

FIGURE 4.9 Examples of dental tools used for sculpting.

of shapes and sizes, this category also covers any miscellaneous tool. (See Figure 4.10.)

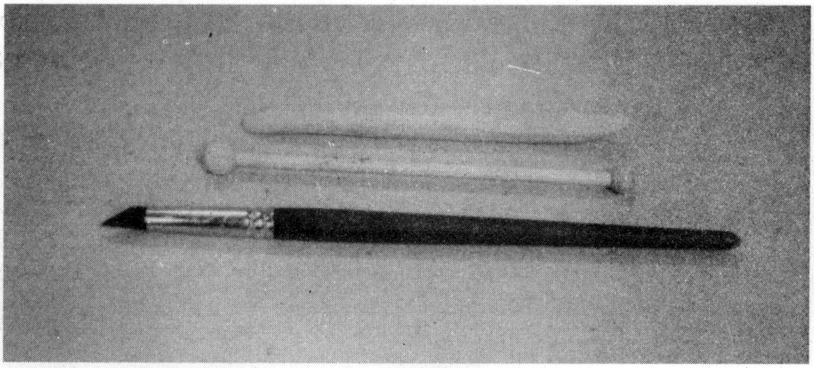

FIGURE 4.10 Examples of modeling tools.

Sponges—Primarily used to apply makeup, these are great for smoothing rough details, finishing a surface, and applying skin texture. Various types and shapes are available in some art supply stores, but they are more prevalent in beauty supply shops or in the cosmetics section in most supermarkets. (See Figure 4.11.)

FIGURE 4.11 Several different types of sponges used in the sculpting process.

Rubber stamps—Usually made by the artist, although some are commercially available, these flexible shapes have an inverted pattern that can be pressed into the clay to make an impression. These are for applying skin texture, wrinkles, and any repeating pattern. (See Figure 4.12.)

FIGURE 4.12 Different types of rubber stamps used for applying texture to a clay sculpture.

Brushes—Available with a variety of bristles and ranging in size and thickness, these are good for smoothing clay, removing debris, and adding detail. (See Figure 4.13.)

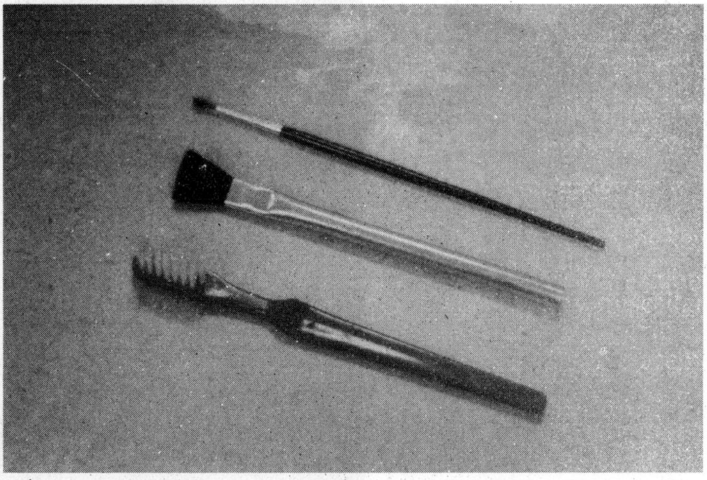

FIGURE 4.13 Examples of different types of brushes.

Thin plastic and squirt bottle—Any ultra-thin, clear, plastic material. Kitchen plastic wrap is ideal. Draping the material over clay permits us to use sharp tools to make soft impressions. A squirt bottle can be used to blast water at soft clay to create delicate detail and to keep water-based clay moist. (See Figure 4.14.)

Ruler and Calipers—These tools, shown in Figure 4.15, are used to maintain symmetry with the armature and sculpture. The calipers are great for measuring uneven surfaces. Simply pinch the ends of both arms around the area to be measured. Use the ruler to get an exact measurement or use it as a guide against another object.

FIGURE 4.14 Thin plastic wrap used to dampen the effects of sharp tools.

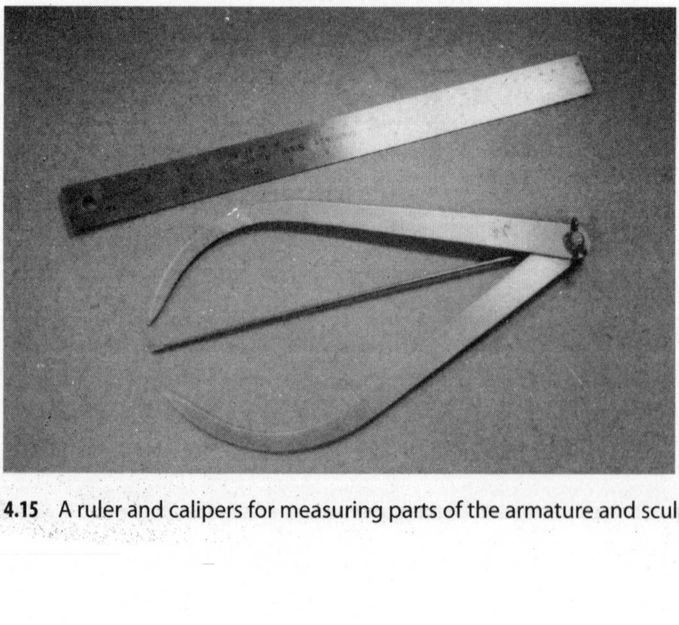

FIGURE 4.15 A ruler and calipers for measuring parts of the armature and sculpture.

ARMATURES

The framework we sculpt upon is called an armature. This structure acts as a skeleton, giving the sculpture form and support. Armatures can be made from various materials as long as they are strong enough to hold the weight of the clay. Your model should not sag during the sculpting process. The armature dictates how the model looks. In life, and in sculpting, the form is built over the skeleton. This makes the construction of the armature critical to the development of the creature. Extreme care should be taken to insure its accuracy based upon the skeletal anatomy of the design.

Almaloy armature wire meets the requirements of the armature. Made of aluminum alloys, this non-corrosive material is lightweight and extremely pliable. It is virtually unbreakable because it resists bending in the same place twice and is also suited for some stop-motion applications. It can be bought in an assortment of thicknesses from 1/14″ to 3/8″ at art supply shops (the thicker the wire, the greater the tension). The wire can also be wrapped to increase its stiffness. See Figure 4.16 for examples of the wire.

FIGURE 4.16 These are examples of different gauges of armature wire.

The gauge, or thickness, of armature wire you use depends on how heavy or thick the sculpture will be. Experiment with different gauges to get a feel for their individual strengths. Portions of your sculpture may be thicker in places, requiring the wire to support more weight in that specific area. Here is the list of items shown in Figure 4.17 needed to build and complete the armature.

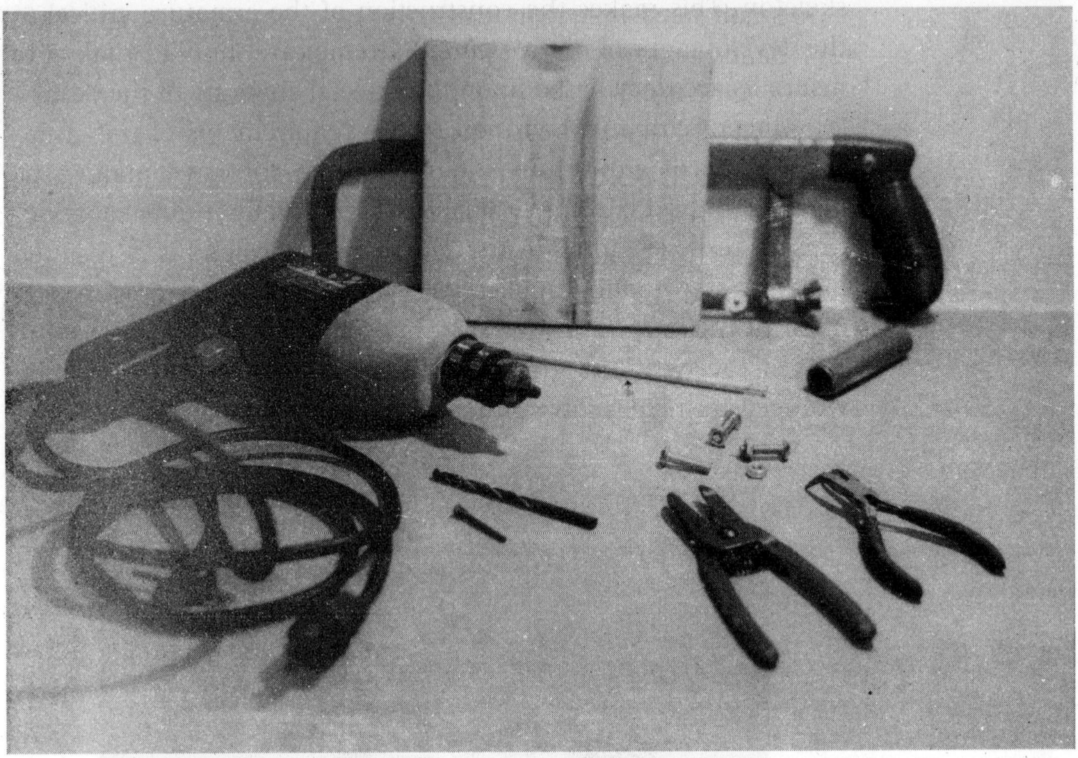

FIGURE 4.17 The basic materials and tools needed to complete the armature.

- A block of wood will be the platform on which we mount our sculpture. It should be large enough to accommodate the anticipated size of our sculpture. It will also have to support the weight of the clay, so get a piece at least 1/2″ thick.

- Machine screws with matching nuts, 1/4″ to 1/2″ longer than the thickness of the wood platform. These are used to bolt the armature to the wood block.
- Epoxy putty can be found at most hardware and auto parts stores. This material is excellent for bonding two separate strands of wire together.
- Wire cutters. You will need these to clip small strands of wire to add fingers, toes, and small detail.
- Small needlenose pliers. These are handy to make intricate bends in the armature wire.
- A hack saw can be used for cutting bolts down if they are too long.
- An electric drill and two bits are needed to bolt down the armature. The first drill bit needs to be the size of the screw shank. The second can be either a milling bit or a standard drill bit the size of the screw head.

TUTORIAL

BUILDING THE ARMATURE

Gather up all of the materials listed above. The armature is built from a single spool of wire by wrapping it tightly around itself to create greater tension.

Step 1: The best place to start is with the hips or shoulders, regardless of the number of arms and legs. Begin with a full spool of wire and estimate about four inches. Make a right angle bend for the creature's hip as shown in Figure 4.18. The remaining portion of wire will be used to create the entire armature.

Step 2: Make a slight bend for the knee and another right angle bend for the foot. (See Figure 4.19.)

FIGURE 4.18 Make a right angle bend for the creature's hip.

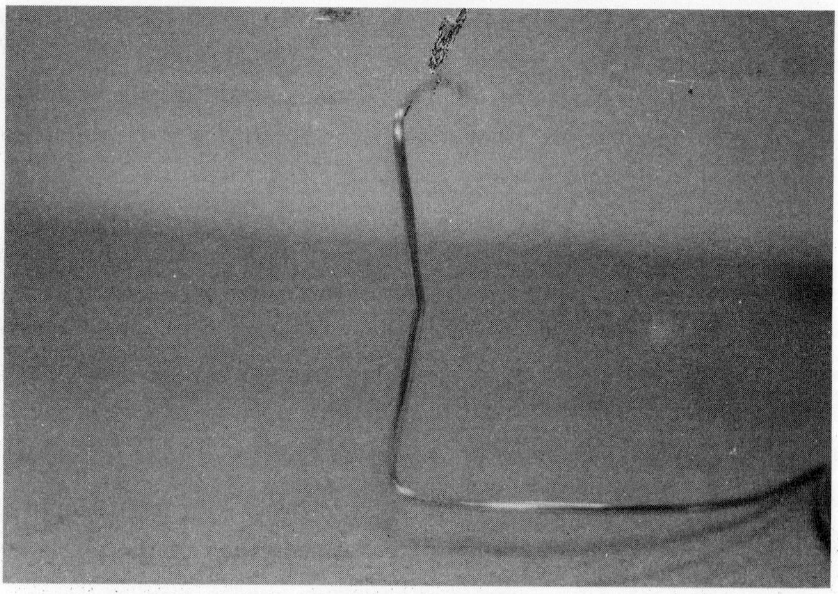

FIGURE 4.19 Make a bend for the knee and for the start of the foot.

Step 3: Wrap the wire around a bolt adequately proportioned to your character. The bend creates a loop acting as the foot (Figure 4.20). The bolt will eventually secure the armature to a platform.

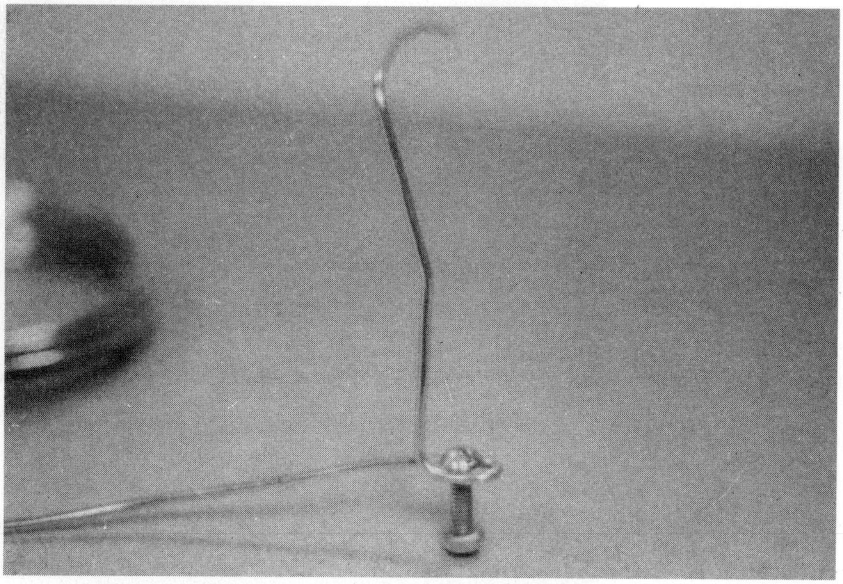

FIGURE 4.20 The loop is created just big enough to trap the bolt inside of it.

Step 4: Remove the bolt and begin wrapping the wire up the leg. (See Figure 4.21.)

Step 5: Continue wrapping the wire tightly around the leg you just created and make your way back to the hips where you began. This completes one leg (Figure 4.22).

Step 6: Continue the wire down the other side, repeating the process to create the other leg. Examine Figure 4.23.

Step 7: After creating the loop for the foot, wrap the wire back up to the hips. During this process you may find that you lose the shape of your legs. This is not a problem; in fact, it is often necessary in order to wrap the wire properly. (See Figure 4.24.)

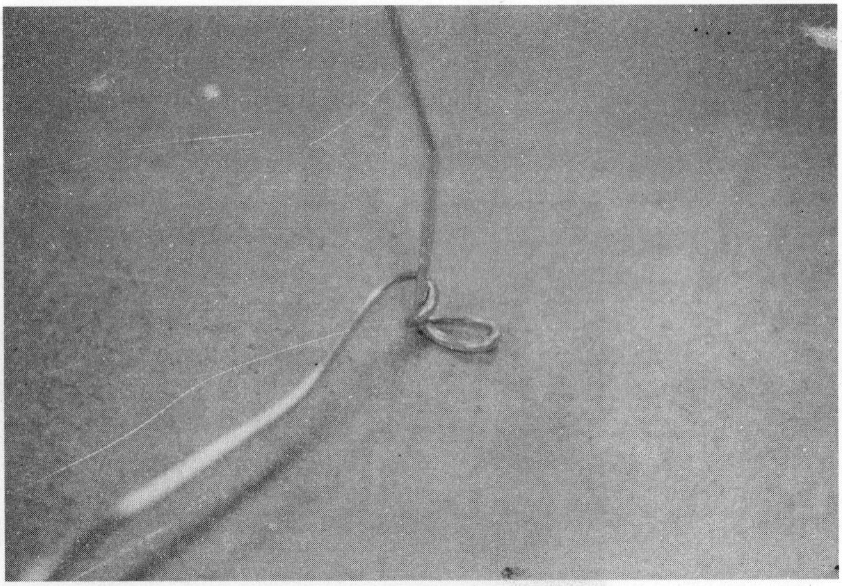

FIGURE 4.21 Wrap the wire around the ankle and continue up the leg.

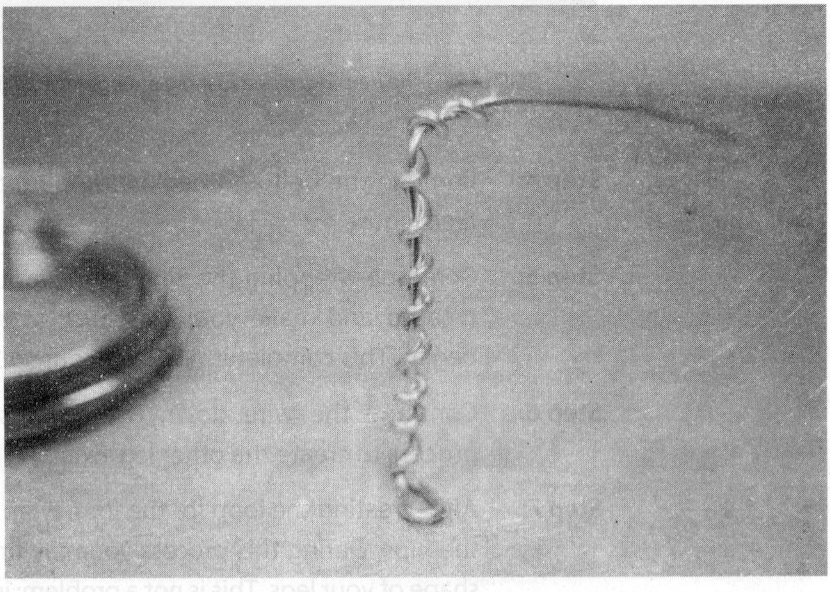

FIGURE 4.22 Wrap the wire up the leg to the hips.

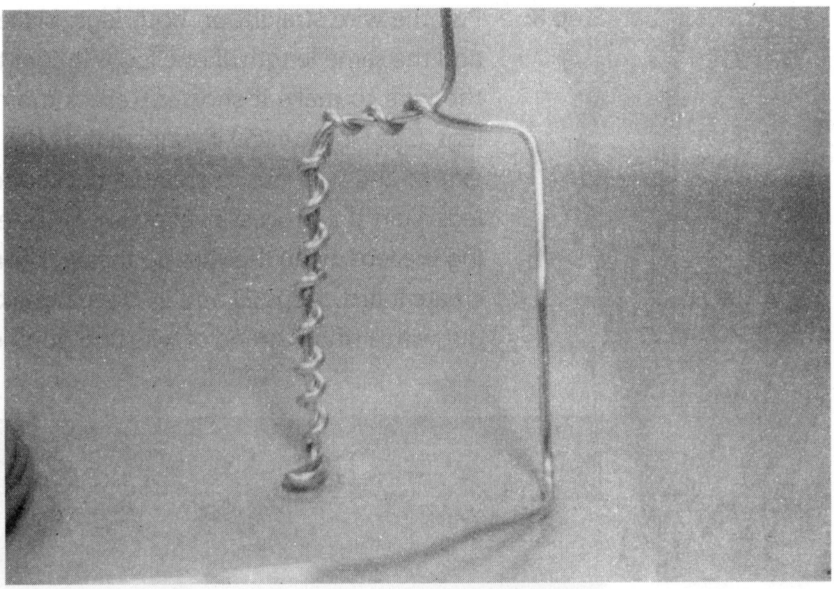

FIGURE 4.23 Shape the other leg.

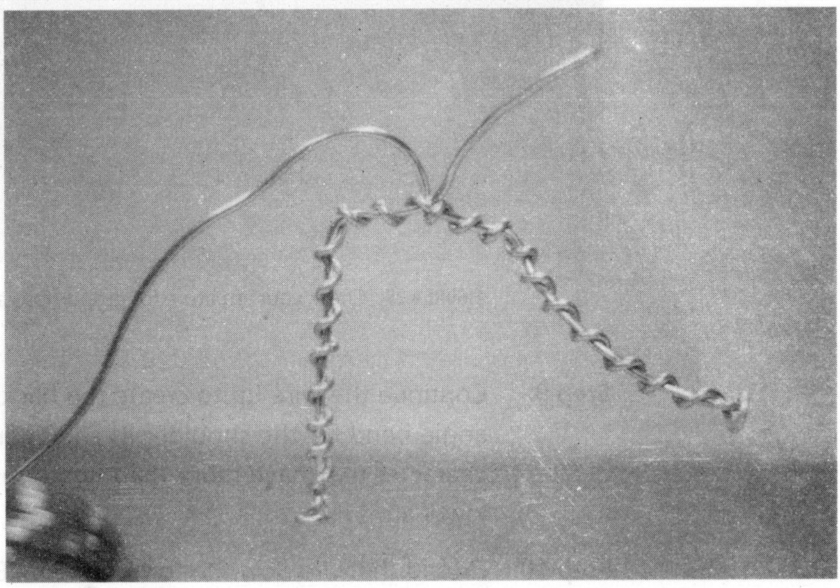

FIGURE 4.24 Wrap the wire from the second leg back up to the hips.

Step 8: Pull the wire straight on both legs. Make sure they are even and the same length. If one leg is longer than the other, twist the wire to make it shorter. Take a moment to reshape the legs. (See Figure 4.25.) If your creature has more than two legs, extend the wire out to create a backbone. At the next set of legs, start the process over again with step 1. Upon completing the legs, wrap the wire up the backbone, but if it has a tail, create it first. Steps 23 and 24 discuss making a tail. Always go out with a single strand of wire and double back on it.

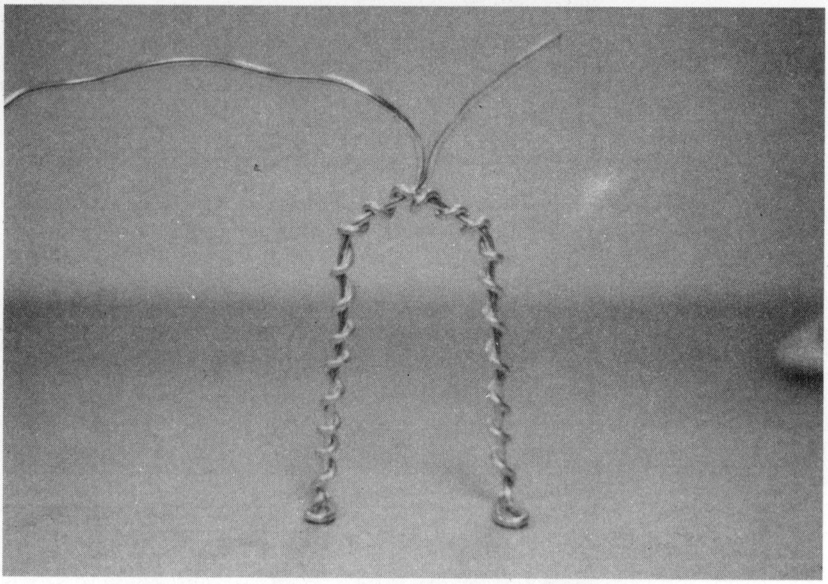

FIGURE 4.25 Check your armature for proportions and shape.

Step 9: Continue the wire up to create the backbone. Make a right angle bend for the shoulder as shown in Figure 4.26. Your character may have more than two arms; simply make the lower arms first.

Step 10: Extend the wire down to form the arm. Bend a loop for the palm of the hand and begin to take the wire back up. The

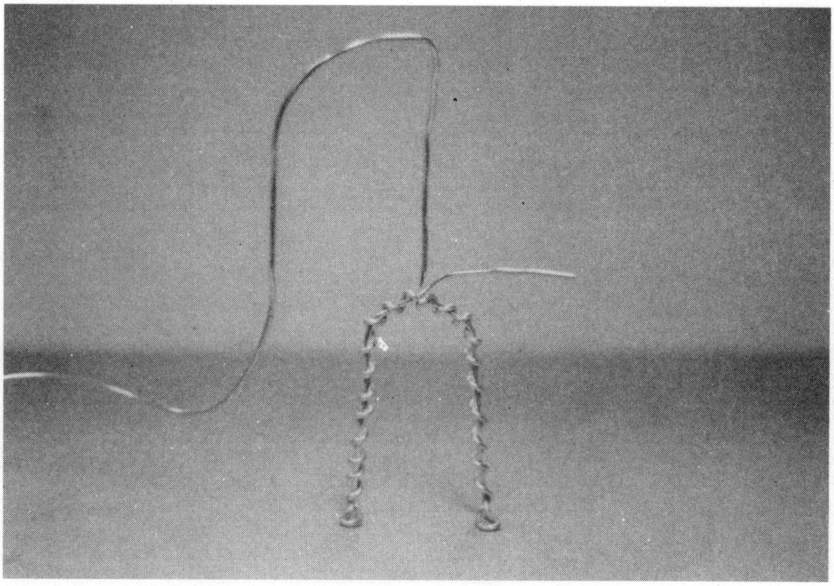

FIGURE 4.26 Create the backbone and the shoulder.

loop, or palm, provides an area from which to extend fingers. Make sure the loop is large enough to accommodate all of your creature's fingers. This is a good spot to examine skeletal reference. You want to avoid spreading the fingers too far apart, and making the loop too large could inadvertently cause this. Examine Figure 4.27.

Step 11: To further refine the palm, use needlenose pliers to create a sharper bend in the hand. Figure 4.28 demonstrates this action.

Step 12: Complete the loop by wrapping the wire back on itself at the wrist. Look at Figure 4.29 to see the squared-off loop. This area is used to attach the fingers.

Step 13: Wrap the wire back to the top of the shoulder. Remember, if you lose the shape of the character, you can always bend it back. (See Figure 4.30.)

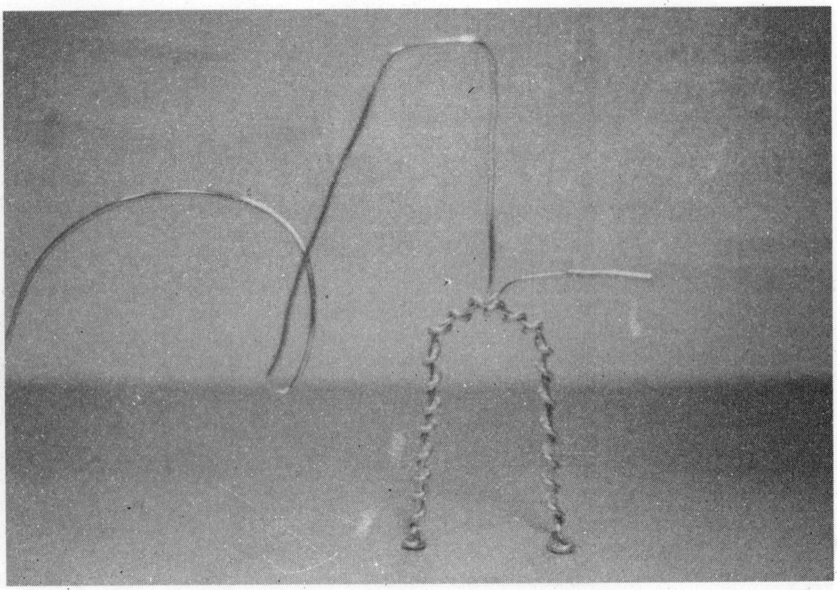

FIGURE 4.27 Make the arm and a loop for the palm.

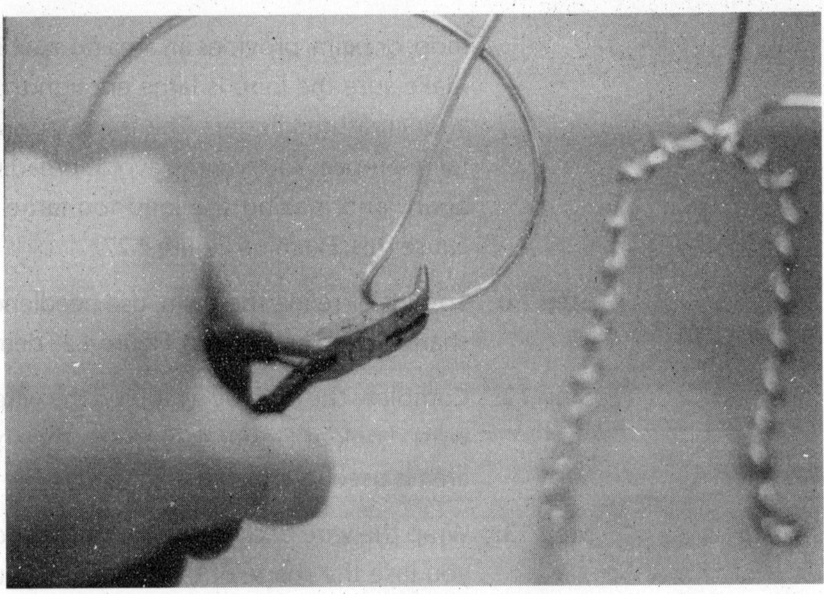

FIGURE 4.28 Use needlenose pliers to precisely bend the wire.

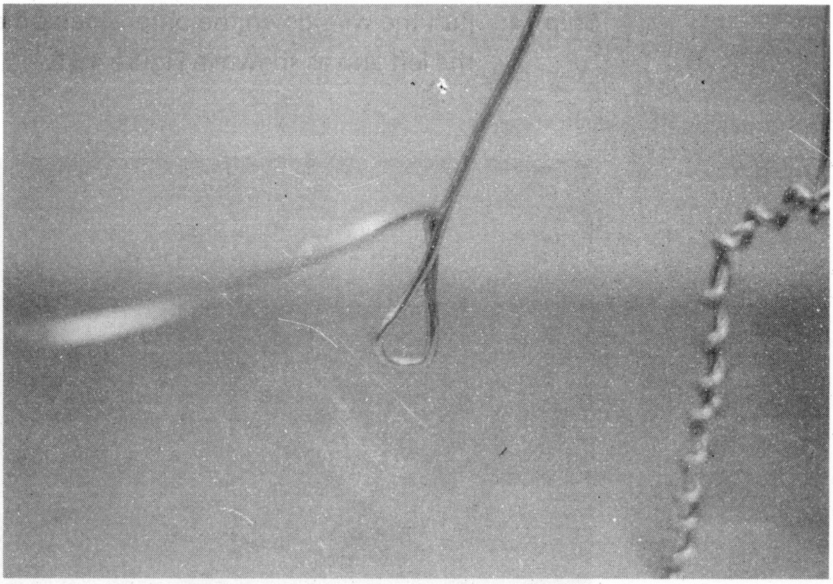

FIGURE 4.29 Bend the wire around itself to create the wrist.

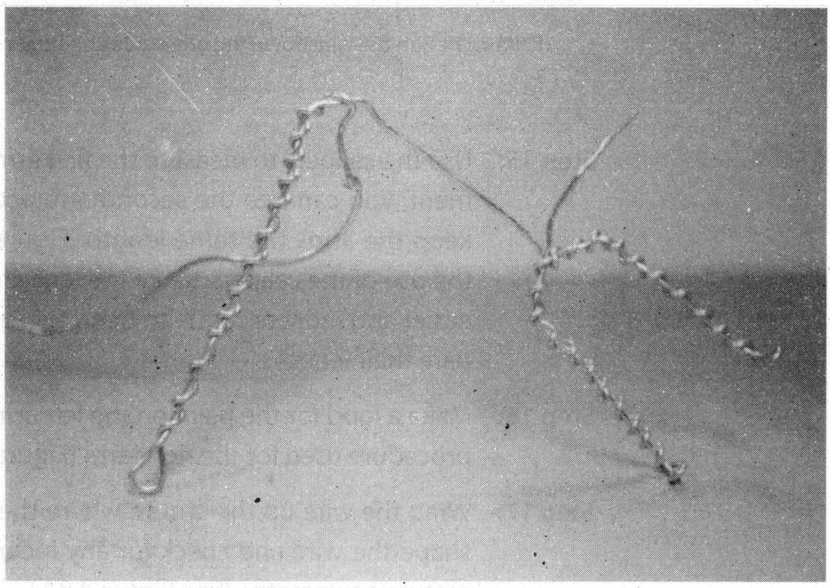

FIGURE 4.30 Complete the right arm and shoulder.

Step 14: Run the wire down the other side of the character to create the left arm as shown in Figure 4.31.

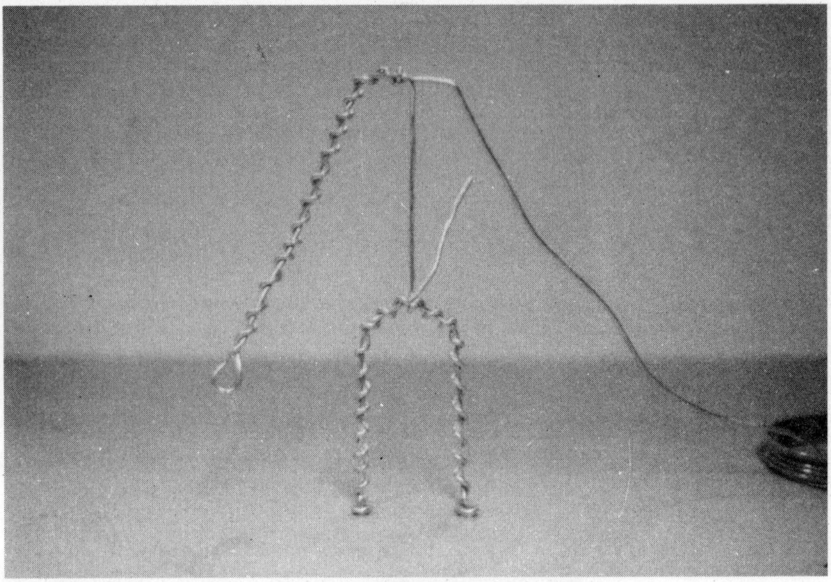

FIGURE 4.31 Run the wire down the other side and begin shaping the left arm.

Step 15: Use the calipers to measure the first arm. With this measurement, you can size the second arm accordingly. This helps keep the arms the same length. Figure 4.32 demonstrates the use of the calipers. Since the legs are close together, it is easier and more accurate to bend the legs straight and compare their lengths.

Step 16: Make a loop for the palm on the left arm following the same procedure used for the right arm (Figure 4.33).

Step 17: Wrap the wire up the arm to where the neck should be. Reshape the wire and check for any inconsistencies in the armature's symmetry. (See Figure 4.34.)

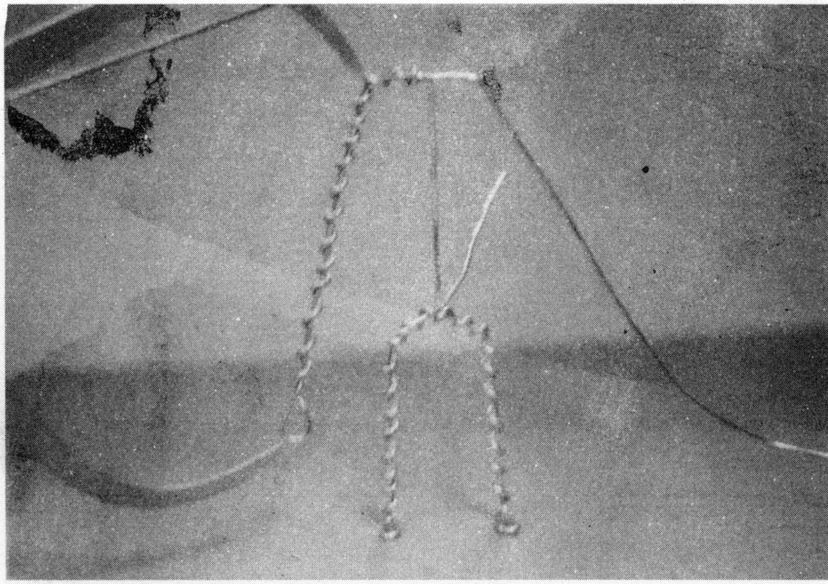

FIGURE 4.32 Measure the right arm with calipers to determine the length of the left arm.

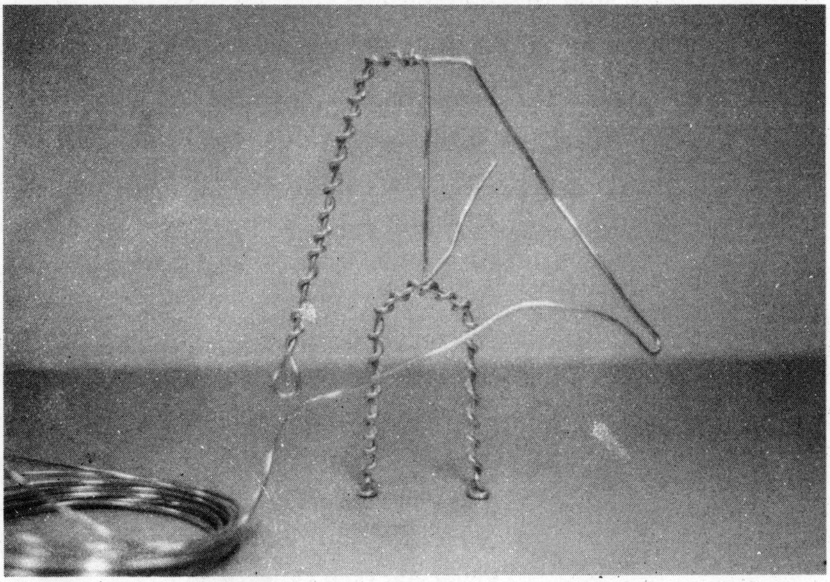

FIGURE 4.33 Make the palm for the left hand.

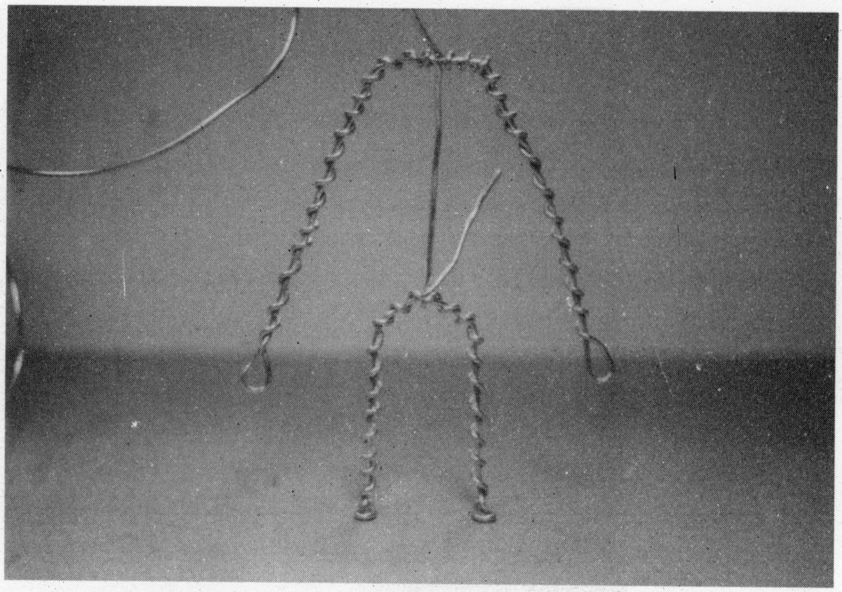

FIGURE 4.34 Tightly wrap the left arm up to the neck.

Step 18: Run the wire out from the body to shape the head as shown in Figure 4.35.

Step 19: Extend the wire to form the character's snout or upper skull. Remember that the wire is for support and the head doesn't normally have thin extremities, so the wire can be as basic as a lollipop-like loop. If your creature bears antennae or floppy ears, shape the wire as if it were a leg or arm. Make a loop, stop at the extremity to extend the wire, double back, and continue the loop. The wire shaping the head does not need to be doubled since the weight of the clay falls on the neck. If your character has a long neck, you might need to reinforce it with another piece of wire that can be added after the armature is done. Complete the head by going three-quarters of the way down the head and run the wire out to form the lower jaw. (See Figure 4.36.)

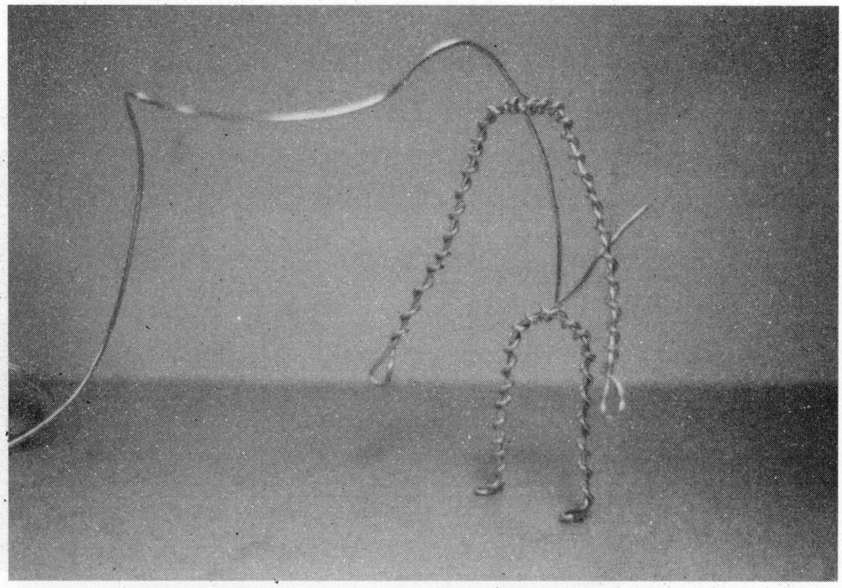

FIGURE 4.35 Run the wire out and begin shaping the head.

FIGURE 4.36 Form the top of the head and the lower jaw.

Step 20: Wrap the wire back down the neck and come up under the shoulders as shown in Figure 4.37.

FIGURE 4.37 Finish the lower jaw and neck.

Step 21: Wrap the wire down the backbone. (See Figure 4.38.)

Step 22: Wrap the wire all the way down to the hips. (See Figure 4.39.)

Step 23: Run the wire behind the creature to form its tail, if it has one. At the desired length, fold the wire over to create a loop. Examine Figure 4.40.

Step 24: Wrap the tail, bringing the wire back up to the hips. (See Figure 4.41.)

Step 25: With the wire back to where we started, tightly wrap it around the hips. Clip the excess from the beginning and end of the wire. Bend any remaining stubs down with the pliers. Examine Figures 4.42 and 4.43.

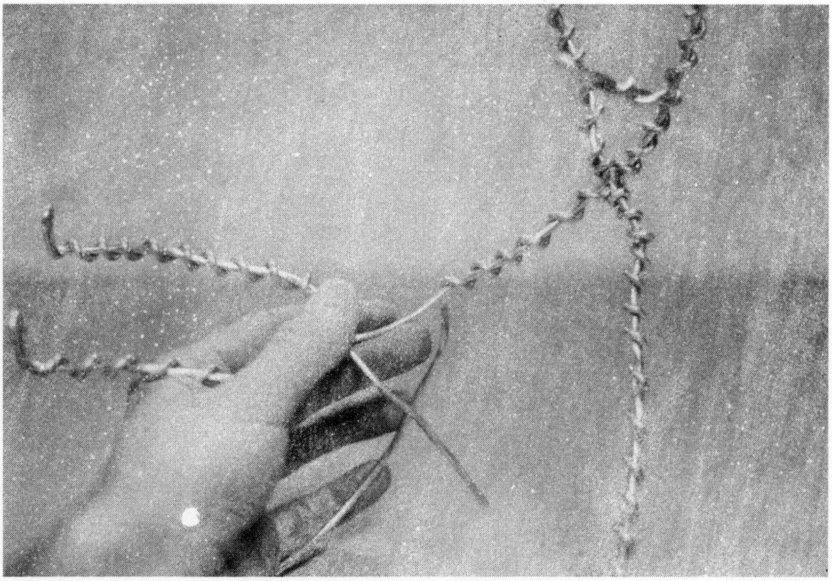

FIGURE 4.38 Tightly wind the wire down the backbone, making your way to the hips.

FIGURE 4.39 Wrap the wire from the backbone around the hips.

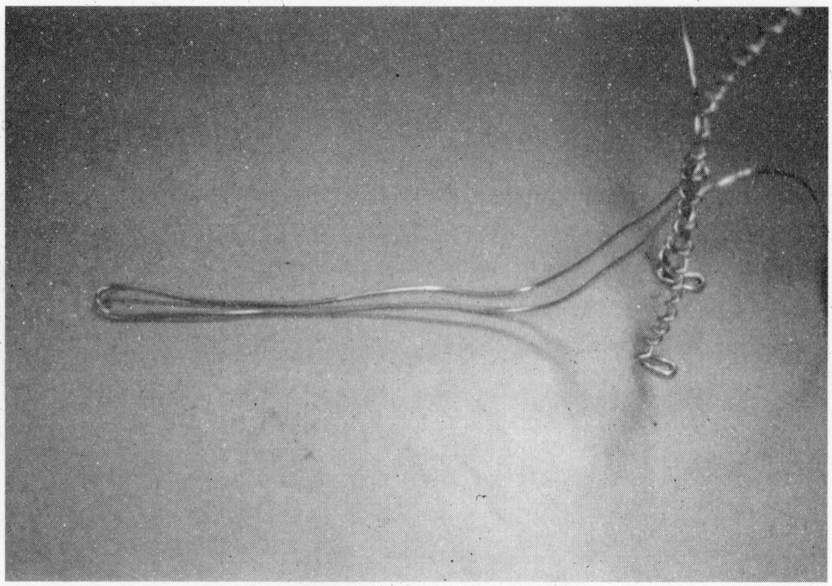

FIGURE 4.40 Shape the tail.

FIGURE 4.41 Make the tail.

FIGURE 4.42 Clip the excess wire with the wire cutters.

FIGURE 4.43 Bend the remaining wire down.

Upon completing the armature, it is necessary to bolt it down. Any wood is acceptable as long as it is large enough to accommodate the size of your creature. If you're going to keep it for posterity or promotion, then it is best to affix it to a black or painted-black material. This helps distinguish your model and makes for a better display. Bolting it down keeps you from handling your sculpture, which could end up destroying a lot of detail. It also prevents your model from toppling over. Depending on your creature, you could decide to elevate it off the platform, enabling you to sculpt underneath it. This works well with creatures that are lightweight. After bolting it down, you can move the armature into its final position, making any last-minute adjustments.

Step 26: Take the platform and drill two holes where the feet will go, using the armature as a guide. The holes you drill should be slightly larger than the bolts used to create the loops in the feet. This allows the bolts to slide in and out of the holes freely. (See Figure 4.44.)

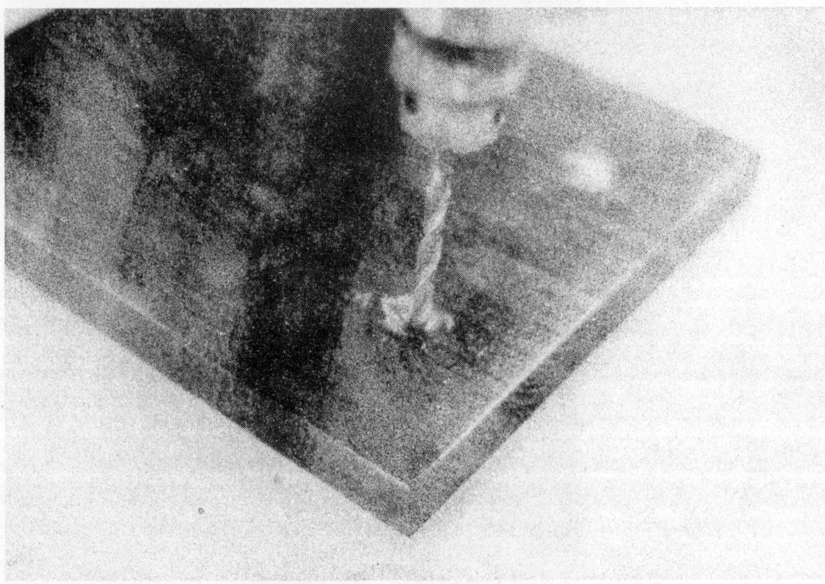

FIGURE 4.44 Drill two holes for the feet.

Step 27: Mill the holes on the underside of the platform so the screw heads are flush with the wood. This way the tops of the mounting screws won't unbalance the platform. (See Figure 4.45.)

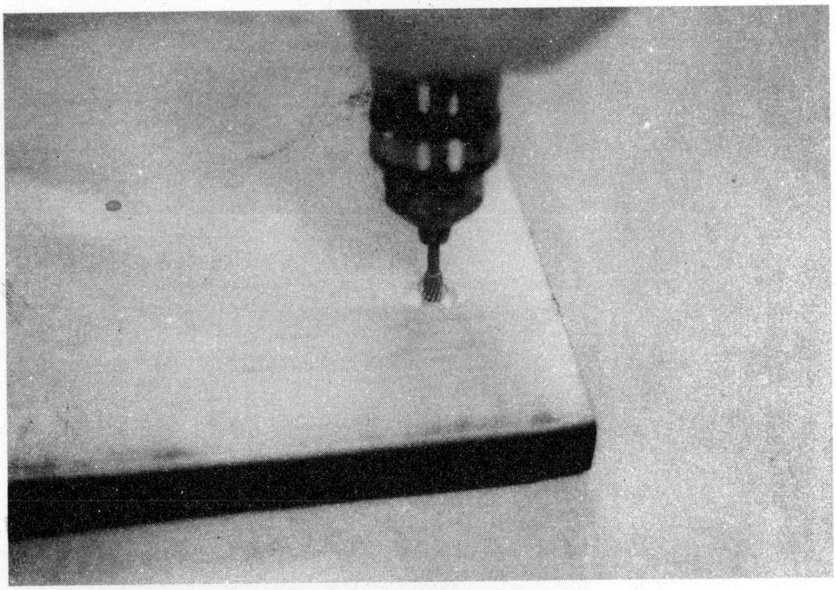

FIGURE 4.45 With a milling bit, carve out holes in which the screw heads can rest.

Step 28: Push the screws through the holes. Make sure they are flush with or lower than the surface of the wood. Examine Figures 4.46 and 4.47.

Step 29: Place the armature over the screws and bolt it down with the nuts as shown in Figure 4.48.

Step 30: Repeat the procedure outlined in steps 26–29 for the tail. Examine Figure 4.49.

Step 31: With the armature securely bolted down, as shown in Figure 4.50, move the character into its final position. Check for symmetry between the arms and the legs and make any final

FIGURE 4.46 Push the bolts into the holes.

FIGURE 4.47 Make sure the screws are long enough to bolt the armature down.

FIGURE 4.48 Secure the armature to the platform.

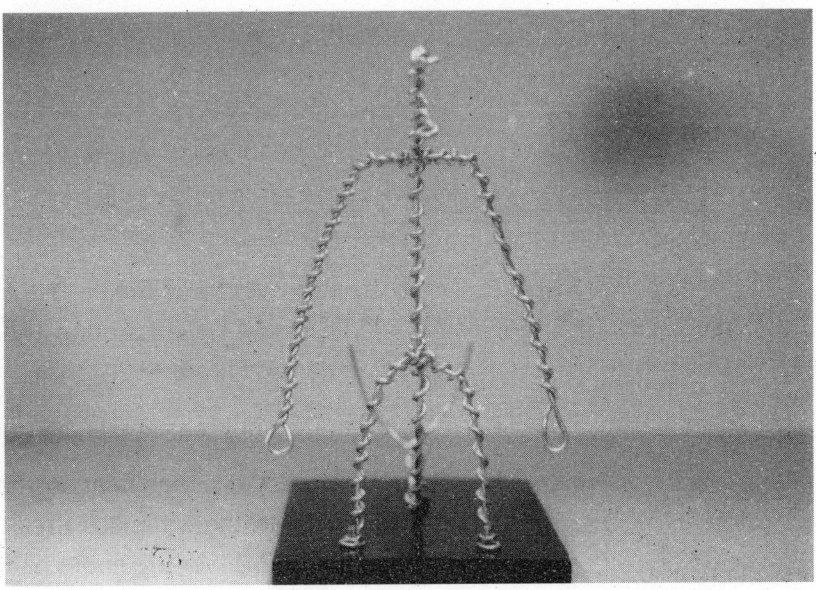

FIGURE 4.49 Bolt down the tail.

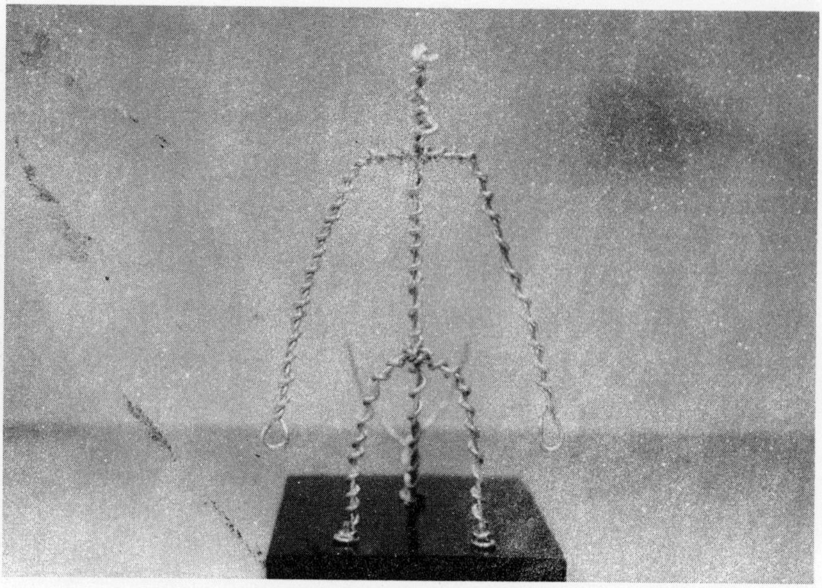

FIGURE 4.50 The Fire Monster's tail has been clipped with wire cutters and shaped into a fork.

adjustments. The design of the Fire Monster calls for it to have a forked tail. To create the fork, clip the wire in the center of the loop and shape the two strands accordingly. (See Figures 4.50 and 4.51.) If your creature has a single tail, clip the wire back on one side only so the skeleton of the tail will not be too thick.

Step 32: Go to the hands and add fingers. Use a smaller gauge of wire and wrap a single strand around the flattened end of the palm as shown in Figure 4.52.

Step 33: Add additional fingers as needed (Figure 4.53).

Step 34: Move the fingers into their final positions. In order to secure the fingers, epoxy them in place. Break off a suitable amount of epoxy putty to cover the entire palm. Mix it together and press it over the palm area. Make sure to firmly cover all sides of the attached fingers as shown in Figure 4.54.

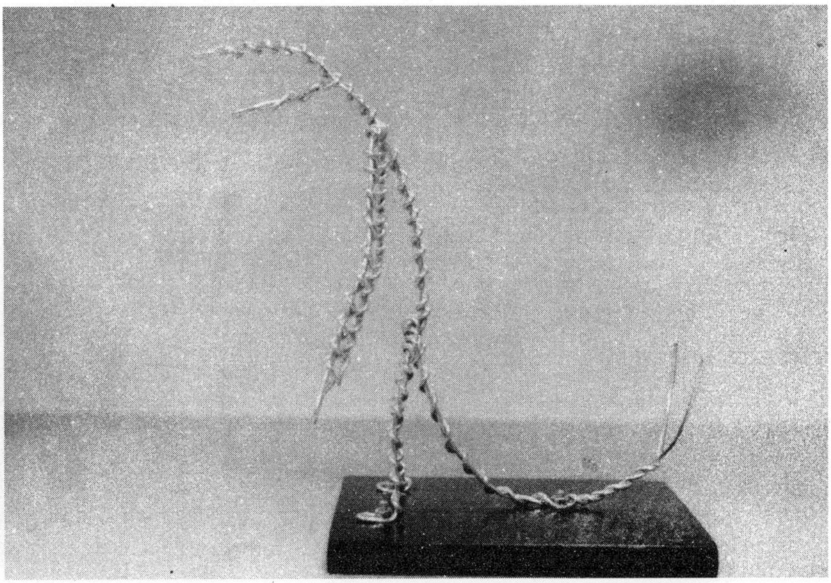

FIGURE 4.51 Move the armature into its final position.

FIGURE 4.52 Wrap a single strand of wire for the first finger.

FIGURE 4.53 Make as many fingers as needed.

FIGURE 4.54 Epoxy the fingers in place.

Step 35: After the epoxy has set, about fifteen minutes, bend the fingers at the joints with needlenose pliers. Figure 4.55 shows an example of this.

FIGURE 4.55 Bend the fingers at their joints with needlenose pliers.

Step 36: Repeat steps 32–35 for the other hand. This will complete the armature as shown in Figure 4.56.

With the armature secured, test each appendage to make sure it has a suitable amount of strength to support the weight of wet clay. This is important in areas that extend away from the creature's center of gravity, e.g., a giraffe-like neck. Simply break off a chunk of clay and mold it around the wire to see if it sags. If it's necessary to reinforce the wire, wrap a piece around a fixed anchor point as close to the center of gravity as possible. Run the wire around the unsupported area. To keep it in place, epoxy the anchor and end positions.

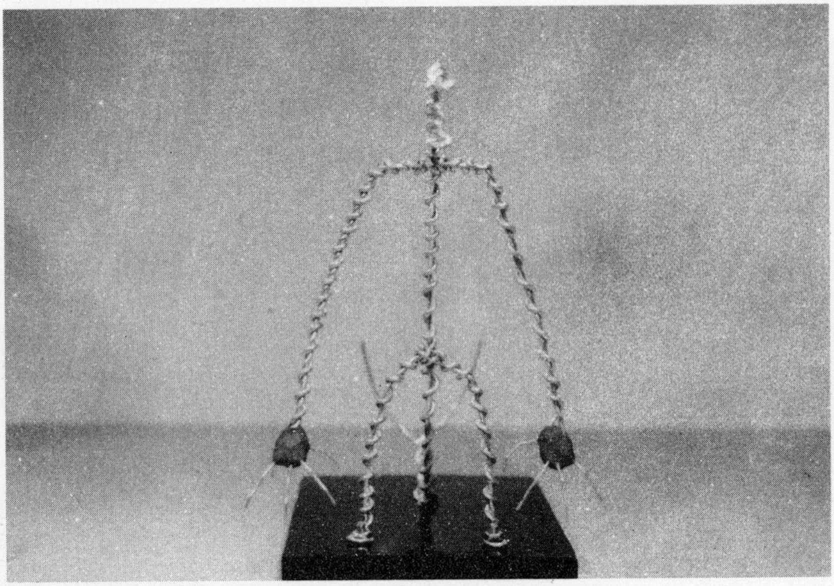

FIGURE 4.56 The armature is now complete.

A sculpting stand or table that allows a model to rotate freely is a wise and extremely useful investment. Many are made with the pottery or ceramic artist in mind. Some come with a drawer suitable for storing clay tools. Figure 4.57 shows an example of such a table. With a rotating platform, it is easy to get access to every side of the sculpture, removing the need to pick up the model and reposition it.

The Fire Monster is sculpted with air-dry clay. As explained in the beginning of the chapter, water-based clay shrinks, and can crack if it shrinks around a solid object. There are two things we can do to help prevent this. The first is to cover the armature in soft oil- or polymer-based clay, giving the wet clay a surface into which it can shrink. Even though the oil-based clay is soft, it doesn't take much resistance to crack the water-based clay. Therefore, it is important to make the wet clay twice as thick as the armature. This is a little harder to gauge but especially effective. The thicker the clay, the less likely it will crack. Keep in

FIGURE 4.57 This is an example of a small sculpture stand.

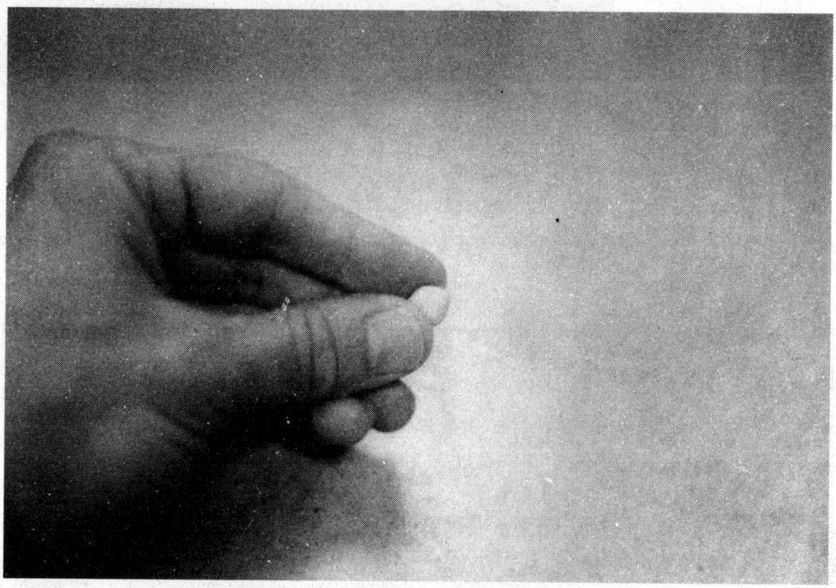

FIGURE 4.58 Pull off a small bead of oil-based clay.

mind however, the thicker the clay, the heavier it becomes, potentially causing the armature to sag or fall.

Step 37: Pull off a small bead, about the size of a large pea, of a soft, oil-based clay. (See Figure 4.58.)

Step 38: Begin covering the armature with small beads as shown in Figure 4.59.

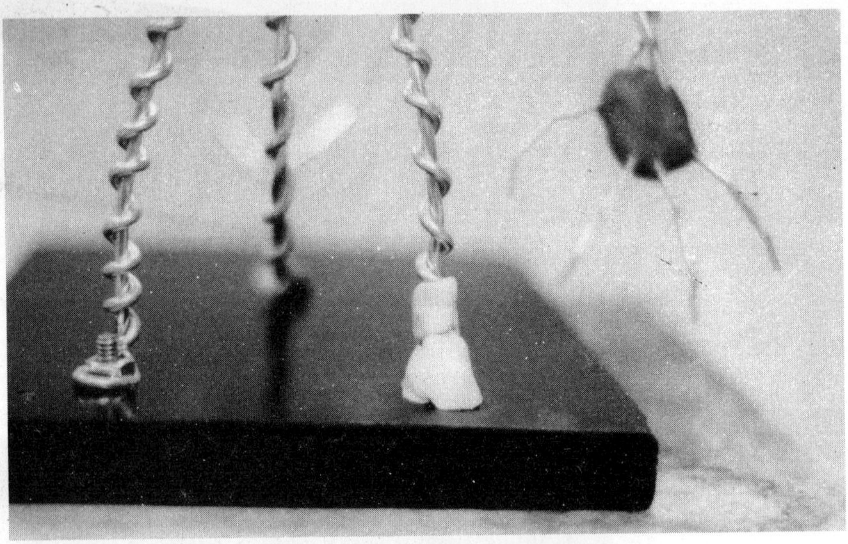

FIGURE 4.59 Apply beads of clay starting with the foot and work your way up.

Step 39: Cover the entire armature with a uniformly thick layer of clay as shown in Figure 4.60.

WORKING ENVIRONMENTS

Evaluate wisely the area you plan on sculpting in. The survival and quality of life for your sculpture depends on it. It's essential to choose a location conducive to sculpting. Pick an area you can

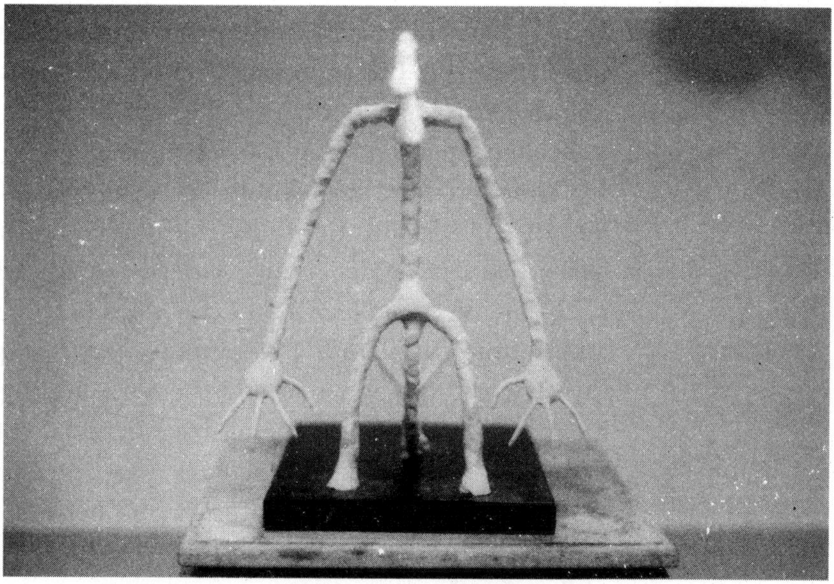

FIGURE 4.60 The armature is covered in a thin layer of oil-based clay.

make your own and be able to surround yourself with 2D reference material. Although your location may vary based on the type of clay you use, make sure you meet the majority of these requirements.

Make yourself comfortable. This is important because of the long hours you will be working in the same location. You will also find yourself twisting and turning to get into every nook and cranny of your sculpture. The area should be spacious and free of obstacles that might prohibit you or your sculptures from moving. You might choose to stand while sculpting, but when it comes to fine detail, you might want to sit to help steady your hand. Chairs can get very expensive, so make sure you don't get carried away with how fashionable the chair looks. Clay freely sticks to fabric, so you might want to go with a vinyl covering. Try to find one with a thick cushion that allows you to adjust the elevation. You will appreciate both of these features. Temperature plays an important part in being comfortable for yourself and for your sculpture. You want a place that is moderately cool, but the last thing you want is to be shivering. If it's too warm, you might get sweat in your eyes. The clay will have its own problems too, resisting soft detail if it is too cold or melting if it is too warm.

Your environment should be clean and safe from falling objects. It should also be a low-traffic area because dust, dirt, and other floating debris, which get stirred up whenever someone walks by, mix readily with all clay. This becomes a problem when attempting fine detail. These micro-particles get embedded into the clay, pulling and scraping the surrounding surface when removed. They also act as detail-blockers when stamping or sponging a texture. Hair and the clay itself are the two biggest offenders. Fragments of clay dry out quickly and become tiny rocks. If they mix back into your sculpture, they tear the clay or get in the way of fine detail.

Choose a location that is well lit. Because clay is a solid color, it can be difficult to interpret elevation changes. The same problem occurs in the computer. When we build our CG model, it will start off with a default shader. We will often rotate the model and alter the lighting to see how the surface is being described. For the majority of the time, we want our clay model to be globally illuminated, removing any dark shadows. A second, mobile light source is advantageous to highlighting particular sections. At certain points in the sculpting process, it is a good idea to turn off your global light source and look at your model in silhouette or with heavy shadows, using your mobile light or a candle to see its contours. This is especially useful when checking the symmetry of your model.

Once you begin your sculpture, you will not want to move it until it is completely dry and ready to be baked or molded. Prematurely relocating your model will cause the center of gravity to shift, possibly bending the armature. This yields unwanted results such as cracking or stress wrinkles. Water-based clay is highly susceptible to this. Furthermore, it increases the chances of a catastrophic accident, like dropping the sculpture or bumping it into something.

Conclusion

Make sure to create a design in 2D before entering the sculpting phase. Start with a character profile, listing attributes you would like to see and those attributes the creature cannot live without. These descriptions help paint the image in your mind, making it easier to draw or find suitable images.

The procedures and tools described in this chapter can be used for any type of character. If you are dealing with a large design, use multiple spools of wire by simply connecting the pieces with the methods outlined for attaching the Fire Monster's fingers. It's best to work with smaller maquettes, as this keeps the cost and weight of the sculpture to a minimum. The larger the model is, the more difficult it becomes to support.

Your fingers are the best tools for modeling the overall surface shape. Resort to tools for fine detail and areas that are inaccessible. When sculpting, anything is a tool. Keep an eye out for surfaces that might make a good texture. Use objects to create patterns and texture instead of trying to resculpt them. Don't get caught up in sculpting intricate detail by hand when it exists in everyday life.

In the next chapter, we will sculpt a maquette of the Fire Monster. The maquette building process requires a few days, so make sure the environment you choose is safe and comfortable. Sculpting can be very therapeutic; play your favorite music or enjoy the solitude. Either way, indulge in what relaxes you. This allows the ideas to flow and your hands to execute them.

CHAPTER

5 SCULPTING

In this chapter, we are sculpting our creature. This is a vitally important phase in the development process and defines how your creature looks and feels. The sculpture, or maquette, provides us with a clear goal. Time is not wasted developing ideas or troubleshooting the character's appearance. In addition, photos of the sculpture are used to help create the CG model.

Water-based, air-dry clay is used to create the Fire Monster. It's a good idea to experiment with all three types of clay covered in Chapter 4. Learn what their strengths and weaknesses are, and get comfortable working with them. Every project is a little different, so your favorite type of clay might not always be practical or economical. Air-dry clay does require extra work to use, however, the benefits far outweigh the few additional tasks needed. You must keep the clay from drying out, which entails covering it when you're not sculpting and spraying it with water regularly. The benefits of air-dry clay are that it doesn't require kneading, accepts extremely fine detail, and can be smoothed with water. With time and practice, you might find the sculpting process easier than modeling in the computer.

BEGINNING YOUR SCULPTURE

The Fire Monster was sculpted using air-dry clay. This type of clay was chosen because it is easily shaped and it accepts fine detail. If you choose air-dry clay, make sure you have a few things handy. Use a spray bottle filled with water to spray the clay about every fifteen minutes to keep it moist and pliable or to saturate sections that you want to blend together. Wrap wet paper towels around the unfinished areas to keep the clay moist for extended periods of time. As long as the towel is wet, the clay stays soft. In the event the clay dries up prematurely, this process also reconstitutes the clay. Lastly, a large, plastic garbage bag is needed to sustain the clay when you are not working on it. The bag needs to be big enough to cover the sculpture from top to bottom. Using all of these techniques can maintain the sculpture almost indefinitely. If you decide to use another type of clay, these items are not needed.

There are three phases in the sculpting process that apply to all types of clay but vary in execution. The first phase is to build the basic shape of your model. Next sculpt the features and fine detail. Lastly solidify the model by leaving it exposed to air, baking it, or making a mold, depending on the type of clay.

The basic shape is achieved using the "build up" method, which entails placing thousands of beads of clay onto an armature. This process is very effective because it gives you the chance to accurately shape your model according to your vision, and it is easier to maintain symmetry. If you use large clumps of clay, you end up having to chisel the sculpture down to get one side to look like the other. This can be more difficult, and you probably won't get an idea of what your creature looks like until it's too late. This might seem excessive and time consuming, but the model will be a closer representation of your vision throughout the process, which saves you an immeasurable amount of time in the long run.

Once you start applying clay to the armature, spray it often to keep it moist and if you need to leave it for a while, be sure to soak it down and cover it with a garbage bag. The bag does not have to be airtight, but it should be free of holes and secured around the bottom of the sculpture. To prevent mold buildup, allow fresh air in once in a while. Once your sculpture is covered, you can leave it unattended for days. It takes a while for the clay to dry completely.

TUTORIAL

THE "BUILD UP" METHOD

Step 1: Apply beads of clay to the armature. You may start anywhere because this process is so incremental; however, the hips give a good indication of the proportions for the rest of the body parts. The beads should be sized to build bulk, not to define detail. Break a pebble-sized piece of clay off the block and roll it between your fingers until it is a round ball. (See Figure 5.1.)

FIGURE 5.1 Apply small beads of clay to the armature, beginning with the hips.

Step 2: Spread the beads outward along the shape of the armature. Try to keep the beads in a single layer. Continue applying them to the rest of the creature's appendages as shown in Figure 5.2.

Step 3: Keep adding beads to the creature's trunk to build up bulk as shown in Figure 5.3.

Step 4: Run clay beads down both arms. Pay close attention to the muscles in the arms, as they usually dictate the shape of the skin. Do not put any clay on the fingers or toes; these areas are very thin and dry out quickly. Use smaller beads to define any muscles. Study Figure 5.4 to get an idea of how this is done.

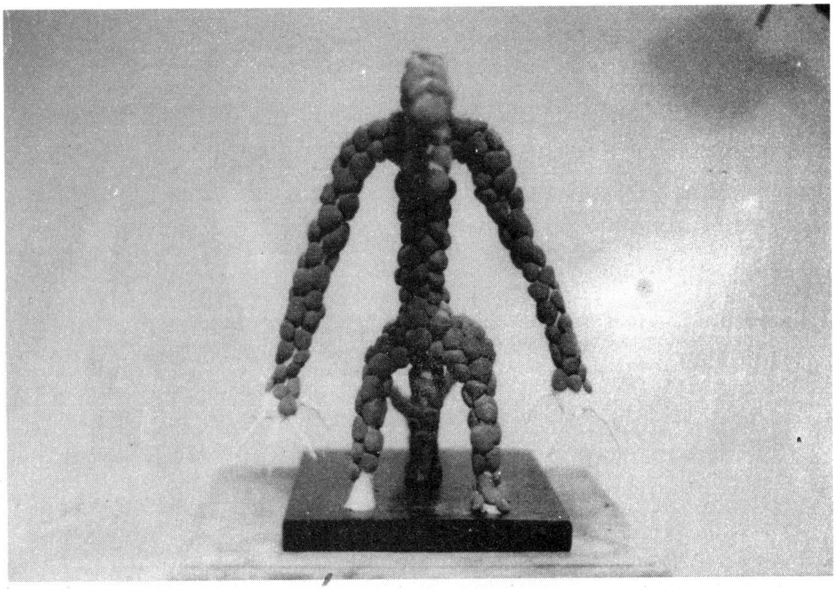

FIGURE 5.2 Clay beads applied to the entire character in a single layer.

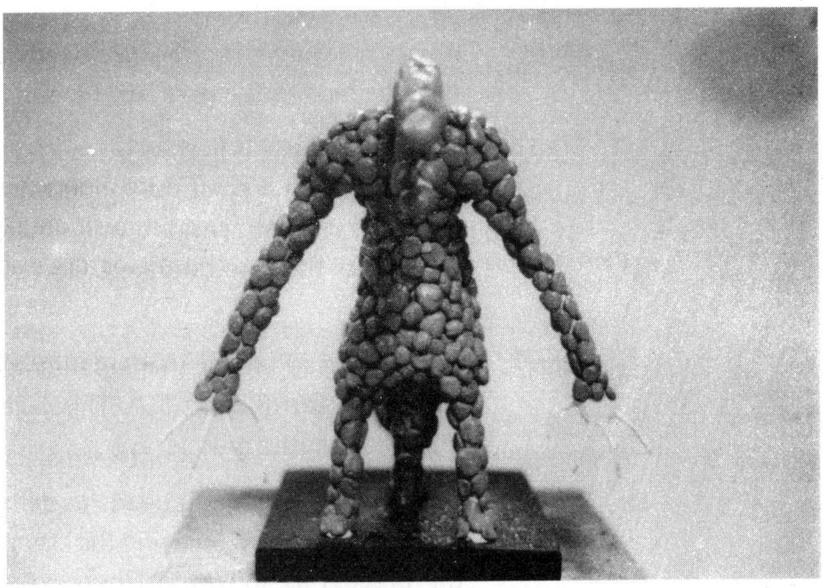

FIGURE 5.3 Clay beads applied to the body to build up bulk.

FIGURE 5.4 Muscle detail has been added to the front of the Fire Monster's arms.

Step 5: If your creature has a tail, run beads down the tail starting near the hips. (See Figure 5.5.)

Step 6: The Fire Monster is fleshed out and ready for some finer detail. Choose an area of the model you wish to work on and cover the rest with paper towels and spray them down with water until they are saturated. Figure 5.6 demonstrates this process.

Step 7: Continue to add small, shape-defining beads to flesh out the creature's skin (Figure 5.7). This layer of beads could be thought of as the muscle layer.

Step 8: Once you have enough beads to define the muscles, begin smoothing the clay. Spraying the clay with a little water helps the process as shown in Figure 5.8. Add muscle-defining beads to the rest of the model and smooth the entire model as shown in Figure 5.9.

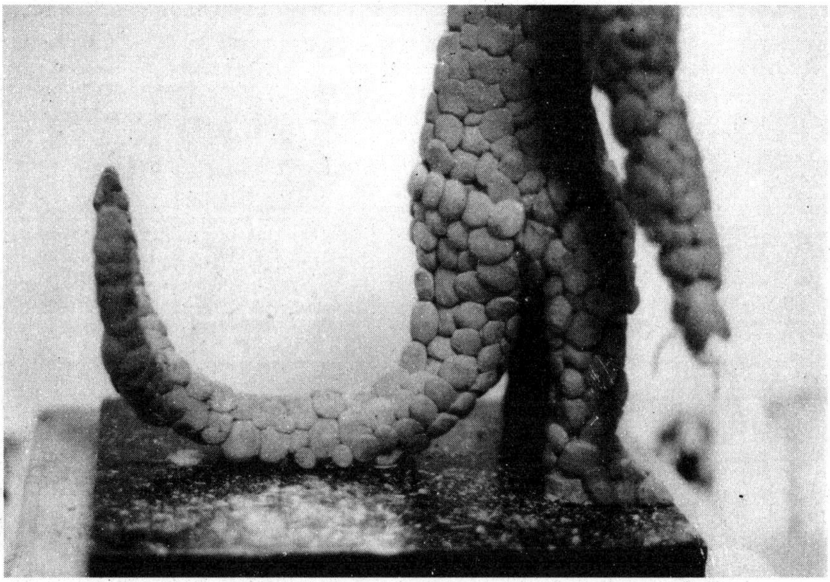

FIGURE 5.5 Apply beads down the tail.

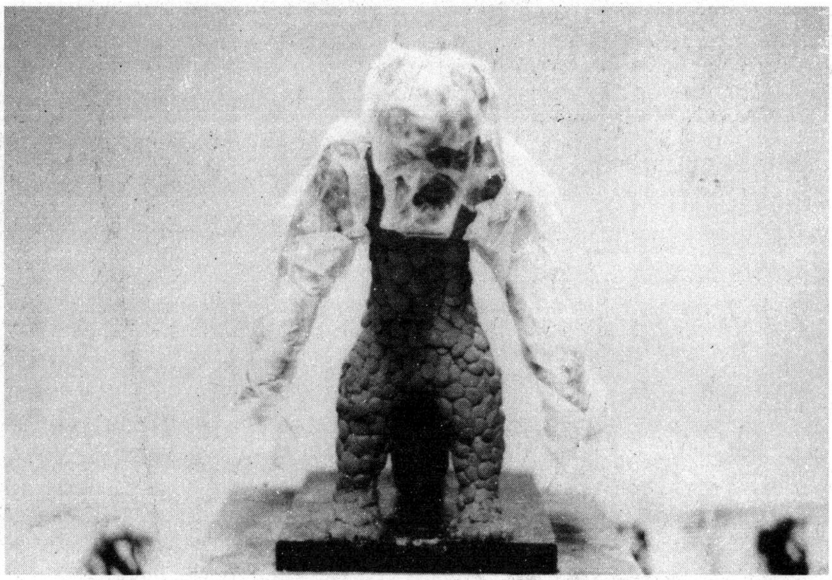

FIGURE 5.6 Cover the parts you're not working on with wet paper towels to keep the clay from drying out.

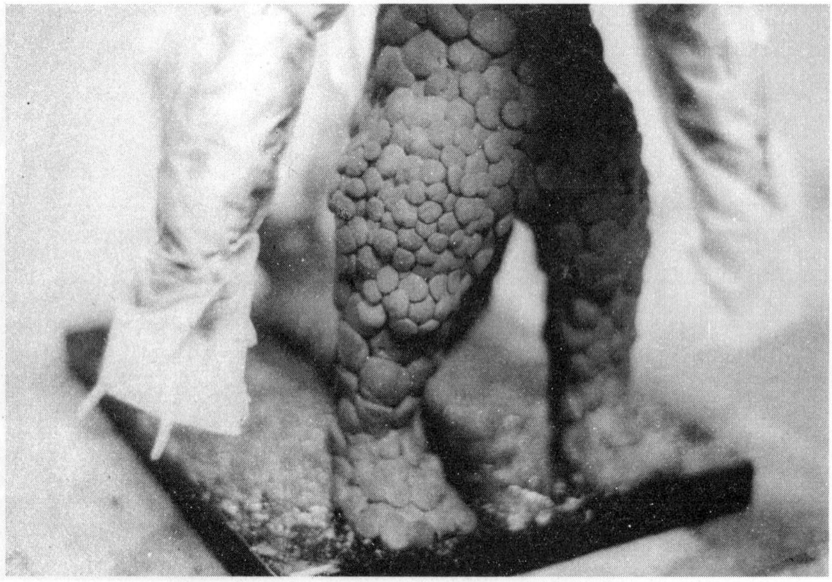

FIGURE 5.7 Add small beads to create the muscle layer.

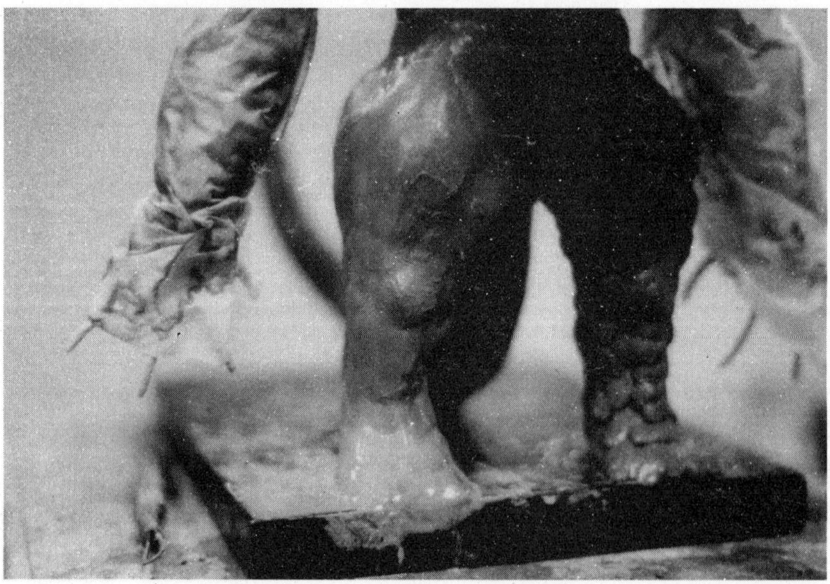

FIGURE 5.8 Spray the beads with water and smooth out.

FIGURE 5.9 The surface of the Fire Monster has been completely smoothed.

Tips and Tricks

If you have never sculpted before, adding detail can be difficult and frustrating. To make this process easier, use existing objects to make impressions in the clay. One way to do this is to make your own rubber stamps. Using liquid rubber, you can copy just about anything. Liquid rubber or latex can be found at most hobby and craft stores. The following tutorial shows you a quick and easy way to make your own rubber stamps.

TUTORIAL

RUBBER STAMPS

Step 1: Find an object that looks similar to the texture you are trying to achieve. The human hand has excellent wrinkles and makes for a really nice stamp. Position your hand to get the best-looking wrinkles. With a small disposable paintbrush, apply some latex between your thumb and index finger as shown in Figure 5.10.

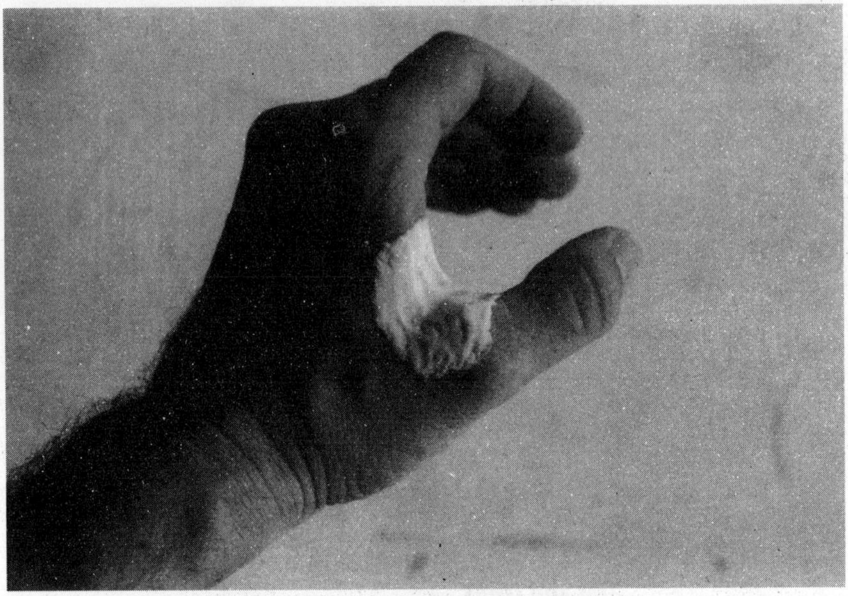

FIGURE 5.10 Paint liquid latex onto a wrinkled part of your hand.

Since latex is a liquid, it will work its way into small cracks and crevices. Therefore it is not suitable on fabrics or around hair or open or healing wounds.

Step 2: Allow this to dry for about five minutes. Use a hairdryer to speed up the process, if you wish.

Step 3: Continue painting layers of latex to reinforce the stamp.

Step 4: When it's dry, peel the latex off. This creates a negative impression of your skin. Press it into soft clay and a positive impression is stamped as shown in Figure 5.11.

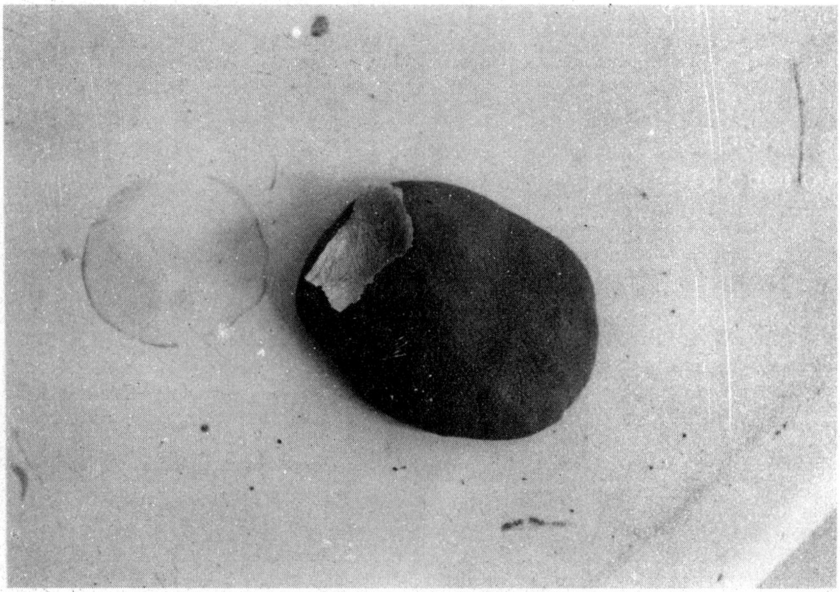

FIGURE 5.11 Peel the latex off your skin and stamp it onto some clay to make a positive impression.

Another technique for adding detail is to build detailed pieces of clay before attaching them to your sculpture. This next tutorial shows how to create a biomechanical vein.

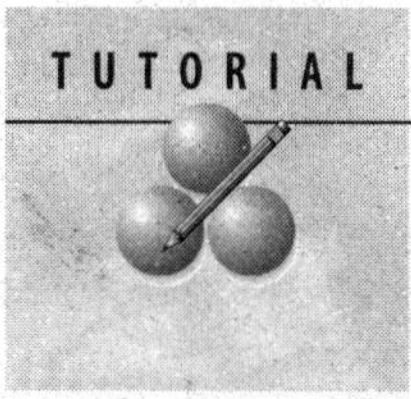

BIOMECHANICAL VEIN

Step 1: Break off a piece of clay. Roll it out into a tube on a smooth surface.

Step 2: Roll a piece of electrical conduit found at the hardware store around the surface. Press hard enough to make deep impressions.

FIGURE 5.12 This is an example of an impression made with electrical conduit.

Step 3: Continue around the entire surface. Try to roll it in a complete circle so the detail lines up with itself. Figure 5.12 shows an example.

SCULPTING

Starting with a smooth clay surface is like a three-dimensional blank canvas. In fact, it is identical to painting 3D texture maps after you have built your geometry. Our next step is to refine the creature's shape and add detail. This part is impossible to work out in your head. By shaping the clay, we can test ideas, realize problems, and formulate new concepts. The character starts to take on a personality. The fascinating part is that the creature develops a mind of its own and may take on a different personality than originally planned.

TUTORIAL

Sculpting

Step 1: Once the entire surface is smoothed out, check the sculpture for symmetry and thickness. It is very easy to make one arm thinner than the other, so use calipers wherever possible, and add more clay beads, if necessary. Check the character to see that all of the skin's contours are represented. If any are missing, add more beads or a piece of clay in the desired shape. Work the clay into the model as demonstrated in Figure 5.13.

Step 2: Detail can now be applied. Start with the head and work your way out. Usually this is the most detailed and challenging area. Completing the head first brings the sculpture to life, making it easier to envision the rest of it. With a clay tool, make oval incisions for an eye, nose, and mouth. Begin

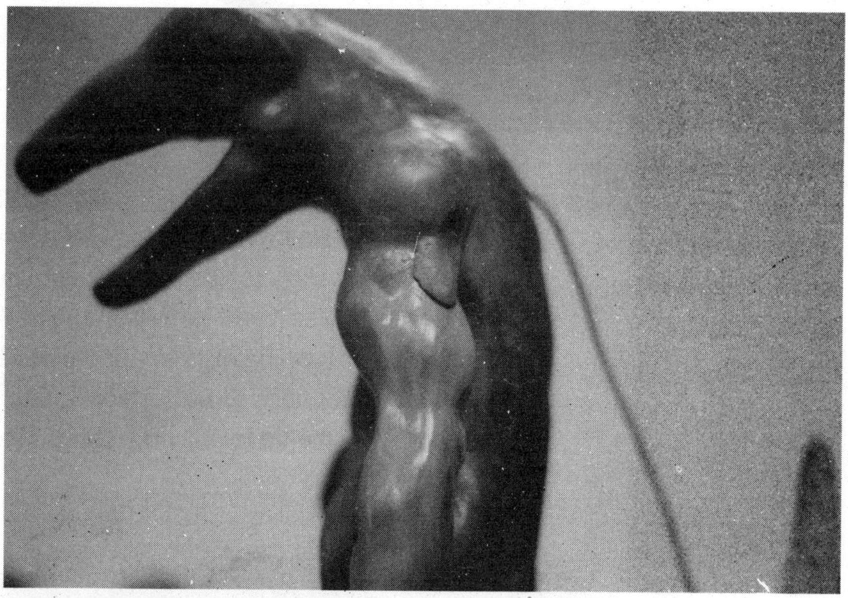

FIGURE 5.13 Add a piece of clay for any muscles or surface detail that are missing. Blend the clay into the sculpture by rubbing down the edges with your fingers.

adding surface detail to the head with additional clay pieces as shown in Figure 5.14. These details might include skin texture, hair, moles, or scars.

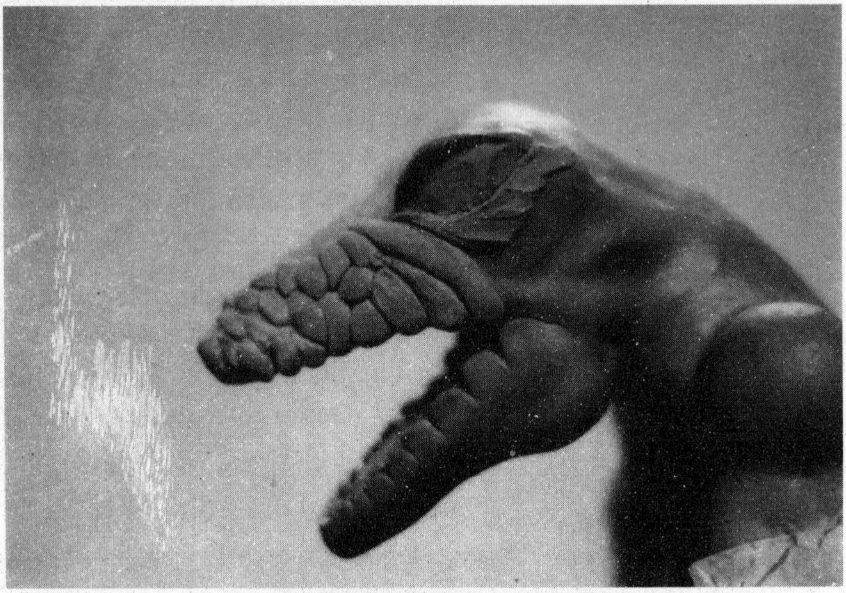

FIGURE 5.14 Add beads of clay for the creature's skin detail.

Step 3: Use a tool like the one shown in Figure 5.15 to blend the edges of the skin detail. It is difficult to blend the edges perfectly with any type of tool, so use a soft touch, and continually move over the clay as if you were painting in Photoshop with a low opacity. Most of the nicks in the clay will be taken care of later, so it does not need to be perfect. Rotate the tool to use different parts of the tip for varying results. (See Figure 5.16.)

FIGURE 5.15 A rubber-tipped modeling tool.

FIGURE 5.16 Tubes of clay are placed under the eye and blended into the skin detail to build up the cheekbones.

Step 4: Spray the head once or twice with water. Using a sponge similar to the one shown in Figure 5.17, pat the area gently to remove any clay artifacts or nicks in the surface of the clay. Press the sponge into the cracks and crevices between the folds of clay to smooth out the area. Use more water if needed. Experiment with different sponges until you find a generic skin texture that you like. Figure 5.18 shows the application. It is good to use a sponge to smooth out the clay periodically, giving you a sense of what the skin looks like. It's also a great cleanup tool, reaching areas other tools and fingers cannot.

Step 5: For detailed areas that need to be indented, scrape out grooves with an open-loop tool (Figure 5.19). For the finer areas, use a rubber-tipped modeling tool. Figure 5.20 shows the results of the tool on the lower jaw.

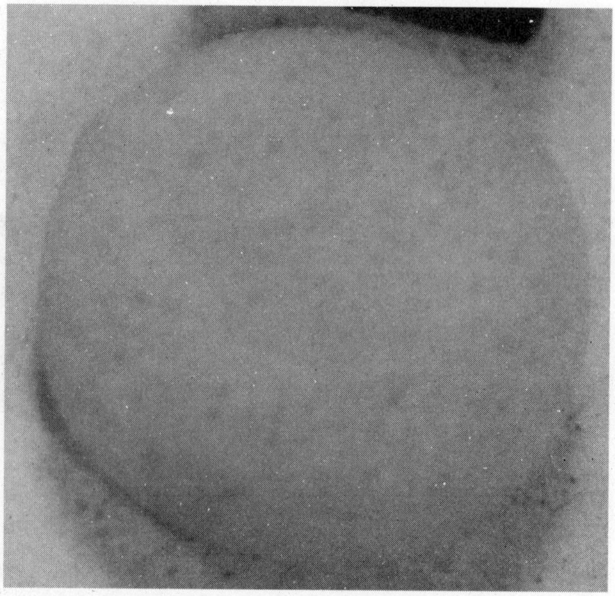

FIGURE 5.17 A yellow hobby sponge used to smooth the clay with generic texture.

FIGURE 5.18 Gently blot the area repeatedly to remove any nicks or defects in the clay. This also provides a neutral skin texture.

FIGURE 5.19 This is an open-loop tool.

FIGURE 5.20 Add surface detail to the lower jaw.

Step 6: Use a sponge like the one shown in Figure 5.21 to smooth out the lower jaw. This type of sponge is used because it has smaller pores, creating a finer texture. To get into cracks, fold the sponge over a thin-line tool. Figure 5.22 demonstrates the action.

Step 7: To create soft creases or wrinkles in the clay, drape a thin piece of plastic wrap over the area you wish to affect. Using a sgraffito tool like the one shown in Figure 5.23, press into the plastic. Make strokes over the plastic to create creases in the creature's skin; if the plastic breaks or tears, get a new piece.

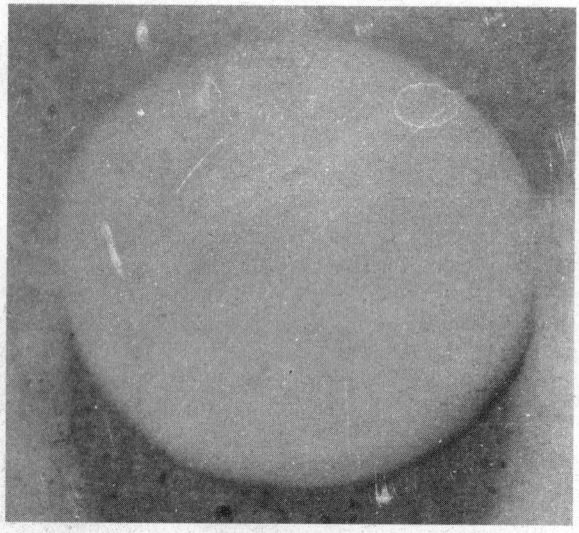

FIGURE 5.21 This is a polyurethane makeup sponge used to smooth the clay on the lower jaw.

FIGURE 5.22 Smooth the surface of the lower jaw with a thin sponge.

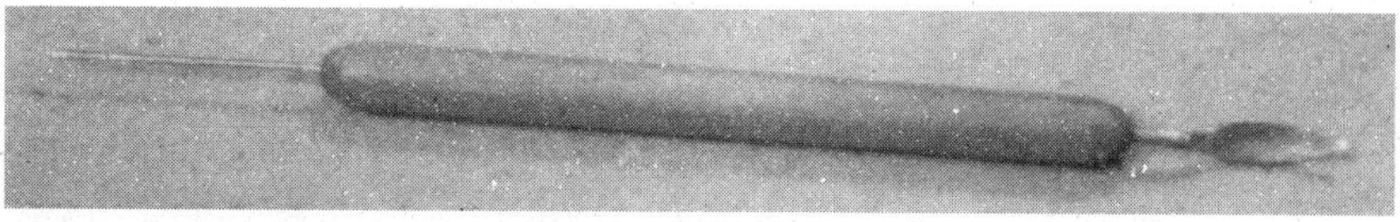

FIGURE 5.23 The sgraffito tool used to make impressions in the clay through the plastic wrap.

The plastic softens the effect of the tool and presses the clay in along the borders of the incision, to create a smooth sloping edge. Practice this on a separate piece of clay to achieve varying results. The type of tool and motion of the slice weigh heavily on the outcome. Figure 5.24 shows the results of using the plastic wrap just under the corner of the eye. Use a sponge to clean the area after removing the plastic.

FIGURE 5.24 Curves have been drawn over plastic wrap in the corner of the eye. The plastic has been removed and the area was cleaned up with a sponge.

Step 8: Once the head is done, move on to a new area. Remember to spray the model with water if you are using wet clay. The pectoral muscle in the chest is shaped with a thin-line loop tool as shown in Figure 5.25. Use the tool to remove clay with a gentle stroking motion. Figure 5.26 shows the muscle after it is shaped with a loop tool. These tools are good to use in tight areas where your fingers and hands can cause damage to surrounding areas. Once you are pleased with the shape, smooth out the area with a sponge.

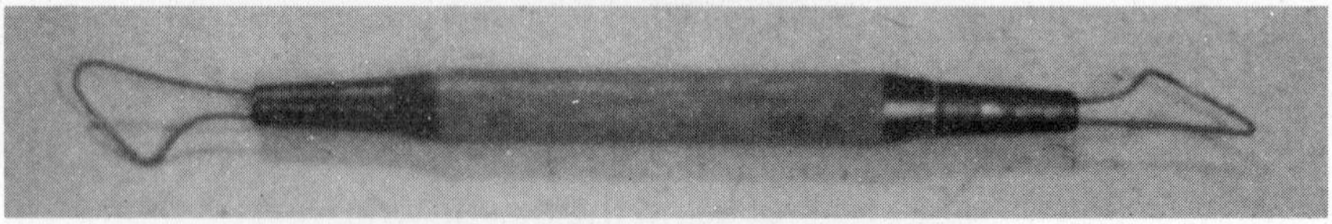

FIGURE 5.25 This is a thin-line loop tool.

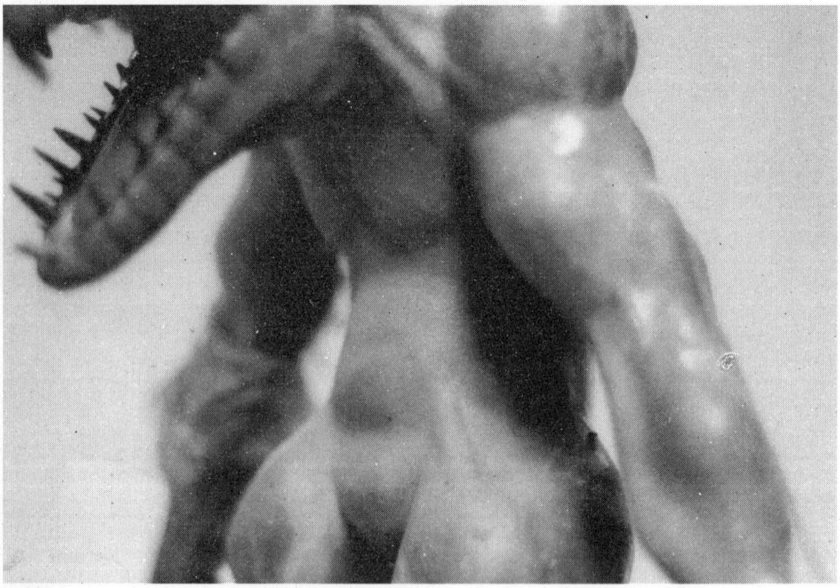

FIGURE 5.26 Using a loop tool, shape the pectoral muscle.

Step 9: To add a coarser type of skin, roll out balls of clay between your index finger and thumb and press them onto the surface of the clay as shown in Figure 5.27.

FIGURE 5.27 Press balls of clay onto the back of the Fire Monster's neck.

Step 10: Spray the newly pressed balls of clay with water. Using a tough sponge, like a greasepaint makeup sponge similar to the one shown in Figure 5.28, firmly blend the beads together. Figure 5.29 shows this action.

Step 11: Along with coarse skin, you might have parts of an exoskeleton emerging from or on top of the skin. To add these features, place strips of clay in the desired shape and press them onto the clay. Do not press too hard or you will damage the shape. Figure 5.30 shows an example of this detail before it is worked into the model.

Step 12: Add any remaining skin detail across the rest of creature. (See Figure 5.31.)

Step 13: Using the same technique and sponge outlined in Step 10, blend the balls of clay into the skin of the creature. If your creature has spikes or parts protruding out of its skin, use a

FIGURE 5.28 This is an example of a greasepaint sponge.

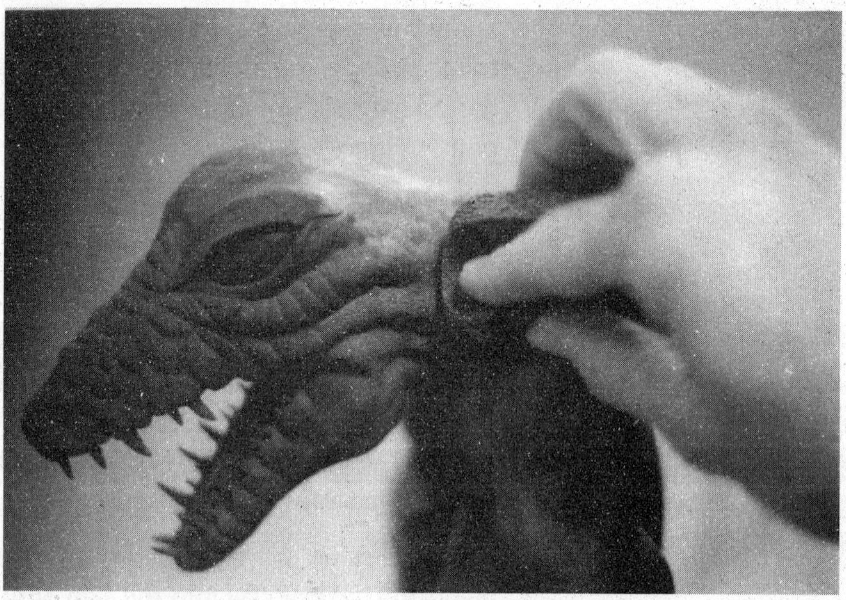

FIGURE 5.29 Blend the balls into the creature's skin.

FIGURE 5.30 Strips of clay and beads are added to the creature's back.

FIGURE 5.31 Fill in the remaining areas with skin detail as needed.

cylindrical tool to push holes into the clay. This creates a holdout area to place the protruding object and is easier than trying to build up from the surface. Teeth are done in the same manner. Figure 5.32 shows the surface after it is blended together.

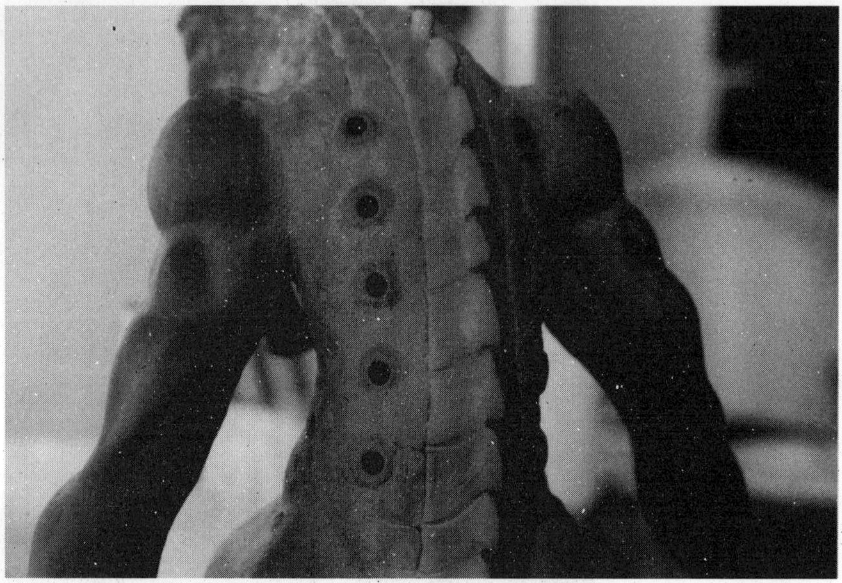

FIGURE 5.32 Blend the clay with the red, rubber sponge. Shape the clay strip into pointy scales.

Step 14: Very few things in Mother Nature end abruptly. Sporadically place extra beads across the skin's surface to blend any rough surface textures as shown in Figure 5.33.

Step 15: To create skin folds, place plastic over the desired area. Carve creases into the skin with a sgraffito tool like the one used in Figure 5.34.

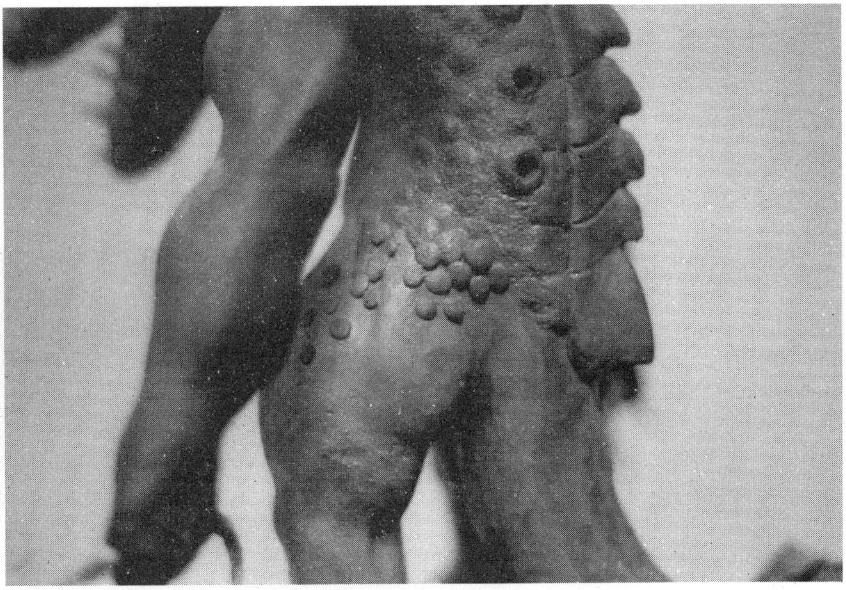

FIGURE 5.33 Place balls of clay across the character's skin. When finished blend in with a sponge.

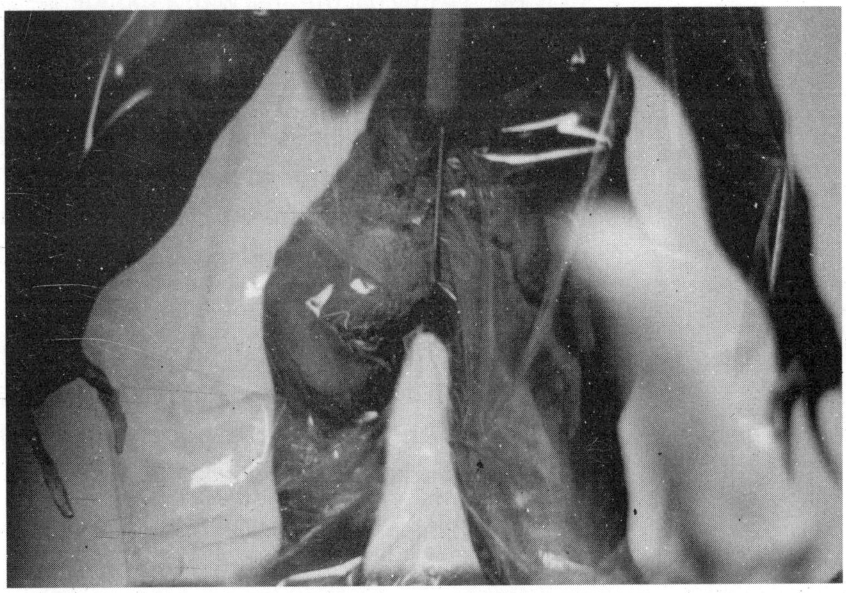

FIGURE 5.34 Firmly run the sgraffito tool over the plastic in a curved slicing motion.

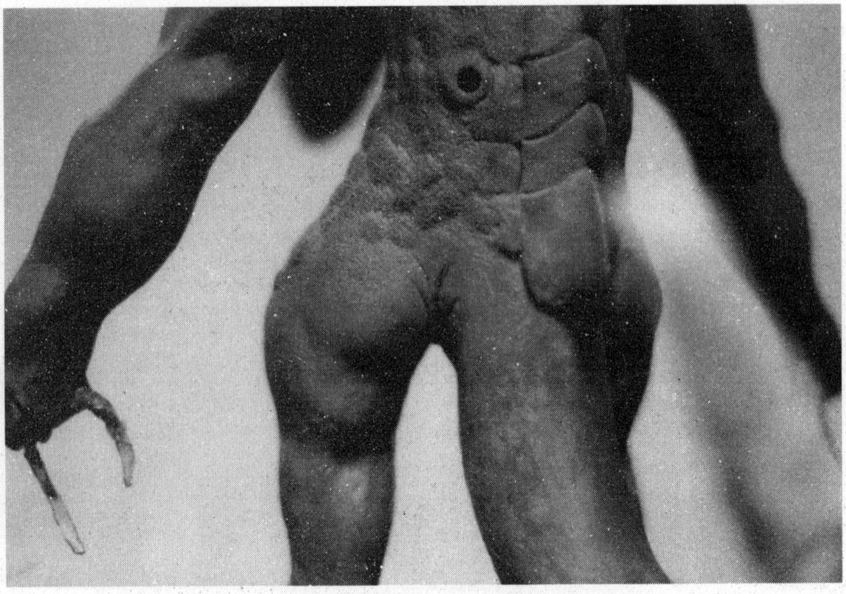

FIGURE 5.35 Pat the newly formed wrinkles with a sponge.

Step 16: Gently pat the area with a sponge. Be careful not to press too hard or you will blend creases out of the clay surface. (See Figure 5.35.)

Step 17: To create light skin texture, such as in the area of the elbow, use the sgraffito tool as you did in Step 15. With the sharp tip of the tool, graze the clay ever so gently. Try it with or without the plastic. Blend the lines gently with a sponge as shown in Figure 5.36.

Step 18: At this point we can go back to the hands or feet. Using the build-up method, add small beads of clay to form the palm and fingers. Smooth the beads out. Apply more beads for the knuckles as shown in Figure 5.37.

Step 19: Blend in the knuckles and carry some of the clay back to the wrist to form tendons in the hand. (See Figure 5.38.)

Step 20: Smooth the surface with a sponge as shown in Figure 5.39.

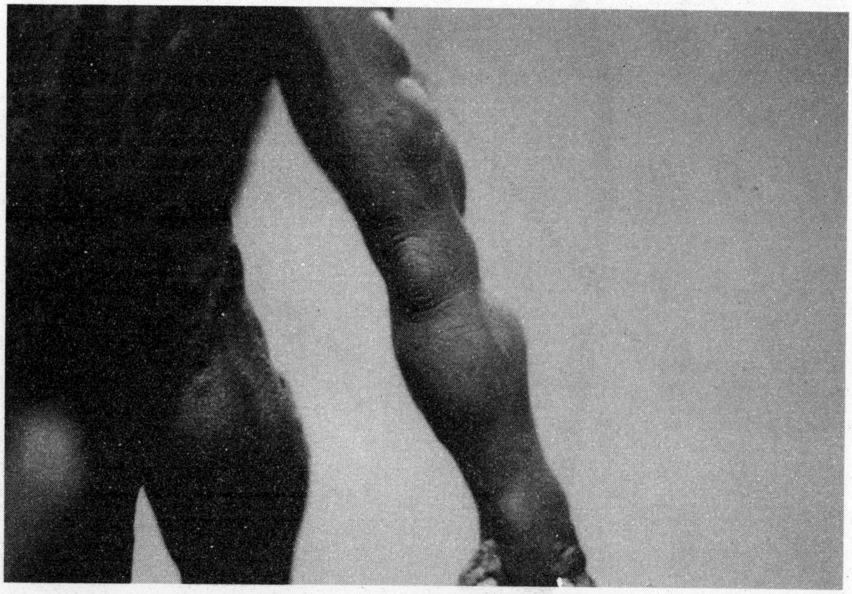

FIGURE 5.36 Carve wrinkles into the elbow. Pat the newly formed creases with a sponge.

FIGURE 5.37 Build up the hand and add beads for knuckles.

FIGURE 5.38 Shape the knuckles and tendons.

FIGURE 5.39 The hand after it has been smoothed with a sponge.

Step 21: Draw small creases in the knuckles similar to the ones you applied to the elbow. Make sure to draw them in the shape of the knuckle for heightened realism. For a final skin effect, lightly glide the point of a sharp sgraffito tool over the surface of the hand. Gently pat with a sponge to remove any artifacts and blend in the detail. Figure 5.40 shows the results.

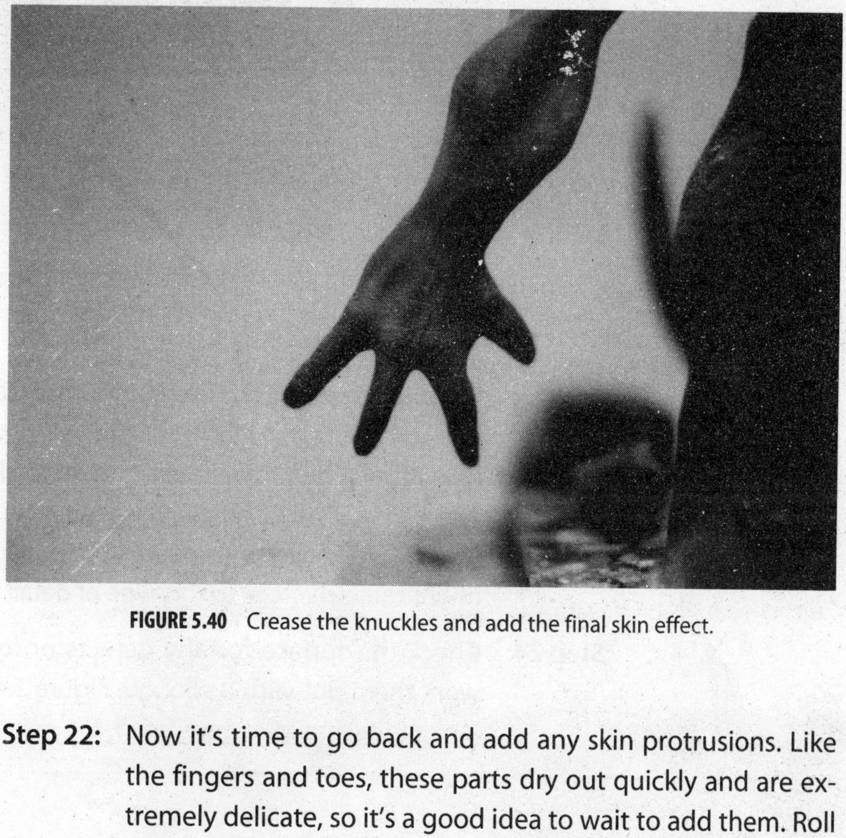

FIGURE 5.40 Crease the knuckles and add the final skin effect.

Step 22: Now it's time to go back and add any skin protrusions. Like the fingers and toes, these parts dry out quickly and are extremely delicate, so it's a good idea to wait to add them. Roll out clay on a smooth surface to create teeth, spikes, or, in the case of the Fire Monster, quills. Let them dry out a little, then insert them into the holes you created earlier. Figure 5.41 shows an example.

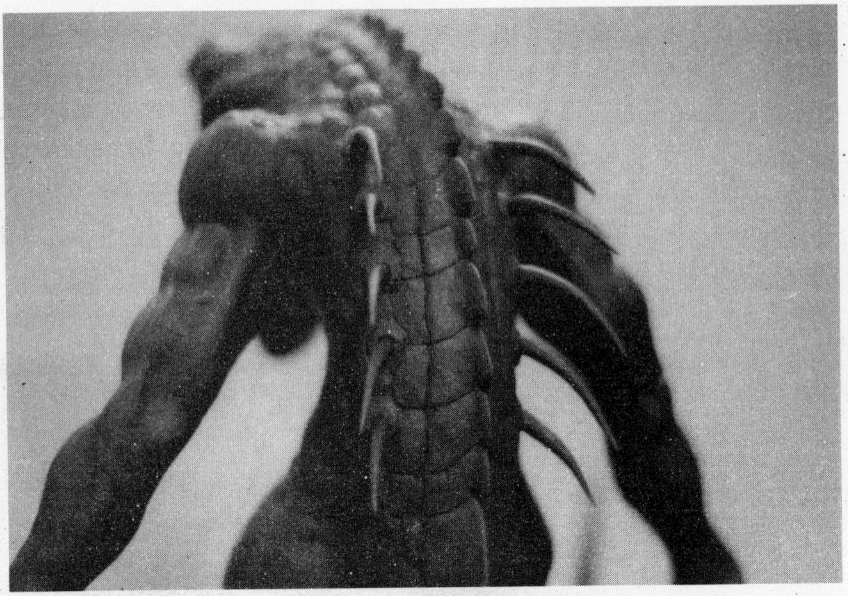

FIGURE 5.41 Put porcupine-like quills down the creature's back.

Step 23: Some of the protrusions might be too small to handle, like the tiny quills along the Fire Monster's tail. Poke or hook them with the end of a tool to help place them as shown in Figure 5.42. These last details should finish off your character. Draping paper towels over these areas or spraying them with water might cause damage to this type of detail.

Step 24: Check the surface for any defects or foreign particles and work them out with a sponge. Figure 5.43 shows a close-up look of the Fire Monster's head.

Finishing Touches

The next stage is to let the clay dry out. Since many precautions were taken prior to this to prevent the clay from cracking, it

FIGURE 5.42 Add any finishing touches to your character.

should be fine, however, some cracks might still appear. The best way to prevent cracking is to let the clay dry out slowly. Liberally mist the entire model with water every hour or so and diminish the amount of water as time passes. Do not cover it. The clay will change colors based upon the thickness. Thinner areas turn a light

FIGURE 5.43 This is a close-up of the Fire Monster's head.

gray while thicker areas darken. If the clay has cracked, the following steps demonstrate how to patch it up.

TUTORIAL

REPAIRS

Step 1: Fill any separation with fresh clay and blend it into the model with a sponge. Once you blend in the edges, be careful not to disturb the model. This could cause the model to shift, destroying the blended appearance.

Step 2: It is highly probable this patch will crack again, so repeat the process until no more cracks appear.

CONCLUSION

The sculpting process is now finished. The sculpture is still very fragile and is best stored in a cool, dry location out of harm's way. Limit moving or transporting it. In the event the sculpture breaks, it can be repaired with Elmer's glue and touched up with additional clay. If a more stable version is required, use any flexible mold-making material to make a cast. Gypsum cement or plaster is not recommended because it adheres to the clay and will crack the sculpture.

The sculpture can be painted once it has thoroughly dried. Acrylic paints are acceptable, and in some cases, it may be necessary to prime the surface with a base color to prevent additional colors from fading or seeping into the clay.

CHAPTER

6 SCANNED DATA

In the previous chapter, you sculpted a maquette to be used as a reference object. To build a CG model from this reference, it is necessary to photograph the object from different angles. The photos are scanned into Maya, allowing you to manipulate geometry over them. Another method to get your physical model into the digital realm is to scan the sculpture directly into three-dimensional information or what is referred to as point cloud data. There are many different types of scanning methods available, ranging from lasers to point-to-point vertex entry. Each of these methods requires external tools and software, but most are too costly for the independent artist. However, there are companies that will scan the model for you. When the model is scanned, the data shows up as millions of floating points shaping your character, and geometry can be built from this cloud of points by connecting the dots.

RAW DATA

Different scanners produce different results, but typically, scanned data is messy and/or extremely dense regardless of the equipment. The generated dense mesh is used as a reference object to create workable geometry. Although the process of sculpting a reference model and then scanning the model for a reference object seems redundant, it does save time. The reference object makes it easy to form a manageable surface. An optimal way to do this is to convert the scanned data into NURBS surfaces. NURBS surface flexibility and resolution independency make it easy to change the quality and amount of detail in the final model. It is then possible to convert the NURBS surface into a seamless polygon or subdivision surface model with uniform geometry.

The type and quality of the scanned data can change the way you decide to make a NURBS surface. Figure 6.1 shows an example of what laser-scanned data looks like. Notice the uneven triangles and bad form. Geometry like this is difficult to texture and animate.

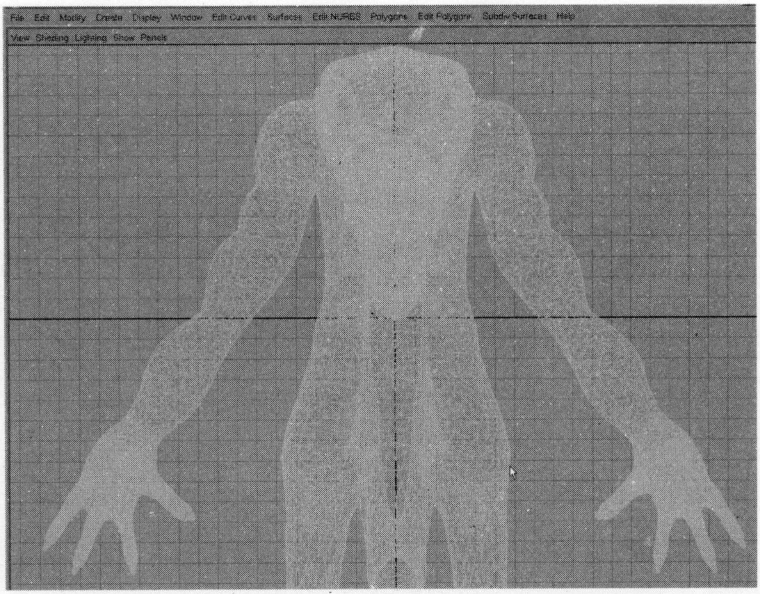

FIGURE 6.1 This is an example of what laser-scanned data looks like.

Figure 6.2 is an example of what point-to-point scanned data looks like. Generating this data entails using a scribe tool to point to every proposed point on the physical model. The end of the scribe is pressed against the model causing a vertex to be plotted in 3D space.

Creating NURBS Patches

In this chapter, we describe two methods to convert the raw geometry to NURBS surfaces. The first is to make the scanned polygon surface live with the Live tool in Maya. Making a surface live allows you to draw curves, from which surfaces are generated, directly onto the surface. The second method is to use the convert tool called SubD to NURBS. This process is more automated but requires large amounts of memory to convert the polygon model to

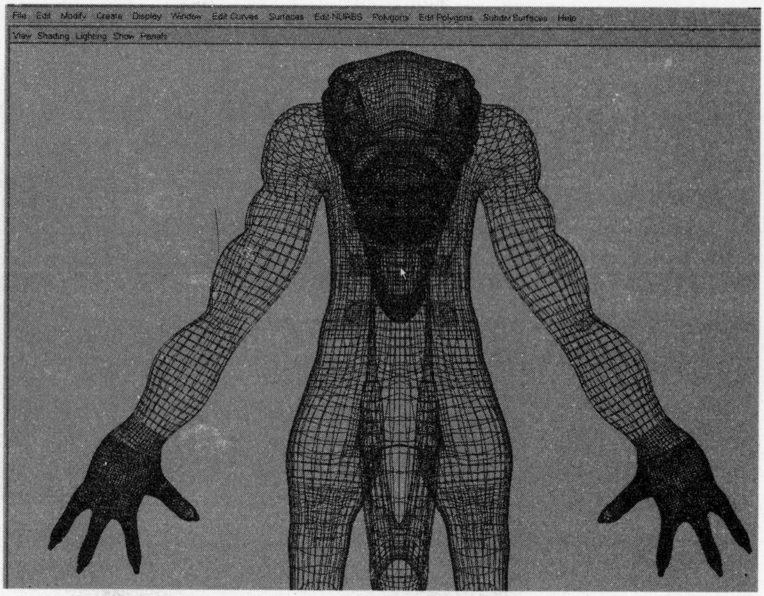

FIGURE 6.2 This is an example of what scanned data looks like with the use of a scribe tool.

a subdivision surface model. This tool is only effective if the original geometry is clean and uniformly spaced.

TUTORIAL

LIVE SURFACES

Step 1: Load the scene file called "LiveSurfaces.mb" from the CD-ROM. This scene file is a representation of scanned data for the Fire Monster character.

ON THE CD

Step 2: Focus on the creature's right arm. Select the surface and choose the magnet icon from the status line to make the surface live. NURBS surfaces must have four sides, making it necessary to divide the surface into multiple patches. For instance, the arm is basically a cylinder, however it attaches to the body more like a rectangle. By breaking the surface into multiple patches, we can square off the connection without distorting the surface or adding excessive geometry. The first objective is to divide the surface into square sections with curves. To do this, draw a curve completely around the shoulder, as shown in Figure 6.3, using the CV Curve Tool from the Create pull-down menu. Make sure the Curve Degree is at least 3 in the tool options, and add enough points to pick up the surface detail. Do not match the ends up exactly; leave a small gap. Choose Open/Close Curves from the Edit Curves pull-down menu and change the shape setting to Preserve. Apply the settings to complete the curve.

FIGURE 6.3 Draw a curve around the shoulder.

Step 3: Draw another complete curve around the arm a few units down as shown in Figure 6.4. Select the curve and open the Rebuild Curve tool options from the Edit Curves pull-down menu. Set the Rebuild Type to Uniform, the Parameter Range to 0 to # of Spans, and the Number of Spans to 20, and then apply the settings. If you are using cubic curves, this gives

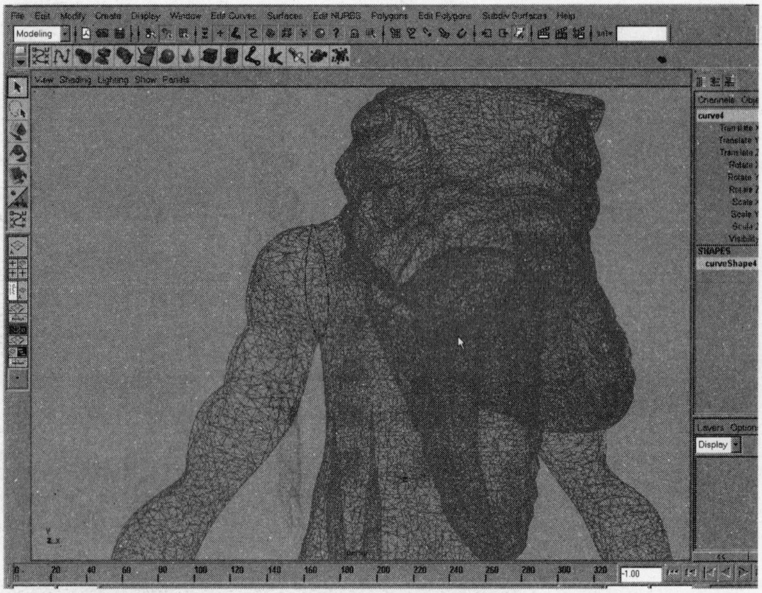

FIGURE 6.4 Draw another curve farther down the arm and rebuild both curves.

you a total of 23 control vertices. When you rebuild the curve, the CVs do not automatically update on the surface. It is necessary to touch or slightly move each CV individually to get them to snap back to the surface. To do this, you must move the center of the translate manipulator. The arrows will move the CV off of the surface. Deselect the curve and select the curve from Step 2. Open the Rebuild Curve tool settings and choose Match Knots. Select the other curve and apply the settings. The first curve selected now matches the parameters of the second curve. This is done to insure clean geometry and to line up the starting point of each curve. If the starting points are not aligned, a NURBS surface created from these curves will appear twisted. Make sure to touch all of the CVs to get them to snap back to the surface.

Step 4: Using both curves as beginning and endpoints, draw four curves down the length of the arm between them to divide the shoulder area into four rectangular sections. Assure that the new curves intersect the old curves by turning on the edit points. This can be accomplished by selecting a curve and opening its attributes. Select the Component Display tab and check Disp EP to display the curve's edit points. You must use the edit points because they actually sit on the curve, unlike control vertices that reside off of the curve. Choose the CV Curve Tool and turn on Snap to Point. Drop the first CV on an edit point and then turn off Snap to Point. Draw the rest of the curve, snapping the last point to an edit point on the other curve. Build three more curves, equally spaced, around the arm. Remember, the goal is to create rectangular patches, so keep the curves as square as possible. When finished, rebuild the curves to Uniform curves with four spans. Touch all the CVs to snap them back to the surface. Use Figure 6.5 as an example.

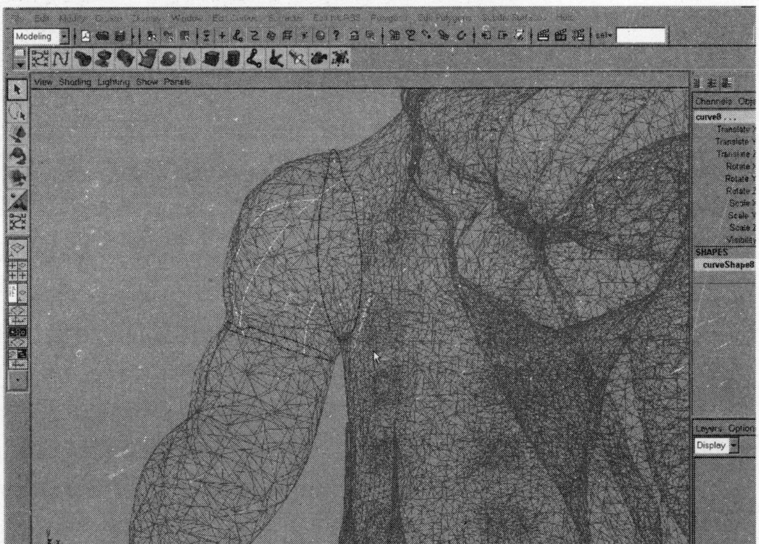

FIGURE 6.5 Draw four curves perpendicular to the first two curves, making sure to intersect their points.

Step 5: Next, move to the body and draw a curve all the way around the midsection just under the arm. Close the curve and select all of the CVs in component mode. Draw another curve perpendicular to the previous curve from the front of the creature's midsection, over his shoulder to the back, creating an upside-down U. Make sure to snap the beginning and endpoints to the midsection curve. Use Figure 6.6 as reference.

FIGURE 6.6 Draw two more curves around the torso and up and over the shoulder.

Step 6: Draw four curves from the ends of the four arm curves to points along the upside-down U curve on the body. Draw the lines as straight as possible. To keep from having to rebuild the curves, draw them all in the same direction and use the same amount of points. Use Figure 6.7 as reference.

Step 7: Draw two more curves underneath the arm to square off the last section. Start these curves where the four splines come together under the arm. Figure 6.8 shows the placement of these two curves.

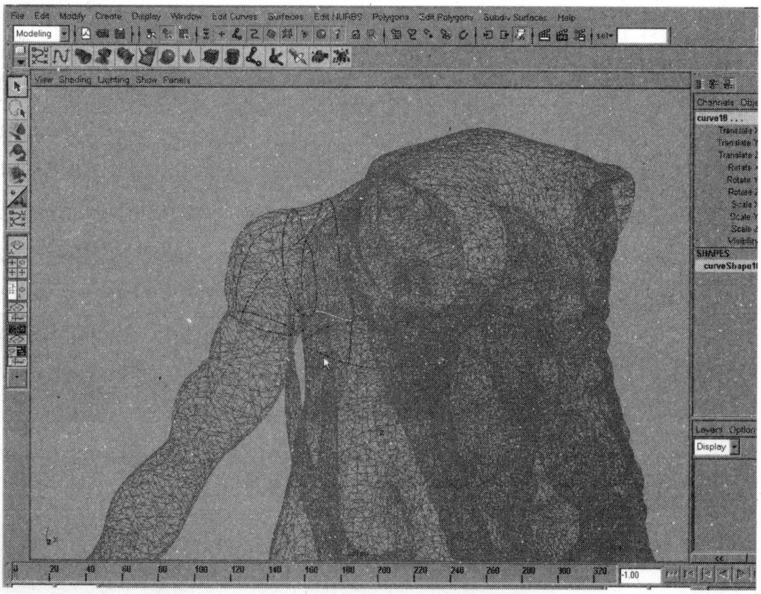

FIGURE 6.7 Draw four more curves from the arm to the upside-down U curve on the body.

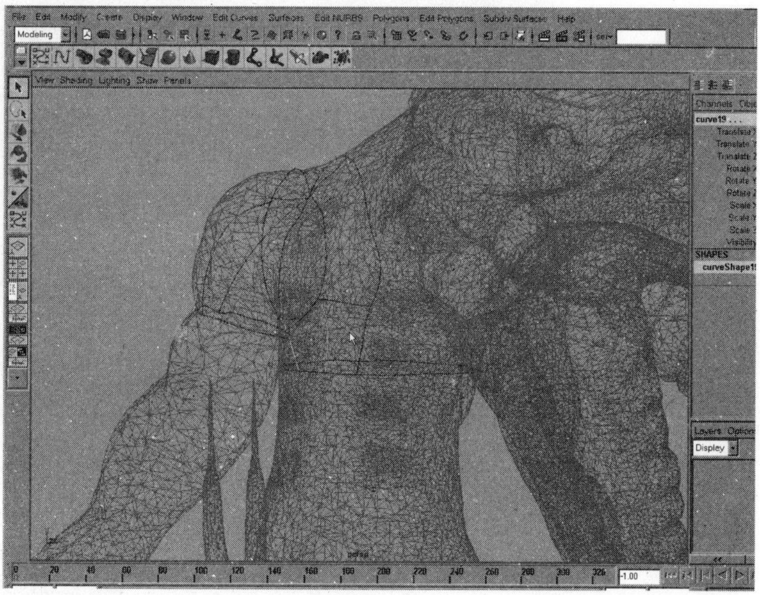

FIGURE 6.8 Draw two more curves to create borders for three surfaces under the arm.

Step 8: The shoulder and its connection to the torso are outlined. The next step is to create profile curves suitable for use with the Birail tool. Go back to the top of the shoulder where we began in Step 2. Birail +3 requires that we have two rail curves and three or more profile curves. The two curves running over the top of the shoulder and going down the length of the arm are our two rail curves. Both of these curves are connected to curves that circle all the way around the arm. Using these curves as reference, draw curves between the two rail curves to be our first and last profiles. To draw the curves more accurately, use the EP Curve Tool under the Create pull-down menu and snap to point. Figure 6.9 shows the curves.

FIGURE 6.9 Create the first and last profile curves between two rail curves.

Step 9: Draw as many additional profile curves as needed between the rails to define the surface. Use the same amount of edit points to create the curves and draw them all in the same direction. Reposition the points after they are drawn, if needed. Always snap the first and last edit point of the profile curve to the rail curve. After you have drawn all of the necessary profile curves, choose Birail +3 from the Surfaces pull-down menu. Select your profile curves in the desired surface direction and press Enter. Select the two rail curves, and Birail creates the surface automatically. If the endpoints of the profile curves are not intersecting the rail curve, then Birail will fail. Simply select the endpoint of each profile curve and snap it to an edit point on the rail curve. Go through all of them whether or not you think they need it. As soon as the points are all intersecting, the Birail surface will complete itself. Go back and adjust the curves to modify the surface, if necessary. Figure 6.10 shows the completed Birail surface.

FIGURE 6.10 Select all of the profile curves and then the two rail curves to complete the Birail surface.

Step 10: Repeat the process for all of the outlined square patches. Remember that Birail is order dependent, meaning you must select all of the curves in the proper order. The surface doesn't fail if the curves are selected out of order, but the results will be undesirable. As you construct surfaces, you might find that the curves have an uneven number of edit points in the rail curves. Redraw these curves using the old ones as reference. Use Snap to Curve to help draw the new curves. You might find certain surface areas small enough that they don't need profile curves. If this is the case, use the Square tool found under the Surfaces pull-down menu. This tool operates similarly to Birail in that the endpoints of the curves must be intersecting. The difference in the tool is that it requires only four curves. Figure 6.11 shows the finished surfaces.

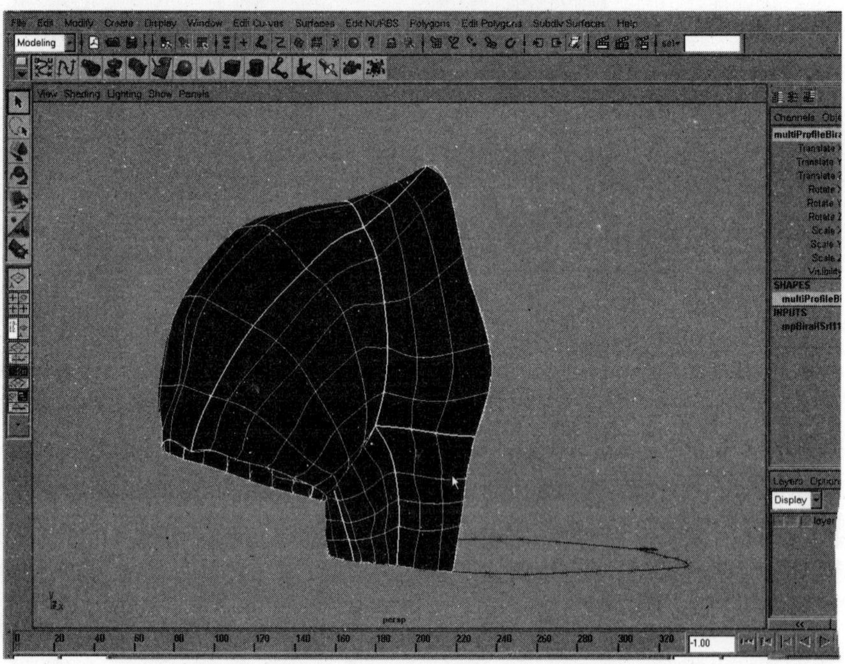

FIGURE 6.11 The completed Birail surfaces for the shoulder.

Step 11: When you are satisfied with the shape and quality of the surfaces, delete the history. Select all the surfaces and open the Edit NURBS pull-down menu. Choose the Global Stitch tool options from the Stitch menu. Use all of the default parameters except for the Stitch Smoothness, which you should change to Tangents, and apply the settings. The edges of all the surfaces stitch together.

Step 12: Using the end profile curves from the Birail surfaces, branch out down the arm and across the body to generate more surfaces until the entire character is finished.

The rest of the character can be created using the patches from the above tutorial. As you create new patches, keep in mind the shape of the surface. Try to place surface edges in natural seams or folds on the character.

TUTORIAL

SubD to NURBS

Step 1: Load the scene file called "SubDtoNurbs.mb" from the CD-ROM. This scene file is a representation of scanned data for the Fire Monster character. The model has been cut in half to reduce computation time. Depending on the processing power of your computer, it might be more advantageous to break up the model further.

ON THE CD

Step 2: Select the model. Choose Convert from the Modify pull-down menu and then Subdiv to NURBS. The model is converted into NURBS patches. You must convert an entire selection; components are not allowed. It also doesn't matter which subdivision level you are on. Figure 6.12 shows the converted NURBS patch model.

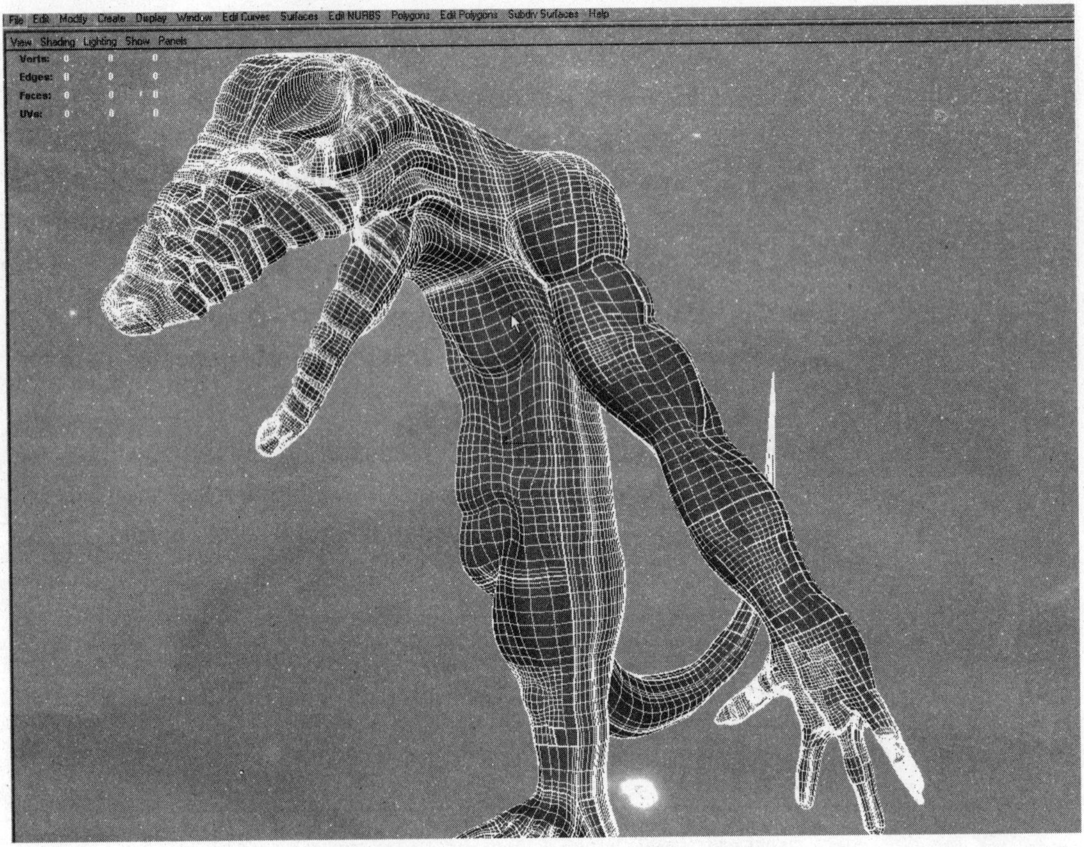

FIGURE 6.12 The Fire Monster after it has been converted into NURBS surfaces.

Step 3: The NURBS surfaces that are generated still need a lot of work. By selecting various parts of the model, you will notice a difference in the number of isoparms in a surface as well as surface size. It is necessary to merge these patches together to create clean geometry. Begin with an area that has large pieces. On the Fire Monster, the arm is a good place to start, so hide all of the surfaces not associated with the arm. The scene file called SubDtoNurbs2.mb already has the arm surfaces set up on a separate layer. Select the last surface on the shoulder and the three surfaces underneath it to create square patches. Use Figure 6.13 as reference. You will notice

ON THE CD

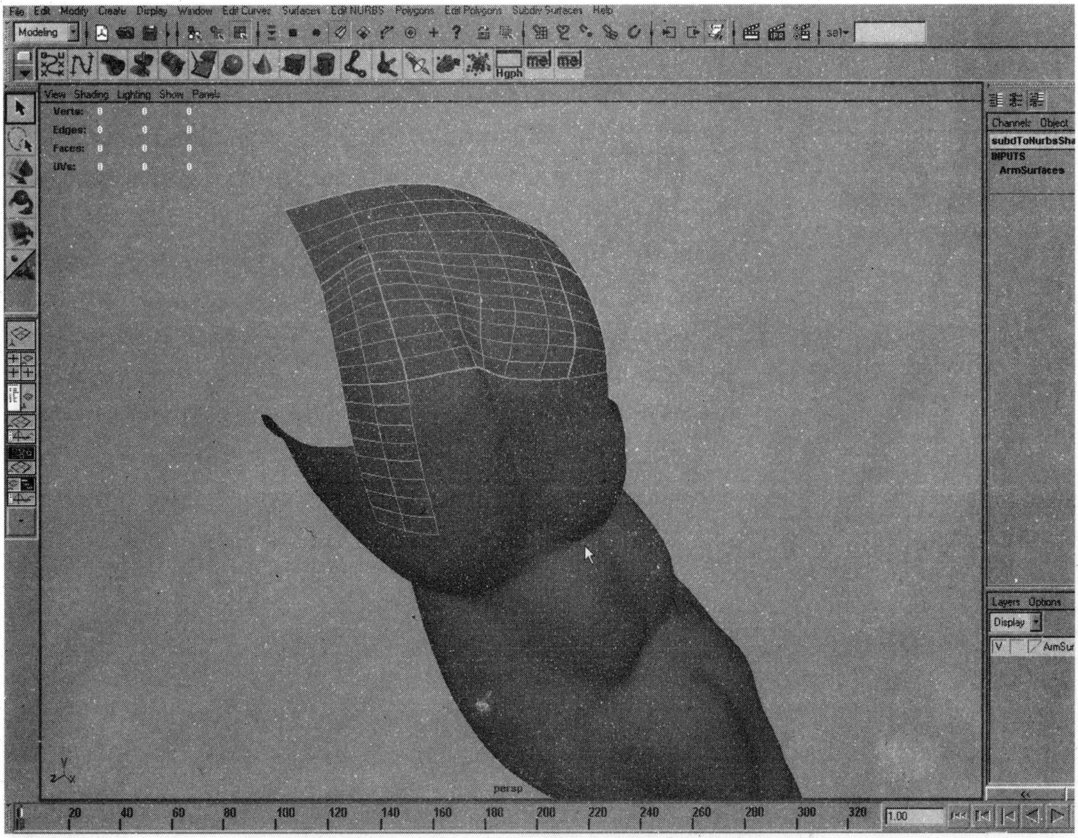

FIGURE 6.13 Detach surfaces to create square patches.

that one surface is longer than the rest. In component mode, choose isoparms and select the isoparms that line up with the surface next to it to form a rectangle. Choose Detach Surfaces from the Edit NURBS pull-down menu.

Step 4: Select the new detached surface and the surface next to it. From the Edit NURBS pull-down menu, open the Attach Surfaces tool options. Select Blend for the Attach Method and apply the settings. Select the next surface in line and attach the surfaces. This leaves two surfaces from the original four. These two surfaces will not attach together without adding unwanted and misplaced isoparms. To fix this, select the surface you made from the first two, and press Ctrl-A on the keyboard to open the Attribute Editor. Look at the Spans UV under the NURBS Surface History tab. Determine which direction is the one you want to attach by counting the isoparms on the surfaces and comparing them to the U and V spans. There will always be one more isoparm than spans. With this surface we want to attach the surface in the U direction, which has nine spans; therefore, both surfaces need to have nine spans in the U. Select the other surface and open the Rebuild Surfaces tool options from the Edit NURBS

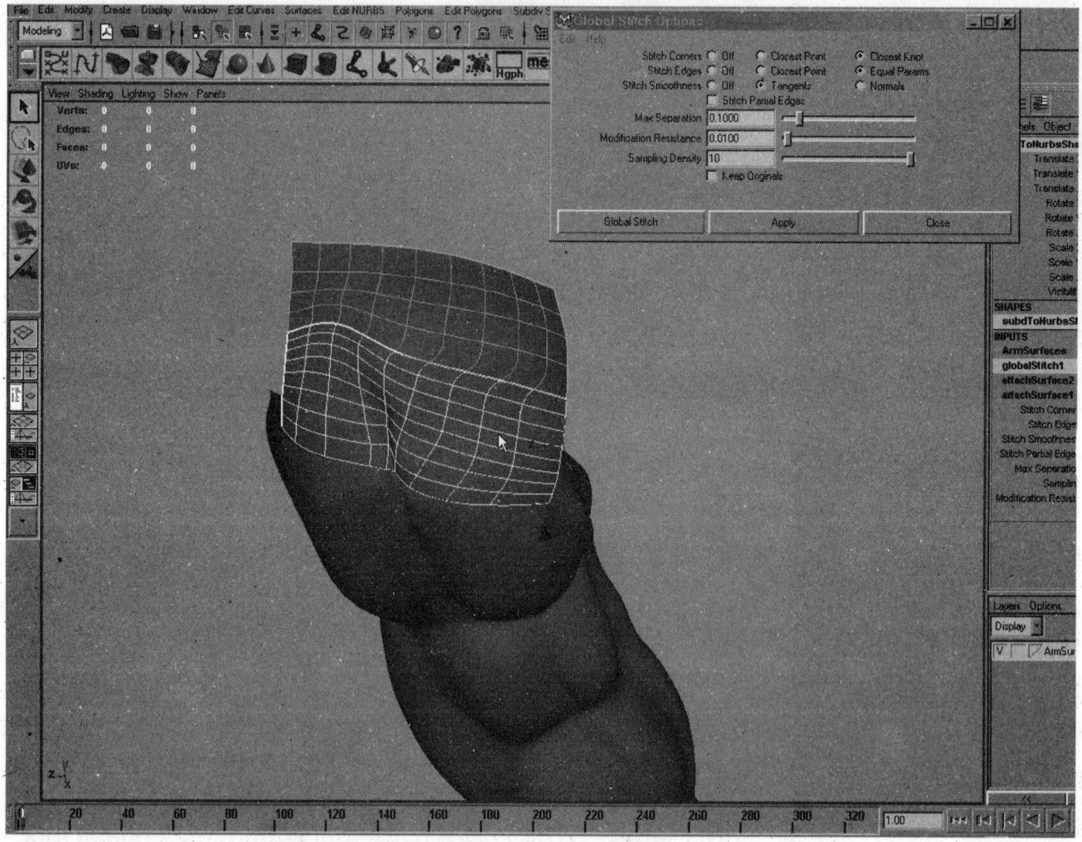

FIGURE 6.14 This is the completed surface on the shoulder.

pull-down menu. Choose Uniform for the Rebuild Type, 0 to #Spans for the Parameter Range, U for the Direction, and set the Number of Spans U to 9. Also make sure nothing is selected for Keep and apply the settings.

Step 5: With both surfaces still selected, choose Attach Surfaces. Figure 6.14 shows the completed surface.

Continue to detach, rebuild, and attach surfaces across the entire model. Place the seams in inconspicuous areas, such as natural seams, creases, and areas not likely to be seen by the camera.

CONCLUSION

Regardless of the type of data you are working with, the goal is to uniformly reconstruct it. Detailed characters usually require hundreds of separate surfaces to complete. Although this seems like a lot, it will only take a day or two to rebuild, while modeling a character from scratch could take weeks or months.

In the next chapter, we will discuss the different tools available for manipulating triangles. We are using subdivision surfaces to build the Fire Monster, but we need to understand polygons and NURBS to fully appreciate the power of SubD. After establishing a tool set, we will begin modeling.

PART

III

MODELING FOR FILM

CHAPTER

7 THE TOOLS

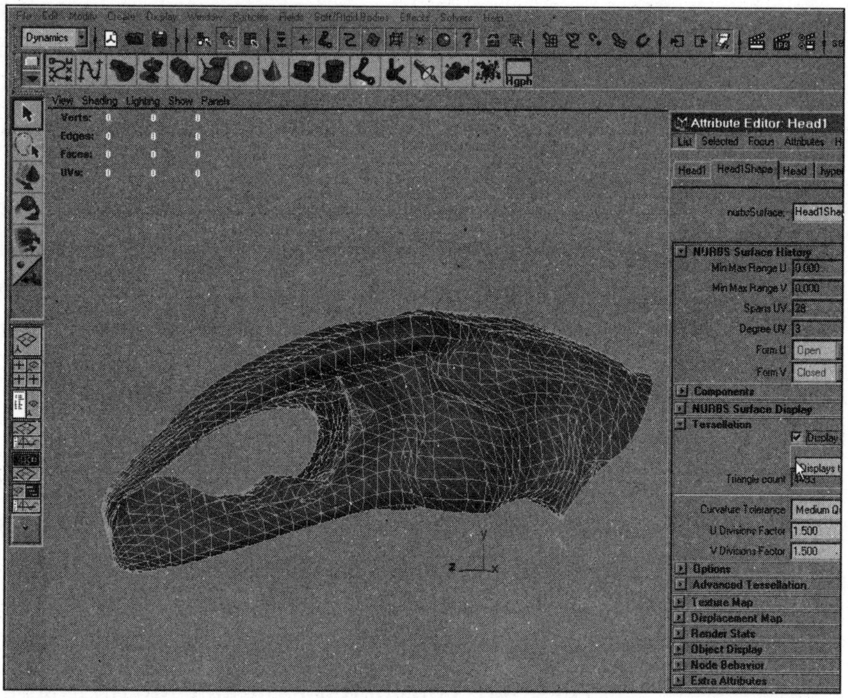

At this point, you should be ready to begin modeling your creature in Maya. Chapters 1 and 2 established a well-organized and solid design of your creature. In Chapter 3, you learned about the anatomy that would bring your design to life. Chapters 4, 5, and 6 were devoted to creating reference material to ease the CG construction phase. Chapter 7 takes a look at which Maya tools are best suited for modeling the creature.

When it comes to building models for film, there are no limits to the tools you can use. Although the floodgates are wide open, you still have to be careful you don't drown. It's a myth that it doesn't matter how much geometry is in the model or what that geometry looks like. Just because you render doesn't mean all is forgotten. Excessive geometry and any triangle not explicitly providing for the shape, form, or detail of a model cause increased render times, let alone the complications with texturing and animating. Just as in the real-time game world, it is essential to optimize your models. The main difference is that accuracy and attention to detail are rarely sacrificed. Visual feedback and the lowest render times obtainable are of the utmost importance.

Many artists get caught up in pushing buttons for instant gratification without ever grasping the concepts behind the fundamentals. Having a thorough understanding of the tools helps in every facet of the production process. It might even eliminate the need for proprietary software. The most basic tools in 3D modeling software are those aiding us in the manipulation of triangles. These are considered basic not for their simplicity, but because they are the building blocks for all that will follow. Three-dimensional geometry is a collection of triangles. The tools used to create and manipulate these triangles are polygons, NURBS, and subdivision surfaces.

The battle is neverending over which one is better, NURBS or polygons. Everyone has his or her own preference and view. Truly the answer to this argument is a matter of choice. When it comes to building 3D models, the answers are not always so clear, but knowing the strengths, weaknesses, and uses for these tools can make the process less painful. In the end, it is the results that matter. If it takes the combination of every tool at our disposal, then so be it.

Subdivision surfaces are used for the creation of the Fire Monster. As compared to the sculpture in Chapter 4, subdivision surfaces are the closest thing to air-dry clay based upon their malleability and the amount of detail achievable. To understand this relatively new tool, it helps to know what comprises these surfaces and how to manipulate them. Subdivision surfaces are a cross between NURBS and polygons, drawing from both of their advantages and disadvantages. Since the Fire Monster is built with subdivision surfaces, or SubD, it is necessary to appreciate and grasp the fundamentals behind polygons and NURBS—not just in modeling, but texturing as well. Let's discuss these tools and learn their characteristics through several exercises.

POLYGONS

By definition, a polygon is a collection of vertices placed in order and connected by edges to form an n-sided shape. By grouping polygons together, you get polygon objects. Regardless of how many sides a polygon object has, it is still fundamentally made of triangles. A quad, a polygon containing four edges, is made up of two triangles. These triangles do not officially become three-dimensional polygons until you assign vertices and edges to them. You may not see the separation between the two in wire frame, shaded view, or in the render, but the computer is drawing them.

Polygons are placed into two classifications: planar and non-planar. Planar describes a polygon whose vertices lie in the same plane, as shown in Figure 7.1. Non-planar refers to a polygon that has vertices in multiple planes, as shown in Figure 7.2. A triangle will always be planar.

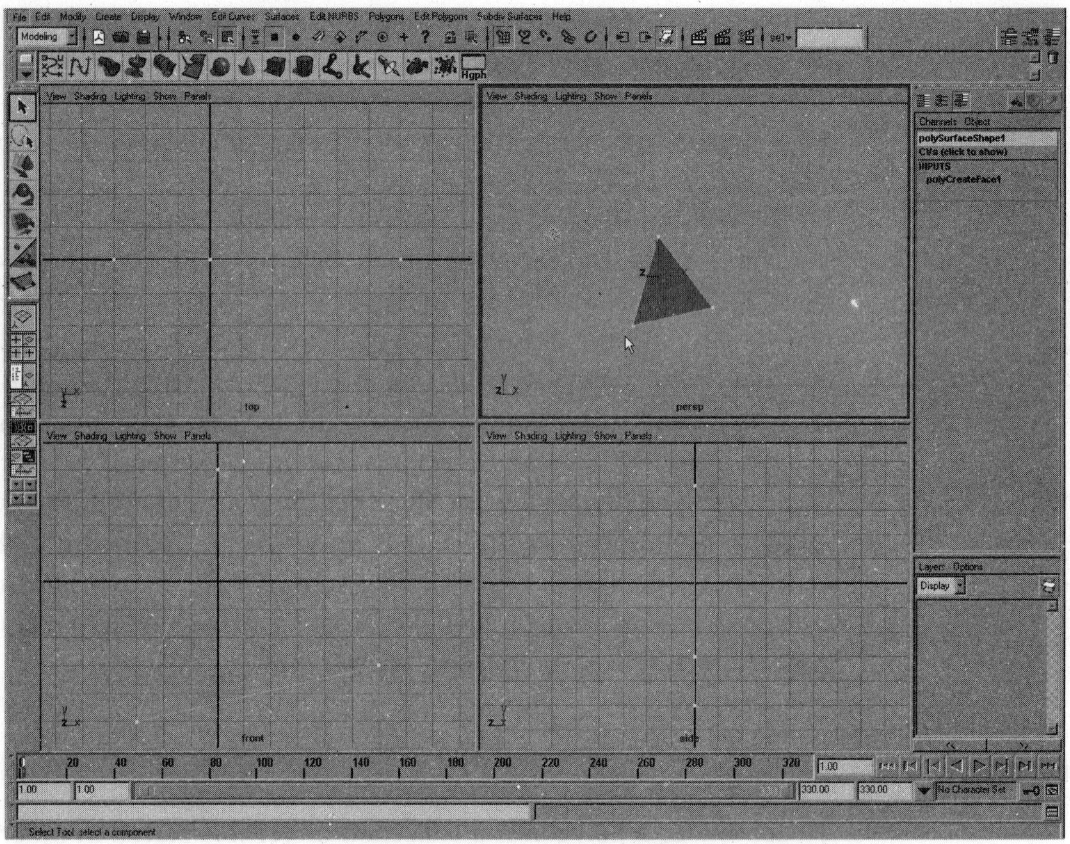

FIGURE 7.1 This is a planar polygon.

Polygon objects can exhibit a trait called non-manifold geometry, which can occur in three different conditions. The first is any polygonal object that cannot be unfolded into a single plane without overlapping itself. In other words any single edge shared by three or more faces. An example of this would be a sphere with an extruded edge as shown in Figure 7.3. If you were to open and flatten the sphere, the extruded faces would overlap other geometry. This is important when texturing. Geometry such as this needs to be textured separately. The second case is when a single vertex connects two or more faces. They do not, however, share any

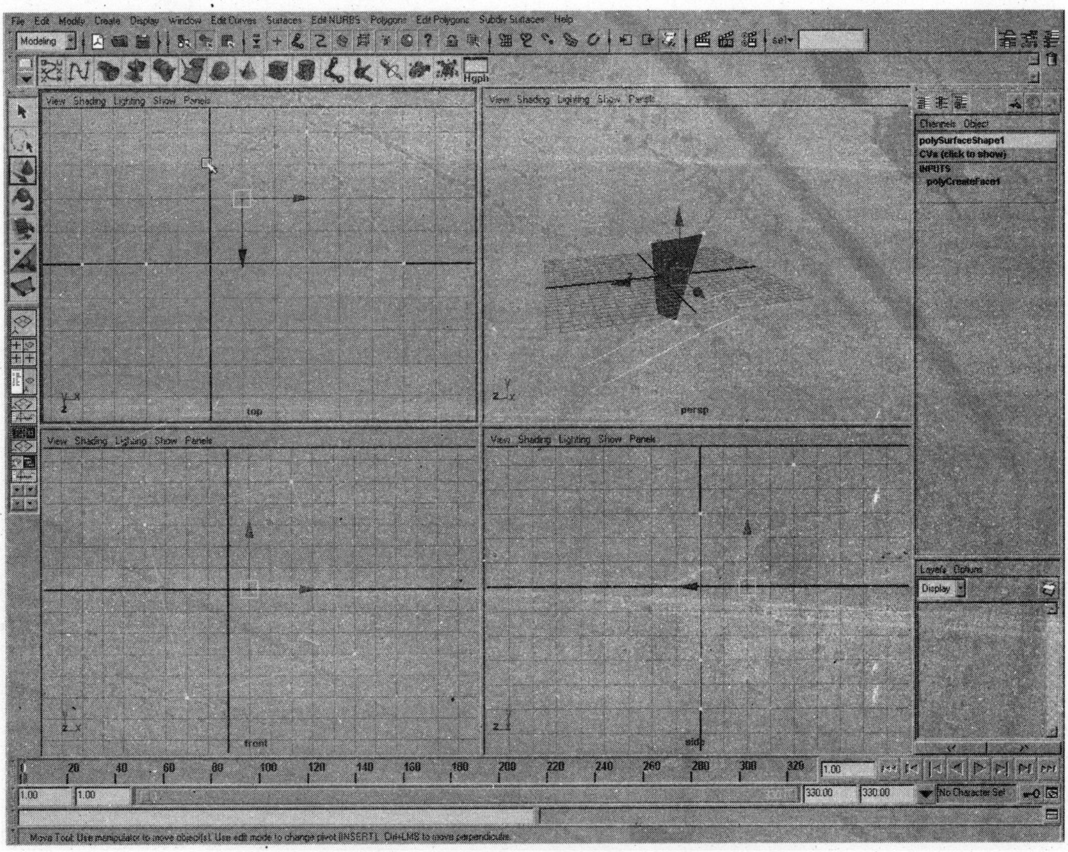

FIGURE 7.2 This is a non-planar polygon.

edges. Figure 7.4 is an example of this. The third occurrence, shown in Figure 7.5, happens when connected faces on a single surface have opposite normals. Although non-manifold geometry is considered legal or valid, it can be troublesome when it comes time to texture the object. At the same time, it can be advantageous by reducing polygon count and supplying additional detail.

Polygons are extremely versatile because you can directly manipulate individual triangles. Providing the most accurate feedback, they take the guesswork out of interpreting surface definition. Polygons also give you a faster response time or refresh

FIGURE 7.3 This is a sphere with an extruded edge, an example of non-manifold geometry.

FIGURE 7.4 This is a single vertex connecting two faces, the second form of non-manifold geometry.

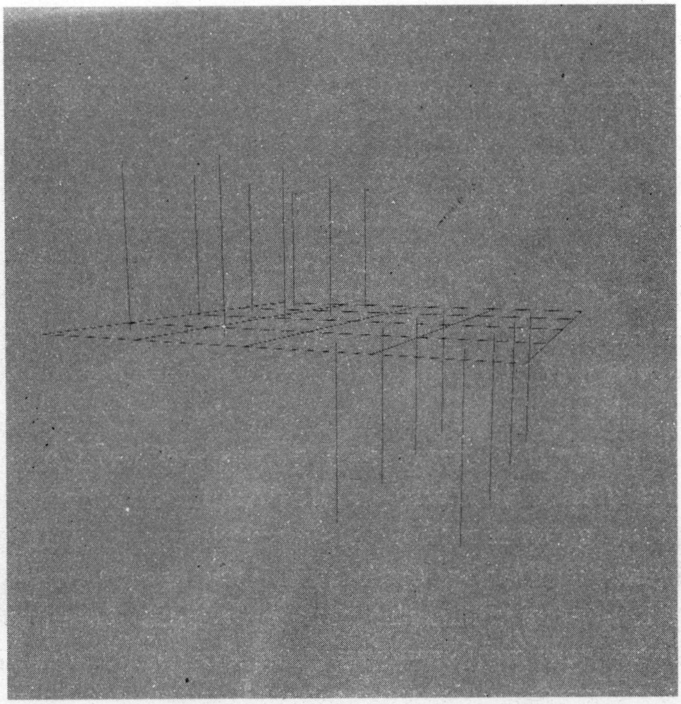

FIGURE 7.5 This is a single surface with opposing normals, the third example of non-manifold geometry.

rate at lower resolutions. There is no smoothing or rounding; what you see is what you get. This means that the computer does not have to do any extra calculations to display the surface. The disadvantage comes with objects that are organic or rounded by nature. Achieving a smooth, curved surface requires the addition of hundreds of triangles before you render, slowing down your computer and the workflow.

Polygon UVs

Every vertex on a polygon model has at least one UV, which is used to place textures. Therefore the more vertices, the more UVs you have, making the model increasingly more difficult to texture.

Positioning UVs is of utmost importance for good texture placement because bad UVs cause stretching and warping. Polygonal UVs must be assigned to the model. They are not generated with the geometry and must be projected onto the surface. This can be done through any of the projection methods (planar, spherical, or cylindrical). The ideal positioning of UVs is consistent with the shape of the face or faces being textured. For example, look at Figure 7.6 and Figure 7.7. The UVs have been pulled underneath the eye, altering the shape of the UVs, but not the shape of the polygon. Notice the difference between the points from the geometry

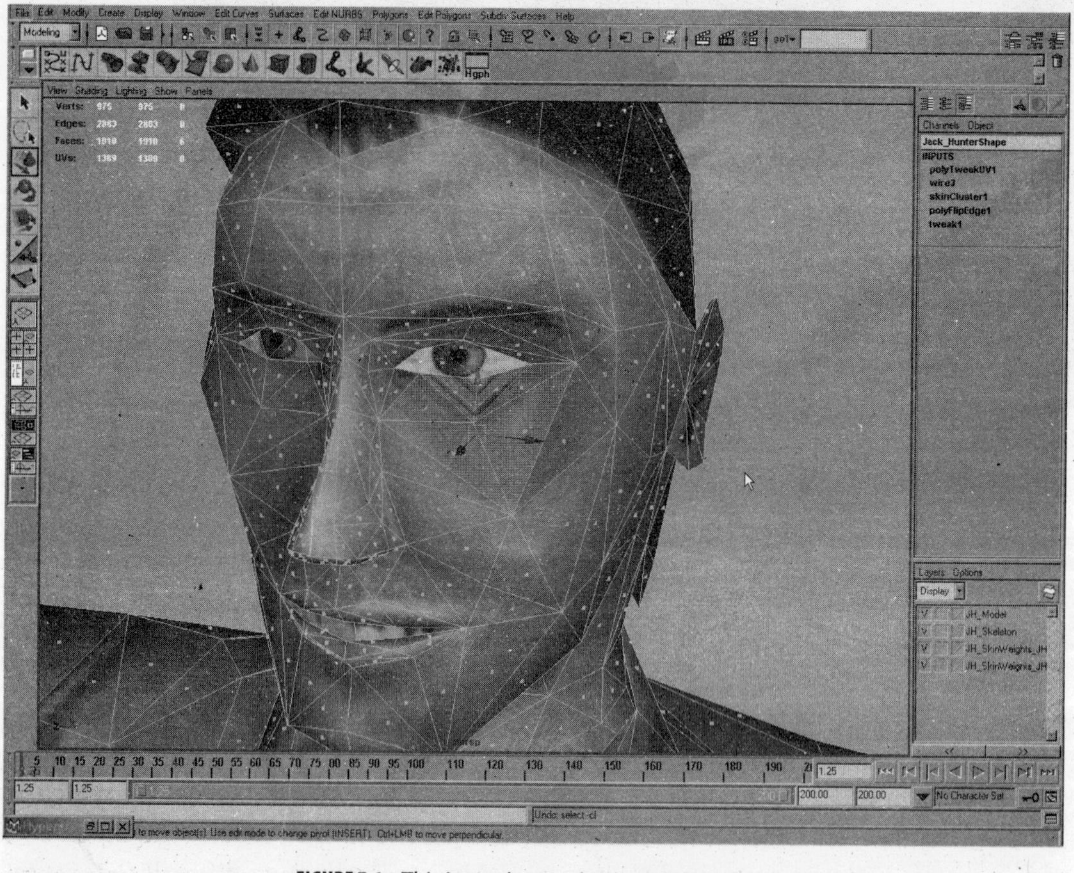

FIGURE 7.6 This is a polygon object with bad UVs.

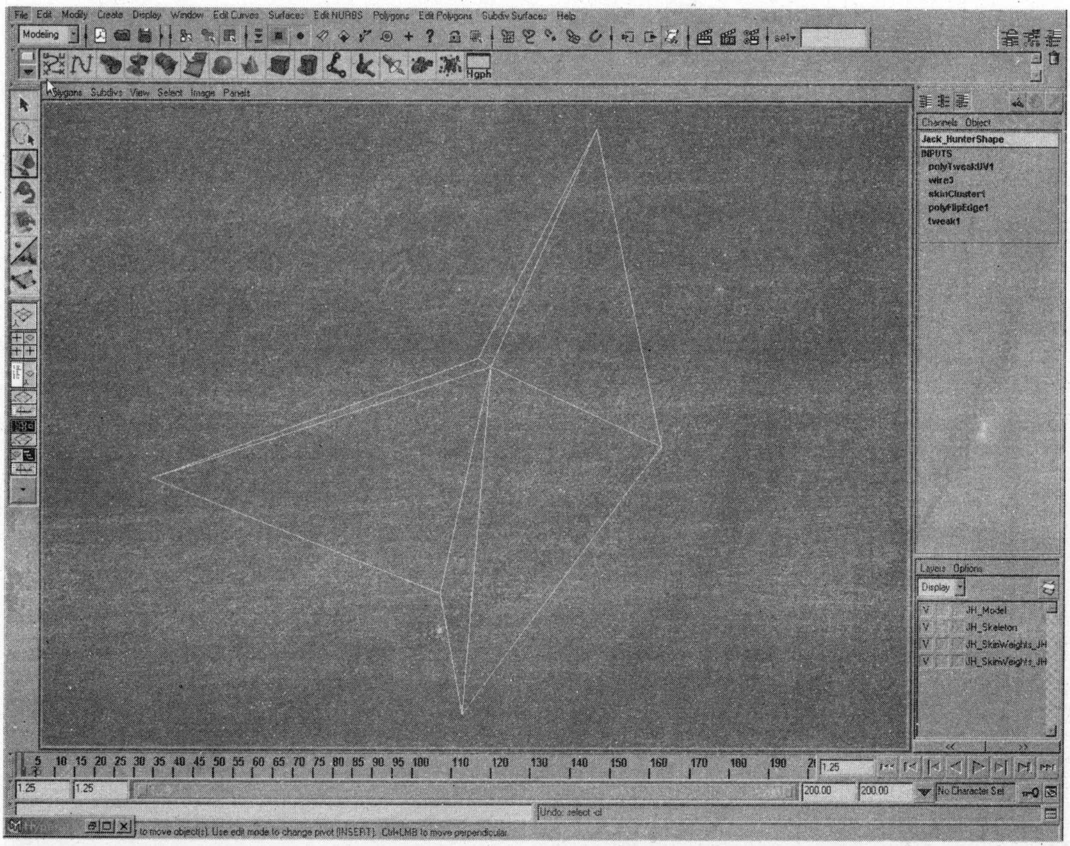

FIGURE 7.7 This is how the UVs for the model in Figure 7.6 look in the UV texture editor.

to the UV placement. To fix this problem, you would move the UVs to match the shape of the geometry, preventing any type of distortion.

When dealing with a complex or organic object it is not always possible to move the UVs into the shape of the geometry. Remember, the UVs come from a three-dimensional object that is now flat. A great amount of distortion is bound to happen. Moving one UV affects others. This is why it is sometimes advantageous to separate UVs into groups, just like with non-manifold geometry, to help prevent warping. When you texture map parts separately, duplicate UVs are created at the separation to keep the borders. Figure 7.8 shows a polygon model with 975 vertices.

However, to map this character properly, it is necessary to break the UVs into groups. Notice the pockets extruded from the jacket of the model in Figure 7.8. This is non-manifold geometry and will need to be mapped separately. In Figure 7.9 you can see the UV placement in the UV texture editor. There are 1,389 UVs to be mapped.

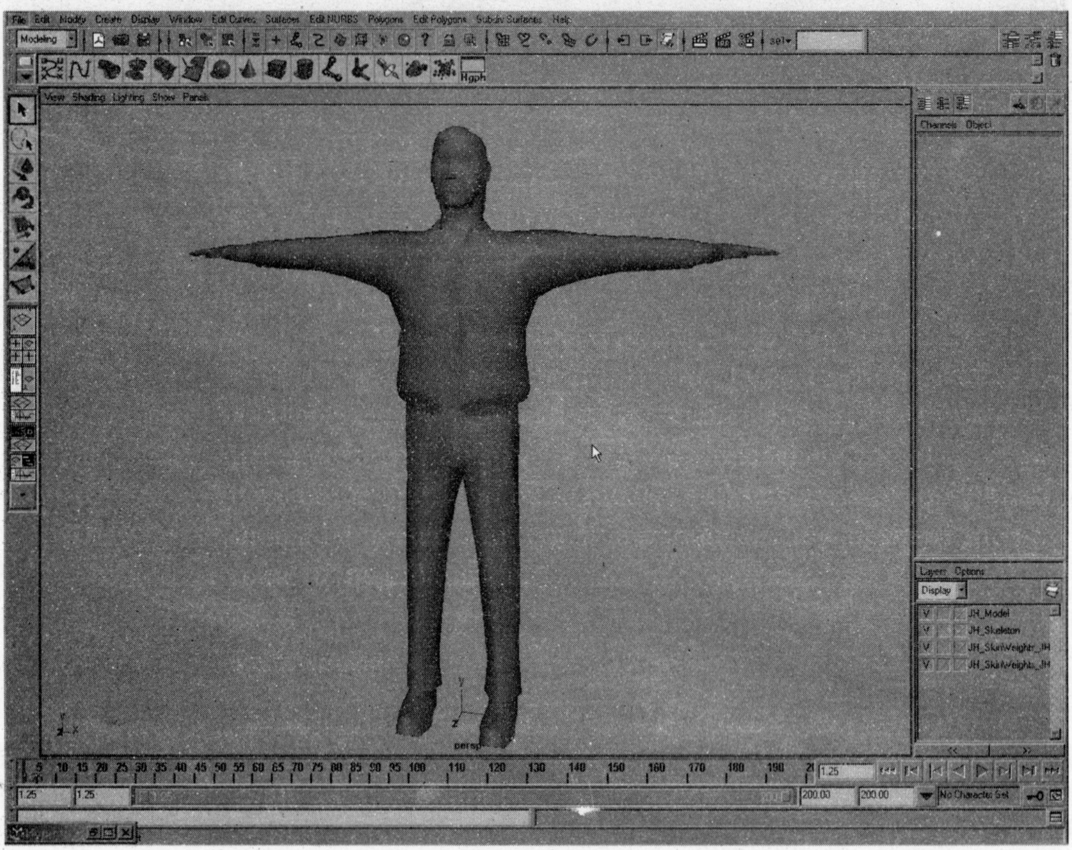

FIGURE 7.8 This is a polygon model with 1,910 faces and 975 vertices.

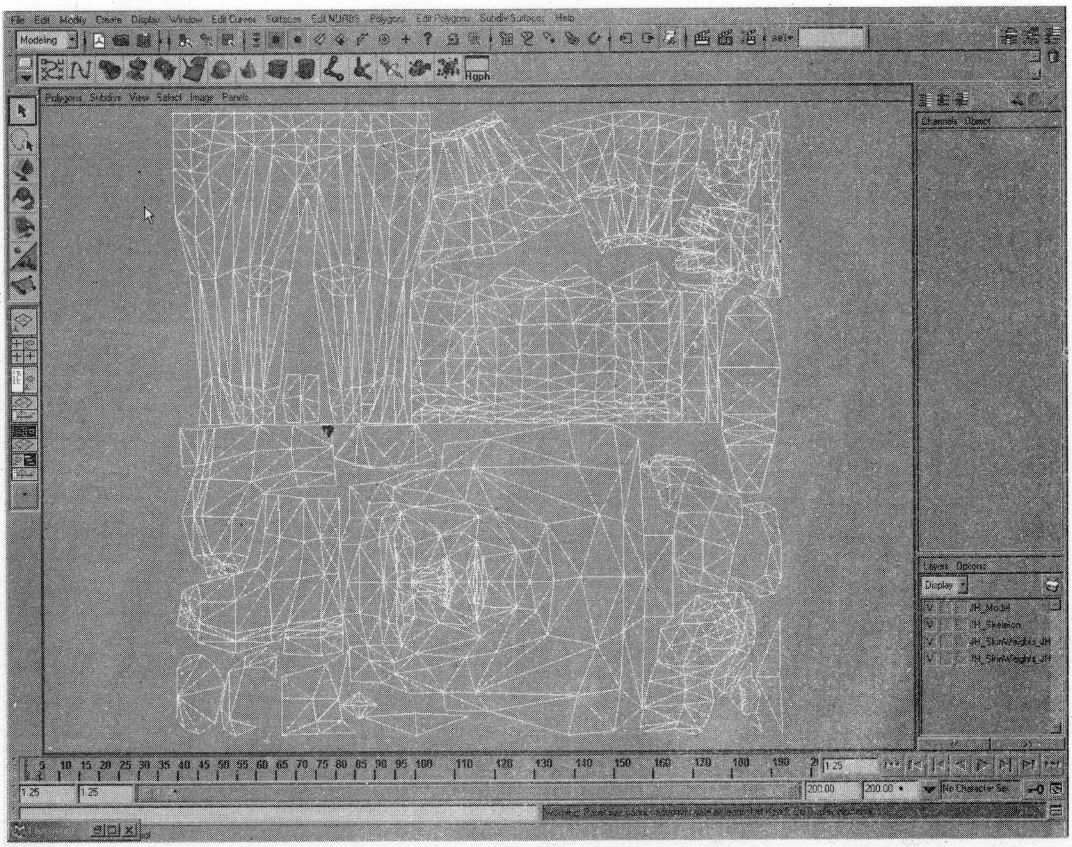

FIGURE 7.9 This shows the UV placement for the polygon character in Figure 7.8.

NURBS SURFACES

NURBS modeling is the process of using <u>N</u>on <u>U</u>niform <u>R</u>ational <u>B</u>-<u>S</u>plines to construct geometric surfaces. The curve, or the control vertices that make up the curve, can be used to shape these surfaces. Generating objects in this manner allows us to manipulate curves or splines to get the desired result from the surface. Like all renderable geometry, a NURBS surface is made of triangles as shown in Figure 7.10.

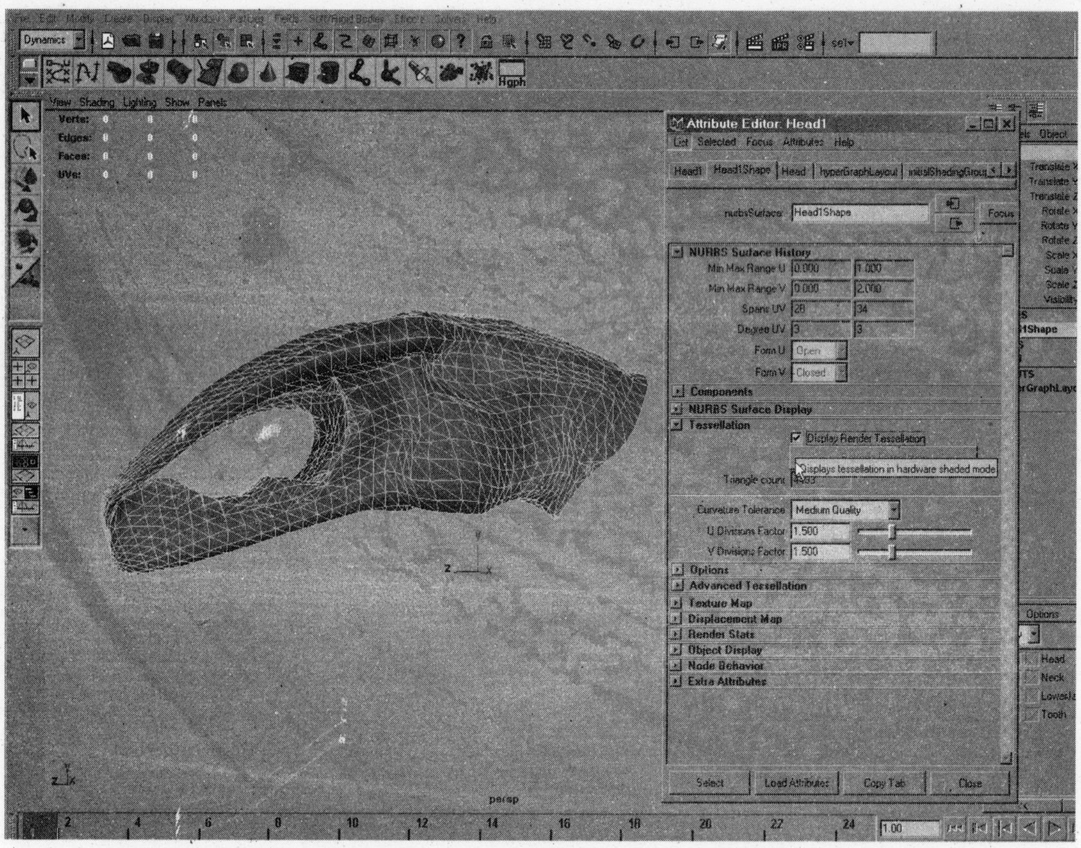

FIGURE 7.10 This is a NURBS surface with its tessellation turned on in hardware-shading mode.

These triangles should not be misconstrued to be polygons, for they do not have edges or vertices. To manipulate these triangles, edit the interconnected curves, or isoparms, that make up the surface. Working with NURBS surfaces allows you to modify more than one triangle at a time. The triangles bend together, keeping the surface smooth and rounded, benefiting us with less on-screen geometry and fewer points to manipulate.

NURBS surfaces are more complicated than polygon objects because you cannot directly manipulate the triangles comprising them. Another complication is that a NURBS surface will always have four sides, which prevents us from creating detailed organic characters with a single surface. In order to achieve a seamless NURBS character, you have to build the character with numerous four-sided NURBS patches stitched together. When dealing with multiple surfaces, you must understand parameterization. This determines a range of numbers used to calculate positions on a curve or surface. These numbers are dependent on the edit points that make up the curve or surface. The values for these edit points change based on the two types of parameterization in Maya, uniform and chord length. If two surfaces have different parameterization, they will not attach or blend together properly. By rebuilding surfaces to match one another, they will align properly and, in the end, create cleaner geometry.

Uniform parameterization assigns each edit point an integer, numbered sequentially regardless of the amount of space between the points. So, the distance halfway between any two points will always be .5. This makes identifying positions along a curve or surface very easy. The isoparms making up a surface are also attached to each edit point. Therefore, you could actually count the number of curves in a surface to find a value. This spacing also dictates how textures stretch across the surface. The values are equal regardless of the distance between points. This means the texture stretches in areas of greater distance and pinches in smaller distances. This may create unwanted results. You can rebuild a surface, forcing the isoparms to be equally spaced, allowing the texture to lie correctly. However this moves the curves and alters the shape of your geometry.

Chord-length parameterization is based on the distance of a curve or surface. The values are numbered according to the distance between each edit point. Floating-point numbers are assigned from the beginning of the curve or surface to the end. Chord-length parameterization defines curves more efficiently. With chord length you can achieve sharper curves with fewer isoparms. When texturing a chord-length surface, the image lies evenly across the entire surface area.

NURBS UVs

Unlike polygon objects, NURBS-surface UVs are automatically created. The only way to alter these is by altering the parameterization. This works to our advantage. When the model is done, so is our UV placement. However, since we cannot directly manipulate the UVs, it's often necessary to paint the texture map in a distorted fashion to fit within the parameterization.

Texture placement can be difficult with a NURBS surface if you are not aware of the parameterization being used. Even more difficult is identifying areas to paint. Since NURBS surfaces do not have projected UVs, you can't directly manipulate them. There is no point of reference to begin painting. However, with a polygon object, you can export the UV placement from Maya and into a 2D paint package, giving yourself a template onto which you may paint. Therefore, a simple solution is to convert your NURBS surface to a polygon object and export the resulting UV image. Figure 7.11 shows an example.

Subdivision Surfaces

"SubD" is basically a hybrid of polygons and NURBS. In a sense, you get the best of both worlds. Subdivision surfaces are approximated to give a smooth interpretation of edges and faces without having to display them all. This is very similar to a NURBS surface. Subdivision surfaces, however, are not limited to rectangular patches like NURBS surfaces are. Because of this there is no limit to the shape of a single piece of geometry. You can create a smooth, continuous surface for a seamless organic character.

Subdivision surfaces work in layers. The surface starts at a base level of 0, and to add more features and detail, select faces or edges and subdivide them. The resulting subdivision is split into quadrangular faces and assigned to a new level. The corresponding level number portrays vertices and faces. Each level can be subdivided

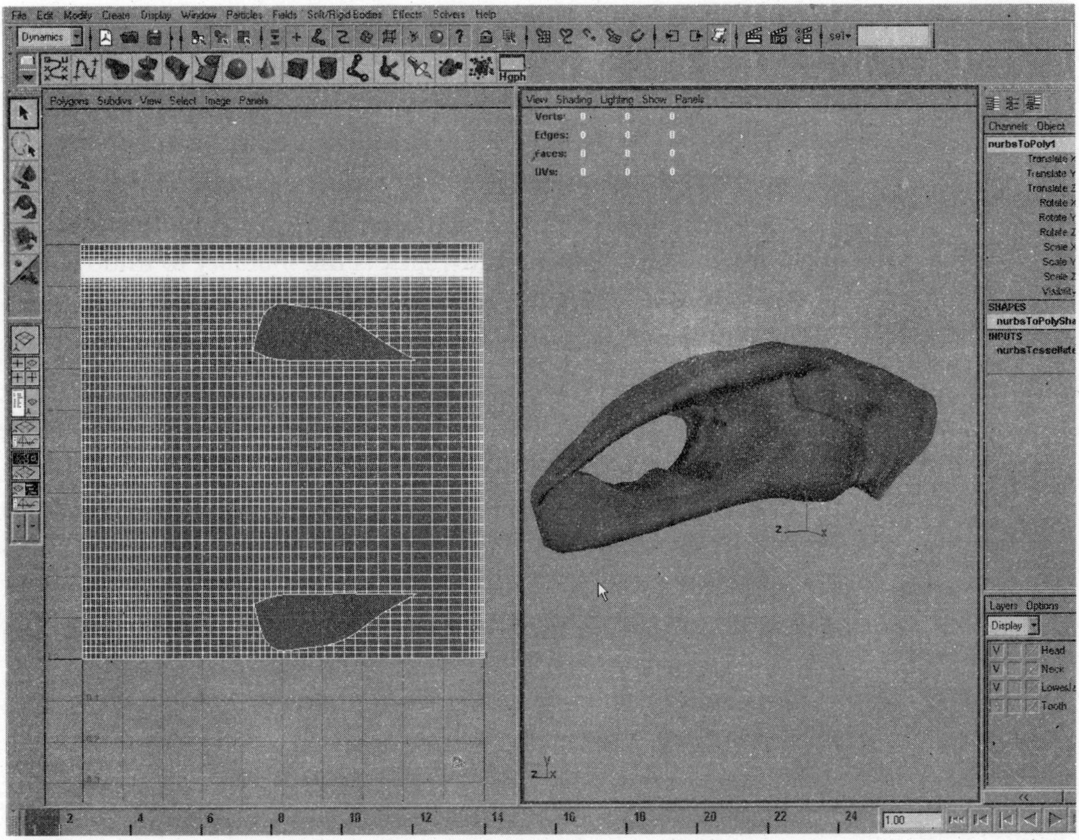

FIGURE 7.11 This is an example of a NURBS surface that has been converted to polygons to export the UV placement.

for finer detail. The higher the level goes, the more the amount of detail. This process would continue until you have enough detail or the software restricts you from creating additional levels. Maya can support thirteen subdivision levels.

Subdivision surfaces act like NURBS surfaces in that their components should be four-sided. In other words, they should be constructed only with quadrangular faces. Although SubD can support triangles, it is not recommended. The model might appear fine all the way up to animating, but when rendered the triangles flicker. By keeping subdivision surfaces constructed with quad faces, the geometry can tessellate properly during rendering.

Although SubD surfaces have the best attributes of polygons and NURBS, they do have some limitations in Maya 4. For starters, unlike polygons, SubDs cannot support non-manifold geometry. This means extra faces are required to mimic the effects of this type of topology. Another drawback is the inability to undo subdivisions. Once you divide an area, there is no turning back. Similarly, geometry cannot be deleted from the surface; extra faces must be added to create the illusion of holes. A similar disadvantage is that they do not support trimmed surfaces. It can be difficult to make selections because subdivision surfaces get complex very quickly. There are no hulls that allow you to select a row of control vertices as there are with NURBS surfaces, so rows of vertices must be selected manually. In addition, using the arrow keys to walk or move up and down your selection is not supported. Lastly, the soft-body or rigid-body tools do not work with SubD models.

To work around some of these limitations, build and model a polygon proxy. Essentially, this is a polygon model converted to a subdivision surface. The proxy serves as the base, or level 0, of the subdivision surface. The construction of the polygon proxy model must adhere to the restrictions of subdivision surfaces, specifically the use of quads and non-manifold geometry. When the SubD model is done, convert it back to polygons for quick editing and soft- and rigid-body support.

Subdivision Surface UVs

UV placement for SubD is similar to that of polygons. However, a major advantage is level 0. By assigning UVs to level 0, you can avoid having to assign thousands of UV points generated from successive detailed levels. Since geometry is divided from level 0, UVs are automatically assigned proportionately within the subdivided face. Therefore, you can texture a low-polygon model and update it to a high-resolution film model as you go.

Once you convert the proxy to SubD, the proxy becomes level 0. Any alterations to level 0 alter the UV placement. To avoid lengthy fixes, lock down the final version of the polygon proxy model and establish the base UVs. Although you can assign UVs to a SubD model, the tools are not as robust as they are for polygons.

CONCLUSION

The largest problem with all of the tools is their flawlessness. Smooth surfaces are at the click of a button. Natural-looking or Mother Nature–designed is difficult. This is where your sculpture becomes an invaluable source of reference. The entire sculpting process helps to generate a more organic and realistic-looking creature. Through imperfections in the clay, irregularities in the armature, and inconsistencies in our artistic ability, we produce natural-looking results. To maximize its usage, photograph several different orthographic views of the sculpture. Try to maintain the distance from the camera to the sculpture for each image. In Chapter 8, the photos are used to build the polygon proxy.

With an understanding of the advantages and disadvantages of the tools, it's time to build the skin of the creature. The Fire Monster is built using subdivision surfaces, allowing his skin to be a single continuous surface. There won't be any seams to stitch or parameterization issues to worry about. SubD requires extra thought and planning to insure a quality surface. Your completed CG model will have hundreds of thousands of triangles. It is very easy to subdivide yourself into a corner. Use your reference material to plot out your model.

CHAPTER

8 THE POLYGON PROXY

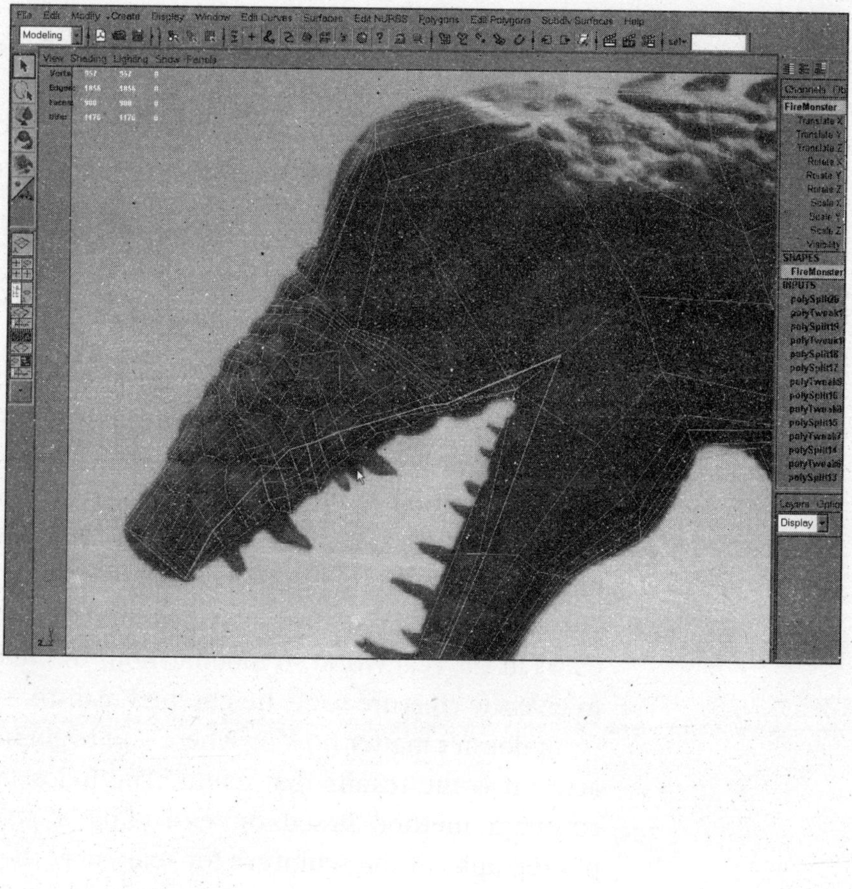

Plan, plan, plan, and then plan some more. It is difficult, if not impossible to anticipate everything, but the more you do in the development or pre-production stage, the better off you are. Your creature will benefit from this, too. There are many paths you can take to get the same results. It is just a matter of finding the one that suits you best.

Every stage of development is crucial in the construction of a film character. Chapter seven established subdivision surfaces as the tool best suited for modeling the Fire Monster. When working with SubD models, it is critical to the survival of your character that it is built with a solid foundation. An error in judgment could result in hundreds of extra triangles or weeks of UV texture placement. The foundation upon which you build the SubD model is the polygon proxy. This is the base level to which all detail is applied.

THE BASE MODEL

The polygon proxy is just that, a basic polygon model. It can be built with any method or tool as long as you end up with a model containing only quadrangular faces and eliminate all forms of non-manifold geometry. When satisfied with the model, convert it to a SubD model. To save time, only half of your creature needs to be built. You can symmetrically duplicate this half to the other side and seamlessly attach the two together. Perfect symmetry rarely exists in the real world so modifications to the duplicate are made to give the creature some heightened realism.

It doesn't matter how or where you begin modeling your character; it is the results that count. The following tutorial demonstrates a method based on extruding a polygon cube. Using photographs of the sculpture for reference, the tutorial constructs half of the Fire Monster's body.

TUTORIAL

MODELING THE POLYGON PROXY

Step 1: Load the Maya scene file called "Poly_Proxy.mb" from the Chapter 8 folder on the CD-ROM, or if you have created your own creature, load the scene with your aligned image planes. Create a primitive polygon cube. Place the cube at the creature's hip. In a bipedal creature, the hip area is the center of the body. Regardless of how many legs your creature has, the center is a good starting position.

ON THE CD

Step 2: Enter into component mode by pressing F8 on the keyboard, and move the vertices on the right side of the cube to the border of the creature. Align the vertices on the left side of the cube with the Y-axis. Figure 8.1 shows the placement.

FIGURE 8.1 Align the cube with the image plane in the front view.

Step 3: Extrude faces down the leg and up the body. Add a new extrusion at all of the major surface changes to rough out the basic shape of your creature. Add extrusions also to skeletal joint areas and areas of deformation. If you can't align the newly created geometry with the extrude tool, go into component mode and move the vertices individually. Do not worry about the alignment in any of the other views at this time; concentrate on one view to establish the character's proportions. Use Figure 8.2 for reference.

FIGURE 8.2 Align each new extrusion with the image plane in the front view.

Step 4: Work your way up the head then down the left arm. Continue to align vertices of the body with the Y-axis. Extrude faces for the left hand and be sure to add a sufficient number of faces to support the intricacies of the hand. If you come up short, you can always add more at a later time. Figure 8.3 shows the construction of the palm and thumb.

FIGURE 8.3 Extrude the palm and thumb.

Step 5: Pull the rest of the fingers out of the hand. Split the faces with the Split Polygon Tool. From the Edit Polygons pull-down menu open the Split Polygon Tool settings. Change the Snapping Magnets to 2 and make sure that Tolerance is at least 10. Snapping magnets cause the newly created vertex to snap to a point along the edge on which it was created. With a setting of 2, the vertex will stop at two locations, evenly spaced, along the edge. This allows the edge to be split evenly into thirds. The tolerance controls the power of the magnet. The higher the value, the faster the vertex snaps to the magnet.

Step 6: Complete the edge across the bottom of the hand. Split the face again with a snapping magnet of 1. This means the vertex will snap in the middle of our newly created face, dividing the original face into thirds. Examine Figure 8.4 to see the effect.

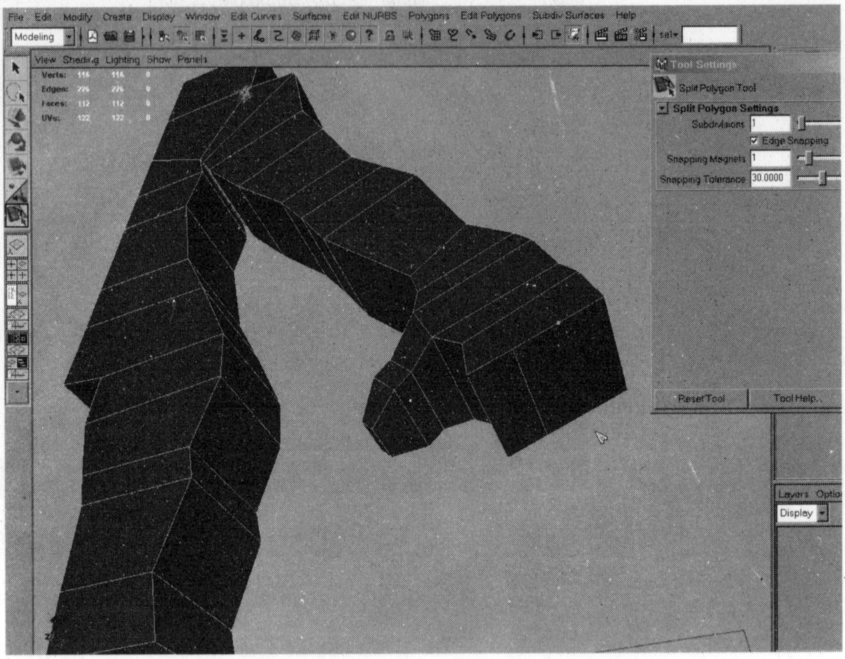

FIGURE 8.4 Split the new face in half.

Step 7: Extrude the fingers and line them up with the reference photo as shown in Figure 8.5.

Step 8: The basic shape of the model is done in the front view. Switch to the side view and shape the body's vertices with the image. Don't worry if the model cannot line up exactly with the photos. With the proportions established in the front view, you can approximate the vertex position for the

FIGURE 8.5 Move the finger geometry to match the background image.

side view. Select the faces for the foot and extrude those out as shown in Figure 8.6.

Step 9: Finish extruding the rest of the creature based on Figure 8.7.

Step 10: Using the Split Polygon Tool, extrude the toes. (See Figure 8.8.)

Step 11: After extruding the toes, the foot is left with faces larger than quads. These must be eliminated. With the Split Polygon Tool, split each face, starting between the toes, all the way around the model until you reach a border edge. The goal is to keep the model made of only quads. Figure 8.9 shows the edges being split.

Step 12: Repeat Step 11 for the hands. Notice in Figure 8.10 how the edges wrap all the way around the model from the fingers and toes. This is to ensure our model is only made of quads. It also adds extra geometry to help support additional detail.

FIGURE 8.6 Match the vertices of the body to the contours of the Fire Monster's back. Begin extruding the foot.

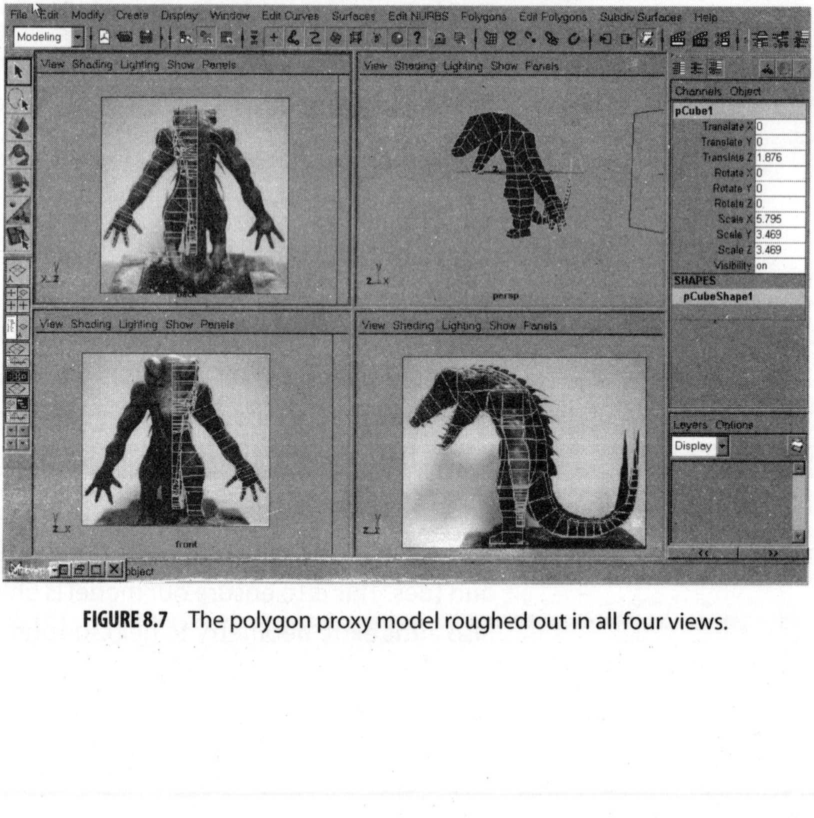

FIGURE 8.7 The polygon proxy model roughed out in all four views.

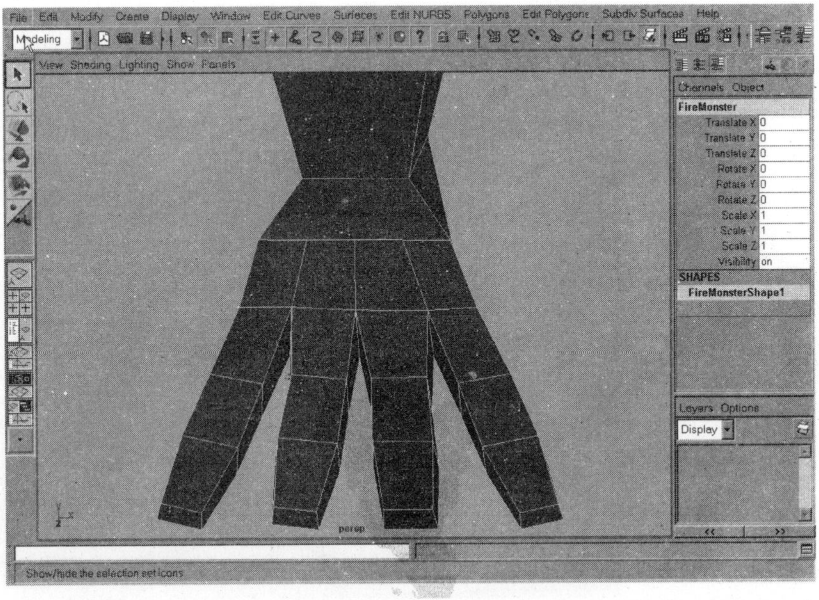

FIGURE 8.8 The foot has been split into fourths and the toes extruded out.

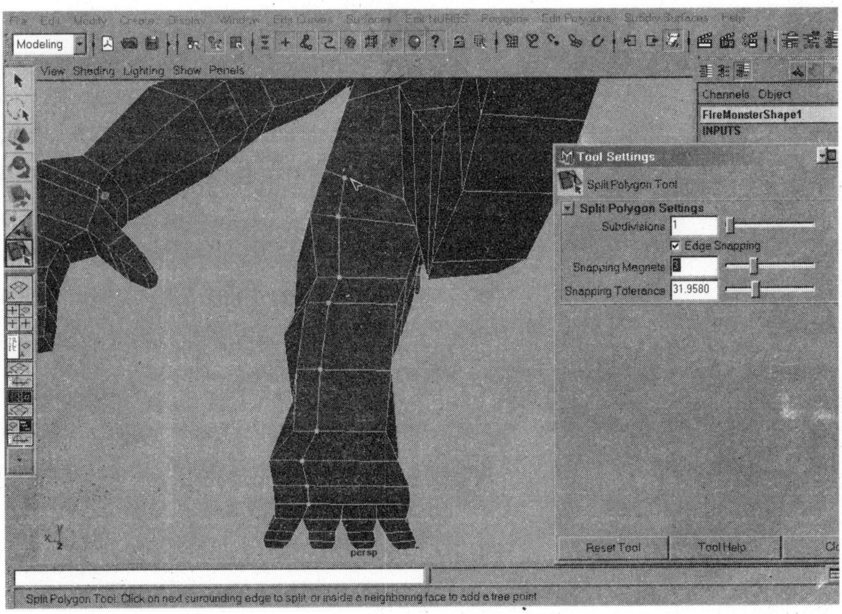

FIGURE 8.9 Split the faces from between the toes to the closest border edge.

FIGURE 8.10 Split faces all the way around the model to keep it made of quads.

Step 13: You might run into a circumstance where you cannot split the geometry evenly to a border edge. You can change the direction of the splitting geometry by adding a junction. Instead of splitting the face from edge to edge, drop a vertex halfway across the face, and another to an adjacent edge. This leaves a vertex floating in the middle of the face. Split the face again from the floating vertex to the next-closest vertex. Figure 8.11 shows the steps for creating this type of junction.

Step 14: The basic shape of the polygon proxy is finished. The model needs to be taken one step further to reduce the amount of subdivided levels needed. Examine your model for large details. On the Fire Monster these are the pads along the creature's snout, indentations along the lower jaw, the mouth

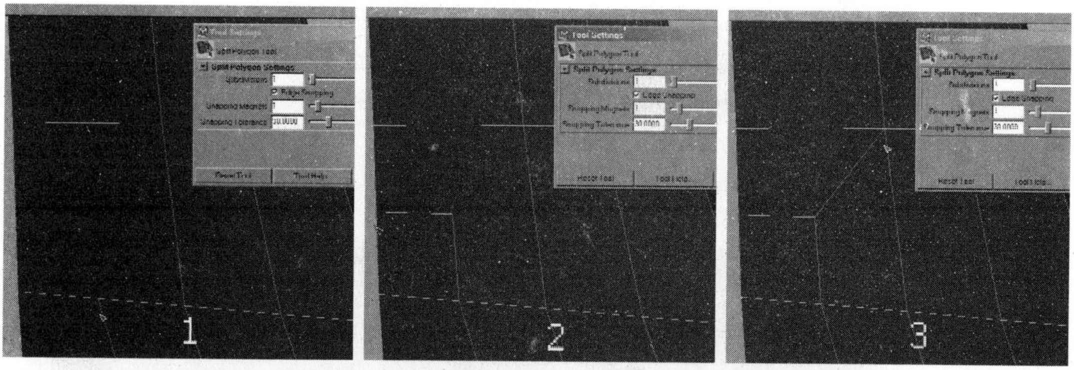

FIGURE 8.11 Create a junction to change the direction of the splitting edges.

interior, and some muscle definition. Figure 8.12 shows how the snout has been divided with the Split Polygon Tool.

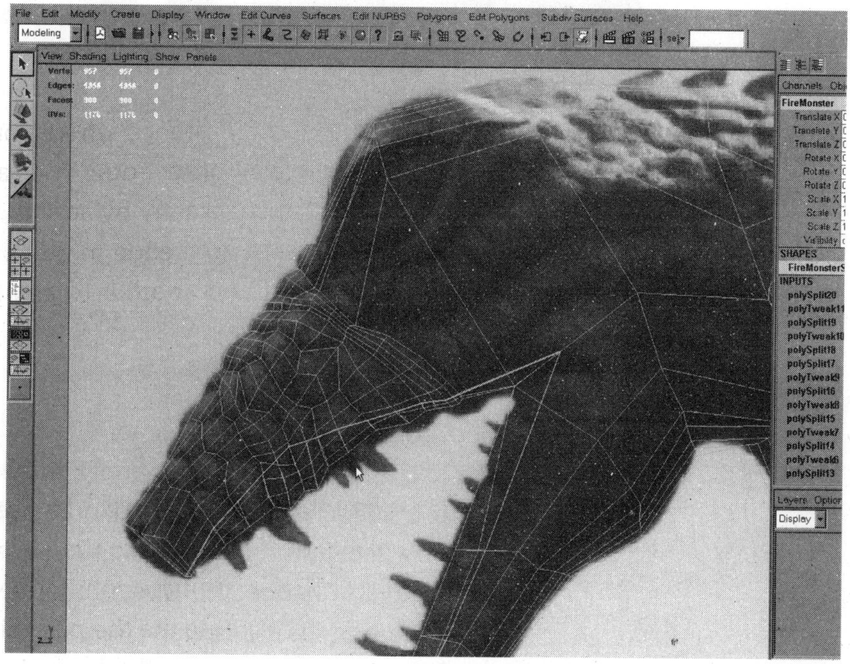

FIGURE 8.12 Use the Split Polygon Tool to add more detail to the snout.

Step 15: By adding extra rows of geometry to the side of the snout, n-sided polygons are created inside the mouth and along the side of the head. Carry the split edges out to a border edge to keep the model quadrangular. See the completed proxy model in Figure 8.13.

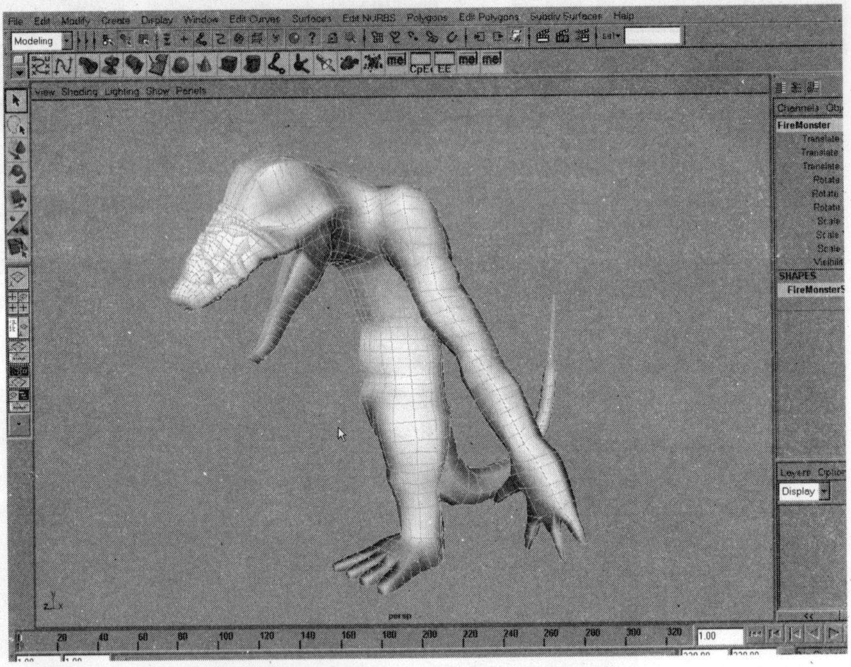

FIGURE 8.13 The proxy model is now finished.

Step 16: Check the model for any geometry that could cause problems to the SubD model, specifically, three-sided faces, five- or more-sided faces, holes, and non-manifold geometry. Open the Polygons pull-down menu and select the Cleanup tool options. Change the operation to Select Geometry. Check the box for Faces with more than 4 sides and Non-Manifold Geometry. Any geometry fitting the settings of the Cleanup tool will be selected. Fix this geometry to fit the parameters outlined in Chapter 7.

Step 17: Review your clay sculpture for distinguishing factors or elements. Identify detail that could be considered an exoskeleton. Decide whether or not these features sit on the skin surface or protrude from it. If there are protrusions, such as exposed teeth or spikes, consider making a hole in the proxy to be filled later with the skeleton model.

THE BASE UVS

In a complex model, projected UVs must be broken up into separate UV groups. It is impossible to flatten all of the UVs together without stretching them. Each significant part of a complex model is mapped separately. Even though UVs are resolution-independent, meaning any size texture map can be applied to them, they must share the same scale. If they don't, pixels appear larger or smaller in comparison to adjacent UV groups.

One way to eliminate this problem is to map all of the UVs into the 0-to-1 texture space and assemble them into separate groups. Next, establish the proper resolution for the collective size of all the UVs. Lastly, normalize each group and create texture maps based upon the resolution of the collective size. This procedure is explained in detail in Chapter 12.

To make the UV placement easier, it is advantageous to create a base set of UVs before converting the model to a subdivision surface. It is easier to do at this point because of the relatively low polygon count. Roughing out the UVs also helps eliminate stretching and warping in the texture map before the model gets too heavy. The UVs are altered as you add and transform geometry at higher levels. However, the basic shape and group remain, making adjustments less complex. The main purpose is to block out how the geometry is to be textured. The following tutorial goes over the basic mapping procedures.

TUTORIAL

Roughing the UVs

ON THE CD

Step 1: Open your proxy model scene file or load "Roughing_Uvs.mb" from the Chapter 8 folder on the CD-ROM. With the model selected, pull down the Edit Polygons menu. Go to Texture and open the tool settings for Automatic Mapping. Set the number of planes to 6 and the Optimize to Less Distortion. Using less distortion generates more UV parts; however, it cuts down on stretching and warping. Set the scale to uniform, which automatically scales the UV pieces so they fit within the texture space. Apply the settings. Open the UV texture editor in a window to examine the results. These are the UVs for the entire model. Figure 8.14 shows the UV texture editor and the mapped UVs.

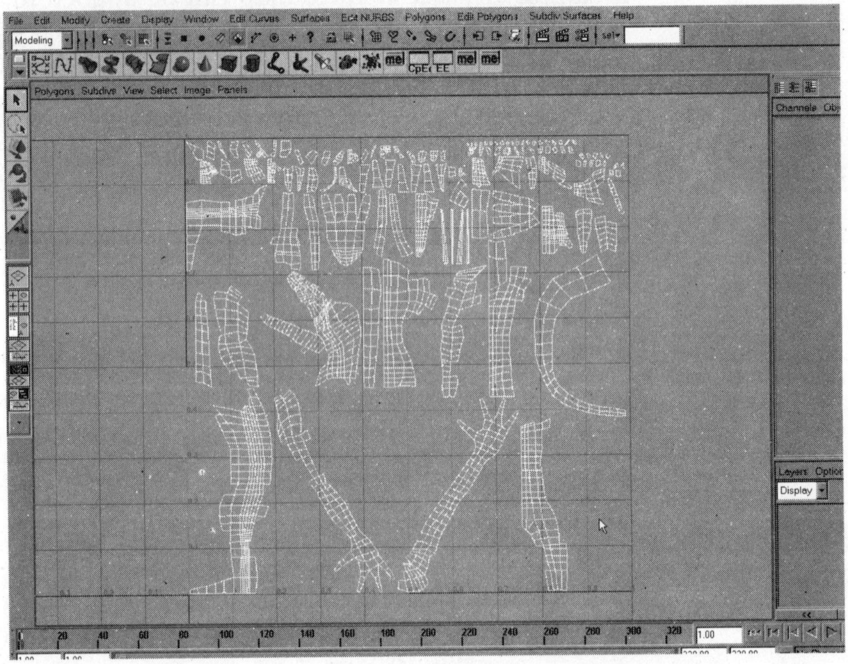

FIGURE 8.14 The results of automatic mapping are shown in the UV texture editor.

Step 2: The UVs must now be put back together with minimal disruption to the UV shapes. First, decide which parts should be mapped separately (head, hand, fingers, etc.). Next, move the associated UVs into groups by themselves as shown in Figure 8.15. It might be necessary to cut UVs in order to group them properly. To do this, select the edge or line of edges and choose Cut UVs from the Polygon pull-down menu.

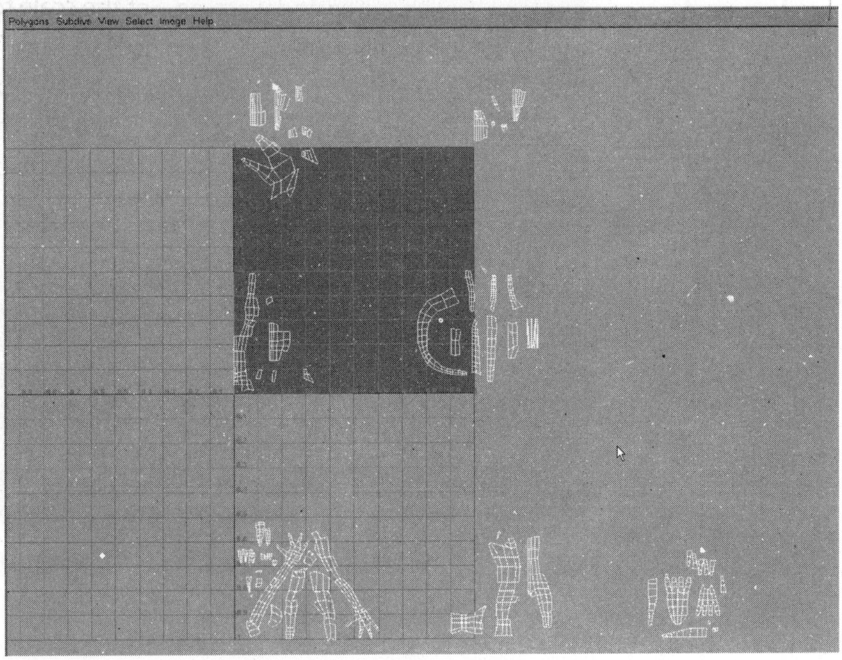

FIGURE 8.15 Move the UVs into separate groups.

Step 3: Begin reattaching the UVs by selecting a border edge in the UV texture editor, which will highlight its corresponding edge. Evaluate these shared edges to see if they can be sewn back together without overlapping or grossly distorting the UVs. Use the Move and Sew UVs tool to hasten the process. Regardless of how the UVs are placed, seams are inevitable.

Try to place seams in inconspicuous areas. On a leg, cut the UVs down the inside of the thigh. On an arm, place the seam toward the body. Figure 8.16 shows the UVs for the Fire Monster's arm and fingers after moving and sewing the UVs.

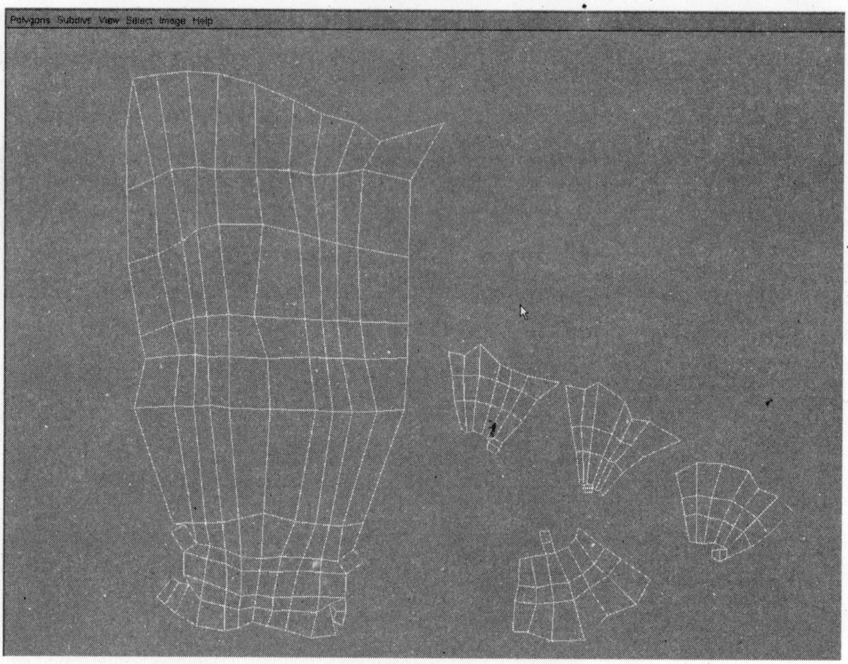

FIGURE 8.16 These are the arm and fingers of the Fire Monster.

Step 4: If the automatic mapping procedure breaks the UVs up too much, re-map the faces with another projection tool. The newly mapped UVs will have to be scaled in proportion to the others. Figure 8.17 shows the basic UV layout for the polygon proxy.

Step 5: Convert the polygon model to subdivision surface by choosing the Modify pull-down menu. Select Convert and choose Polygons to Subdiv. You might have to raise the Maximum

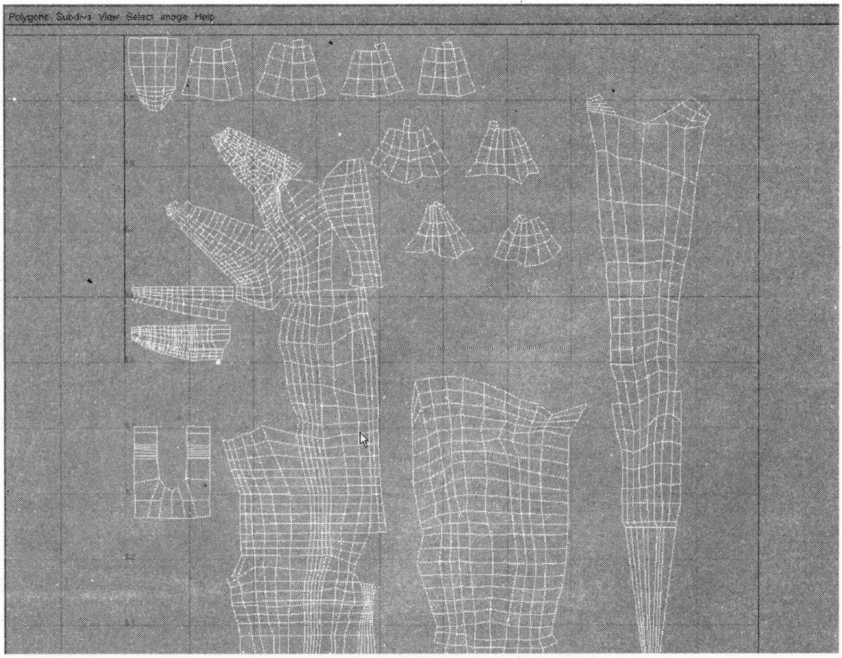

FIGURE 8.17 This is the basic UV layout for the polygon proxy.

Base Mesh Faces depending on the polygon count of your model.

CONCLUSION

The polygon proxy model, or SubD level 0, is extremely important. It determines the success of the subdivision surface model. Determining how much detail should go into the proxy is challenging, but keeping half of the proxy model under two thousand faces is a good guideline. Study the model for sharp elevation changes and basic shape. Differentiate between fine detail and surface shape.

Evaluate and optimize the proxy model when you are done. The Cleanup tool under the Polygons pull-down menu can help you find illegal geometry for subdivision surfaces. Use this tool prior to converting the proxy. To further test the geometry, it is a good idea to periodically convert the model to SubD. This allows you to make sure you have enough geometry to work with and shows any awkward subdivisions.

Saving your scene files is important at every phase. Make sure you keep the final version of the proxy model. During the SubD modeling phase, it might be necessary to return to this version. If you find you are subdividing vast surfaces beyond level 3, go back, add more detail to your proxy, and start over. Although it is a step backward, it keeps the model's face count lower, saving you time during every phase after.

Level 0 is done. From here on out, additional modeling is done to level 1 or higher. Your goal should not be to reach the highest level. The lower you stay, the better your model will perform. Think hard before subdividing any face. With experience, it will become second nature.

The next chapter involves the construction of your character's skeleton. The polygon proxy provides reference to mold the bones. This also helps refine the proxy model. As you build the skeleton, you might find anatomic inaccuracies. These issues can be dealt with prior to converting to subdivision surfaces.

CHAPTER

9 MODELING THE SKELETON

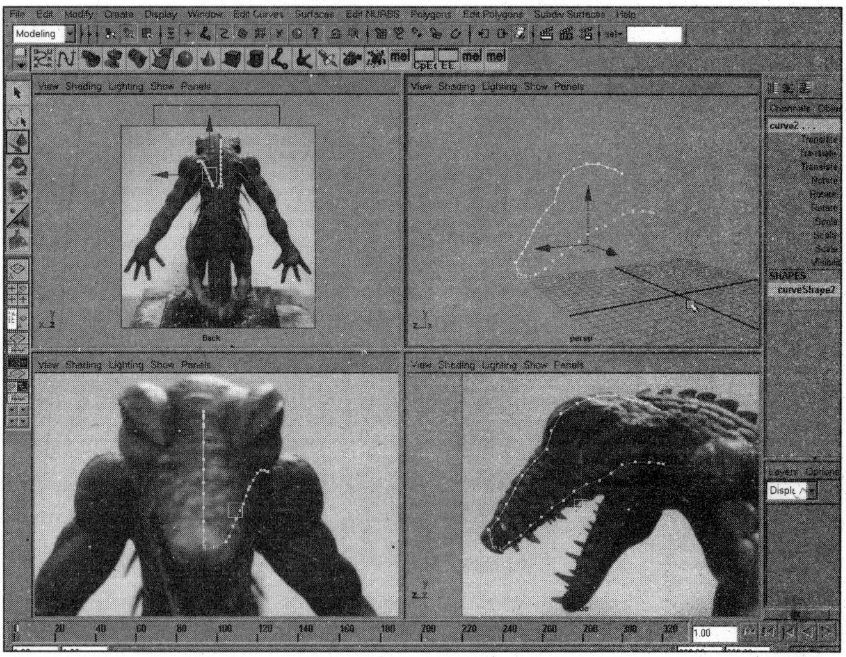

The bones of our character are there to provide accurate muscle placement, anatomically correct animation, and surface deformation. They will never be a part of the final render except in the case of an exoskeleton. Each bone making up an articulated joint must be modeled separately. Joints that do not move, such as those in the skull, can be modeled as one object. Polygons and NURBS are both suitable for the construction and implementation of the creature's bones. Subdivision surfaces are useful for the construction, but cannot be made into a rigid body, therefore must be converted to a polygon object.

THE SKELETON MODEL

Regardless of the tool, the bones should be smooth and devoid of sharp edges. The flatter the surface, the better the deformation. Except for those making up the exoskeleton, the bones will never be seen under the creature's skin, so they do not require a tremendous amount of detail or accuracy. A lot of time could be wasted easily in modeling the bones too perfectly. Keep in mind that the denser the geometry, the more taxing it is on your computer, thus slowing it down. The goal is to create the basic shape of individual bones. Many fully illustrated anatomy books are available providing excellent reference material.

The best reference is the modeled character. It provides us with scale, joint placement, and overall shape. Think of the character as a solid volume that needs to be filled. The bones should be proportional to the creature's body. Making them too small might cause them to pop out of the creature's skin by avoiding collision detection. Making them too large may not leave enough room for muscle. Feeling your own body is a great way to judge the depth of bone and the thickness of the surrounding tissue.

The following steps outline the construction of the bones in the arm, which are modeled using various tools. Any tool in Maya is acceptable to use as long as the outcome conforms to the guidelines in the above paragraph.

TUTORIAL

THE ARM

Step 1: Load your character into Maya. Create a new layer with the layer editor located under the channel box on the right hand side of the screen. Click on the Layers pull-down menu and choose Create Layer. Double click on the new layer, which will bring up the Edit Layer box. Rename this layer to "Skin" and choose a color that resembles the creature's skin. Save the settings. Change the Display type to Template by clicking once in the empty box to the left of the layer's name. Templating the geometry will display a light-gray wire frame of the model. This makes the model and its components unselectable until you change the layer back to a normal display.

Step 2: Choose an area to begin; it really doesn't matter where you start because the character dictates position and scale. The arm is probably the most complex area so it is a good place to start. The first bone to model is the humerus. This is located in the upper arm and is connected via a ball-and-socket joint to the bones of the shoulder. Model this bone using the Loft tool. Move to the center of the world and, in the top view, draw a circular curve with the CV curve tool located under the Create pull-down menu. Duplicate this curve and move it down in the front view a few units. Continue duplicating curves for the bottom of the bone. Repeat this procedure for the top. Shape the curves to resemble the outline of a humerus bone. Select the curves in order from top to bottom and choose Loft from the Surfaces pull-down menu. Figure 9.1 shows the curves and the lofted surface. If

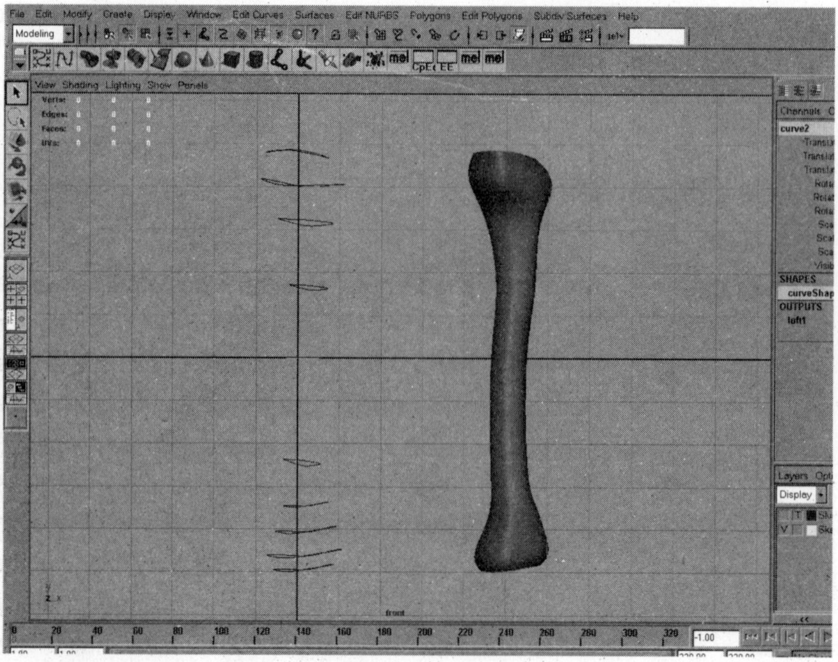

FIGURE 9.1 After drawing curves in the shape of the bone, loft them into a surface.

the surface doesn't look the way you expected it to, modify the original curves. With history turned on, the surface updates automatically. This is very useful as it can be easier to shape the curves after you create the surface because you can immediately see the results.

Step 3: Once you have the desired shape, delete the history and the curves. Notice the surface is open on the top and the bottom; these must be closed. Select the last row of CVs or hull in component mode. Turn grid snapping on and translate the center of the selection to the Y-axis. Turn grid snapping off and reposition the row so it is centered with the geometry. Repeat this procedure for the bottom. Figure 9.2 shows the top of the humerus closed.

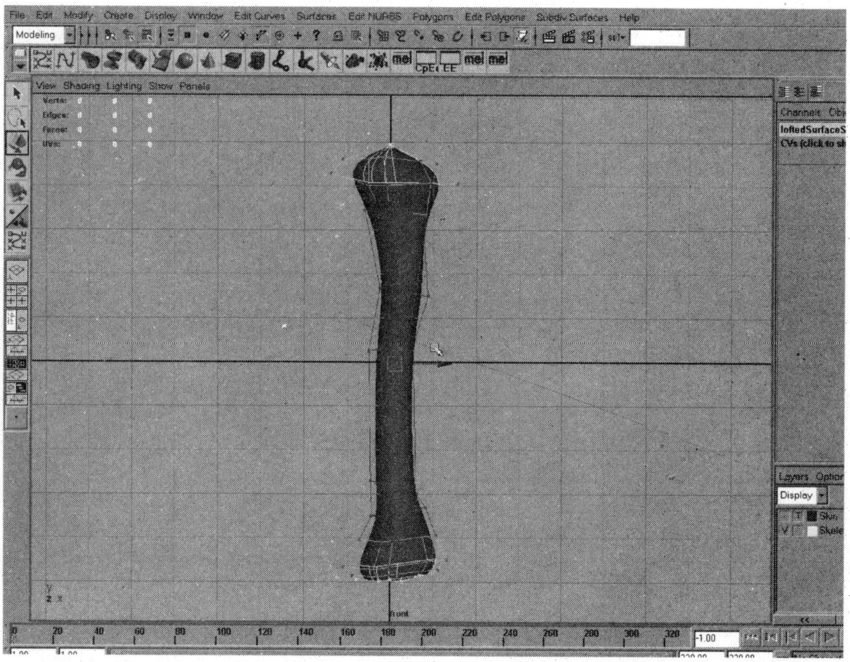

FIGURE 9.2 Snap the last row of CVs together for the bottom and the top.

Step 4: You need to rebuild the bone if it is a NURBS surface. Open the Options box of the Rebuild Surfaces tool located under the Edit NURBS pull-down menu. Under the Edit menu choose Reset Settings. This returns the options to their default settings. Change the number of spans in the U and V to 12. Rebuild the surface to spread out the isoparms evenly and to add more CVs. This aids in collision detection. Figure 9.3 shows the tools and the outcome.

Step 5: Place the bone into its proper position inside the skin of your creature. Once it is placed, delete the history and freeze the transformations.

Step 6: Create the radius and the ulna in the same manner. Create another layer and name it "Skeleton," and assign the bones

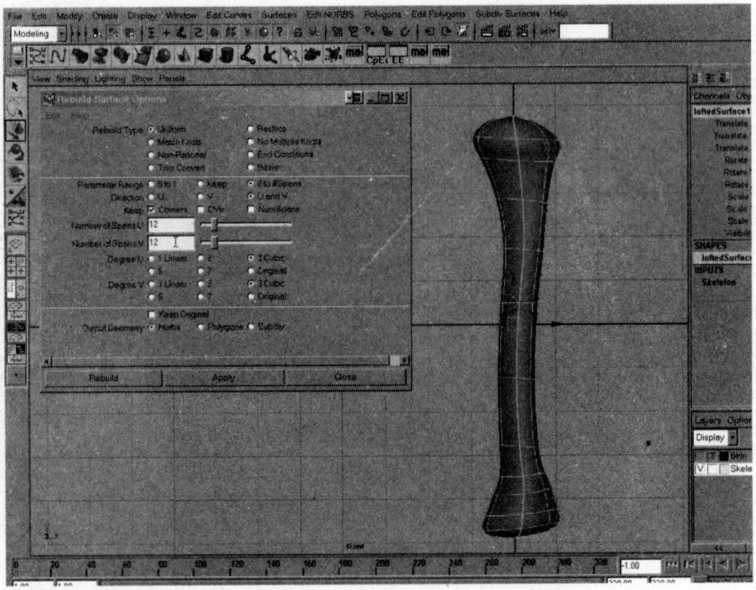

FIGURE 9.3 Rebuild NURBS bones to uniform geometry.

to this layer. Figure 9.4 shows the three finished bones positioned inside the skin.

Step 7: The next bone is actually a group of eight bones. The carpal bones sit at the end of the forearm and comprise the wrist. This group can be modeled as one, for they do not need to be articulated. Create a primitive NURBS sphere from the Create pull-down menu. Squash and stretch hulls until you get a wedge-like shape, and position the object in the wrist. Shape the carpals so they fit snugly under the skin.

Step 8: Now move on to the metacarpals and phalanges. These bones possess radial symmetry, therefore, you can use the revolve tool to model them. In the front view, draw one-half of a metacarpal bone. Don't worry about making it perfect; it is easier to modify after the surface is generated. Using the default settings, choose Revolve from the Surfaces pull-down menu. Move the new surface into the positive X-axis

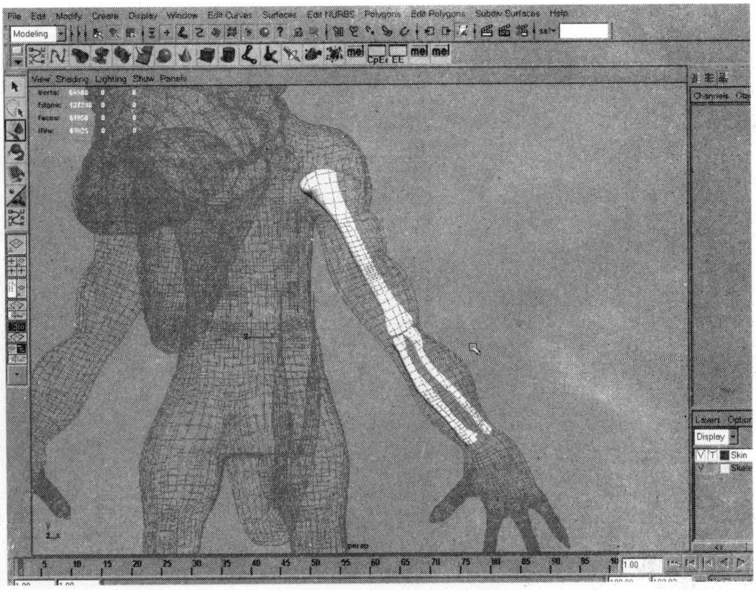

FIGURE 9.4 These are the humerus, radius, and ulna.

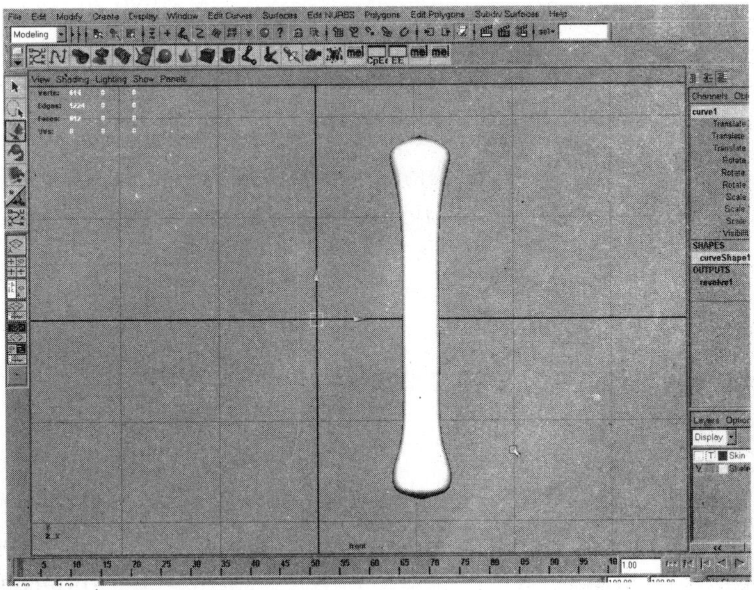

FIGURE 9.5 Use Revolve to generate radially symmetrical bones.

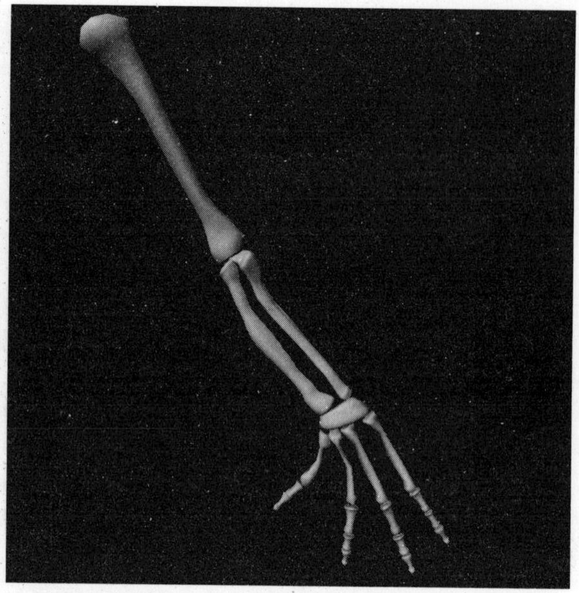

FIGURE 9.6 This is the complete skeleton for the arm.

for easy access to the curve. In component mode, push and pull CVs to get the desired shape. Figure 9.5 shows the revolved bone and its curve.

Step 9: Build all of the bones in the hand. You only need to build one complete finger because the rest can be scaled versions of the original. Figure 9.6 shows the complete skeleton for the arm.

THE SKULL

To build the skull, use the Birail +3 tool. This tool requires two rail curves and as many profile curves as needed. Think of it as a flexible railroad track. The rail curves act as a guide for the surface to follow, while the railroad ties, or profile curves, connect the two together. Birail +3 is a loft with two outer curves to control the shape of the surface border.

Step 1: Draw two rail curves in the shape of your character's skull profile, using your image planes as reference. Regardless of your character's shape, the first curve runs from the upper palate to the back of the head. The second curve runs from the upper palate to the back of the throat. Make sure you leave space between the two curves at the start because you will need to insert a profile curve between them. Reshape the lower curve to follow the contours of the exterior skull or gum line. You may use Figure 9.7 for reference. When finished, it is necessary to rebuild the curves so they have the same knot spacing. This makes the results of the birail predictable by

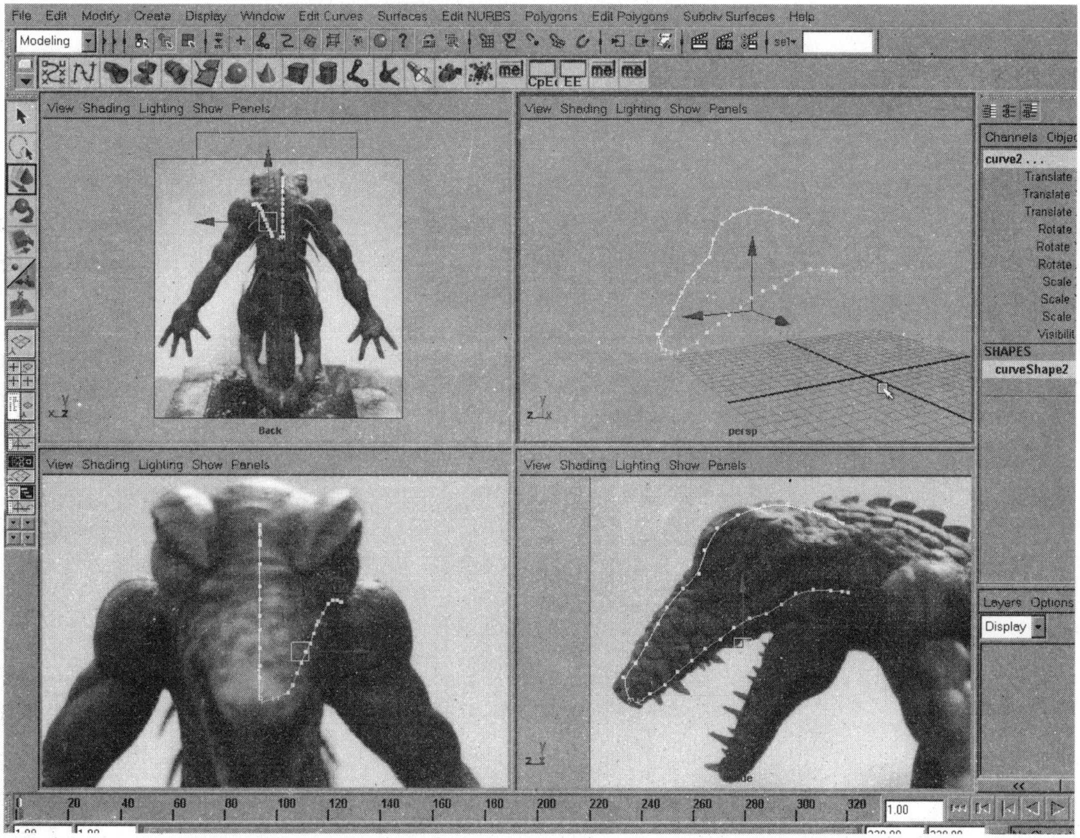

FIGURE 9.7 Draw two rail curves for the upper left quadrant of the skull.

only adding an isoparm at each knot. If this is not done, the Bi-rail tool adds as many isoparms as it sees fit to match them up, usually resulting in a surface with excessive geometry. Choose the Rebuild Curve tool settings from the Edit Curves pull-down menu. Change the Rebuild Type to Match Knots and make the Parameter Range 0 to # of Spans. Select the curve you want to modify and then the curve with the proper knots. Apply the settings.

Step 2: Draw as many profile curves as needed between the rail curves. You only need to insert these curves in areas requiring a surface change, such as the nose and eyes, places that can't be defined with the rail curves alone. Draw the basic curves, then go back and shape them to accurately fit the shape of your character's head. Add a small lip where the teeth go to give the bone some thickness. Figure 9.8 shows an example.

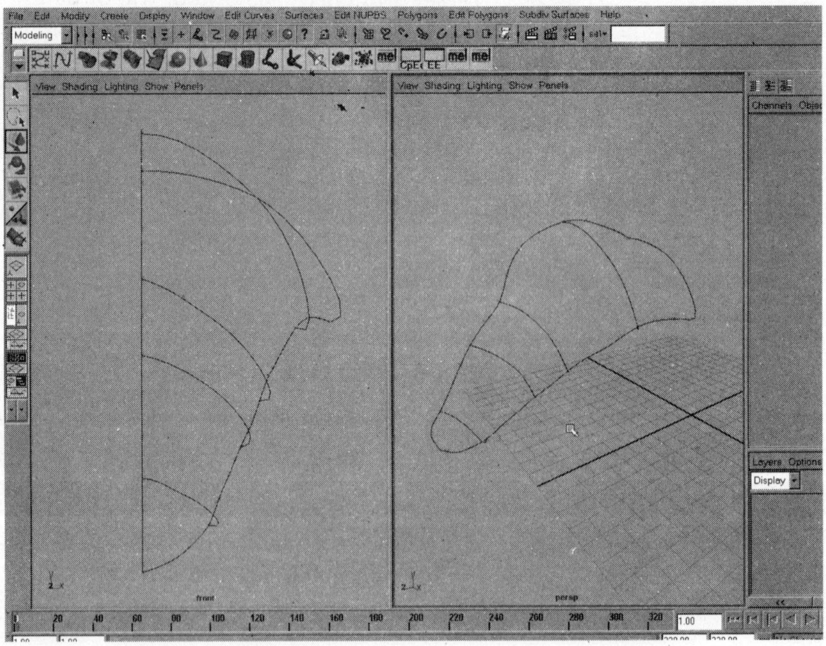

FIGURE 9.8 Draw as many profile curves as needed.

Step 3: In order for the Birail tool to make the surface, the profile curves must be intersecting the rail curves. There are two ways to make this happen. The first is to turn on the edit points of the curves. Select the last edit point of the profile curve and snap it with Snap to Point to the closest edit point of the rail curve. You must snap to edit points; snapping to CVs does not work. The second method is to snap to a curve. Select the last CV or edit point of the profile curve. Turn on Snap to Curve or hold down C on the keyboard. Hold the middle mouse button over the rail curve. The point automatically snaps to that curve. If you continue to hold the middle mouse button, you can move the point along the curve. Make sure all the curves are intersecting.

Step 4: Run Birail +3, and if it fails, check the curve intersections again. Modify the surface to fit inside the polygon proxy by moving control points on the curves. You must move the intersecting curves as one or the birail breaks apart and fails. If this does happen, simply re-snap the points together. Once it is shaped, delete the history on the surface and delete the curves. Rebuild the surfa e so the isoparms are evenly spaced as shown in Figure 9.9.

Step 5: Under the Edit pull-down menu, choose the Duplicate tool options. Change the scale in X to −1 to create a mirrored duplicate of your model, and apply the settings. Select both surfaces and choose the tool options for Attach Surfaces from the Edit NURBS pull-down menu. Choose Blend and turn off Keep Originals. Apply the settings. Figure 9.10 shows an example.

Step 6: Next, you need to create an opening for the eye socket. Make the surface live by selecting it and choosing the Magnet icon from the status line. In the side view, draw a curve in the shape of the eye socket. Use Open/Close Curves from the Edit Curves pull-down menu to close the curve. Modify the curve as needed. Figure 9.11 shows an example.

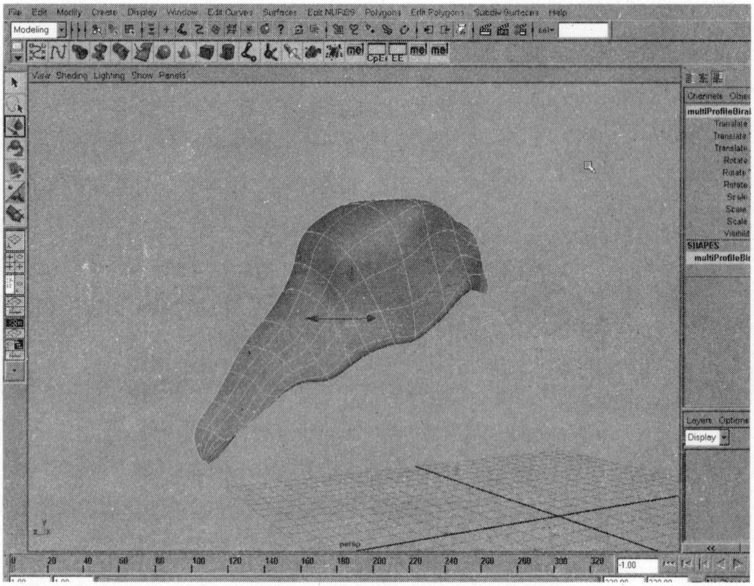

FIGURE 9.9 Modify the surface to more accurately depict the shape of your creature's skull.

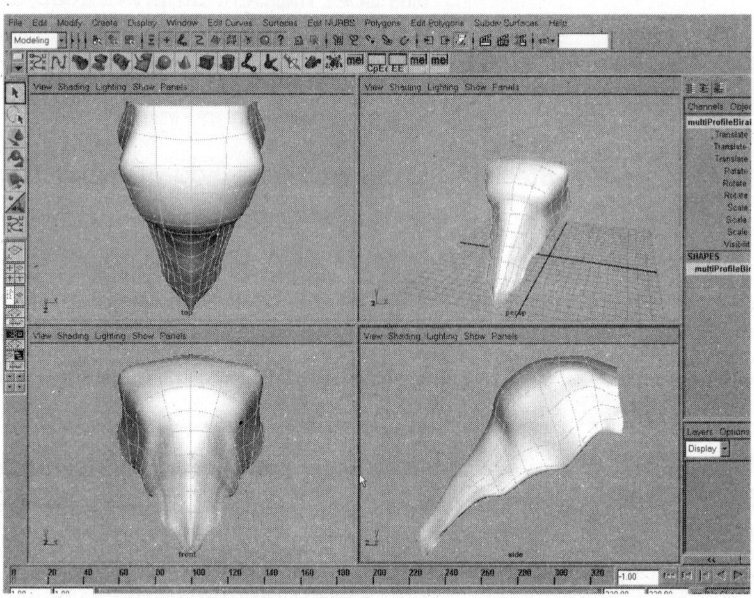

FIGURE 9.10 Create a mirrored duplicate and attach the surfaces.

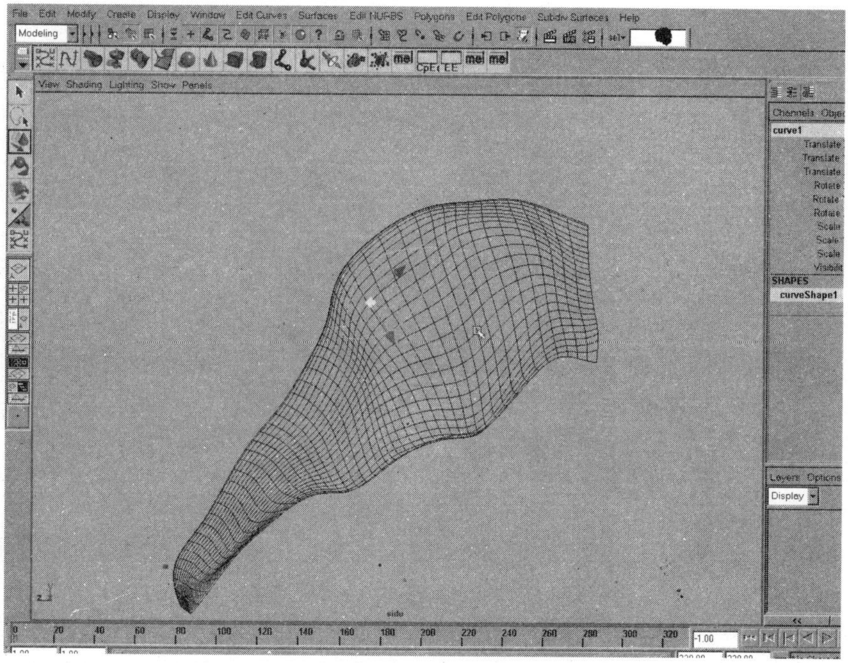

FIGURE 9.11 Draw a curve for the eye socket.

Step 7: To create a curve for the other side of the skull, choose Duplicate Surface Curve from the Edit Curves pull-down menu. Choose Duplicate from the Edit pull-down menu and duplicate it with a scale of –1. The mirrored duplicate now needs to be put back on the surface. Make sure you are in the side view and choose Project Curve on Surface from the Edit NURBS pull-down menu. Delete the other curves, leaving two curves on the surface of the skull.

Step 8: To cut out the sockets, open the Trim Tool options from the Edit NURBS pull-down menu. Make the Selected State Keep, and apply the settings. Figure 9.12 shows the results.

Step 9: Build the jaw in the same manner as outlined in Steps 1 through 8. Figure 9.13 shows the final skull for the Fire Monster.

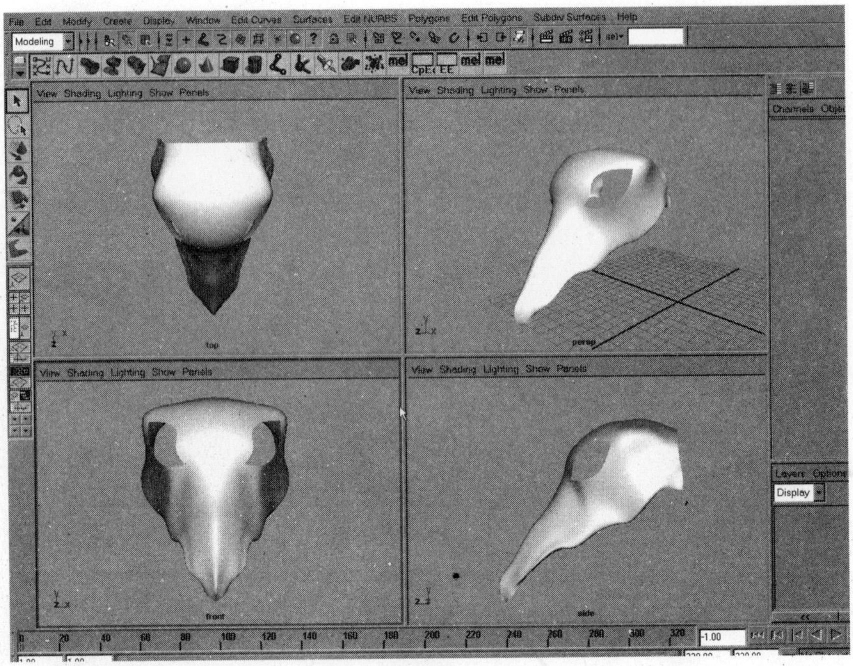

FIGURE 9.12 Use the Trim Tool to remove the eye sockets.

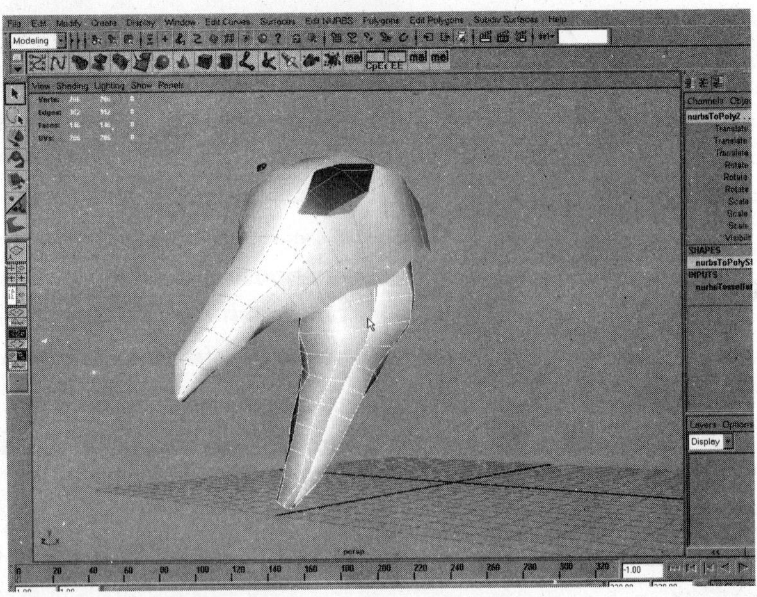

FIGURE 9.13 This is the Fire Monster's skull.

Using the tools and methods outlined, you can quickly generate the entire skeleton. Pay special attention to bones more apparent under the surface of the skin, e.g., the rib cage and elbow. Make sure these bones are smooth and a little larger than they actually would be in real life. This helps deform the skin more accurately. Figure 9.14 shows the completed skeleton for the Fire Monster.

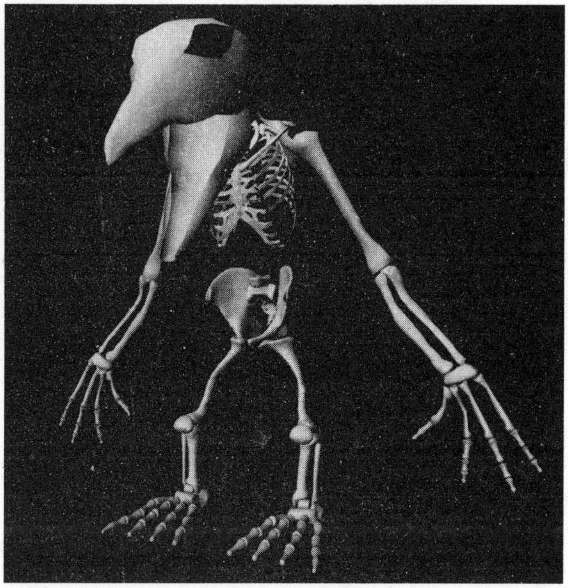

FIGURE 9.14 This is the completed skeleton of the Fire Monster.

CONCLUSION

It is a good idea to optimize the skull by converting it to polygons. The trimmed surface will carry over to the polygon model. By converting it, you will also eliminate any conflicts with the trim and the Rigid Body tool. To do this, select the model and choose Convert Nurbs to Polygons from the Modify pull-down menu. In the tool settings change the type to Quads and the Tessellation Method to Count. Start with the minimum amount of faces. The jaw used 50 faces and the skull 100 faces as seen in Figure 9.15.

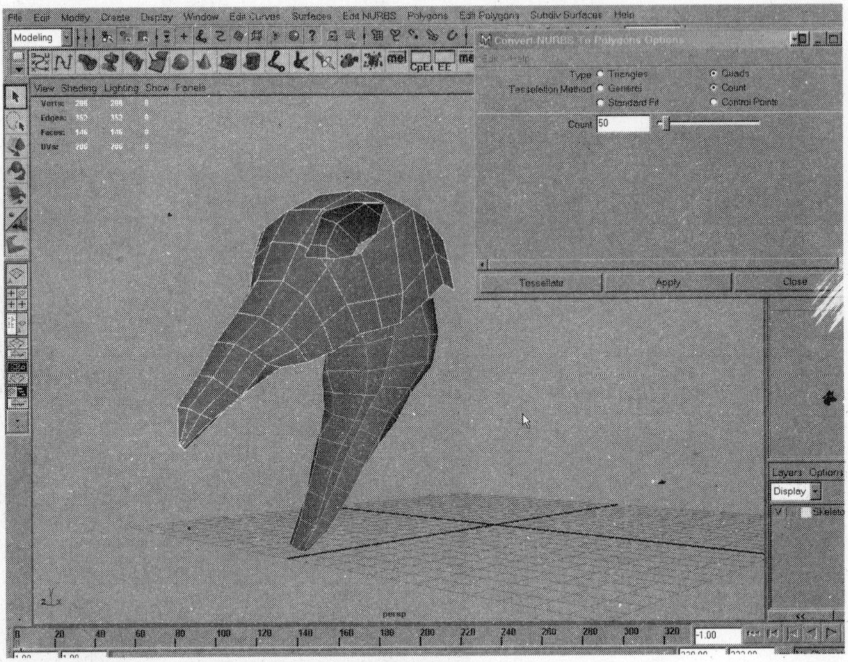

FIGURE 9.15 Convert the NURBS skull to polygons.

The next chapter is devoted to modeling the skin. To finalize the proxy model, line it up with your skeleton. Make sure the skeleton sits inside the proxy. If any part of the skeleton sticks out, alter one of the two surfaces based on anatomic accuracy. If you haven't already done so, convert your polygon proxy to subdivision surfaces.

CHAPTER

10 MODELING THE SKIN

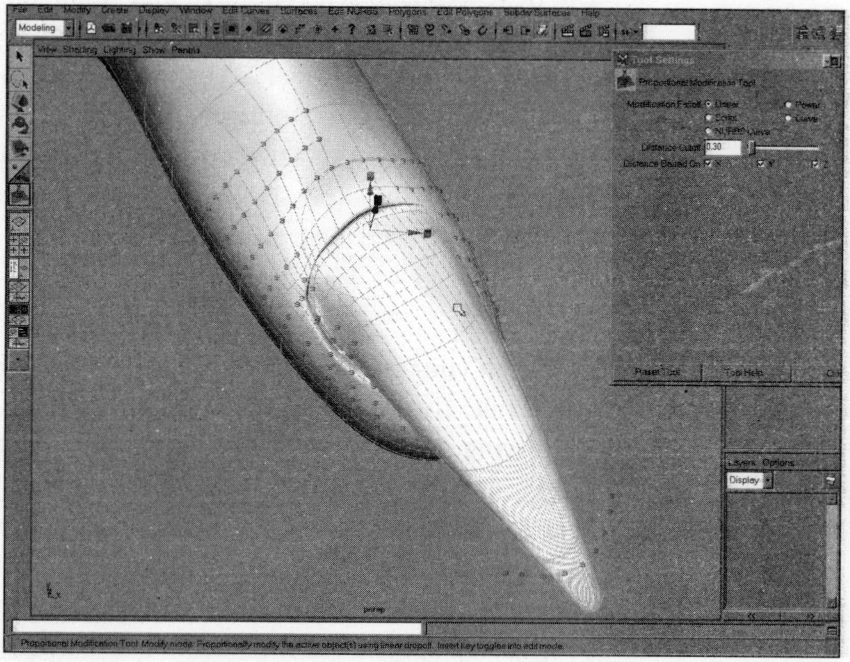

In Chapter 8, you built the polygon proxy, or level 0. This level should be locked down and rarely altered. Modeling in SubD is typically a forward process. Once you complete a level, move on to the next one. Going back to previous levels, however, can be an incredibly powerful benefit to subdivision surfaces. With lower-numbered levels you can quickly reposition or shape large, detailed areas on a higher level.

When modeling a character in SubD, the first step is to establish a level 0. This level is the base shape for any subsequent detail. The next step is to select an area and subdivide it to level 1. Make all the adjustments possible using the geometry created in level 1 before subdividing to level 2. The more detail that can be placed on lower levels, the more efficient the model will be. This process continues until you're satisfied with the amount of detail in that area. Move on to a new section and begin again.

THE SKIN

Block out your creature to determine which part is skin and which part is not. The skin needs to act as a continuous elastic surface. By identifying skin, it's possible to break the model up into sections or layers, making it easier and faster to model. Human characters have few extra parts. The more fantastic your creature is, the more parts you may have. The Fire Monster has armored plating, or an exoskeleton, over its eyes and down its back. These objects need to be modeled apart from the skin to allow them to react differently. This way the skin could bunch up around the plates.

The head of any character usually has the most detail. By starting with this area first, the construction technique is established for the rest of the body. After converting from polygons to subdivided surfaces, three levels were generated. Maya subdivided the corner of the creature's mouth in order to smooth the surface properly and to support existing detail. With characters this usually happens around appendages, e.g., fingers, toes, arms, and legs.

This is unavoidable in certain situations and doesn't affect the outcome of the model. It is safe to assume that the amount of detail in the Fire Monster will push the model beyond level 2. The optimal goal is to stay at level 3, using a fourth and fifth level only in isolated areas.

The following tutorials demonstrate modeling techniques that can be applied to your character. The main objective is to grasp the tools and principles associated with a specific part of anatomy. Follow along with the tutorial while modeling your creature or practice with the provided scene files.

TUTORIAL

The Nose

Open the scene file in the Chapter 10 directory on the CD-ROM named "Nose.mb". The Fire Monster has more of a snout than a nose, but the same principles apply. The snout has a considerable amount of surface detail. Each individual pad making up his skin is defined by geometry. To keep the amount of subdivisions to a minimum, the pads have been outlined in the polygon proxy, or level 0. The current geometry, however, doesn't have any real definition. Using the sculpture, you can identify defining lines or creases and replicate those with the crease tool.

ON THE CD

Step 1: Select edges from level 0 making up a crease in the snout. Use the background image in the side view and Figure 10.1 for reference. Note where the crease starts and stops. It is important to make sure only the edges needed for the creases are selected. You may undo the operation in Step 2, if needed.

Step 2: From the Subdiv Surfaces pull-down menu select Partial Crease Edge/Vertex. The selected edges are now subdivided as shown in Figure 10.2. A dotted line now represents the creased area. The surrounding geometry is stepped up to level 2.

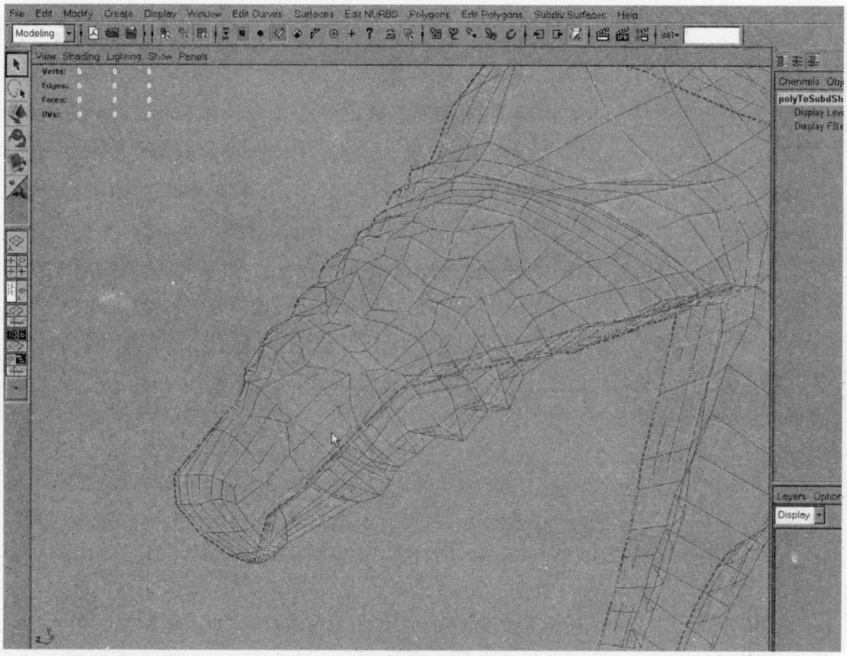

FIGURE 10.1 Select a row of edges corresponding to a crease in the snout.

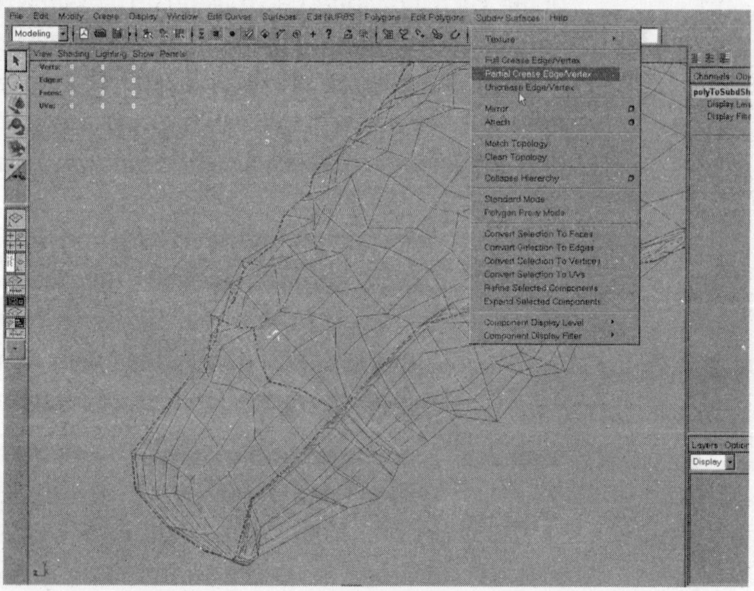

FIGURE 10.2 Crease the area along the selected edges.

Step 3: Switch the Display level to 1 by using the Finer option in the Component Marking menu, or in the Channel Box. Align the vertices of the creased edge in level 1 to the crease in the side view image. Do not modify level 2 at this point. See Figure 10.3 for reference.

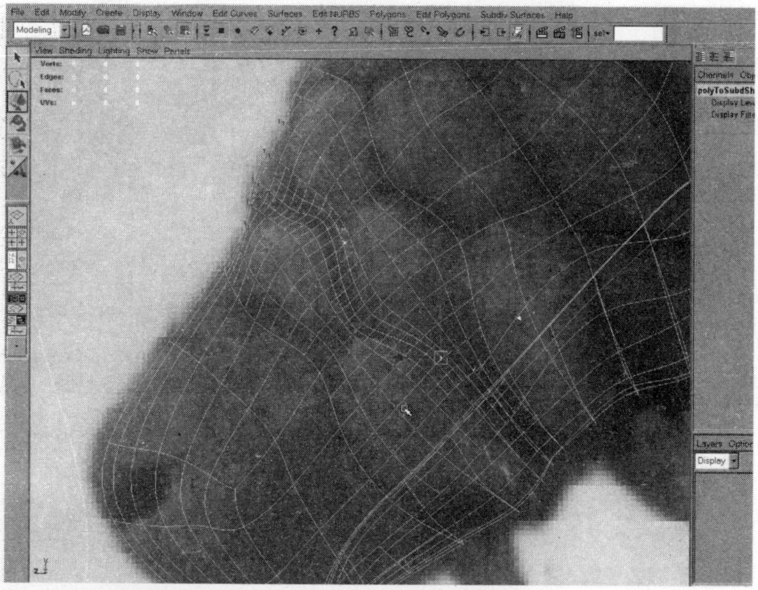

FIGURE 10.3 Move the vertices of level 1 to correspond to the crease in the background image.

Step 4: Pinch the vertices closer on either side of the crease. This makes the crease more prominent. Select the creased edges or vertices and pull them toward zero in the X-axis as shown in Figure 10.4.

Step 5: Go back to level 0 and select edges for the next crease. The Lasso tool can make the selection process much easier. Select it from the tool bar or use Ctrl-Q on the keyboard. Repeat the partial-creasing process for all of the snout detail both horizontally and vertically as shown in Figure 10.5. Some horizontal creases will not have defined edges to crease on

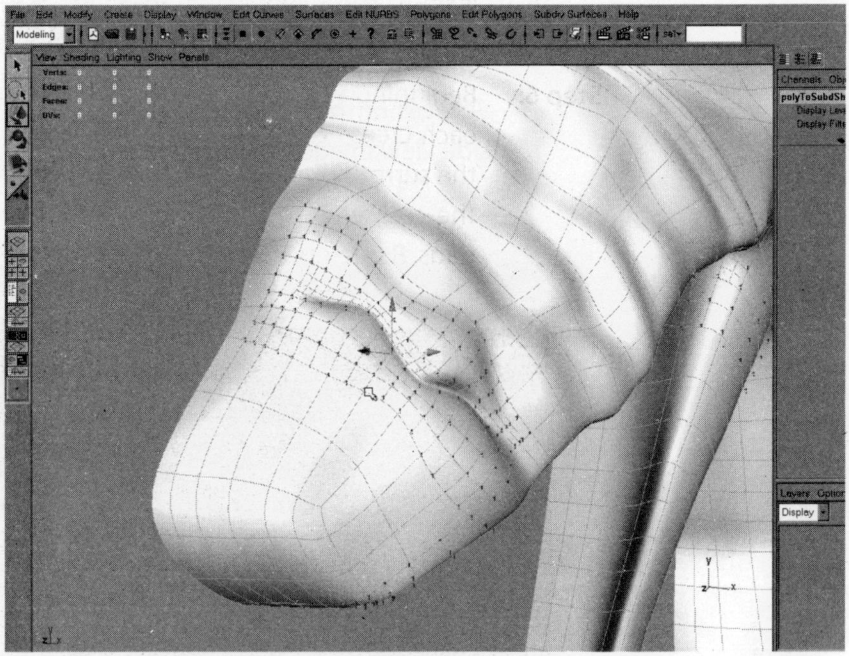

FIGURE 10.4 Pull vertices to deepen the crease.

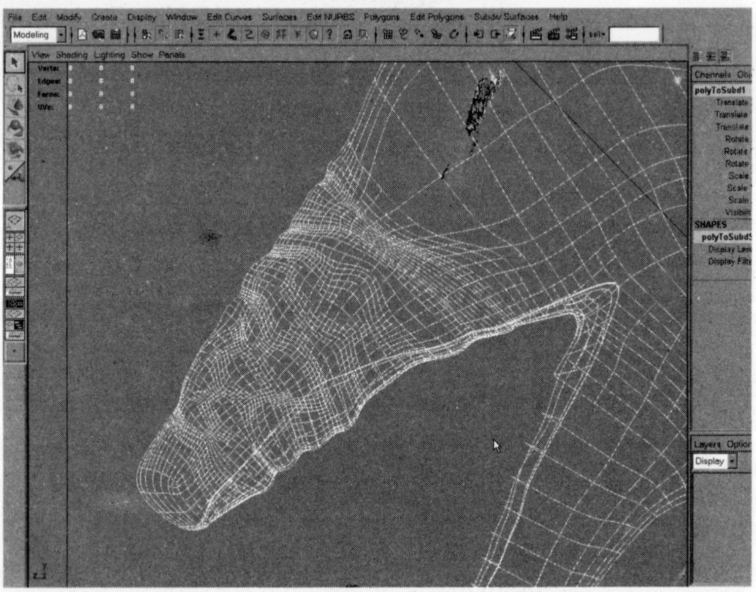

FIGURE 10.5 Crease the edges for the snout detail.

level 0. These edges can be defined using geometry from level 1, and you will not need to crease them.

Step 6: Beginning at the start of the snout, pinch the vertices around each crease on level 1. Push the creased edges in, and pull the surrounding skin out. Move down to the upper lip using the creases as guides. Figure 10.6 shows five shaped skin pads. Remember to use vertices from level 1 only.

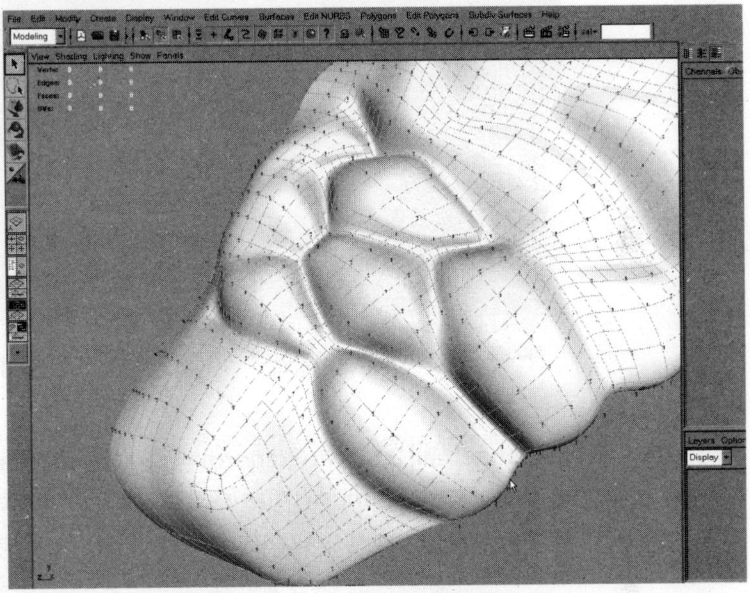

FIGURE 10.6 Five of the pads are done.

Step 7: Certain areas may not be subdivided to level 1. As you move vertices adjacent to these areas, they are subdivided automatically in order to support the new detail. Figure 10.7 shows an example of an area not yet subdivided.

There are three creasing tools available to be used on vertices or edges: full, partial, and uncrease. A full crease creates a hard edge or point in the surface. This is useful for spikes or for separate objects, such

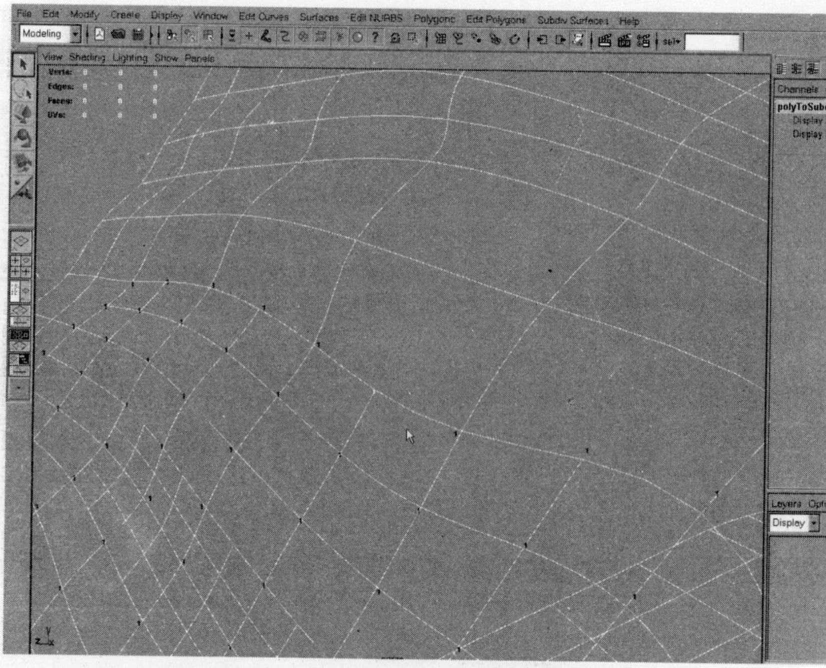

FIGURE 10.7 Moving this vertex will subdivide the neighboring face automatically.

as a fingernail. You would normally use a full crease to denote a change in surface makeup, such as skin to nail or armored plate. The partial crease keeps the surface appearance soft or sloping. Typically a partial crease is used for soft edges to depict a continuous surface. For example, adding wrinkles or skin folds to a character would require a partial crease. Uncrease removes the sharpness of the creased edge. It does not, however, remove the geometry; in fact, it may add geometry. Continue to experiment with the crease tools.

Step 8: At the end of the snout or nose are the nostrils. Go to a level that has a sufficient amount of faces to define the basic shape of the nostril hole. Pull the geometry back into the snout to create a hole. Select the edges around the hole and partially crease them. You can choose to crease at a different level. This can help limit the amount of subdivided geometry. Figure 10.8 shows the nostrils. Human noses are done the same way. Create a partial crease around the border of the nose as it sits on the face. Pinch and pull vertices to form the nostrils.

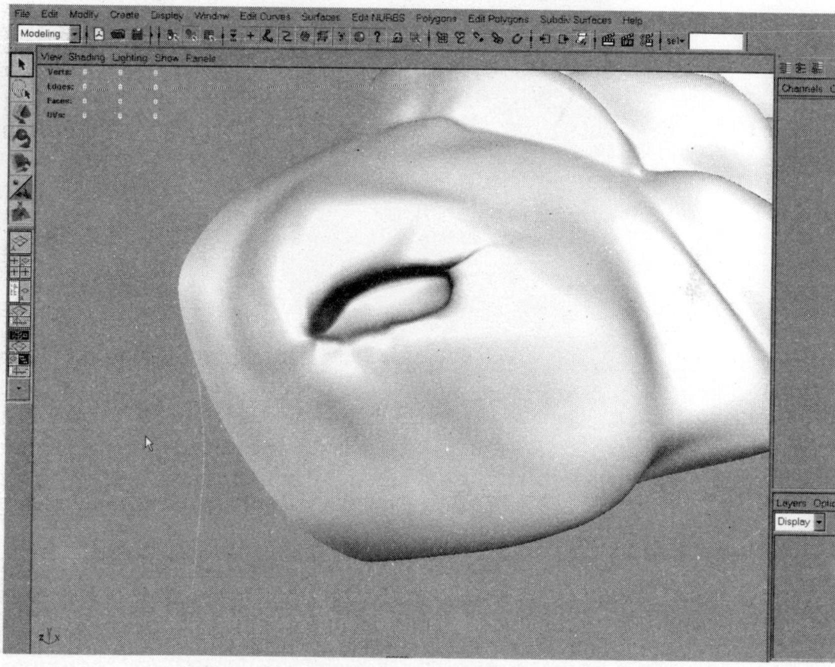

FIGURE 10.8 Pinch and pull vertices to form nostrils.

After the snout or nose, the rest of the features of the face can be modeled. Aging human characters have prominent creasing around the mouth, under the eyes, and on the forehead. Young to middle-aged human characters have little to no creasing in the face. Around the nose, lips, and eyes are probably the only areas that need partial creasing. Figure 10.9 shows the side of the Fire Monster's face.

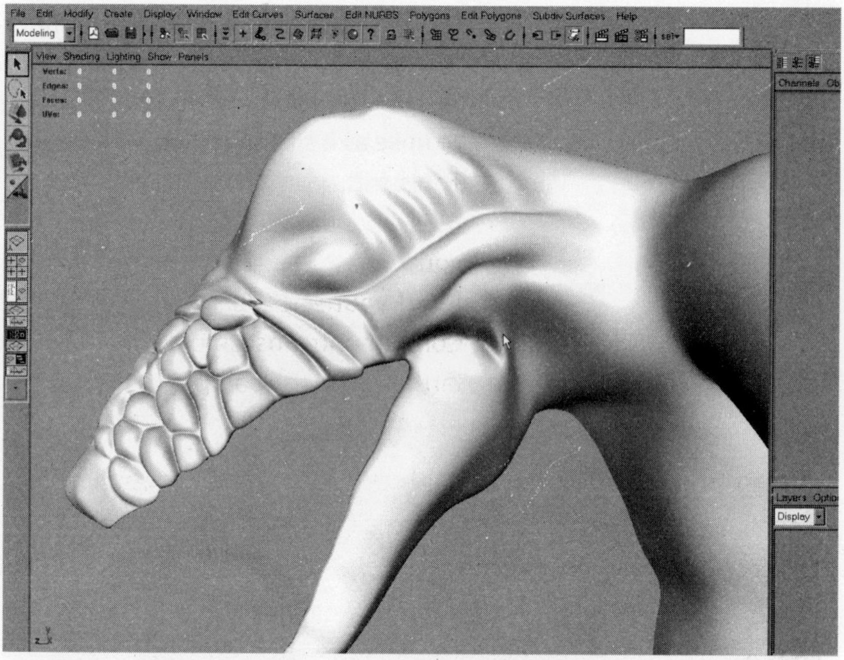

FIGURE 10.9 This is the side of the Fire Monster's face.

TUTORIAL

THE EYE

The eyes and surrounding area can be problematic. Age plays a significant factor in the shape of the eye. Our expectations of how the eye animates also weigh heavily on our construction techniques.

CG eyes must be able to tell the whole story; they give life to our creatures. To model them, look to Mother Nature to guide you. There are three parts to the eye. The first, the sclera, or eyeball, is the white of the eye and is the perfect spherical shape. This round shape is important because it allows us to rotate the eye without it popping out of our head. Next comes the iris, the colored ring that controls how much light enters the eye. The last layer is the lens. Black in color, it absorbs light.

Step 1: Before you build the eyeball, you must have a place to put it. Select a row of vertices or edges the length of the eye socket. Move these components into the head with the Proportional Modification Tool located under the Modify, Transformation Tools pull-down menu (Figure 10.10). Open the tools attributes, and change the distance cutoff based upon the area you want to affect. This linear value decreases from the center of your selection to 360 degrees of the cutoff distance. Components closest to the center are affected the most. The farther away the component, the less it is influenced.

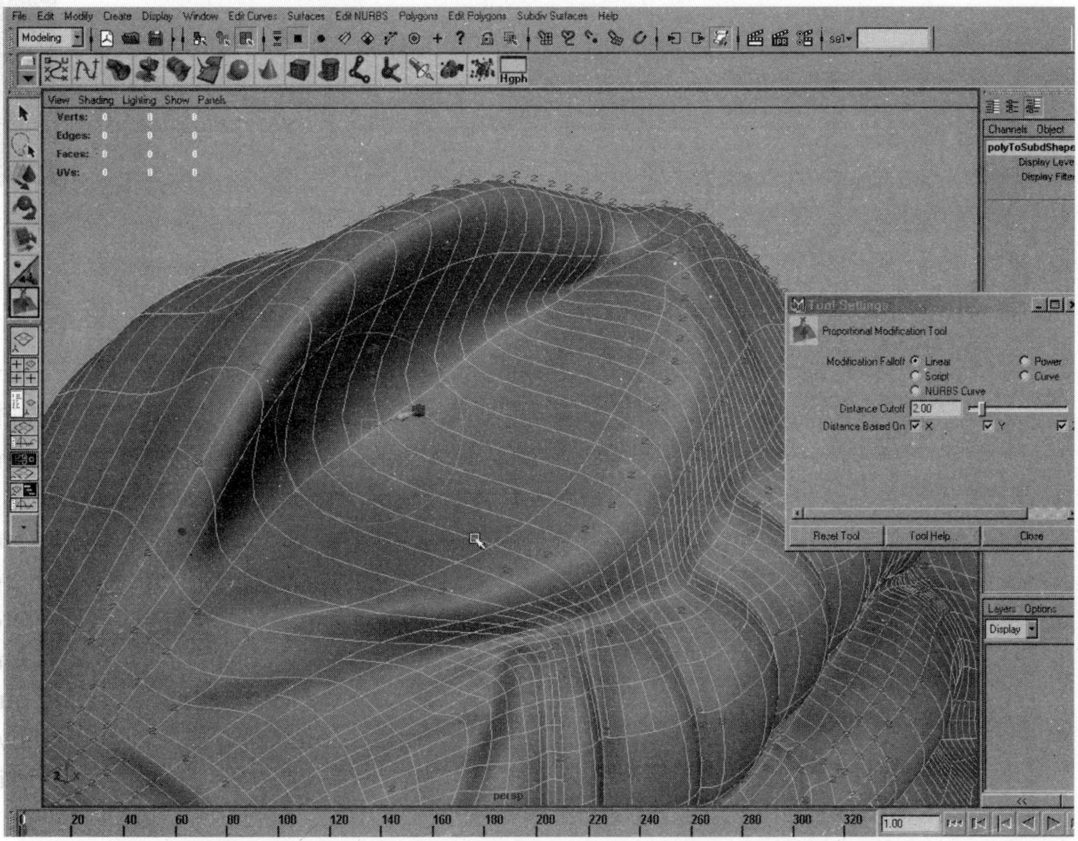

FIGURE 10.10 Push a row of vertices the length of the eye socket inward.

Step 2: Select a row of vertices to make up the border of the eye socket. Crease these edges as demonstrated in Figure 10.11.

Step 3: Pull the resulting creased edge out slightly to imply a bulge from the eyeball itself. Figure 10.12 shows an example.

Step 4: Smooth out the surrounding surfaces. Shape up the inner socket area by creating a bubble in the head. Use Figure 10.13 for reference.

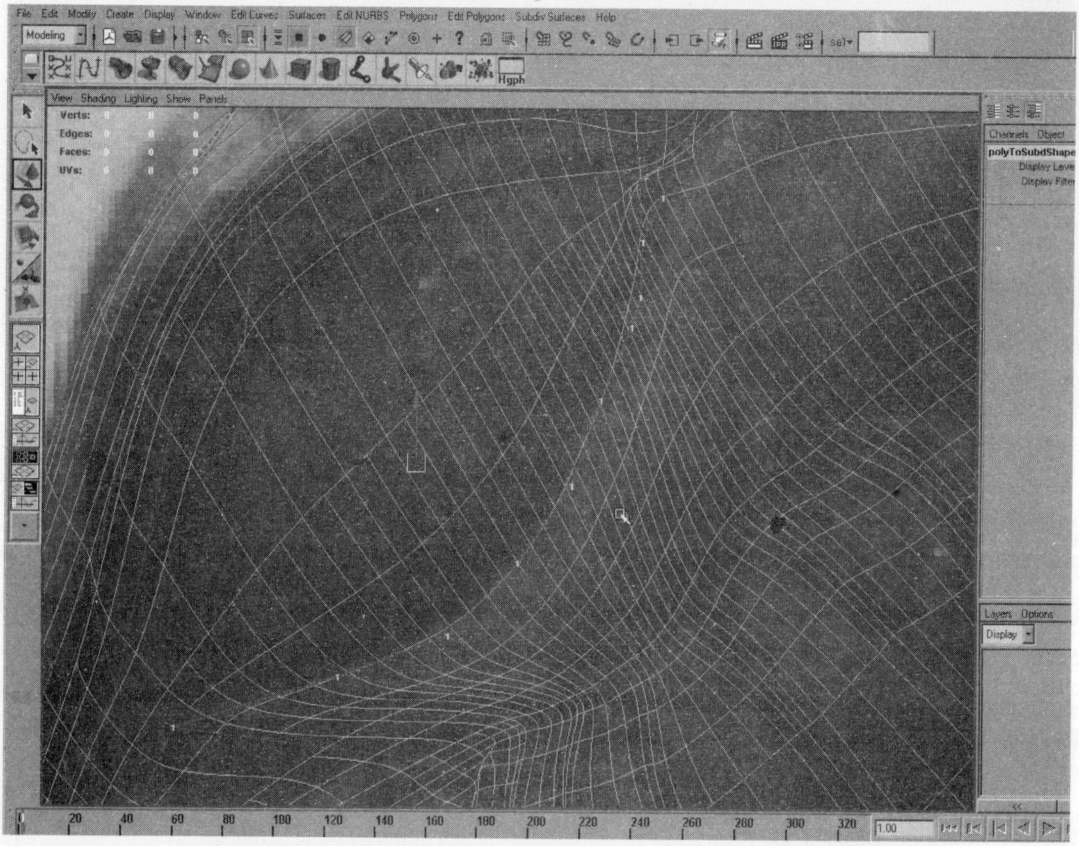

FIGURE 10.11 Crease a row of edges to define the border of the eye socket.

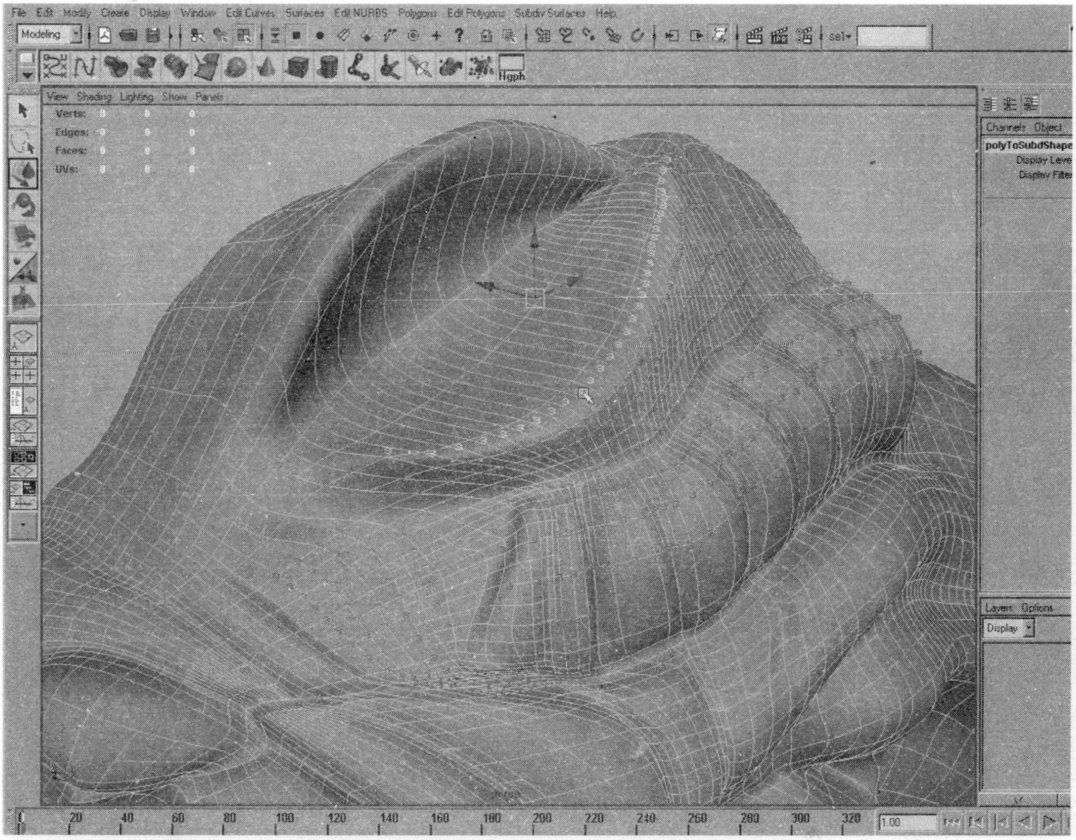

FIGURE 10.12 Create a bulge in which the eyeball can sit.

Step 5: Create a primitive NURBS sphere, and scale it to match the interior bubble in the creature's head. Use the sphere as reference to shape the rest of the eye socket. Remember the eyeball remains round; it is the surrounding skin that gives it an oval appearance. Name this sphere "ScleraLft". Duplicate the object and name the duplicate "IrisLft". Hide ScleraLft. Figure 10.14 shows an example.

Step 6: Scale IrisLft down 2–3 percent, and rotate it so that its poles are facing out. Select a row of hulls and walk up the selection to the top of the pole. Press Delete on the keyboard to remove it. This leaves a small hole in the eyeball as shown in Figure 10.15.

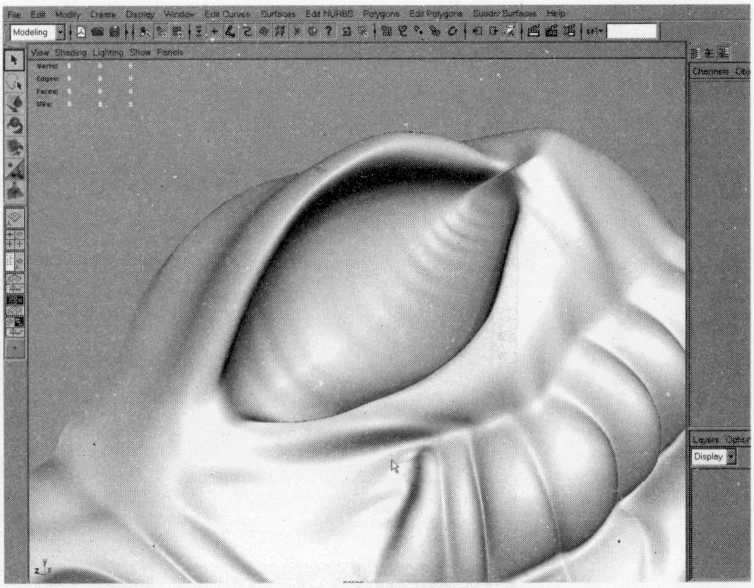

FIGURE 10.13 Smooth out surrounding surfaces and shape up the inner socket area.

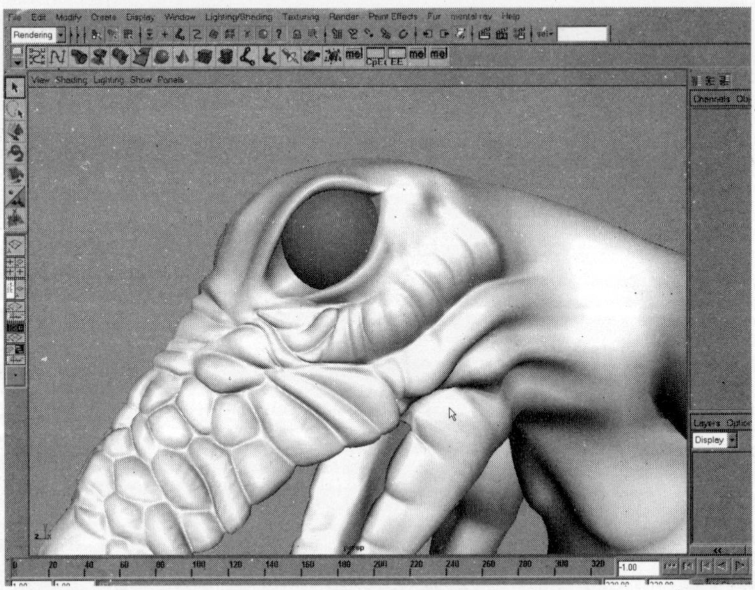

FIGURE 10.14 Create a primitive sphere for an eyeball.

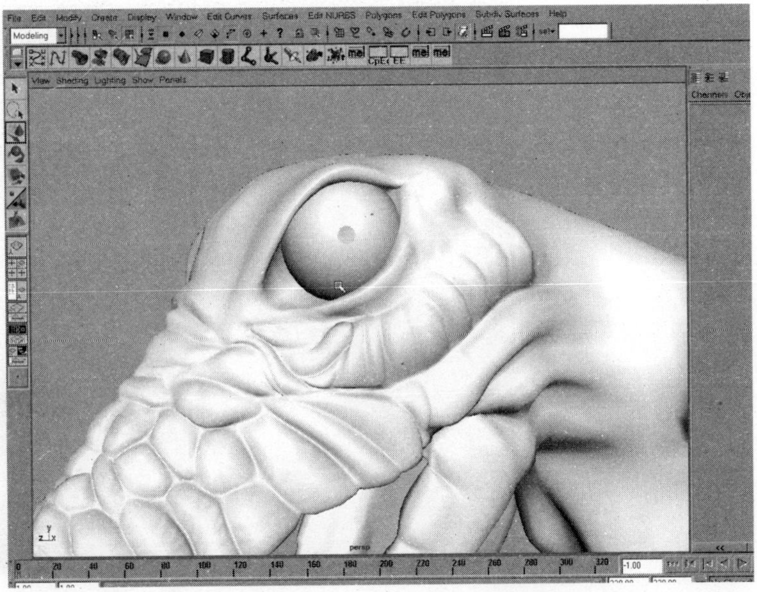

FIGURE 10.15 Delete the last row of hulls on the pole facing out.

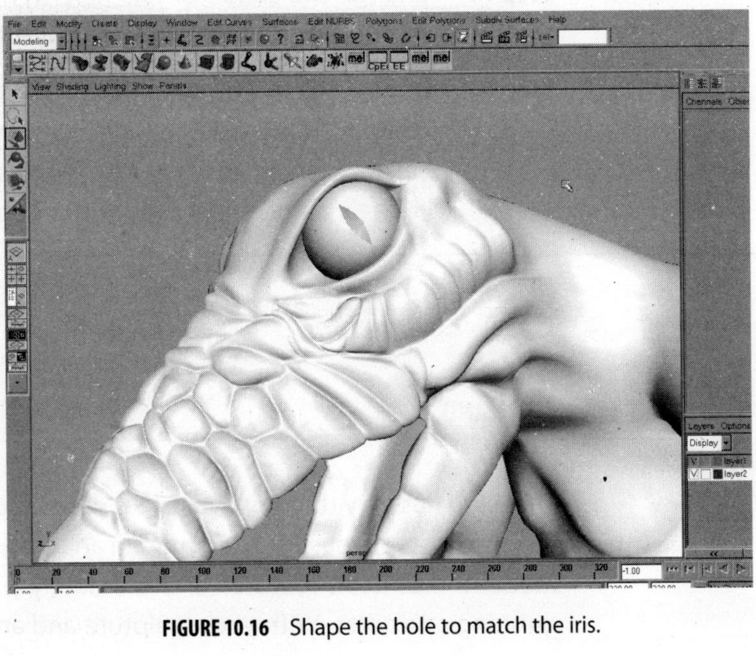

FIGURE 10.16 Shape the hole to match the iris.

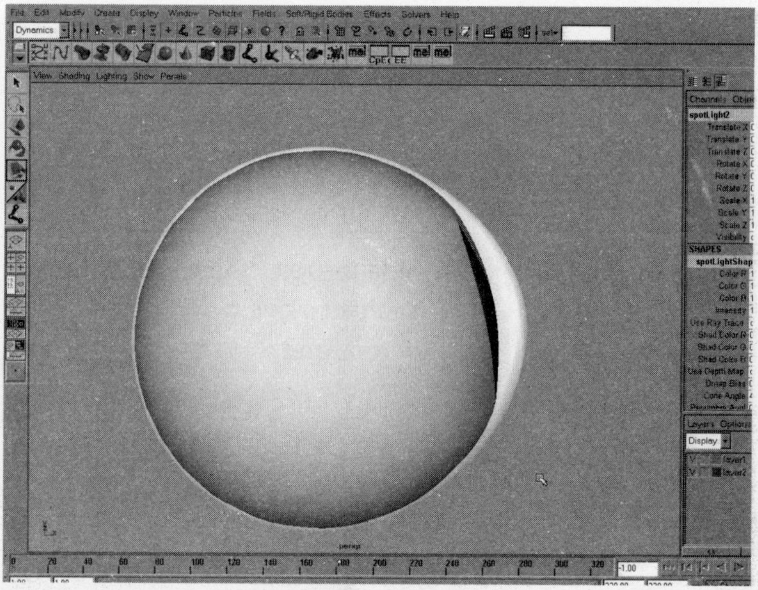

FIGURE 10.17 Create a small dome in the sclera in front of the iris.

Step 7: Change the shape of this hole to match the shape of your creature's iris. Figure 10.16 shows an example.

Step 8: Unhide ScleraLft, and duplicate it again. Name the duplicate "LensLft," and scale LensLft 2–3 percent smaller than IrisLft. Select ScleraLft and translate the CVs in front of the iris out to create a dome effect. Figure 10.17 shows an example.

TUTORIAL

THE HAND

The hand has very thin skin. Veins, tendons, and bones play a huge role in defining its shape. Studying human anatomy can help you when you model the difficult features and ultimately provide the most distinguishing attributes. With your sculpture and anatomy reference, begin

ON THE CD

modeling the hand. Or if you prefer to practice, load "Hand.mb" from the Chapter 10 folder on the CD-ROM.

Step 1: The hand contains areas, just like the snout, that have not been subdivided at level 1. It is not always necessary, but to support the amount of detail needed for the hand, subdivide the rest of the geometry so it is all at the same level. Instead of moving a vertex to invoke the subdivision, choose a vertex, and then select Expand Selected Components from the Subdiv Surfaces pull-down menu. Figure 10.18 shows an example.

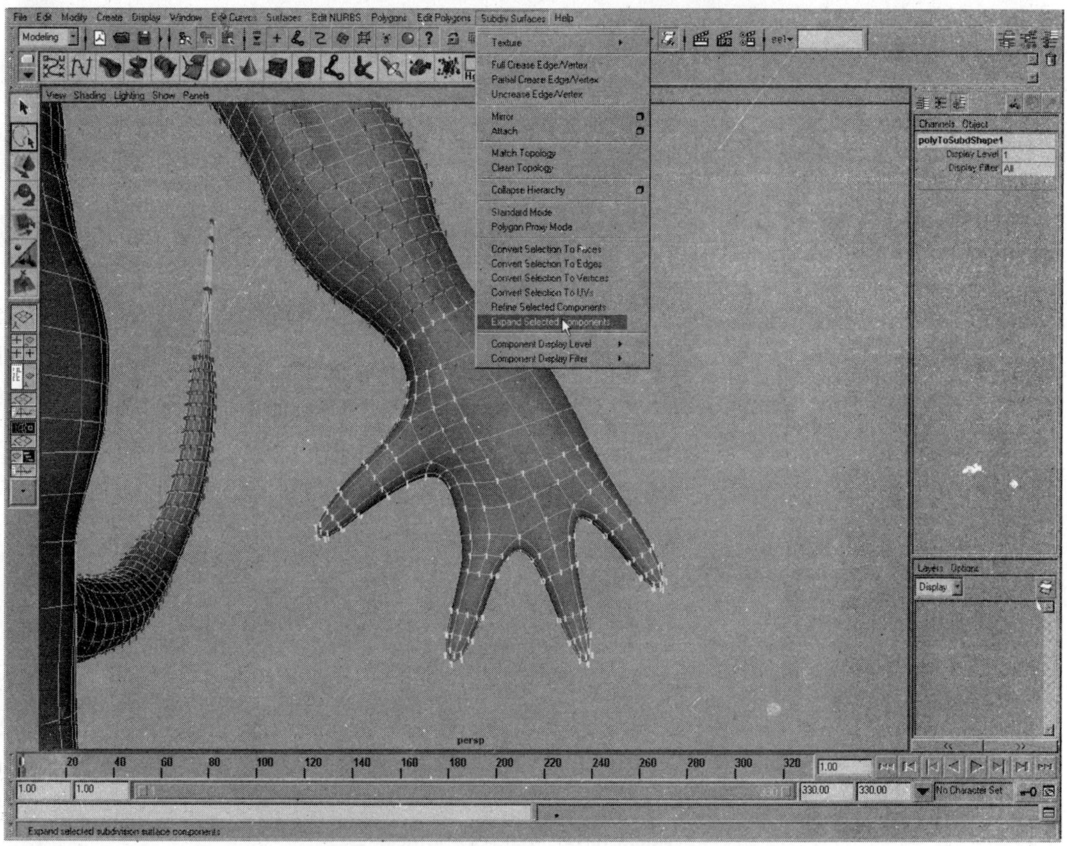

FIGURE 10.18 Choose vertices you wish to expand.

Step 2: Once the hand is all at the same level, you can isolate faces on which to work. Select all of the faces in the hand. From the Show pull-down menu in the viewport choose Isolate Select and then View Selected. Any geometry not selected is hidden.

Step 3: Articulated joints are larger than the long bones that comprise them, especially in the knuckles. Pull vertices to shape the knuckles and the area around them as shown in Figure 10.19. Pay attention to the model position. The knuckle is more prominent when the fingers are bent.

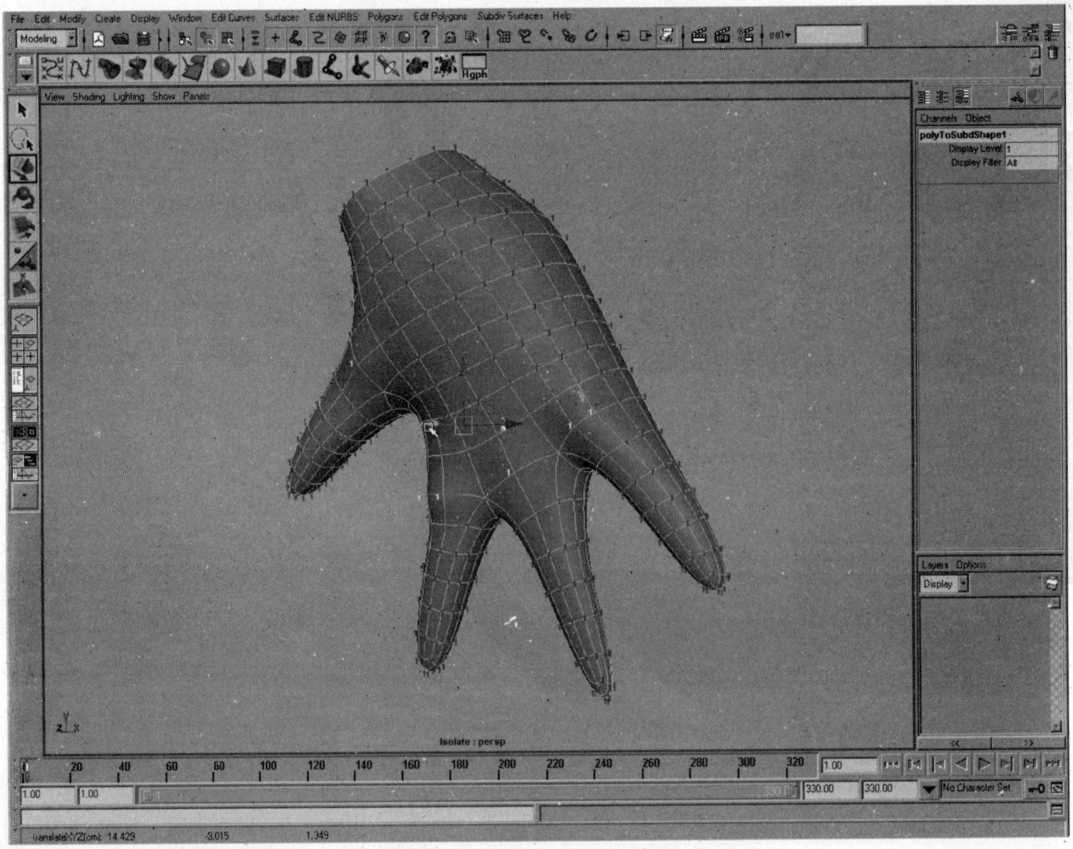

FIGURE 10.19 Shape the knuckles.

Step 4: Indent rows of vertices for all of the joints in the fingers as shown in Figure 10.20. Remember that creases in the skin usually indicate deep tissue connections. These areas will eventually be creased for finer detail.

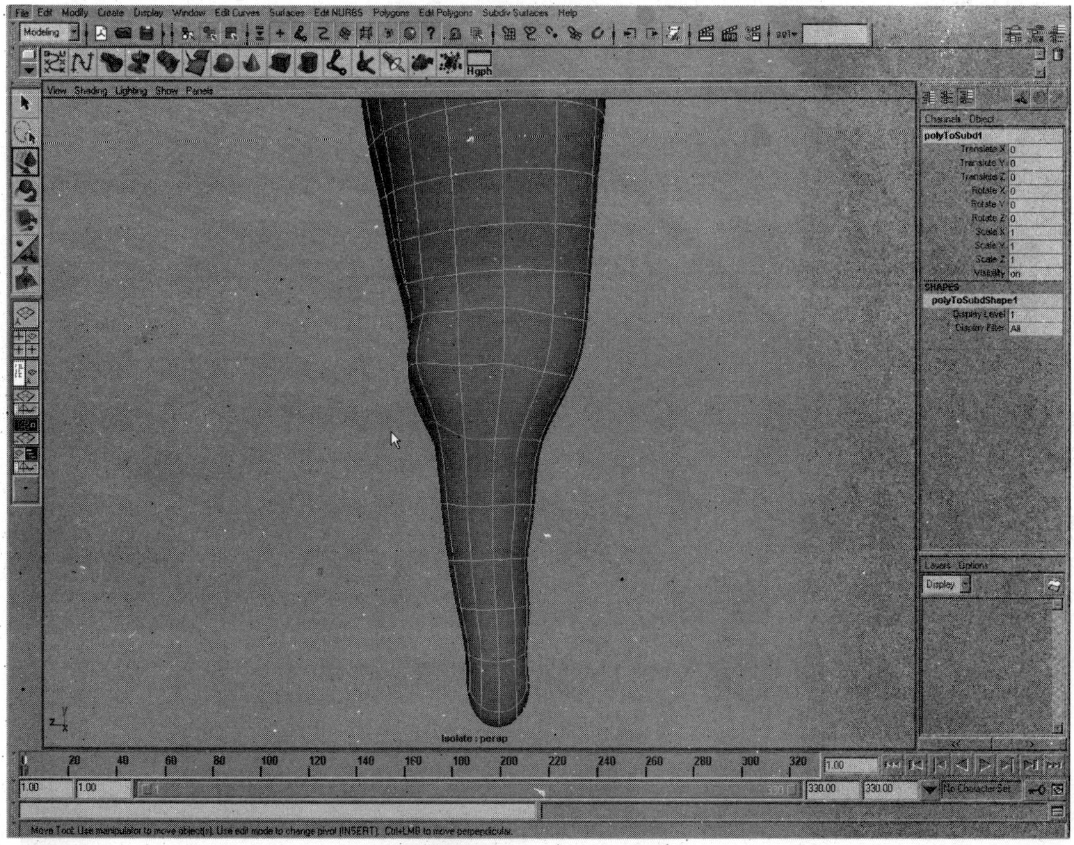

FIGURE 10.20 Shape the natural sloping indentation around the joints in the fingers.

Step 5: The long bone that lies between each joint narrows in the middle. The skin is shaped by this factor. Scale vertices in to create this look as shown in Figure 10.21.

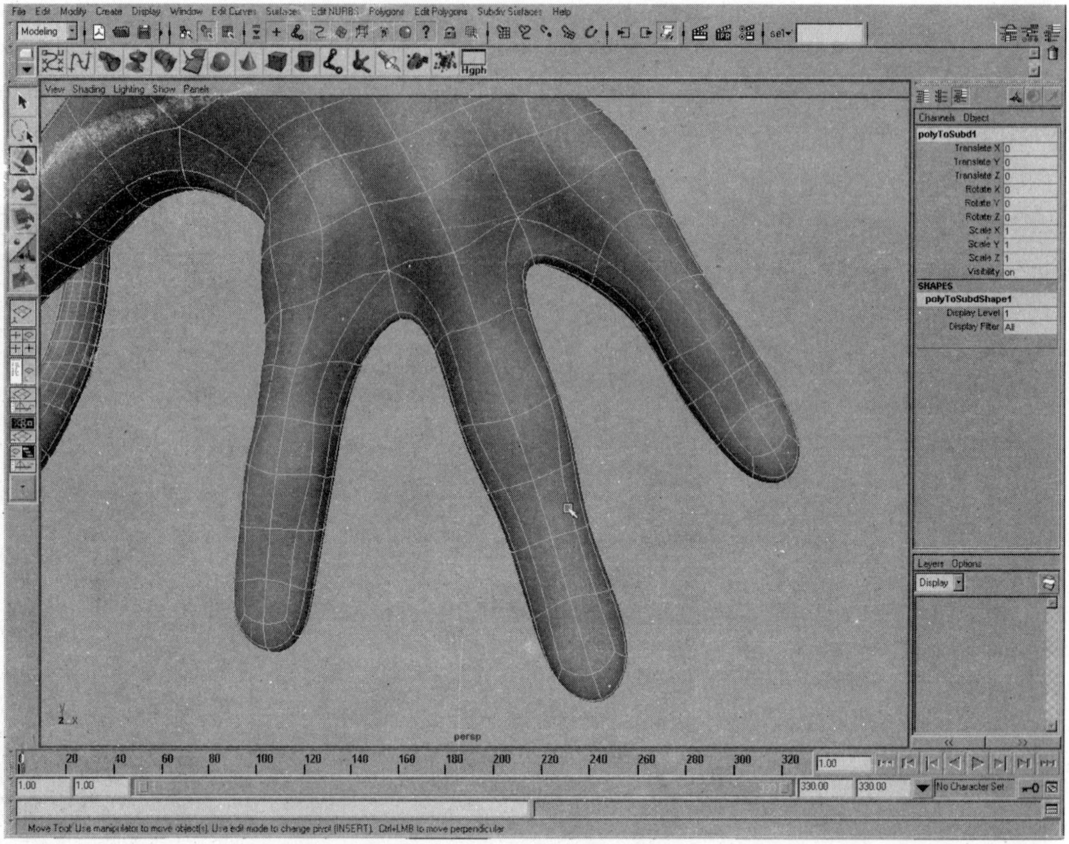

FIGURE 10.21 Scale vertices inward in the shape of a long bone.

Step 6: Continue to shape the rest of the hand based on its proposed anatomy. Pay close attention to the shape of the thumb. Its characteristics are very different from the rest of the fingers. (See Figure 10.22.)

Step 7: The border for the fingernails already exists within the geometry. Select the edges and partially crease them as shown in Figure 10.23.

Step 8: Move up to the next subdivided level, and select the edges making up the border edge between the skin and the nail.

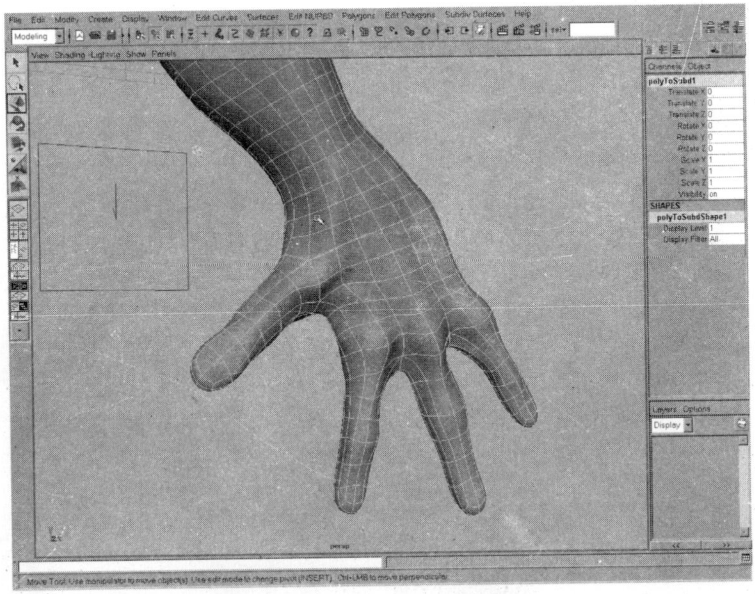

FIGURE 10.22 Shape the rest of the hand with its anatomy in mind.

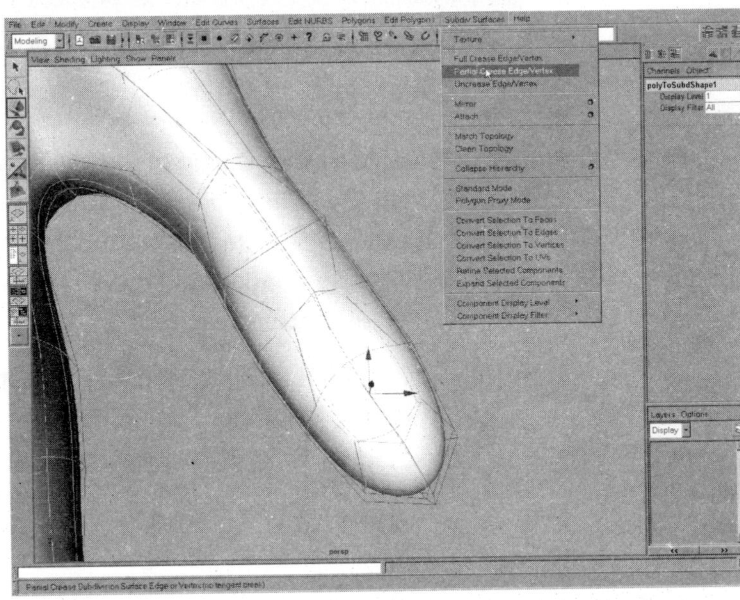

FIGURE 10.23 Partially crease the edges for the fingernails.

Raise these edges slightly with the Proportional Modeling Tool. Figure 10.24 shows an example.

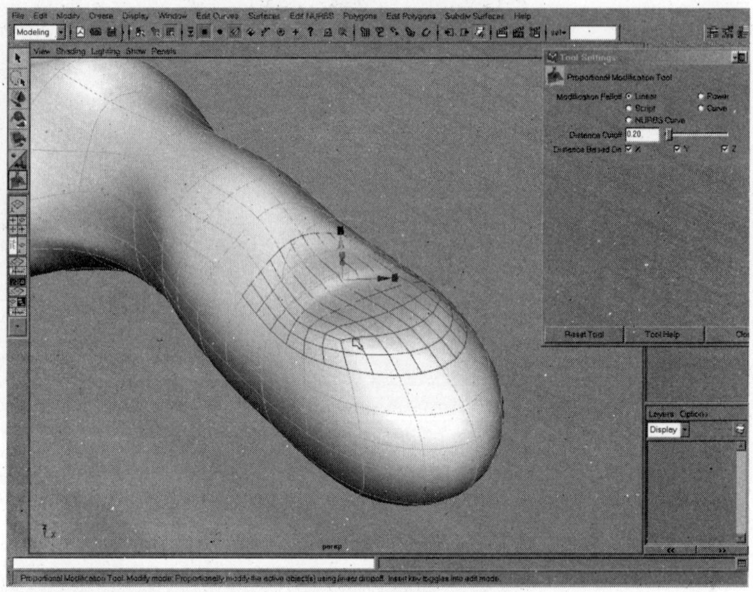

FIGURE 10.24 Raise the border edge to separate the nail from the skin.

Step 9: Select a row for the tip of the nail and pull it out. The Proportional Modeling Tool from Step 8 can help shape the nail. Use Refine Selected Components from the Subdiv Surfaces pull-down menu to add more geometry if necessary. Figure 10.25 shows an example.

Step 10: Full crease the edges all the way around the nail. Use the Proportional Modeling Tool to smooth and shape the surface. Use Figure 10.26 as reference.

Step 11: Now go back and add partial creases in between each articulated joint as shown in Figure 10.27.

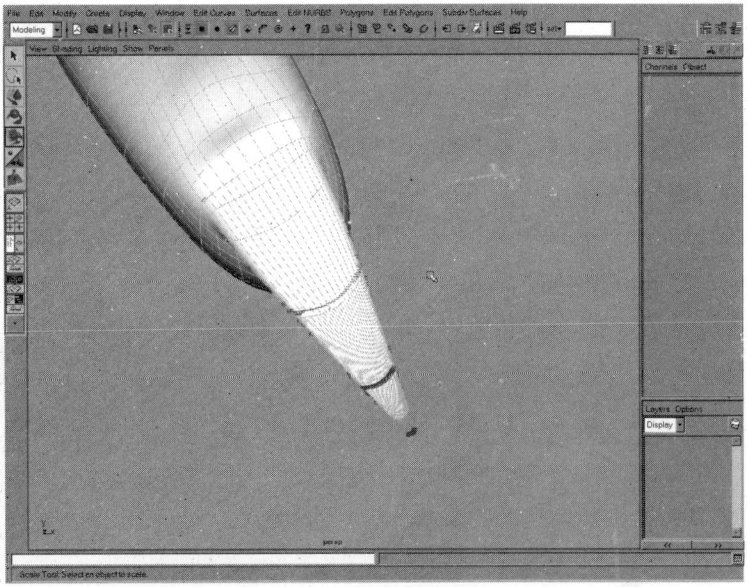

FIGURE 10.25 Partially crease the edges for the fingernails.

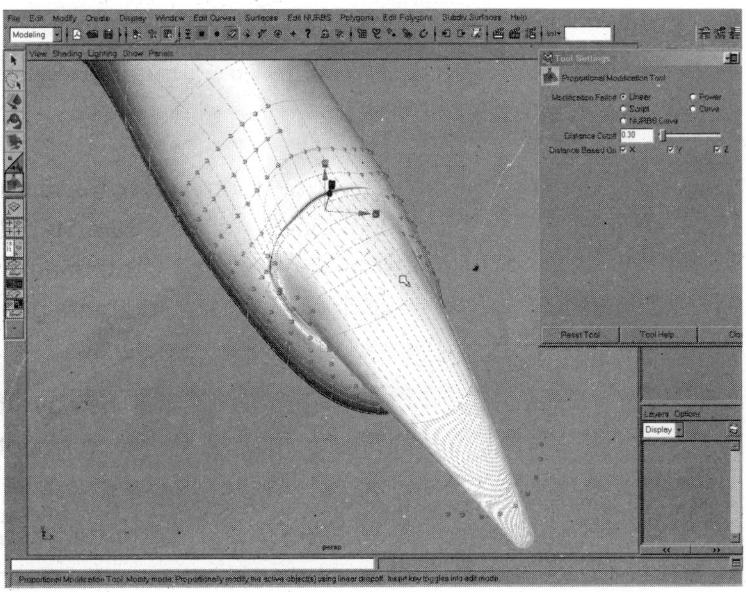

FIGURE 10.26 Full crease the border of the nail.

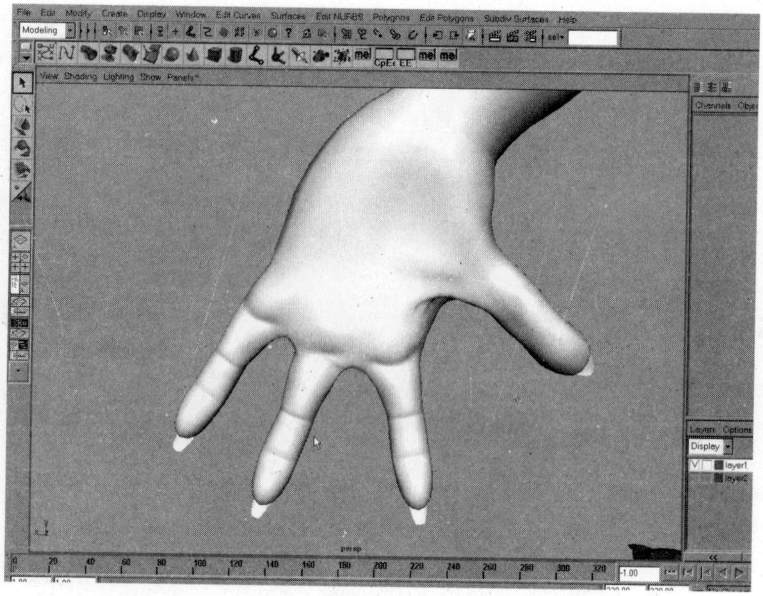

FIGURE 10.27 Partially crease all of the articulated joint areas.

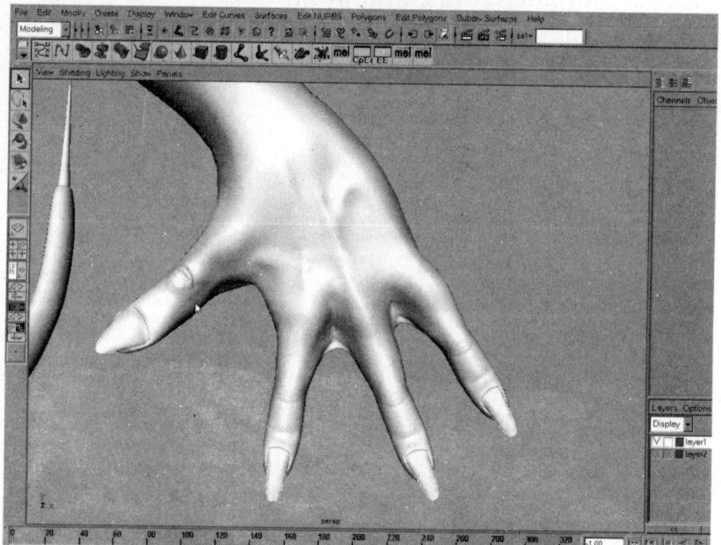

FIGURE 10.28 Finish the hand off by adding tendons and veins.

Step 12: For the finishing touches, partially crease the tops of the joints to form wrinkles in the skin and pull rows of vertices up for tendons and veins. Figure 10.28 shows an example.

CONCLUSION

Continue modeling the skin until you achieve the desired level of detail. Think in terms of reality and only model what is included in the skin. In some cases it is easier to model elements not part of the skin as skin, for example the nails in the hand. These could have been modeled separately and fitted to the skin, however, it was easier to maintain their shape by including them. Once modeled, the nails can be separated for greater control.

The interior of the mouth could be deemed as an object apart from the skin. This would include the upper and lower palates, tongue, gums, and as far down the throat as you want to go. Excluding these elements from the skin makes them easier and faster to model.

In Chapter 11 you will get ready to texture map by establishing UVs and image resolution.

PART

IV TEXTURING FOR FILM

CHAPTER

11 RESOLUTIONS

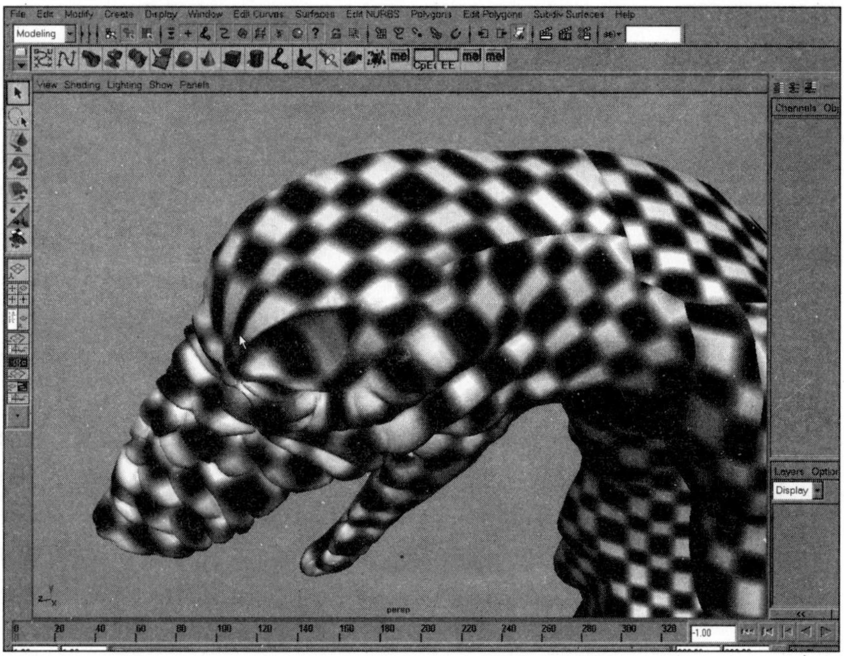

In the previous chapters, you designed and modeled a photo-realistic creature. Detail has been modeled into the creature's skin, but surface texture and color are still missing. The final look of the character is dependent upon the textures and shades applied. To complete this look, it's necessary to paint texture maps. Before you paint anything, though, you must know what size image to paint, which can be a difficult and confusing process. But with foresight and a little math, you can make sense of it.

UV Placement

Texture maps are laid on or wrapped around a surface based on U and V coordinates. UVs on polygonal objects must be projected or assigned to the geometry. In Chapter 8, a rough set of UVs was created to help organize the thousands of UV points generated throughout the modeling process. These groups can now be fine-tuned. The goal of UV placement is to remove any stretching or warping visible when a texture is applied. This way texture maps can be seen the way they were painted, smooth and full of crisp detail.

UVs are not just for texture maps; they also dictate the placement of extra features such as hair or fur. Good UV placement is used to distribute strands of fur across a surface. Several tools, such as the weighting tools, also require good UV placement. Maps can be painted using the UV template to distribute vertex weights by color.

One pitfall to using SubDs in Maya 4.0 is the lack of texturing tools. It is necessary to convert the model to polygons at this point. Under the Modify menu choose Convert and then open the tool options for Convert SubDiv to Polys. Select Adaptive and 1 Division per face to convert the SubD model to polygons exactly as you see it. The following tutorial takes you through the process of how to obtain good UVs on a polygonal object. Follow along while constructing a UV template for your creature or practice with the tutorial.

TUTORIAL

Mapping UVs

Step 1: Figure 11.1 shows a comparison of UVs for the Fire Monster's head. The panel on the left shows the basic UVs from Chapter 8. The panel on the right shows the UVs after detail has been added to the geometry. Notice the border edges are the same.

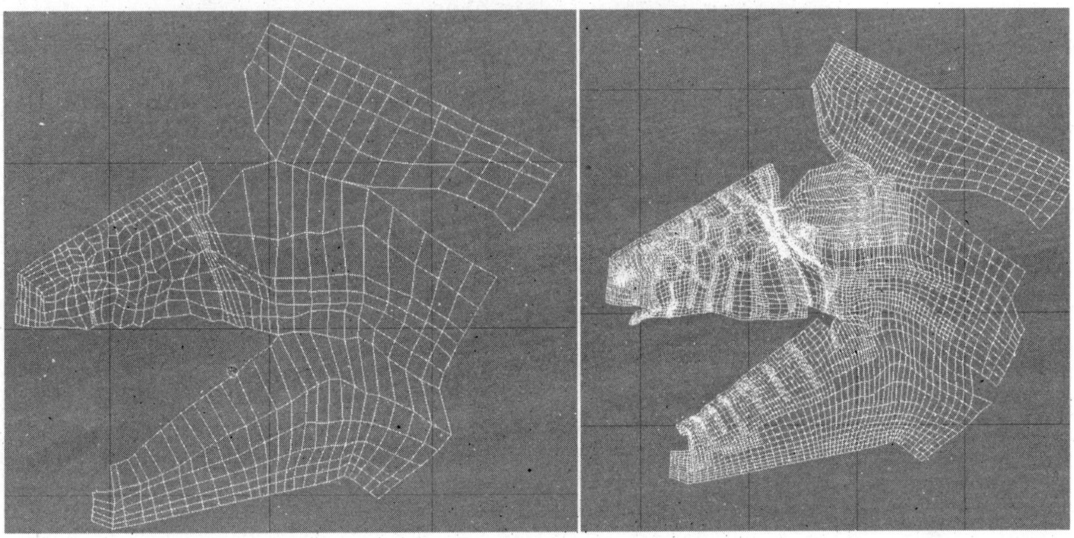

FIGURE 11.1 This is a comparison of the UVs from the low-res model to the hi-res model.

Step 2: Assign a Lambert material to the geometry. In the Color Attribute Channel, apply a procedural texture, such as Checker, to see the quality of the UVs. Change the Repeat UV to 25 and insert 25 in the procedural textures placement node. This makes the checker pattern smaller on the model and allows us to identify stretching or warping easier. Go into the material attributes and open the Hardware Texture tab. Change the Texture Quality to Highest. The texture updates in the 3D views to a more accurate representation of the pattern. The UV Texture Editor is updated as well. Notice the texture is clipped based on the UVs. Examine the model closely for any stretching or warping. Figure 11.2 shows an example.

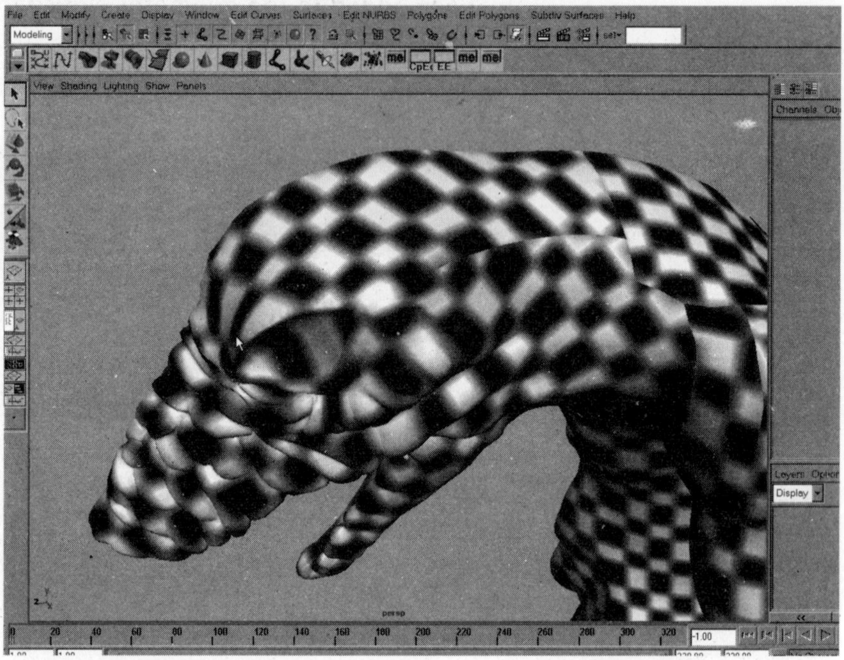

FIGURE 11.2 There is some stretching and warping on top of the head.

Step 3: The UVs for the head do not work. The main problem is the two gaps in the head group on either side of the eye. These gaps will show up as a seam in our final texture. Although it is possible to paint out the seam, the fewer you have, the better off you'll be. Since you already designated the UV group, you can solve this problem relatively easily. Select the row of edges where the UVs break away at the back of the creature's head. Choose Cut UVs from the Polygons pull-down menu from inside the UV Texture Editor. Select a single UV on the cut portion and choose Select Shell from the Select pull-down menu. Reposition the UVs using the Translate and Rotate tool. Use Figure 11.3 for reference.

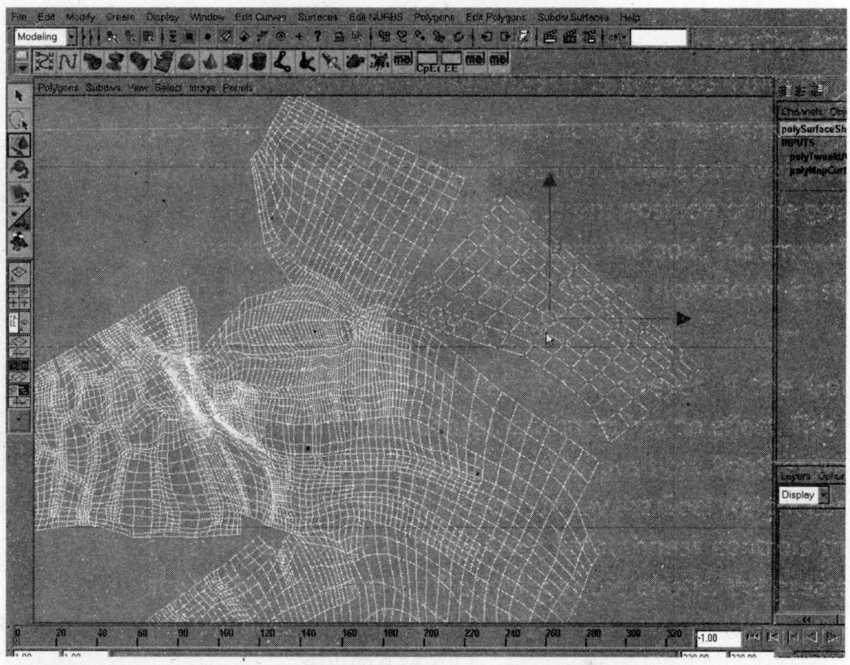

FIGURE 11.3 Reposition the cut UV group to fit better with the rest of the head.

Step 4: Choose Convert Selection to Edges from the Select pull-down menu. This highlights all of the edges of the cut section and its corresponding edges on the head. Deselect the two border edges not associated with the side of the head by simply marquee-selecting around them. It doesn't matter if any of the interior edges are still selected because they are not borders and are unaffected by sewing operations. From the Polygons pull-down menu choose Move and Sew UVs. The cut section snaps into place as shown in Figure 11.4.

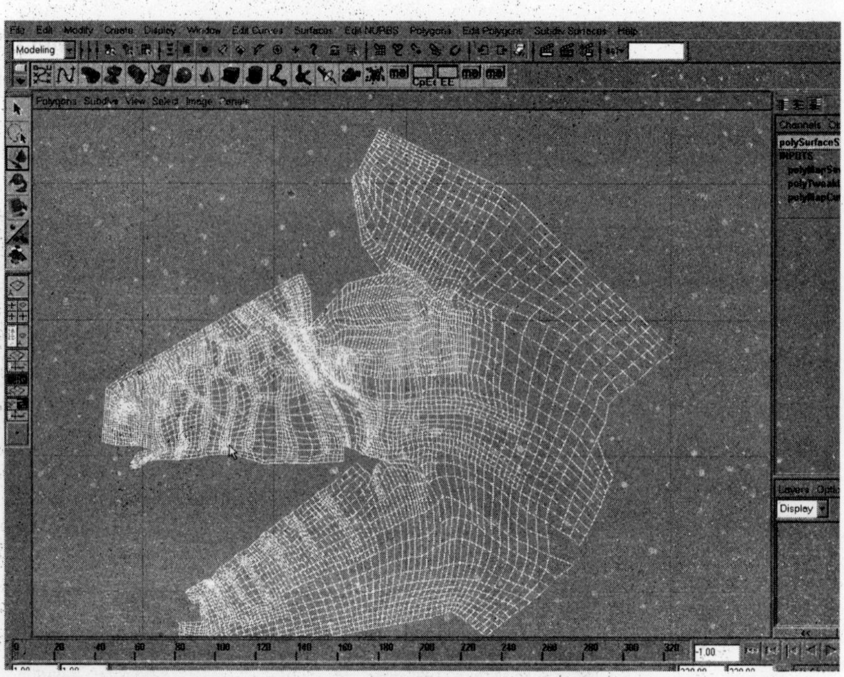

FIGURE 11.4 Move and sew the cut section into place.

Step 5: Repeat the process for the area in front of the eye. Use Figure 11.5 as a guide.

Step 6: Notice that there are UVs overlapping. This can be fixed automatically with the Relax UVs tool, but first you must establish a good UV border. Relax UVs is a powerful tool with the ability to smooth UVs based on the original geometry's shape and designated fixed UV border. Using the geometry for reference, position the UVs along the border edge only. Examine the length of each edge and direction of adjacent edges. Try to match these as closely as possible, ignoring all the interior UVs. Use Figure 11.6 for reference.

Step 7: Move the UVs as far as you can. Do not expect to get them perfect right away. Once they're close, select all of the UVs for the head. Open the options for Relax UVs under the Polygons pull-

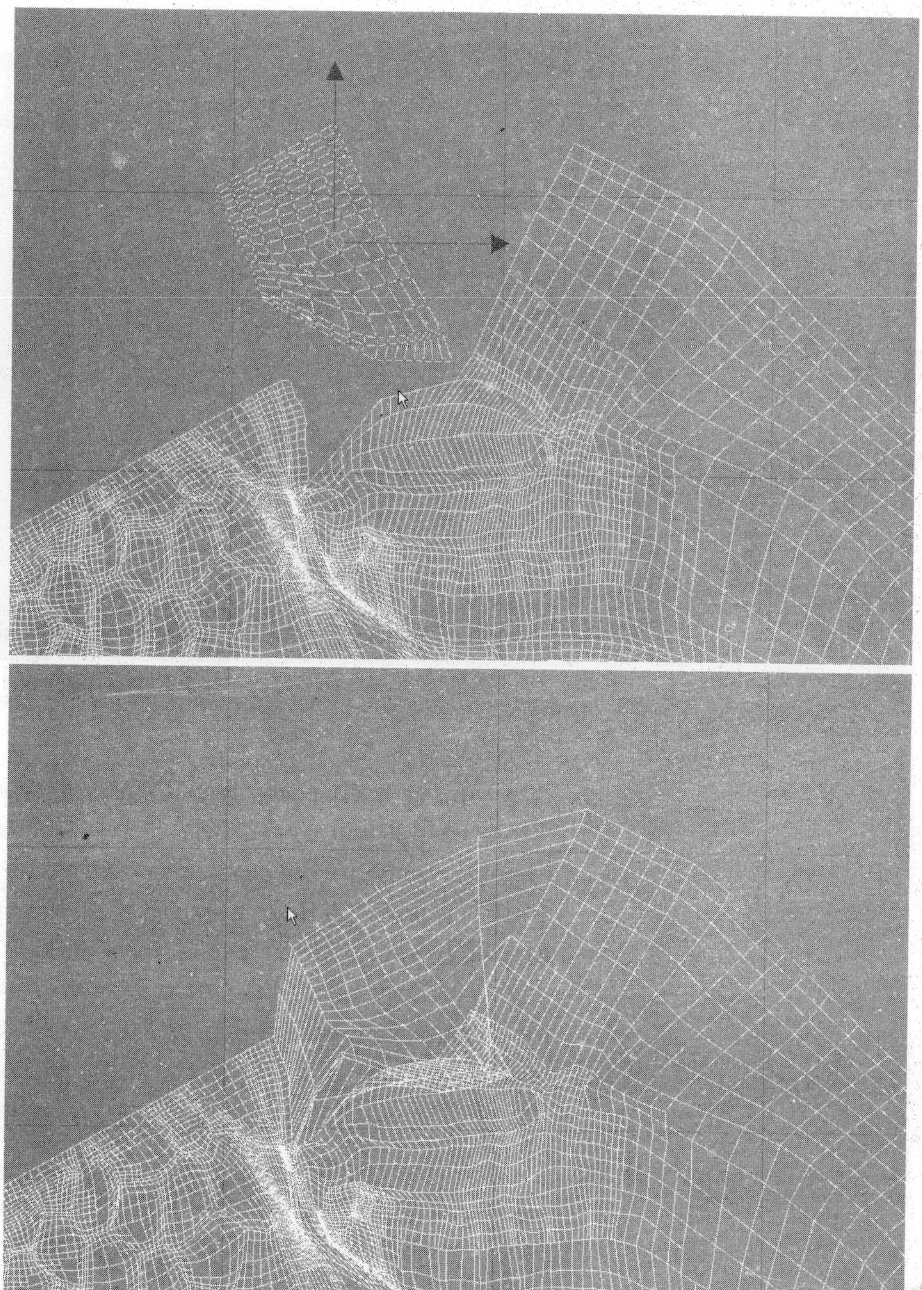

FIGURE 11.5 Cut the UVs, select the border edges, and move and sew them into place.

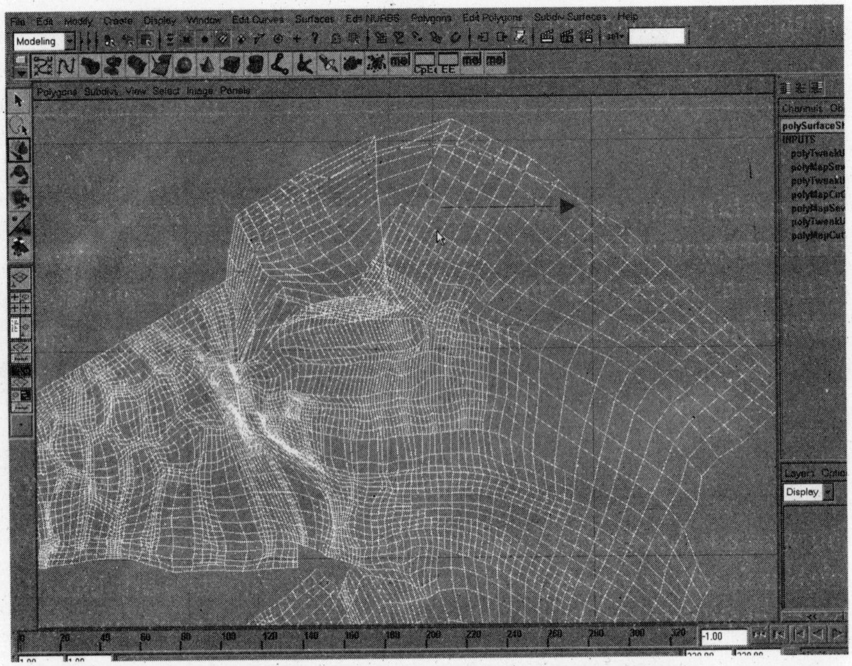

FIGURE 11.6 Move the border UVs to match the size and shape of the geometry's border.

down menu. Change the Edge Weights to World Space. This forces the relax tool to keep the angles designated in the model. Choosing Uniform wouid cause the angles to be evenly spaced. Since our geometry is not evenly spaced, this option does not provide us with sufficient results. Next, click on Pin UV Border and Pin Unselected UVs. The Relax tool affects every UV on the model. By pinning unselected UVs, the others remain stationary. Set the iterations to 10 and choose Apply. Keep selecting Apply until the UVs stop moving. Figure 11.7 shows the results.

Step 8: Compare the border edge to the model's border edge; if necessary, continue to adjust the UV border to match the geometry shape. Use the Checker texture for reference as well. In order for the internal UVs to be good, the border must be accurately depicted. Reshape the border and relax the UVs until they are perfect.

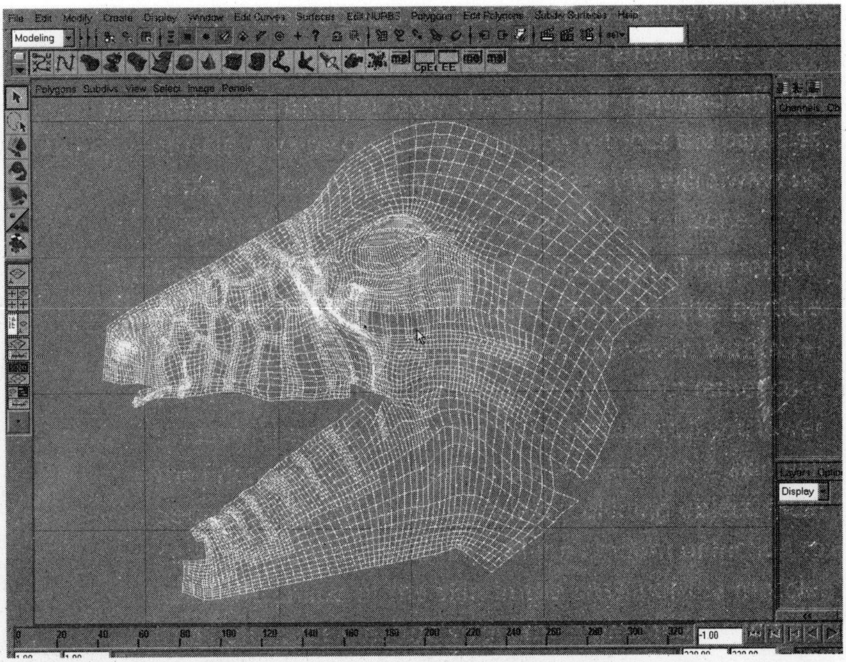

FIGURE 11.7 The UVs after they have been relaxed.

Step 9: Examine the rest of the model. Reshape and relax all of the UV groups. When you're done, the checkerboard pattern should look uniform and square across the entire model.

Step 10: Attach as many groups as you can to each other to ensure that the pixels line up across seam areas. Figure 11.8 shows the complete UV set for the Fire Monster.

OUTPUT RESOLUTION

With UV placement established, it's time to determine the resolution of the textures. This depends on how you plan to output your CG. If you are going to video, use NTSC resolution or 720 × 480 to

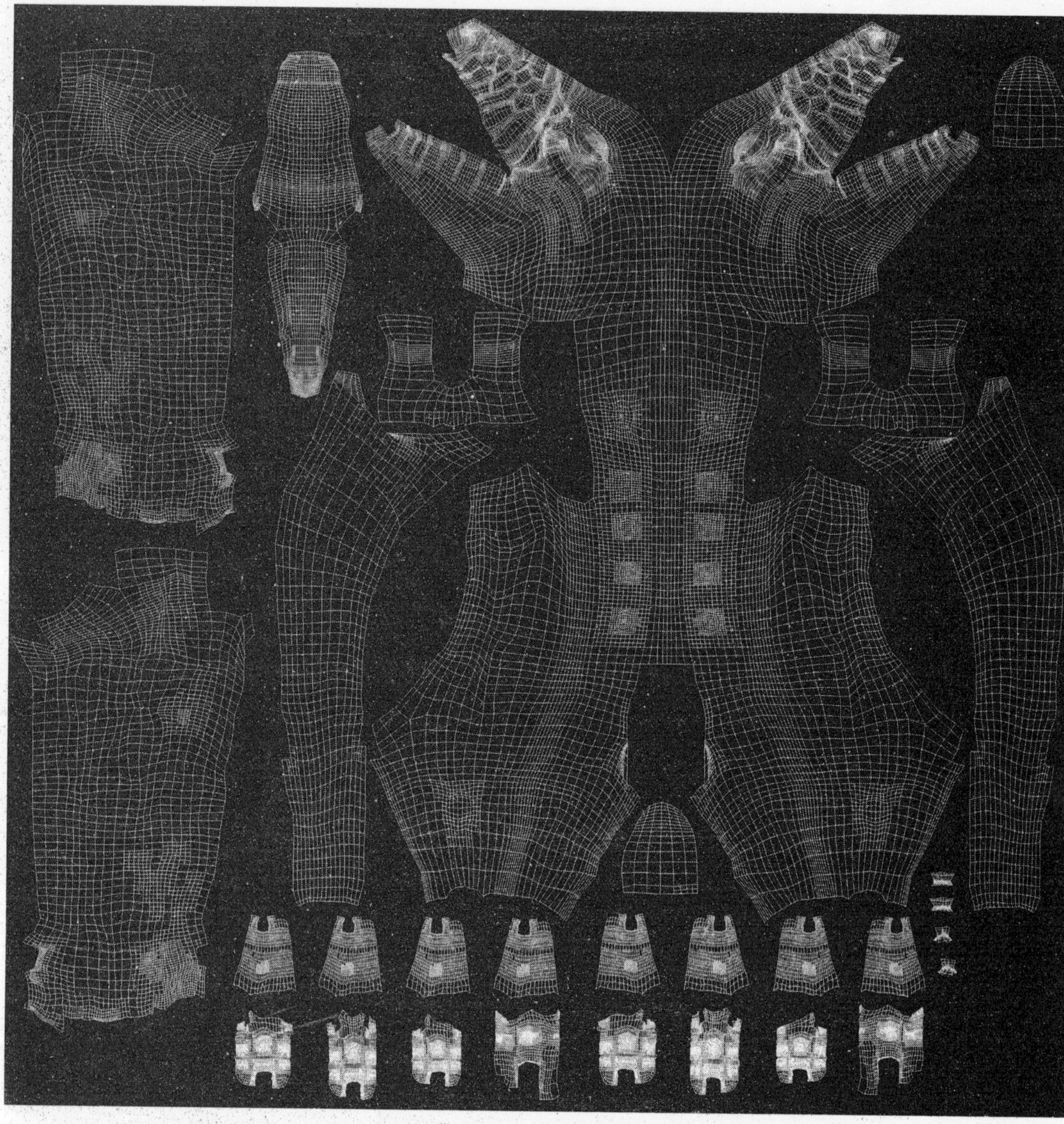

FIGURE 11.8 The Fire Monster's final UV set within the 0 to 1 texture space.

figure texture size. The Fire Monster is going to HD720 or 1280 × 720. The following tutorial uses this resolution to create templates for each part.

TUTORIAL

DETERMINING RESOLUTION

Step 1: Using storyboards or animatics determines the smallest distance the camera gets to the creature. Usually the closest spot is the character's face. This is a good part to use because, most likely, it is going to be under the most scrutiny. In Maya, open the Render Globals from the Status Line. Under the Resolution tab change the Presets to the proper output resolution.

Step 2: Select the model and find the group of UVs most prominent in the perspective view. Select the shell as faces.

Step 3: In a camera, or perspective, viewport select the View pull-down menu and choose Camera Settings. Select Resolution Gate. Mimic the camera shot or size the character up in the resolution gate based on the pre-established distance. Enter into component mode and choose UVs for the component type. Make a marquee-selection around the resolution gate. Figure 11.9 shows an example. The Fire Monster will not be seen any closer than the existing shot. The selection's straightest point from end to end measures 1280 pixels long in the viewport. In the UV Texture Editor it spans across two squares. This means each square is 640 pixels long.

Step 4: Since tools in Maya work best with square textures, use the length for the width as well. This gives you 640 × 640 for each square in the UV Texture Editor. However, the surface of the creature is not perfectly flat, so you need to compensate

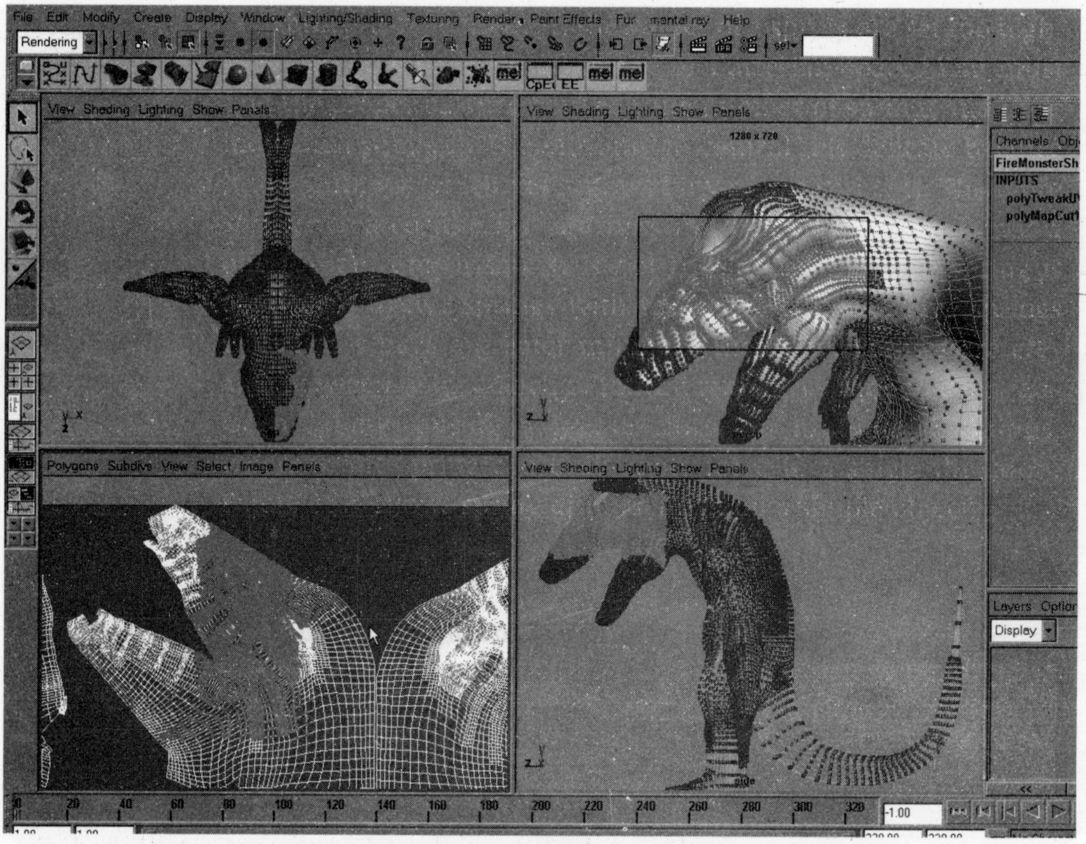

FIGURE 11.9 This camera angle dictates how close it gets to the Fire Monster.

for the bumps and grooves. It can be difficult to determine how curvy a surface is. To eliminate the guesswork, increase the texture size by 50 percent. This is enough to cover any surface. One square works out to be 960 × 960. Using the default grid settings in the UV Texture Editor gives you a 10 × 10 grid, making the total texture size 9600 × 9600.

Step 5: Take a snapshot of the template by choosing UV Snapshot from the Polygons pull-down menu. The maximum size exportable is 2048 × 2048. Use this size and increase it to the

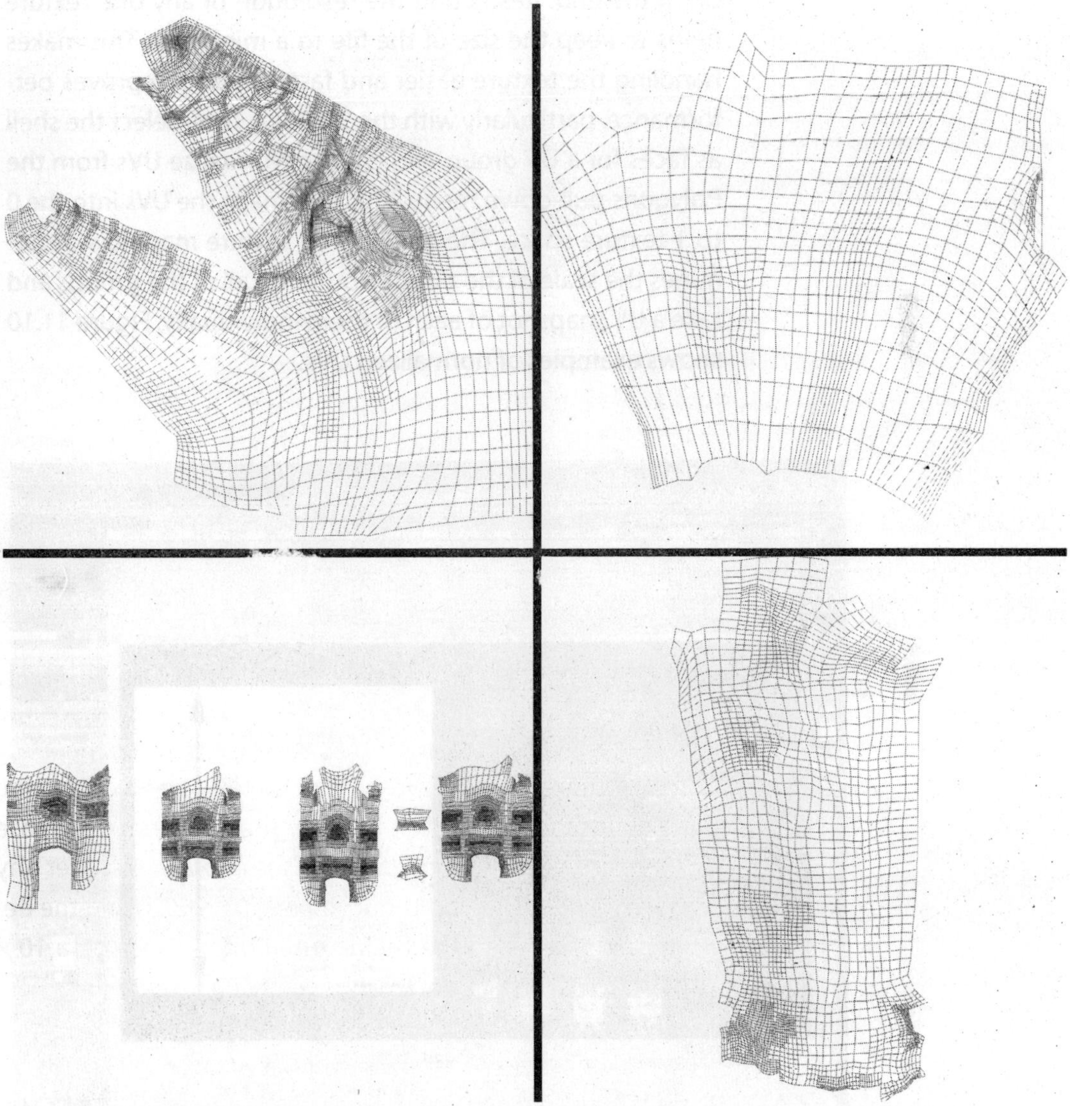

FIGURE 11.10 Each of these group's was normalized to fit within the 0 to 1 texture space.

proper resolution inside Photoshop. This image is the master UV template.

Step 6: In Maya, break up the UVs into groups smaller than or equal to 2048 × 2048. This might seem daunting at first, but it pays off in the end. Restricting the resolution of any one texture helps to keep the size of the file to a minimum. This makes handling the texture easier and faster. It also improves performance, particularly with the 3D Paint Tool. Select the shell as faces for a UV group and choose Normalize UVs from the Polygons pull-down menu. This tool maps the UVs into the 0 to 1 texture space. The scale of the texture map now determines the scale of the pixels. Normalize all of the groups and take a UV snapshot of each of them individually. Figure 11.10 shows examples of normalized UVs.

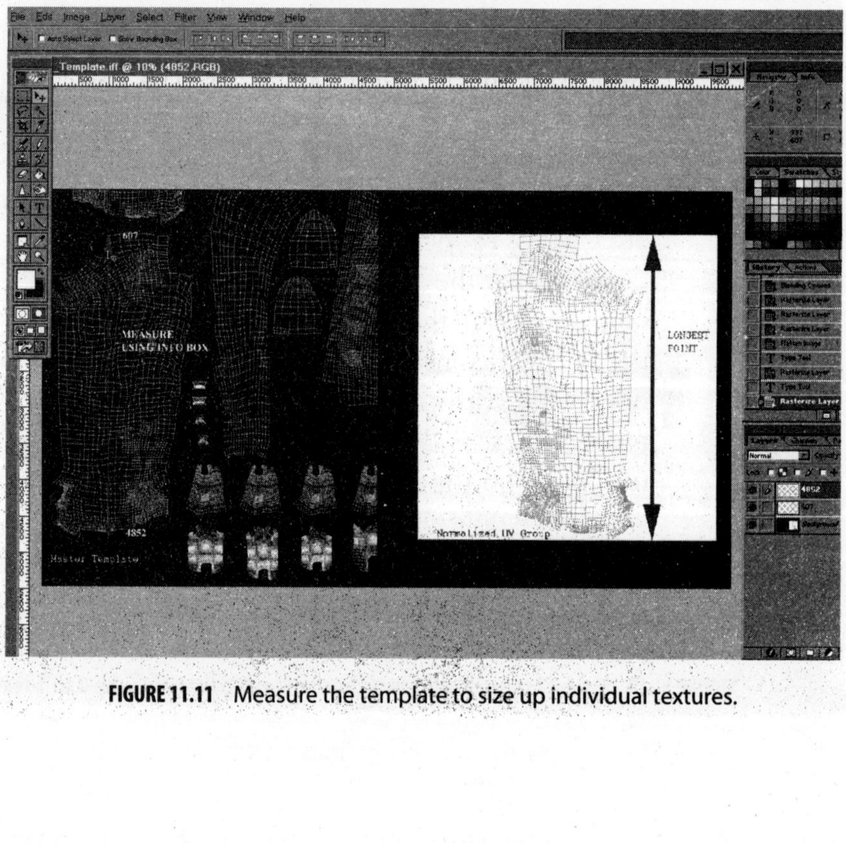

FIGURE 11.11 Measure the template to size up individual textures.

Step 7: The size for the creature's head is now used to determine the size of the rest of the UV groups. Open the master UV template and one group of normalized UVs in Photoshop. Select Show Rulers from the View pull-down menu. Open the Preferences from the File pull-down menu and choose Units & Rulers. Change the Units to pixels. Examine the normalized UV group to determine the longest point. Measure that distance with the help of the Info box on the master UV template. The resulting dimension becomes the length and width of the texture for the normalized UV group. Scale the image to match. Use Figure 11.11 for reference.

CONCLUSION

Creating UV templates can take time but is well worth the effort. Good UVs make for good textures. The objective is to keep your textures square and under 2 kilobytes. By doing this, you are able to take full advantage of painting tools in Maya. A limitation with this tool is that map size must be in powers of 2 (128, 256, 512, etc.). Maya rounds up or down to the closest number.

Now that the UV templates are done for half of your creature's body, duplicate the geometry by mirroring it to the other side. Use the Mirror Geometry tool under the Polygons pull-down menu. Do not Merge with the Original as this attaches the UVs as well. The problem here is that your creature ends up sharing the same texture maps on the right side as it does on the left side, meaning the left hand would also be mapped to the right hand. To eliminate the symmetry, manually merge vertices or edges after the duplication.

In the next chapter, you will be using your UV templates to paint a variety of maps for your creature's head.

CHAPTER

12 MAKE IT REAL

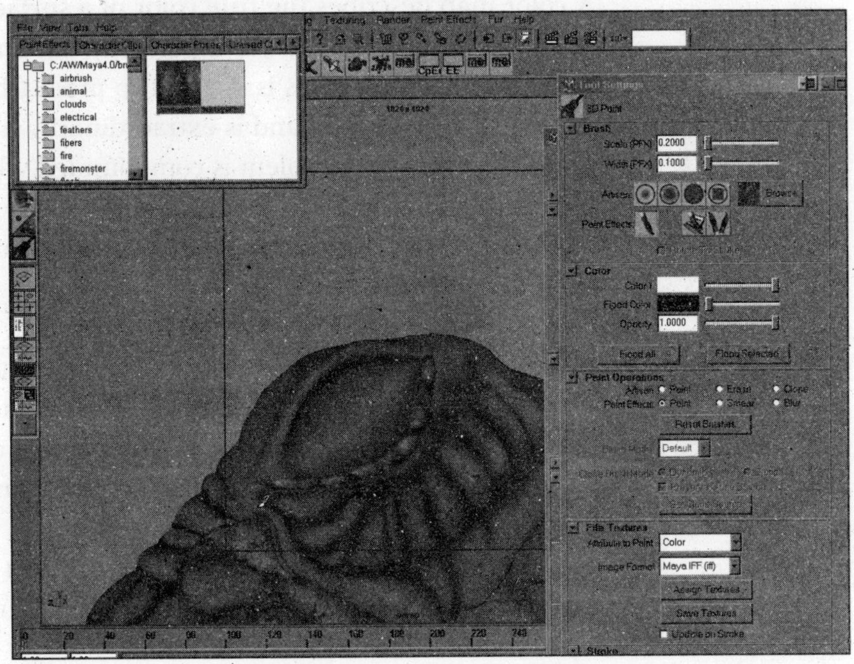

Texturing a surface gives the final look to the character. Textures can make a character look wet, rough, soft, or rubbery. The possibilities are limitless. In the previous chapter you created UV templates. The goal of this chapter is to paint maps for your creature's head using a combination of color, diffuse, specular, bump, and displacement maps to achieve the final look.

Color Maps

A color map describes the true color of a surface, or what the surface would look like if it were perfectly flat and lit without shadows and highlights. This is difficult to predict because this type of condition doesn't exist and is extraordinarily hard to reproduce in the real world. The problem is compounded when building a fictitious creature; there is no point of reference.

A good place to start painting the color map is the creature's head. Usually the most difficult and detailed, it establishes a precedent for all the other body parts. Regardless of the type of character, it's a good idea to paint isolated areas first and paint out any seams in the texture last. Using the UV templates created in Chapter 11, you can select a single part to map and delete the rest. This helps performance and feedback by only having to deal with one texture and a limited amount of geometry.

The following tutorial shows how to paint the Fire Monster's head. These same techniques can be used for any character.

TUTORIAL

The Color Map

Before painting the color map, it is helpful to create a guide for specific detail. Working in conjunction with the UV template, the "guide map" provides reference for detail placement. To hasten the process, isolate the geometry.

ON THE CD

Step 1: To isolate the geometry, select a UV on one side of the creature's head. Your character's head may not be split into two halves, but this doesn't matter. It only means you will have more geometry on screen. Open the UV Texture Editor and from the Select pull-down menu choose Select Shell. From the same menu choose Convert Selection to Faces. Press F8 to enter Component mode and choose Faces for the component type. In the perspective view, Shift-select the entire character to toggle the selection. This selects all of the unselected faces. Press Delete on the keyboard; the remaining faces are those to be textured. The geometry at this point doesn't matter. The only thing you are interested in is creating texture maps. As long as you use the UV templates as guides and don't alter the vertices or UVs, the maps you paint will line back up with the master model. In the scene file called "Color_Map," in the Chapter 12 folder on the CD-ROM, the Fire Monster's head has already been separated from the rest of the model.

Step 2: Exit the component mode by pressing F8 again. Open the Hypershader. From the Create pull-down menu select Materials and create a Lambert material. This is not the final material; the Lambert shader is temporarily applied so the color map can be seen in its purest form. Rendering textures assigned to materials with specular highlights can be misleading. Perfect the color map and then add a more advanced material. Drag and drop the new material with the middle mouse button onto the creature's head.

Step 3: Press F5 on the keyboard to go to Rendering. Select the creature's head. Open the tool options for the 3D Paint Tool from the Texturing pull-down menu. Scroll down and click on the File Textures tab to open it, and choose Assign Textures. Based upon your output resolution, choose the proper settings. The maximum texture size with the 3D Paint Tool is

2048 × 2048 pixels. If you are unsure of texture size, use the largest setting and reduce it later. Texture maps can be safely scaled down, but not up.

Step 4: Using a shade of gray lighter than the assigned texture, outline the details of the creature's head. Paint lines for creases or skin folds. Outline important areas like the eye, nostril, and lips. You can interactively scale the brush in the viewport by holding down B and the left mouse button. Move the mouse from side to side to begin painting. Figure 12.1 shows an example.

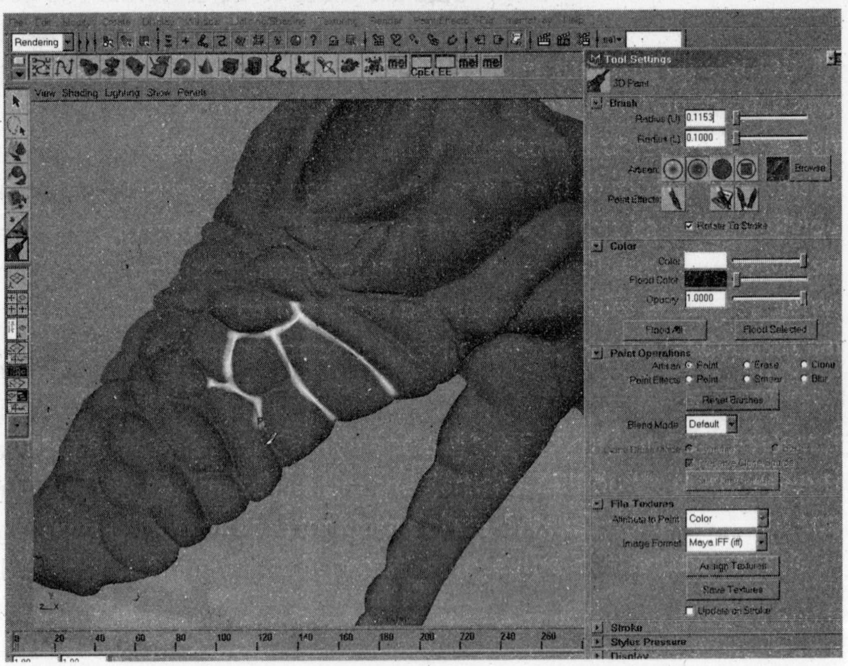

FIGURE 12.1 Paint lines or borders for detail placement.

Step 5: When you are finished, choose Save Textures from the 3D Paint Tool options box. Open the guide map and the corresponding UV template in Photoshop. Click on the guide map to make it current. From the Select pull-down menu choose

Select All. Press Ctrl-C on the keyboard to copy the image. Click on the UV template to make it current. Press Ctrl-A on the keyboard to select all. Press Ctrl-V to paste the guide map as a new layer over the UV template. Change the opacity of the guide map in the layer window. Figure 12.2 demonstrates the merger.

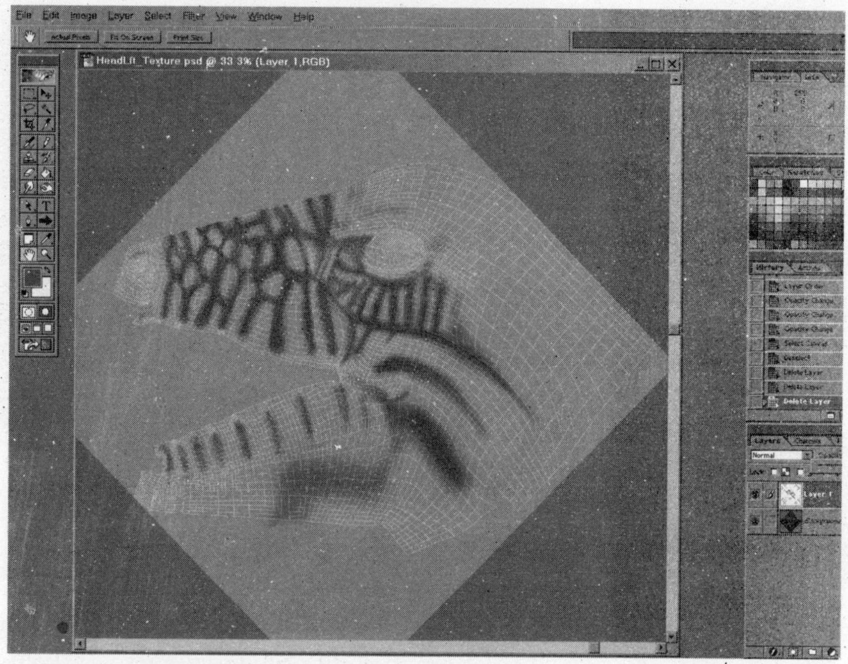

FIGURE 12.2 Paste the guide map over the UV template and lower its opacity. The canvas has been rotated 45 degrees counterclockwise for easier viewing.

Step 6: Start with a base texture. Paint a swatch of color in a new window, depicting the general look of the surface of the entire character. This is the base on which all other detail is painted. Figure 12.3 shows a 600 × 600 swatch of color that was generated from a scanned photo of an alligator. This square was used to paint a base for the entire character.

FIGURE 12.3 This swatch of color, created from scanned photos, was used to paint a base for all the color maps.

Step 7: Select the entire image with Ctrl-A. Choose Define Pattern from the Edit pull-down menu. Make the guide map current and create a new layer on top of it. Choose the Pattern Stamp or Clone Tool from the tool window. With opacity at 100 percent, use the pattern stamp tool to paint over the wireframe areas. To remove any repeatable pattern, lower the opacity by 40 percent and spot-paint areas. Figure 12.4 shows an example.

Step 8: If you are using scanned images, copy parts from the original with any one of the lasso tools and paste them to a new layer on the color map. Use the guide map as a template to line up

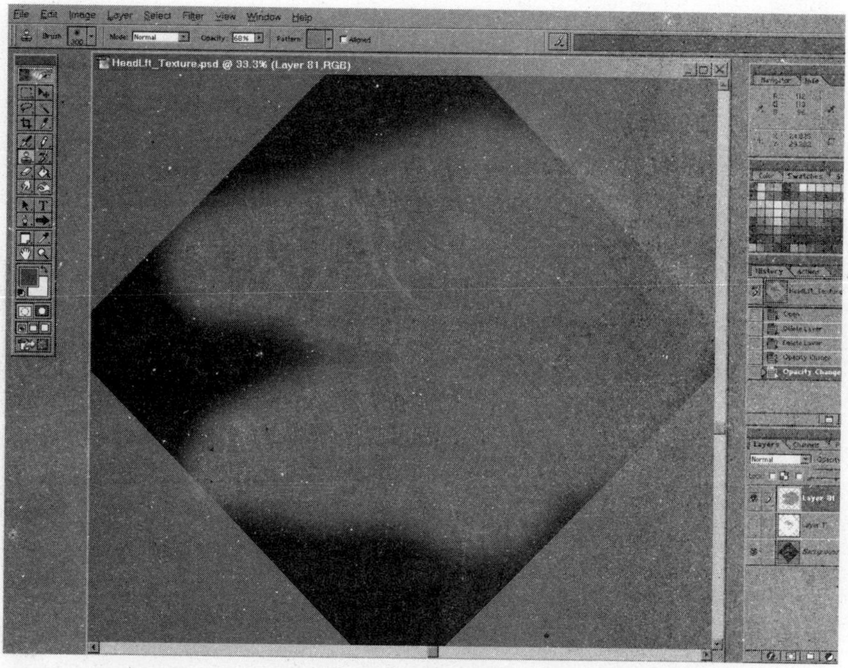

FIGURE 12.4 Paint the base color using the UV template as a guide.

detail. With the Eraser Tool and low opacity—the lower the better, brush over the edges of the clipped image. Continue to brush over the image until you achieve the desired result. Figure 12.5 shows a pad blended in on the Fire Monster's snout.

Step 9: It's a good idea to periodically check the progress of the color map in Maya. This helps to get a feel whether or not you are heading in the right direction. Change the opacity of the layers to expose the colored areas. Choose Save As from the File pull-down menu, and save the image in a Maya-acceptable format. By saving this way, the layers are compressed in the newly saved file only, avoiding any disruption in your Photoshop workflow. Load the image as a color map into the geometries material. Figure 12.6 shows the Fire Monster's progress.

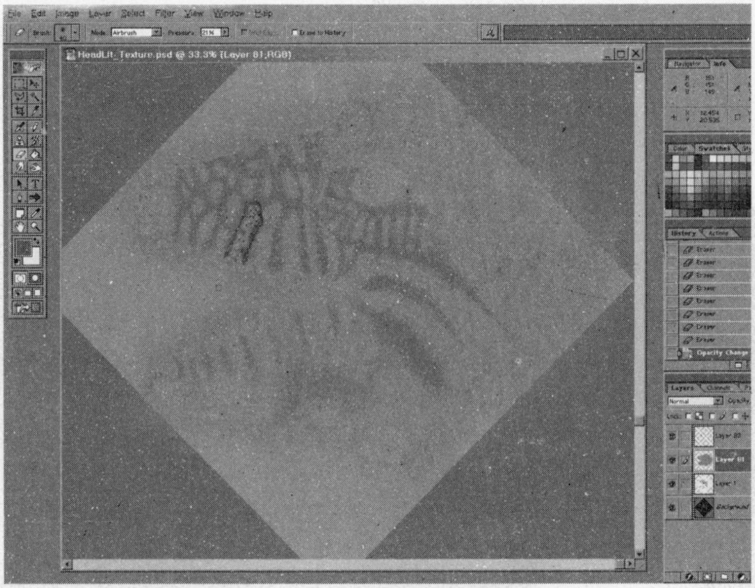

FIGURE 12.5 Blend clipped images with the Eraser Tool.

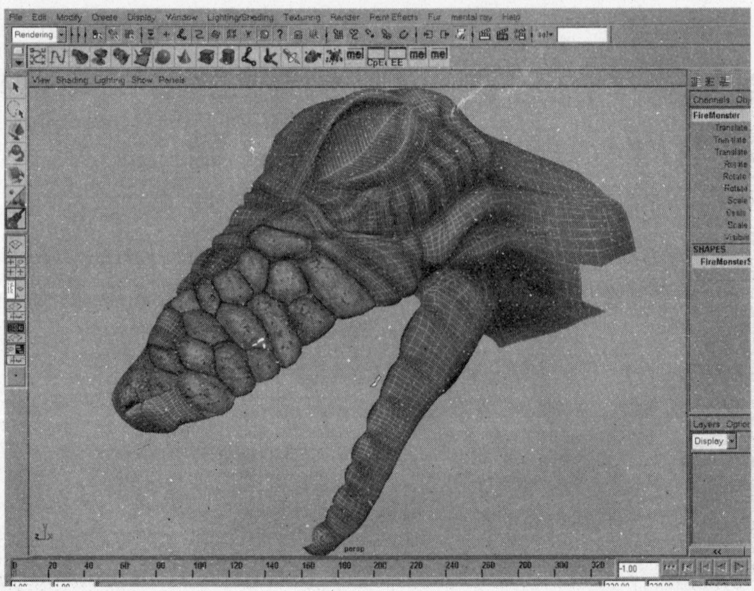

FIGURE 12.6 Periodically check the progress of the color map in Maya.

Step 10: Although the color map should be devoid of any highlights or shadows, it still contains lighter and darker areas. On skin, these areas are a reflection of the skin's exposure to the sun and other elements. The skin also changes color, usually to a

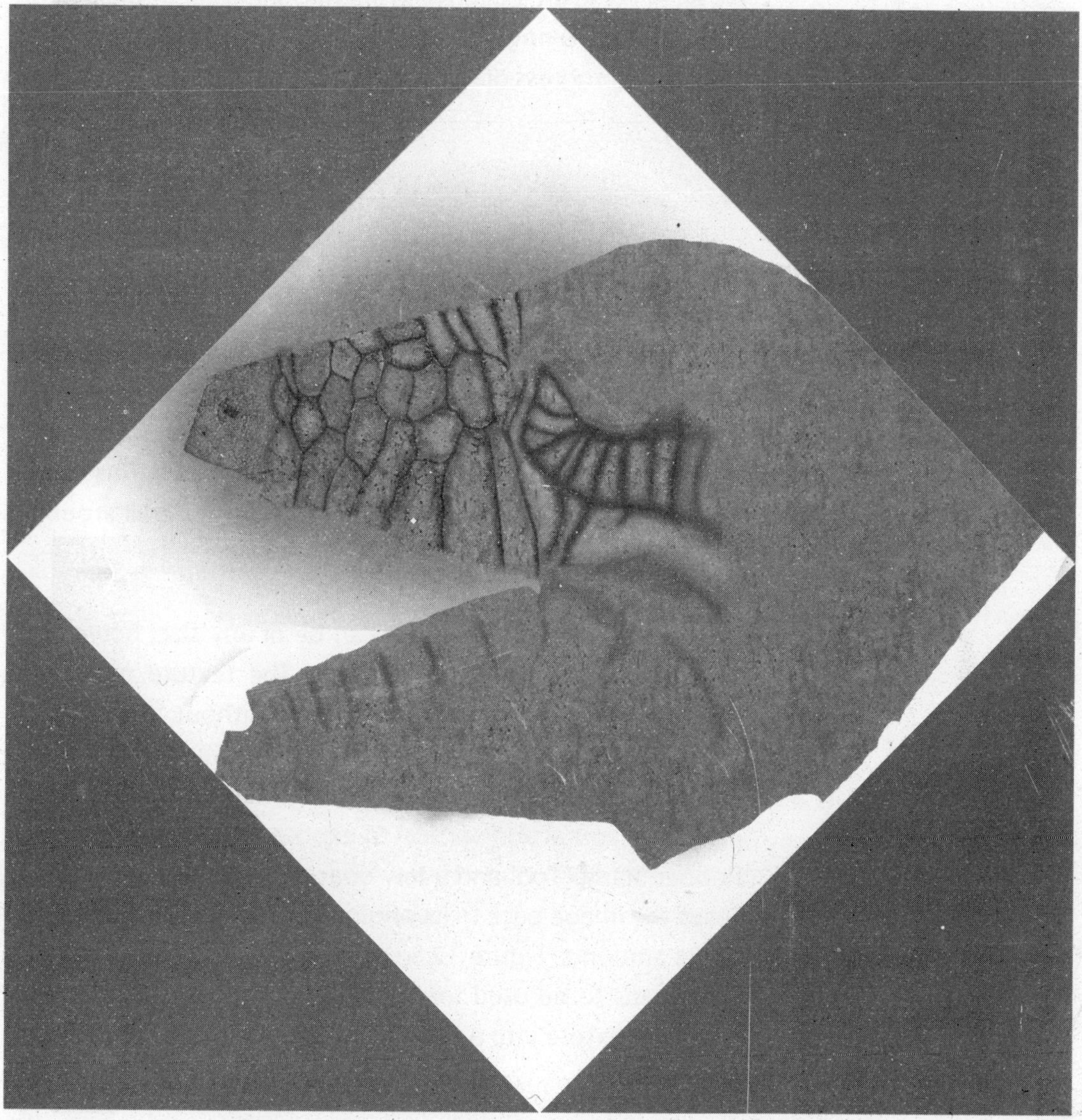

FIGURE 12.7 The left side of the Fire Monster's head is almost finished.

darker shade, where wrinkles form. The Dodge and Burn tools allow you to increase or decrease the intensity of the color values for highlights, midtones, and shadows. Similar versions of these tools are also found under the Mode pull-down menu of the painting tools, such as Airbrush and Pencil. All of these are effective in altering the color of the pixels without destroying the detail of the image. Figure 12.7 shows the progress of the color map.

TUTORIAL

PAINT FX

It is important to remember the advantages of painting in 3D as you paint in Photoshop. Maya has another unbelievably powerful tool called Paint FX. Although the tool comes with a wide variety of brushes, its true power is that you can create and customize your own. This tutorial goes through the steps for creating a brush to paint detail around the Fire Monster's eye.

Step 1: Create a swatch of texture. It can be of any size; however, smaller images are more efficient. The texture must be tileable, meaning it can be repeated without incurring a seam. In Photoshop, from the Filter pull-down menu choose Other and then Offset. Move the image ten to twenty pixels in the horizontal and vertical to expose the seams. With the Rubber Stamp Tool and a low opacity, paint out the seams. Move the image back to its original position by inverting the offset amounts. Figure 12.8 shows a 24 × 100 color map of three pads to be used for detail around the creature's eye. Save the texture into a brushes folder in the current project directory.

FIGURE 12.8 This is a small swatch of texture to be used as a brush in Paint FX.

Step 2: In Maya, press 8 on the keyboard to open Paint FX in a window. Choose Paint Canvas from the Paint pull-down menu. Click on the Edit Template Brush icon to edit the current brush, which should be the default. In the Paint Effects Brush Settings window, click on the arrow to open the Shading menu and then click to open Texturing. Click on the check box for Map Color, and change the Texture type to File. Open the browser next to the Image name text box and choose the swatch of color you created in Step 1. Try out the brush in the canvas window as shown in Figure 12.9.

Step 3: Analyze the painted stroke. Depending on the direction of the image, you might need to rotate the file in Photoshop and resave it. You might also need to adjust the Repeat in the U and the V to properly proportion the texture. To save the brush, create a new directory named for your character in the Visor, typically located in C:\AW\Maya4.0\brushes\. From the Paint Effects pull-down menu choose Save Brush Preset. Give the brush a name and choose to save to the Visor. Type

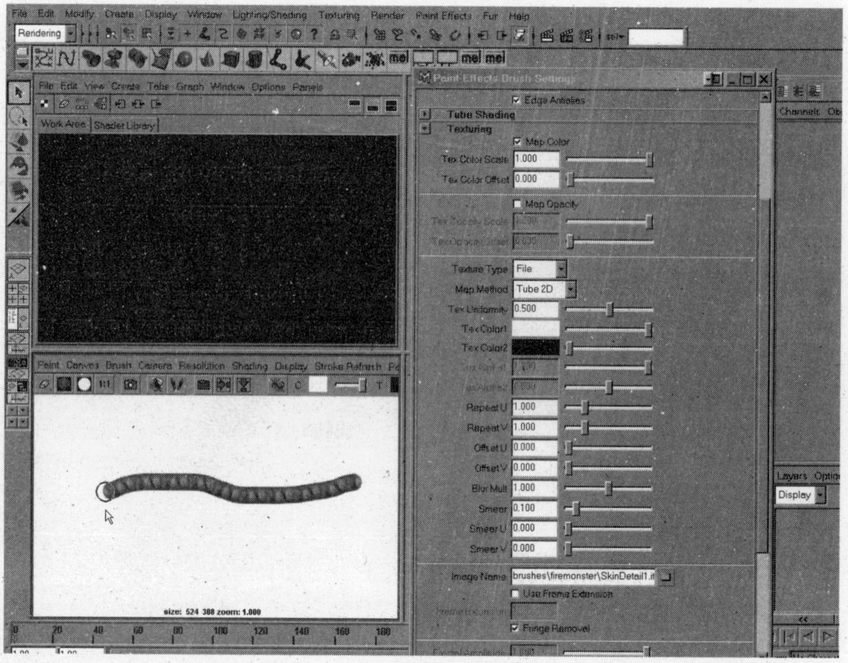

FIGURE 12.9 Test the brush by painting a stroke in the canvas window.

in the name of the directory you created in the Visor Directory text box. Click on the Grab Icon button, and in the canvas window with the left mouse button, create a marquee around a sample of the brush. Releasing the mouse button loads the marquee selection for the icon. Choose Save Brush Preset. The brush is now available through the Visor. Use Figure 12.10 for reference.

Step 4: You have two options at this point. You can create a new texture the same size as your color map and apply it to the geometry or you can apply your existing map to the geometry. Either way, chances are you will be touching up the painted strokes in Photoshop as a new layer. Select the geometry, and open the 3D Paint Tool settings from the Texturing pull-down menu. The color map has already been as-

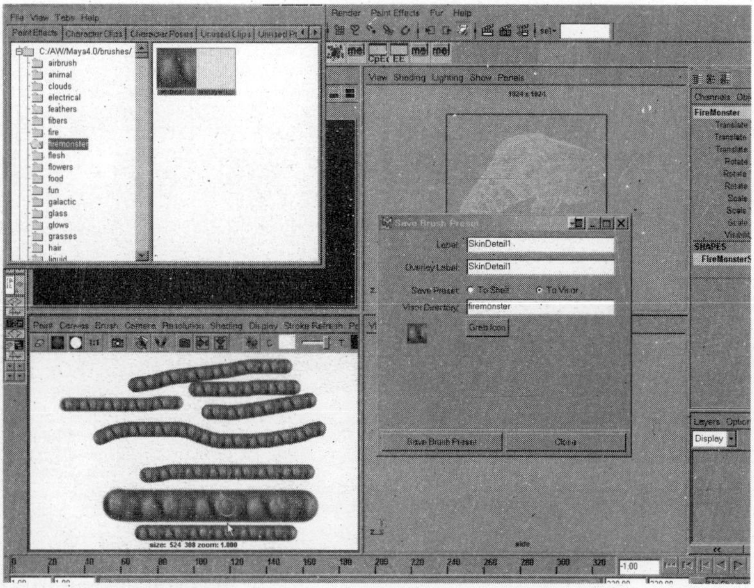

FIGURE 12.10 Save the custom brush to the Visor.

signed to the Fire Monster. Choose the Get Brush icon under the Brush tab and select the custom brush. In the 3D view, paint with the brush as shown in Figure 12.11. You might find the stroke doesn't look the same as it did in the canvas window. This is because you are painting to UVs instead of to a flat image. To correct any distortions, change the brush size and the Repeat in the U and V.

Step 5: The Paint FX tools can be used to create a variety of brushes and effects. Between Photoshop and Maya, highly detailed color maps can be created. Figure 12.12 shows the final color map for the left side of the Fire Monster's head.

Once half of the head is finished, copy it, and flip it horizontally in Photoshop. Map this image to the other side of the head.

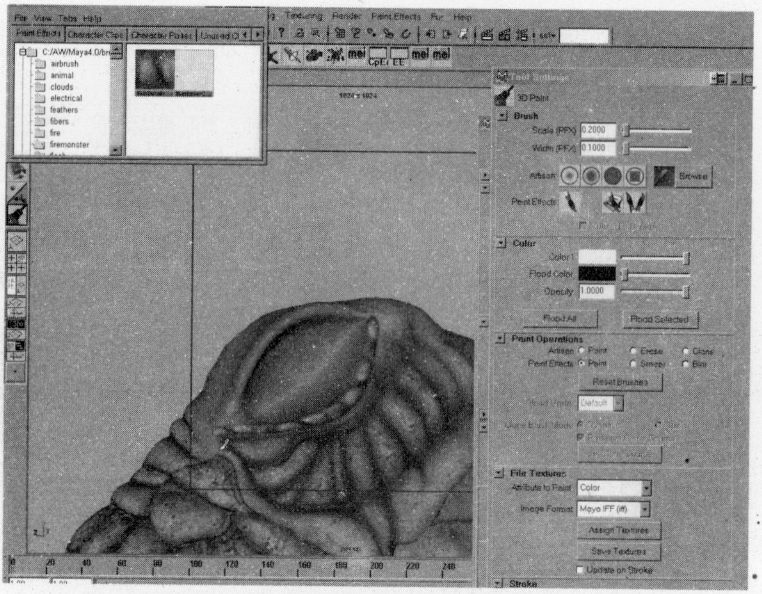

FIGURE 12.11 Paint detail with your new Paint FX brush.

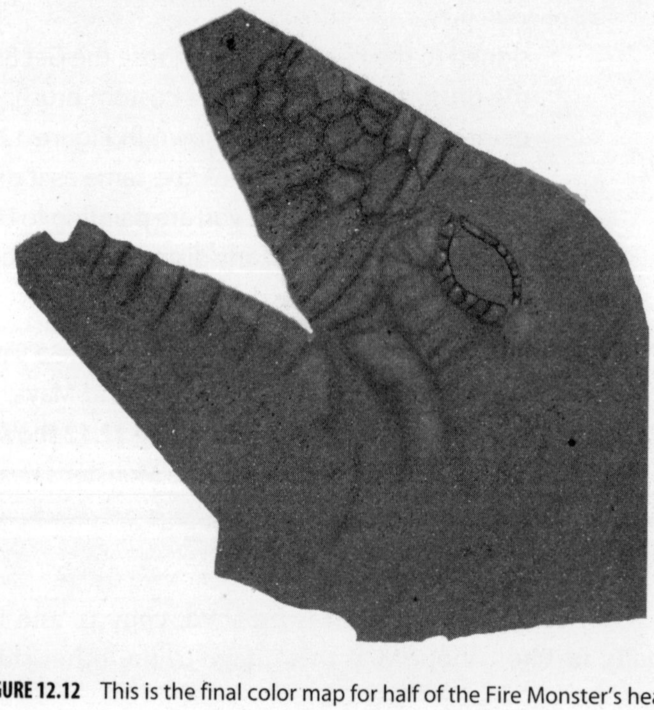

FIGURE 12.12 This is the final color map for half of the Fire Monster's head.

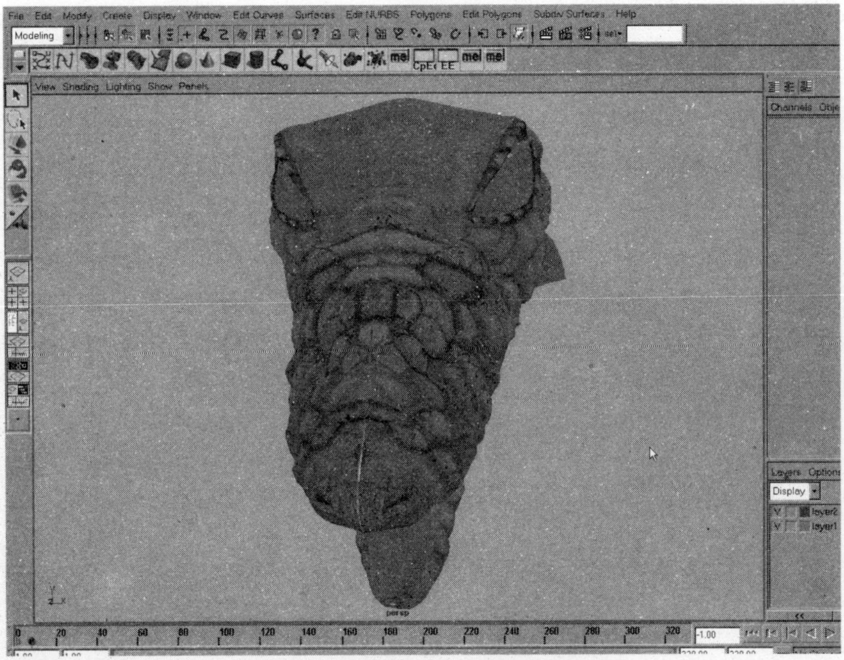

FIGURE 12.13 The two textures create a seam down the middle of the Fire Monster's head.

View the model with its maps to check for seams. Two problems are apparent in Figure 12.13. First, the textures form an awkward pattern where they meet, and second, the pixels don't line up. There are gaps at the end of the snout. To remove these problems easily and effectively, use the 3D Paint Tool to paint across both textures. The following tutorial shows you how.

TUTORIAL

PAINTING OUT SEAMS

Step 1: Isolate the geometry by deleting all of the parts not to be textured as discussed in Step 1 of the Color Map tutorial. To practice on the Fire Monster, open the scene file called "Painting_Seams" from the Chapter 12 folder on the CD-ROM.

ON THE CD

Step 2: Select the model and open the 3D Paint Tool options from the Texturing pull-down menu. Zoom up to a seam and under the Paint Operations tab choose Clone. There are two options to choose with the clone tool: Dynamic and Static. Dynamic cloning moves the cloned source with your brush while Static samples one area and paints continually with it. Choose Dynamic and click on the Set Clone Source button. Pick a generic location from which to clone. You want to avoid highly defined areas. Set the opacity to .8 and paint strokes across the seam or in a circular pattern. Painting in 3D is computationally expensive. If you move too fast, the brush skips. Take your time and go slow. Use Figure 12.14 for reference.

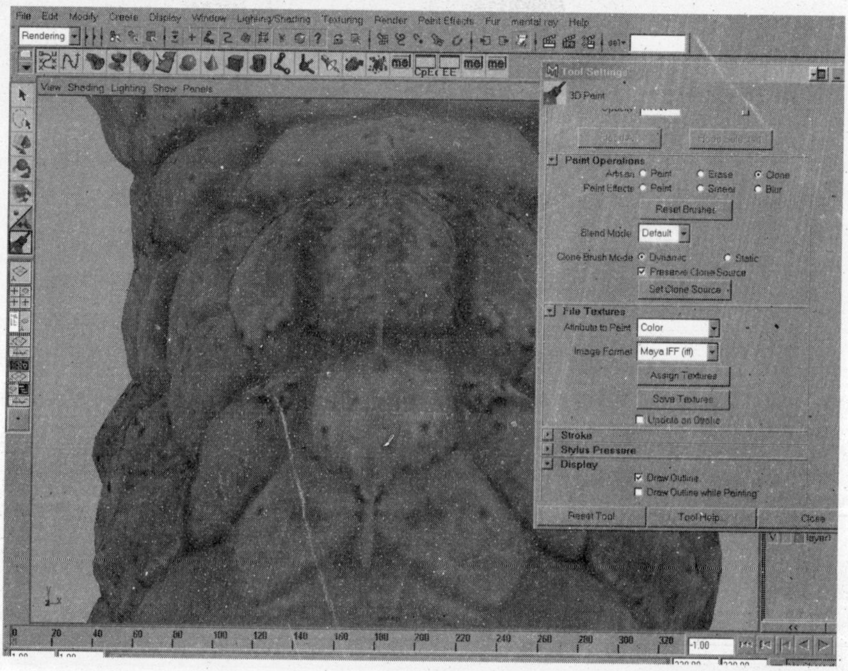

FIGURE 12.14 Select an area to clone and begin painting across the seam.

Step 3: The hardware texture view is an approximation of the texture map applied. In order to see the full results, you must

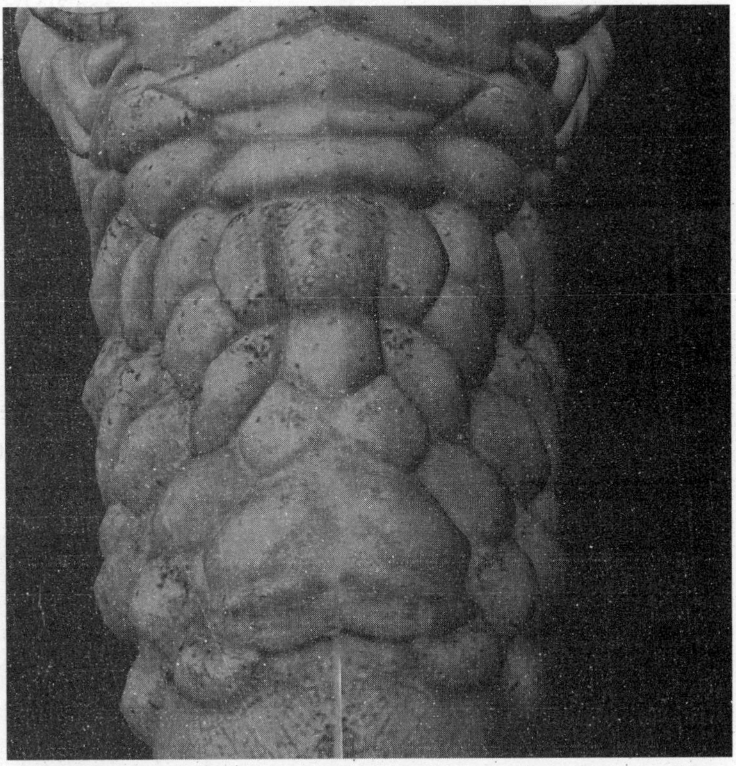

FIGURE 12.15 The seam in the middle of the snout has been painted out.

render the image. Save the texture before rendering to make sure it updates properly. Figure 12.15 shows the seam in the middle of the snout painted out.

DIFFUSE MAPS

Diffusion is the amount of light allowed to reflect off a surface. This is does not pertain to the reflectivity as in a mirrored reflection, but to how a material absorbs light. A value of 0 will absorb all light and appear black. A value of one, or the color white, will bounce back the light, displaying the material's true color.

Instead of a solid color, a grayscale texture map is used to define color intensity in specific areas. This map can be derived from the color map. The following tutorial demonstrates how to create and apply a diffuse map.

TUTORIAL

DIFFUSE

ON THE CD

Step 1: Open your color map in Photoshop or use the maps supplied on the CD-ROM in the Chapter 12 folder under "sourceimages." Under the Image pull-down menu choose Adjust and then Desaturate.

Step 2: Depending on the grayscale values, adjust the Brightness and Contrast of the image. This tool is found just above Desaturate. Increase both of these values to blow out the base skin tone. The majority of the map is white as seen in Figure 12.16. Save the image.

Step 3: Open the materials Attribute Editor in Maya. Click on the map icon at the end of the Diffuse channel. Choose File and load the diffuse map. Figure 12.17 shows a render of the Fire Monster's head with just the diffuse map applied.

Step 4: Select the geometry and open the tool settings for the 3D Paint Tool. Under the File Textures tab change the Attribute To Paint to Diffuse. Select Artisan Paint under the Paint Operations tab. Above that, under the Color tab, set the color to black and the opacity to .2. Shade the areas between folds, cracks, or depressions in the skin to heighten the effects of the diffuse map. The darker the gray, the darker the color map appears. Use Figure 12.18 for reference.

FIGURE 12.16 This is the diffuse map.

SPECULAR MAPS

A surface shines with a highlight when a light is cast upon it, depending upon its color and makeup. Specular maps dictate the highlights of a material. When dealing with organic material, it is important to define the specular color and how light intensities are distributed across the surface.

Take a moment to examine different materials under a light. Objects made of plastic have white specular highlights. Light on actual skin intensifies the color of the skin. By assigning the color map to the specular color channel, it forces the surface to shine with its own skin tone. Figure 12.19 is a render of the specular map only.

FIGURE 12.17 This is a render of the creature's head with only a diffuse map.

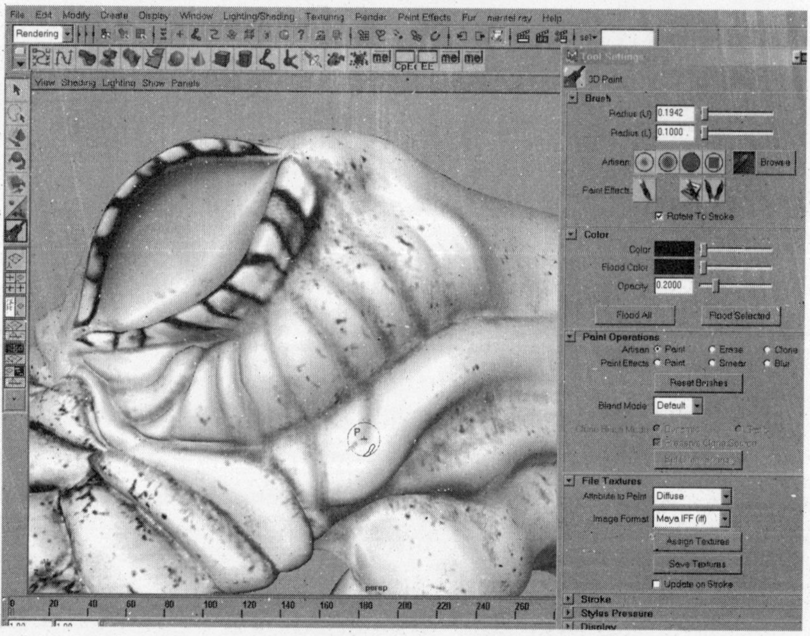

FIGURE 12.18 Shade areas on the diffuse map based on details in the geometry with the 3D Paint Tool.

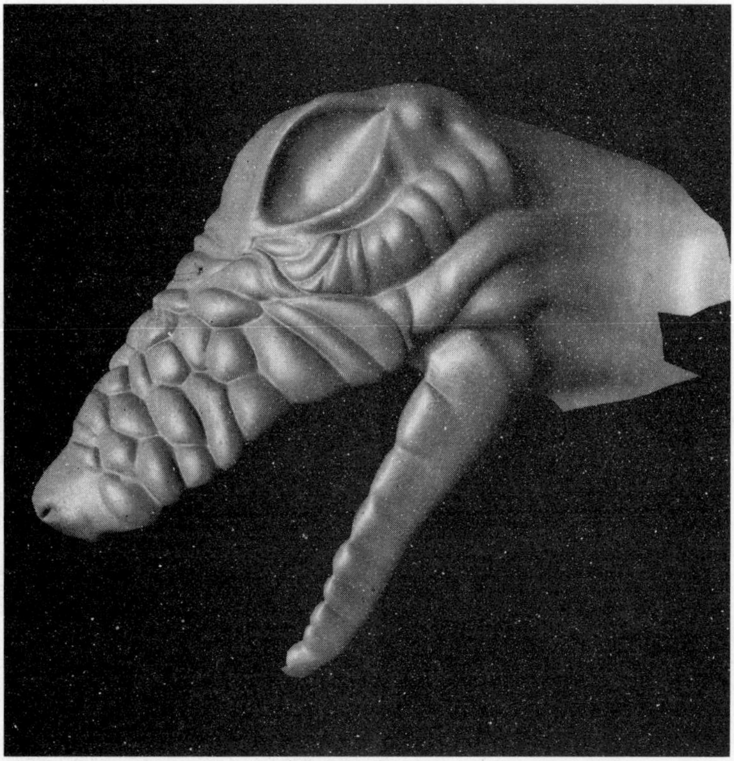

FIGURE 12.19 This is a render of the specular map only.

Bump Maps

Bump maps alter a surface's appearance by shifting the normals. This gives the illusion of depth in order to make a surface appear irregular. Bump maps do not alter geometry; therefore they should be used only for subtle effects.

Bump maps can be created directly from the color map. It is best to "desaturate" the map, or convert it to black and white. The resulting grayscale image can be interpreted. Black values decrease and white values increase the surface elevation. By manipulating the brightness and contrast of the image, you can change the effect of the bump. Bringing the grayscale values closer together smooths out the bump. As long as the values do not create pure white or pure black, the bump affects the surface. Smoothing the bump in this manner creates a subtler, natural-looking effect. Figure 12.20 shows three different renderings with their corresponding bump maps above them. The same values were used in applying the map, only the brightness and contrast were adjusted. Notice in the first and last images the unaffected white and black areas.

Your sculpture from Chapter 5 is invaluable for determining the look of the bump map. All of the sculpture's minute details accomplished with a sponge should be added to a bump map. If feasible, you should take photos of the sculpture, scan them, and use them to help build the bump map. The following tutorial creates a bump map for the left side of the Fire Monster's head.

TUTORIAL

BUMP MAP

Step 1: Load your color map into Photoshop or use the maps supplied on the CD-ROM in the Chapter 12 folder under "sourceimages." Desaturate the image.

ON THE CD

Step 2: Open the Brightness/Contrast tool. Raise the brightness and contrast of the image to create a balance between the blacks and whites.

Step 3: Certain areas of the color map might come across too rough because the texture has noise. Eliminate these areas by smoothing or blending the pixels with the Smudge Tool. Using a pressure value of 20 percent, smudge the texture in a circular pattern. This blends the pixels together without creating a smearing effect and also leaves some detail. (See Figure 12.21.)

Step 4: After the area is smooth, trace any cracks or folds with the Burn tool to make them sharper. Figure 12.22 shows the before and after.

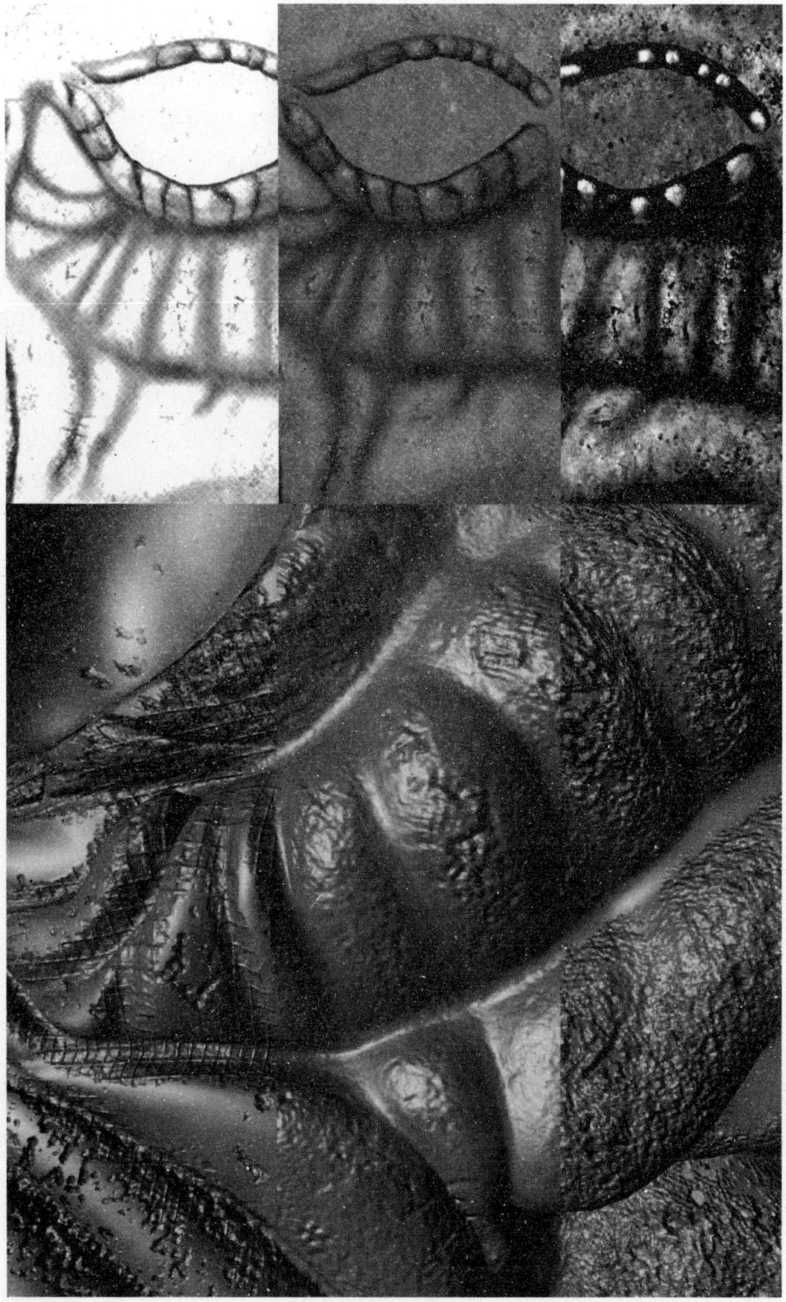

FIGURE 12.20 This is a comparison of three different Brightness/Contrast settings.

FIGURE 12.21 Using the smudge tool, smooth out noisy areas in the bump map.

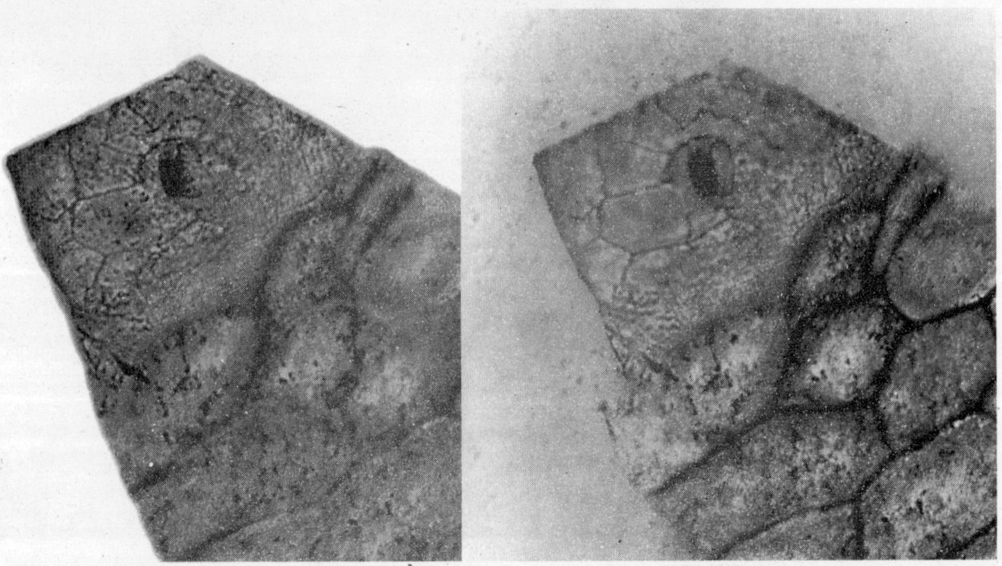

FIGURE 12.22 The bump map with noise (left) and the bump map after it is smoothed (right).

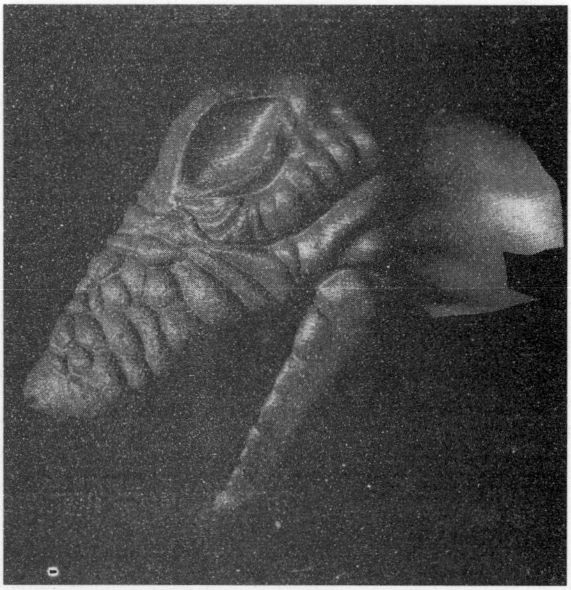

FIGURE 12.23 This is the left side of the Fire Monster's head with only a bump map applied.

Step 5: In Maya, apply the bump map to the material. Render the bump map with all other maps turned off to clearly see the effects. If need be, use the 3D Paint Tool to modify the bump map further. Figure 12.23 shows the Fire Monster's head with just one bump map.

Displacement Maps

A displacement map is similar to a bump map, however, it actually adds geometry to alter the look of the surface. It also has an effect opposite to that of a bump map. Where bump maps make a surface look like it is being pushed in, a displacement map pulls the surface out. Working off the alpha values of a texture map, triangles are added based upon intensity variations. This makes it possible to carve a surface using a texture map. Displacements are extremely useful to create detail too difficult or time consuming to model. Since it alters the shape of a surface, you can view it from any angle and with any lighting setup. In Maya, there are two types of displacement maps: feature-based and non-feature-based. Non-feature-based displacement works off of the existing triangles in the model. Feature-based allows you to sample areas based upon a texture map. Only the painted areas with a value greater than 0, or black, are displaced. Triangles are added based upon the sample settings and color variations in the texture map. The higher the variation, the more triangles are added. This can make feature-based displacement mapping more efficient than actually modeling the surface, especially when modeling in NURBS.

Displacement maps establish the height of displacement. The color black does not push triangles inward. Black is where the surface originates; therefore, blending your textures to black lowers the displacement height to be level with the surface. With the default settings, you can only raise triangles off the surface.

The following tutorial shows how to do this by making the texture around the Fire Monster's eye a displacement map.

TUTORIAL

DISPLACEMENT HEIGHT

Step 1: The area around the Fire Monster's eye has a lot of detail not part of the actual geometry. To add photo-realism and change the shape of the geometry, make the texture in that area a displacement map. In Photoshop, cut out the area to be influenced from the color map or the bump map, whichever defines the shape best, and place it on a black background. Figure 12.24 shows the area around the eye cut from the color map.

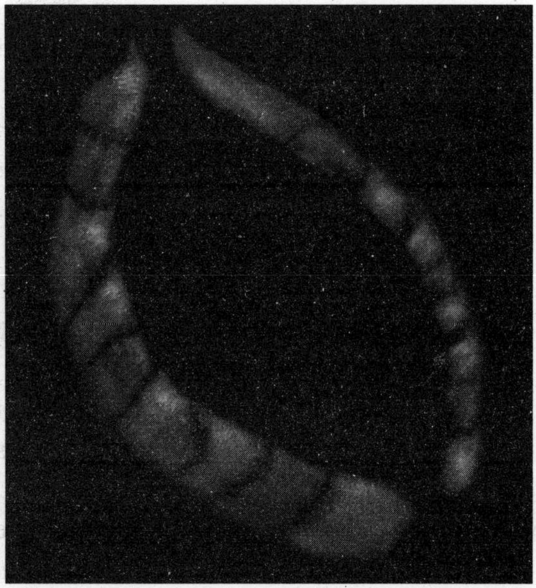

FIGURE 12.24 Cut out the area to be displaced.

Step 2: Remove all of the fine detail or noise in the texture with the Smudge Tool. By making small circles with the brush, smear out the detail. The circular motion leaves the grayscale color information without causing too much damage to the surface. The goal is to retain the elevation information. Figure 12.25 shows an example.

Step 3: Smooth and feather the border edges of the map, depending on how sharp a blend is needed between existing and displaced geometry. With a low pressure setting, use the erase tool to blend the borders to black. Figure 12.26 shows the final map.

Step 4: Open up the Hypershader in Maya. Open the Attribute editor for the material of your character. Click the right mouse button on any of the attributes assigned to a file texture and choose Ignore When Rendering. This turns these channels off so they

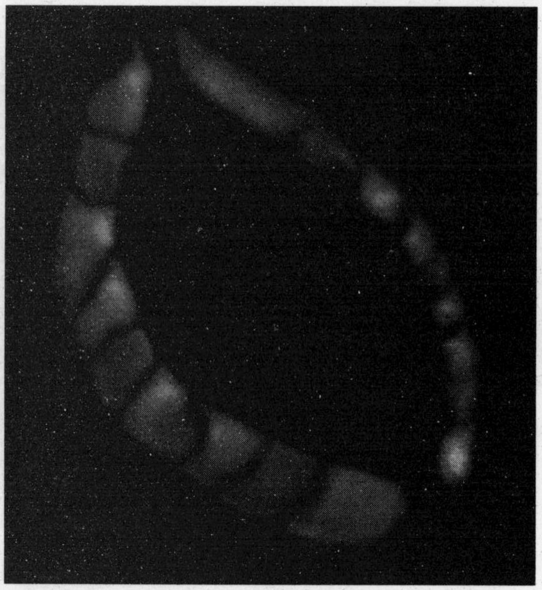

FIGURE 12.25 Smear the detail on the cut out texture.

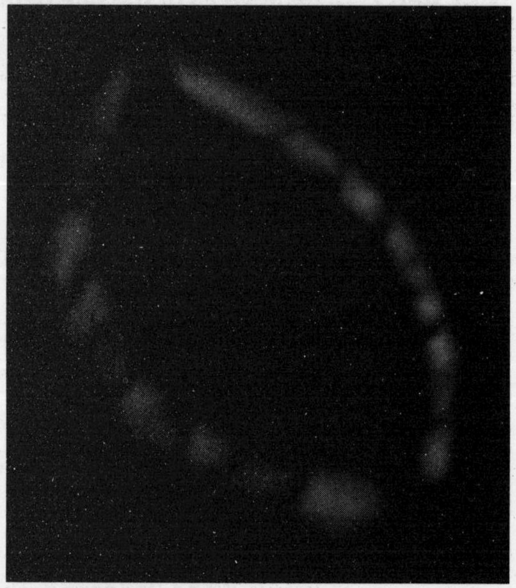

FIGURE 12.26 The displacement map after the edges have been blended to black.

won't show up during render. By doing this, only the effects of the displacement map appear on the rendered surface.

Step 5: Open the Create pull-down menu and create a 2D File texture node. Load the displacement map for the image. With the middle mouse button, drag and drop the file texture onto the material node. Choose Displacement Map from the drop-down menu. The file texture is now applied to the shading group of the surface and does not run through the material node.

Step 6: Select the surface and open its Attribute editor. Click on the Displacement Map tab and make sure Feature Displacement is checked. Use the default settings and render the map. Figure 12.27 shows the effects of the default settings.

FIGURE 12.27 Using the default settings, render an image of the displacement map.

Step 7: The displacement in Figure 12.27 is larger than desired. To modify the height of the displacement, lower the texture's alpha values. Open the Attribute editor for the texture map and click on the color balance tab. Lower the Alpha Gain to .2, which reduces the alpha intensity. This has the same effect as lowering the brightness on the map itself. Render the image again as shown in Figure 12.28.

Step 8: The next attributes to modify are located under the Displacement Map tab in the Attribute editor of the surface.

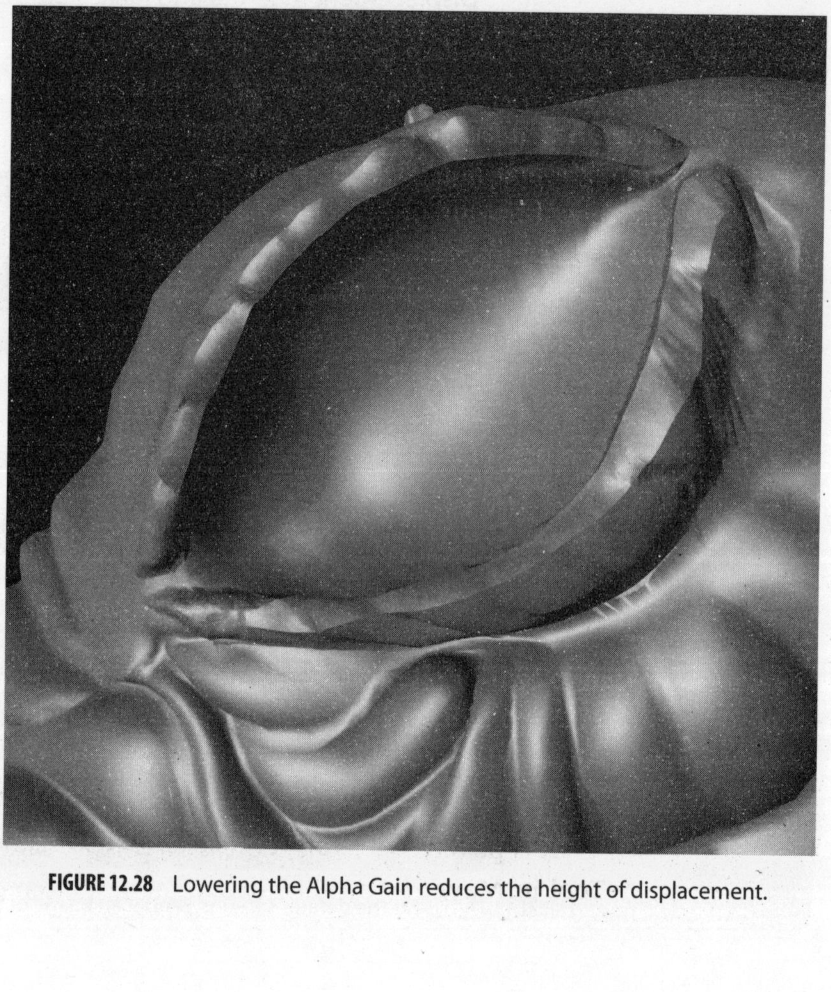

FIGURE 12.28 Lowering the Alpha Gain reduces the height of displacement.

Initial Sample Rate—Analyzes the displacement map for variations in color. The difference in these values determines the amount of triangles added to achieve displacement.

Extra Sample Rate—Refines the geometry added by the initial sampling rate. It's best to use this setting sparingly due to increased render times. Start with a value of 0 and work your way up.

Texture Threshold—Eliminates values less than the setting. The attribute is not needed if you smooth your texture first, removing unnecessary noise.

Normal Threshold—Determines the normal difference between two adjacent triangles. If the difference is higher, the resulting edge will appear sharper. This function is similar to the Soften Normals tool under the Edit Polygons menu.

In Figure 12.28, hard edges exist along the upper and lower eye. To remove these, modify the Normal Threshold. Move the slider bar in increments of thirty, re-rendering each time to check the results. When the edges are smoothed, modify the Initial Sample Rate by first setting the Extra Sample Rate to 0. Continue to change the Initial Sample Rate until the basic displacement is achieved. Try not to exceed a value of 6. After you are satisfied with the overall shape, add to the Extra Sample Rate. If the texture is noisy, 0 may do the trick. Make sure the results are noticeable between each render; otherwise you will just be increasing render times. Also be sure to look in the Output window in Maya to see how many triangles are being rendered. Figure 12.29 shows the displacement with a Normal Threshold of 120. The Initial Sample Rate is 5 and the Extra Sample Rate is 3.

It is possible to paint the displacement map using the 3D Paint Tool in Maya. To do this, delete the displacement node and turn

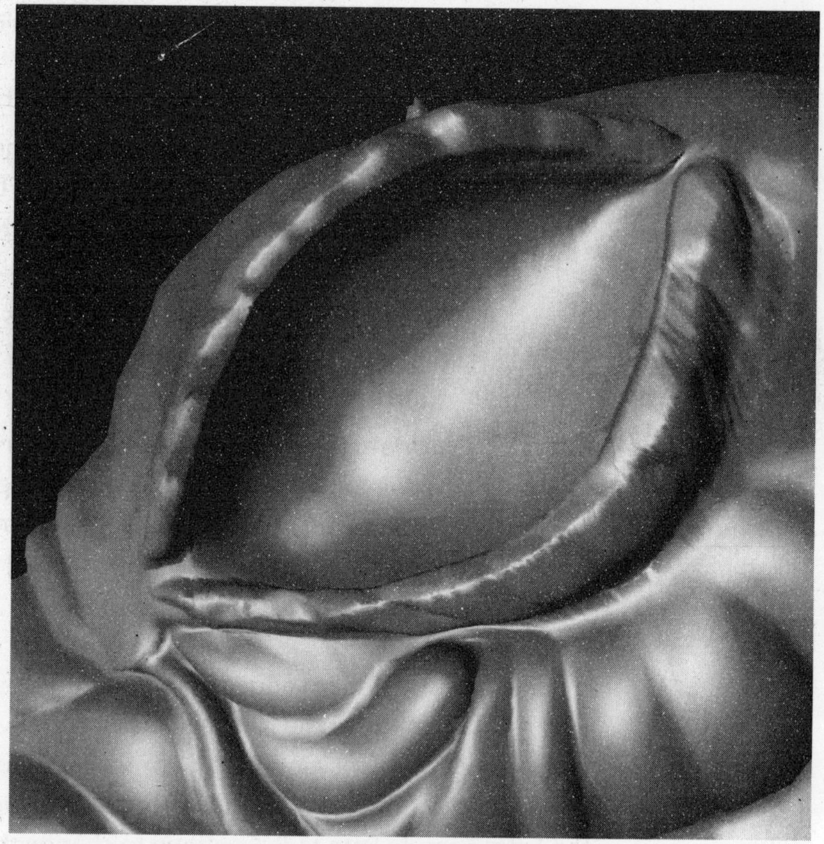

FIGURE 12.29 The results of the final values on the displacement map.

off Feature Displacement. Drag and drop the texture back onto the material and assign it as a displacement map. This time, a bump node is generated and connected between the material and displacement nodes. Open the 3D Paint Tool and choose Bump from the Attribute To Paint pull-down menu. You can now paint directly to the displacement map and render it to see the results. Make sure the bump channel is renderable in the Material Attribute editor. When done, reapply the displacement map with feature-based turned on to free up the bump channel.

It is often necessary to use multiple displacements to achieve different height values. Using a layered texture, you can add as many maps as needed. The following tutorial shows the process.

TUTORIAL

MULTIPLE DISPLACEMENT MAPS

Step 1: Open the Maya scene file called "Multiple_Displacement_Maps." Open the Hypershader. From the Create pull-down menu choose Layered Texture.

Step 2: Click on the node to open its attributes. Add the file texture called "displacement1" to the Color channel and change the Blend mode to Add.

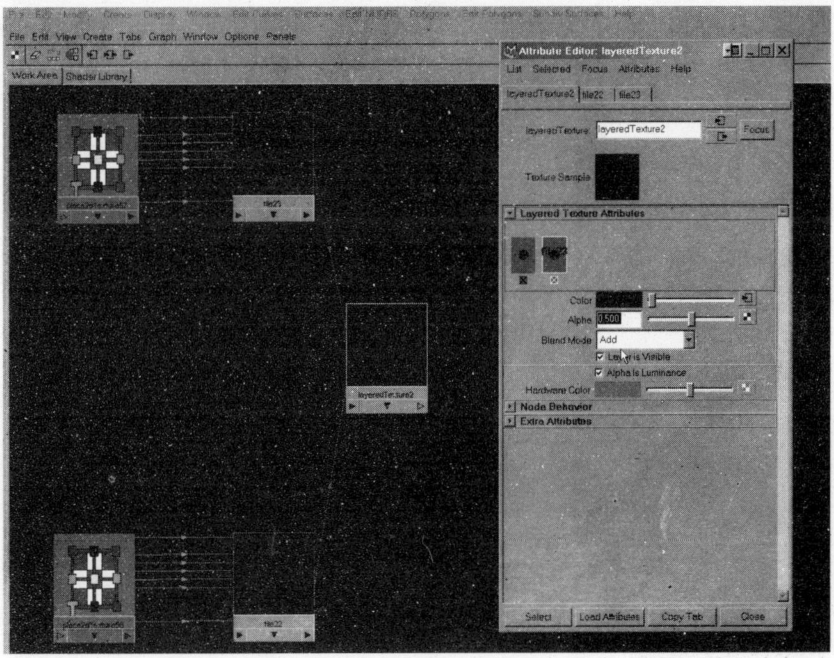

FIGURE 12.30 This is the setup for multiple displacement maps using the Hypershader.

Step 3: Add another file texture called "displacement2" by clicking in the red square under the Layered Texture Attributes tab. Choose the new icon, and add another file texture to the Color channel. Change its Blend mode to Add.

Step 4: Instead of altering the displacement height through the Alpha Gain of the texture map as discussed in the Displacement Height tutorial, change the Alpha values through the Alpha slider bar for each of the layered textures. Make sure the Alpha Gain is at its default setting of 1 for each texture map. Use Figure 12.30 for reference.

CONCLUSION

ON THE CD

When you use a combination of attributes and separate details into different texture maps, surfaces take on a more photo-realistic look. Located on the CD-ROM is a collection of images, named for the map they represent, showing the left side of the Fire Monster's head in its progression from simple shaded to displacement.

PART

V ANATOMICALLY CORRECT

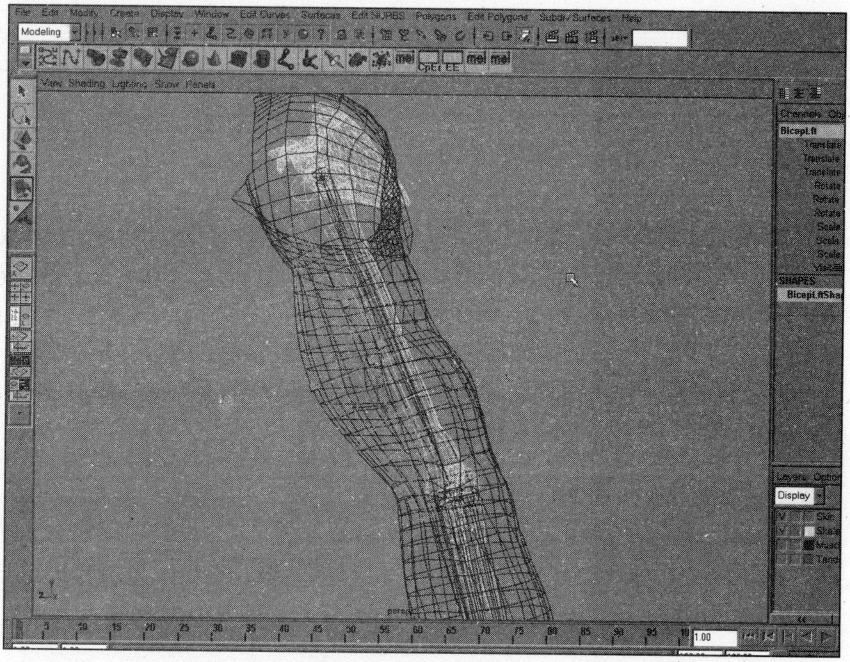

CHAPTER

13 SKELETONS

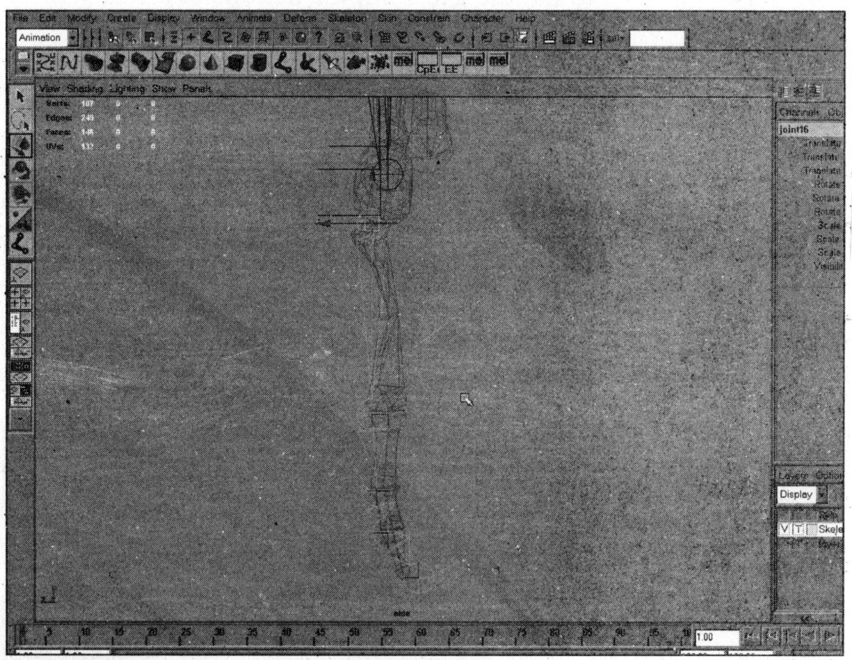

The skeleton is the backbone of all characters and most life Regardless of whether it is an exoskeleton or endoskeleton, an IK system or collection of deformers, characters need some type of structure to support their motion. This infrastructure, or "rig," can range from simple to immensely complex. Creating rigs for film requires a degree of complexity to enable the animator to move the character freely. In this chapter, we will examine the Fire Monster's skeleton and how it relates to characters in general. The primary focus is on the creature's arm, building a suitable rig to handle the complex actions of a real-world wrist.

Skeletal Motion

Skeletal bones in living organisms are connected together and separated by various tissues forming what is called a joint. There are many different types of joints in life; however, only four provide significant movement for our characters. They are hinge, pivot, ball-and-socket, and saddle joints.

Hinge joints—As the name implies, these joints swing in one direction or in a single plane. Hinge joints are considered uniaxial, meaning they can only rotate in one axis. This type of joint can be found in fingers, knees, and elbows. Figure 13.1

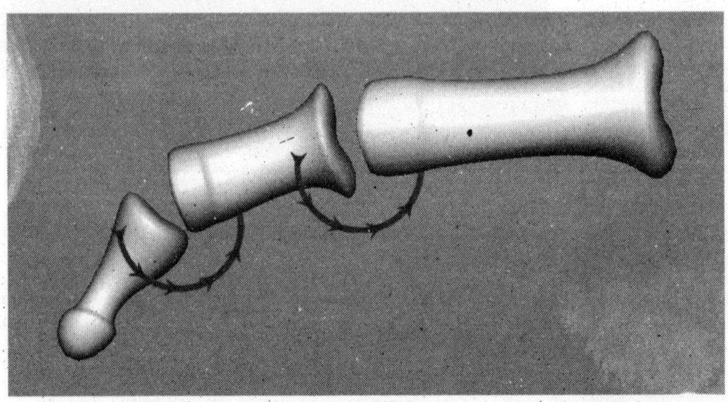

FIGURE 13.1 This is an example of a hinge joint.

shows the rotation of a finger joint. The separation between the bones is where the actual joint tissue would be.

Pivot joints—This joint allows a bone to move around another or rotate about its own axis. Pivots are also considered uni-axial. An example of this type of joint is the motion found in the rotation of the wrist. The radius rotates in a single plane around the ulna. Figure 13.2 illustrates this action.

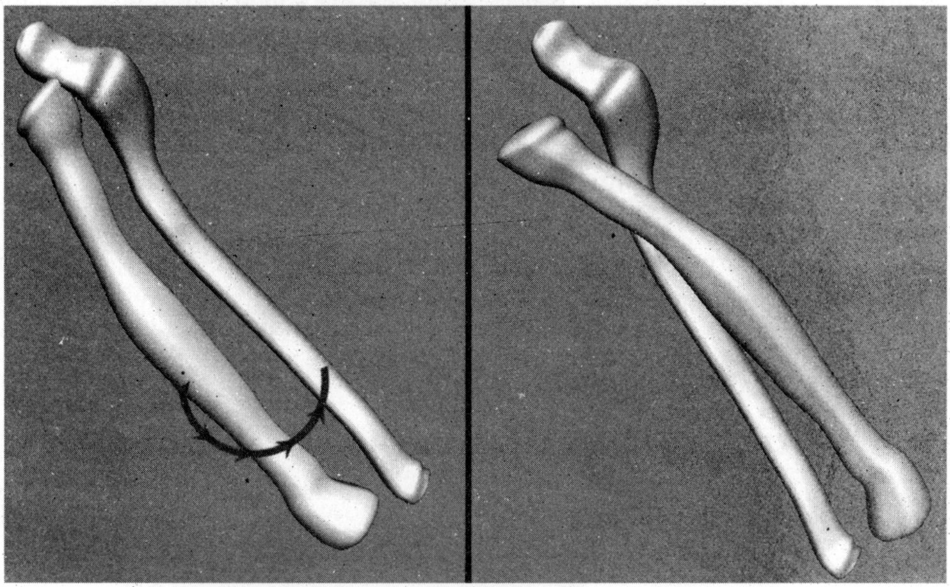

FIGURE 13.2 This is an example of a pivot joint.

Ball-and-Socket joints—In this type of joint, one bone has a rounded, ball-like end cupped by an opposing bone. This provides three degrees of freedom or rotation in multiple axes. The shoulder and hip are examples of ball-and-socket joints. Figure 13.3 shows the rotation of the humerus bone.

Saddle joints—The bones in these joints fit together like two saddles with the tops facing each other with one saddle rotated 90 degrees. This allows the joint to be bi-axial. An example of this

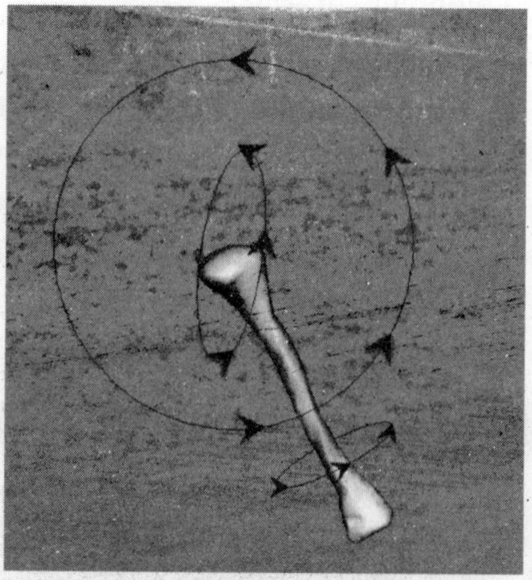

FIGURE 13.3 This is an example of a ball-and-socket joint.

type of joint is where the thumb connects to the wrist. Figure 13.4 shows the basic rotation of a saddle joint.

Building an IK System

With the skeleton complete, creating a system of Maya joints is nothing more than connecting the dots. As discussed earlier in this

FIGURE 13.4 This is an example of a saddle joint.

chapter, the space between each bone is the joint. From joint to joint is exactly where you want to draw the beginning and end of the IK. Positioning of the Maya joint is important, but how the joint rotates is most critical. They must imitate real-world joints as much as possible. To accomplish this, you must understand how IK works just as you did with real-world joints.

IK has three parts, the ball—which is the joint, the extended triangle—which is the bone of the previous joint, and the handle—which controls all of the joints. The first joint drawn is the root. Examine the diagram in Figure 13.5.

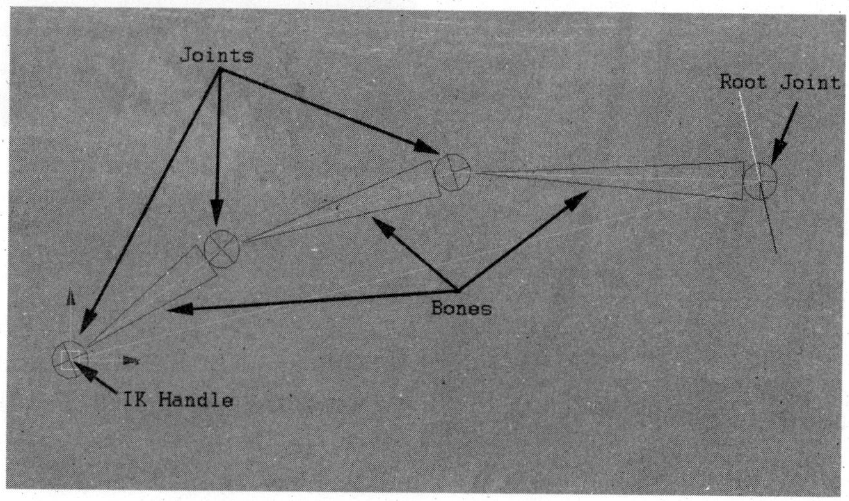

FIGURE 13.5 This is an example of an IK skeletal system.

The root joint is a three-dimensional joint, meaning it can rotate in all three axes. All of the joints thereafter are planar or uniaxial. The length of individual bones helps determine the amount of rotation. Joints should be drawn at the angle in which you want them to rotate—the sharper the angle, the greater the rotation. Figure 13.6 shows the difference in rotation based upon the size and angle of the middle joint.

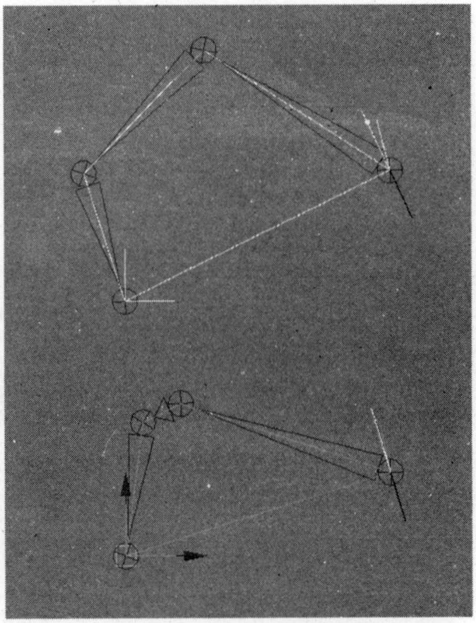

FIGURE 13.6 This example shows the difference in rotation achieved by modifying the middle joint.

IK skeletons are easier to position after they have been drawn. It is best to draw the joints in a planar view and then modify them accordingly, adding an IK handle only to test the rotations. The following tutorial adds IK to the Fire Monster's arm and hand, starting at the shoulder.

TUTORIAL

IK ARM

Step 1: In the front view, draw three joints. Place the first joint at the top of the humerus. The second goes at the elbow and the last at the wrist. Translate the root joint in the side view to align it with the humerus bone. Using the down arrow key on the keyboard, scroll to the elbow joint, and translate this joint to match the elbow position. Repeat the process for the wrist. Use proper naming conventions to rename the joints, "UpperarmLft," "ForearmLft," and "PalmLft." Figure 13.7 shows the final position of the joints.

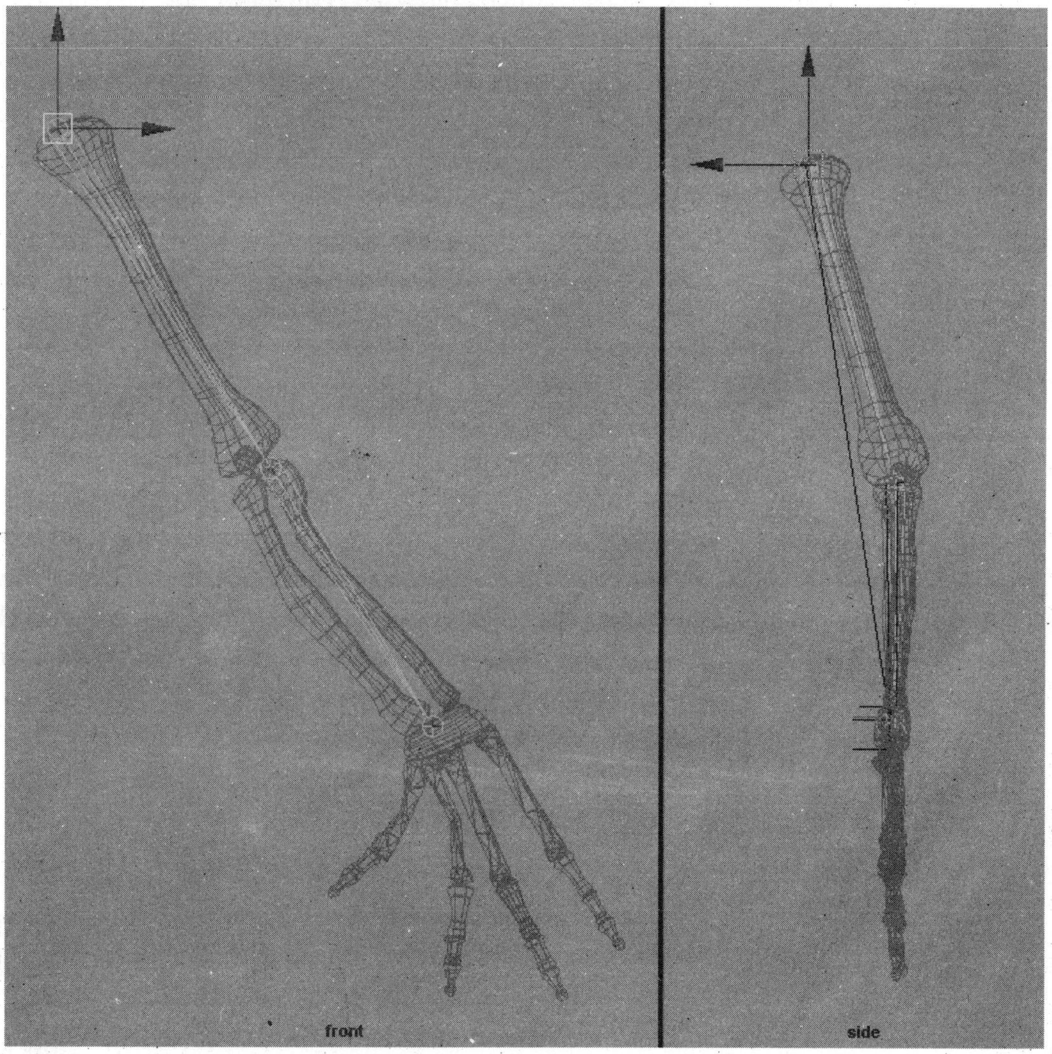

FIGURE 13.7 This shows the joints making up the shoulder, elbow, and wrist in the front view and the side view.

Step 2: If you scale or rotate the joints into position, you need to freeze the transformations and then reorient the joints. Select all of the joints or the root joint. Choose Freeze Transformations from the Modify pull-down menu and freeze, translate, rotate, and scale. It is normal for the translate values to return to zero. Joints are animated by rotation values and not translate values, so this has little effect on them. However the scale and rotate must be set back to their default values. This helps when adding expressions. When you freeze the transforms or modify a joint's position, the local axis of the joint becomes aligned with the world. This must be reoriented to place the first axis, the X-axis by default, down the center of the bone in order for the joint to rotate properly. To reorient the axes use the following Maya embedded language, or MEL, script:

```
joint –e –oj xyz –zso –ch;
```

The script calls out the joint command and opens the selected joints for editing (joint –e). The next flag and proceeding argument (–oj xyz) states orient joint to the following order, xyz in this case. The –zso flag reorients the scale manipulator and the –ch flag reorients all the children of the root joint. The script is needed throughout the creation of the skeleton. Make a MEL script out of it by first typing it in the script editor. Highlight the entire line and, holding the middle mouse button down, drag and drop it onto a shelf. From here on out, simply select the root of the IK skeleton and click the MEL script icon.

Step 3: Next draw the fingers. Create the first joint at the base of the metacarpal on the index finger. Place a total of five joints. Reposition the joints so they line up with the bones. It might be necessary to rotate the joints outside of the bones in order for them to rotate properly. The tip of the finger should angle the most. Use Figure 13.8 for reference.

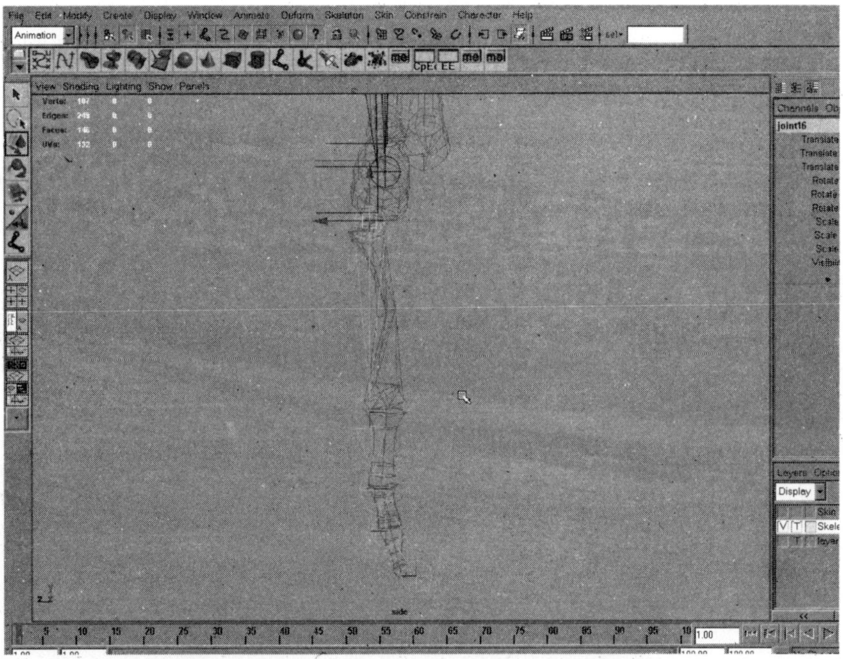

FIGURE 13.8 This is the skeleton for the index finger.

Step 4: Before continuing onto the other fingers, test the rotations of the index finger. Draw an IK handle with the IK handle tool under the Skeleton pull-down menu. Click the second joint from the root and the last joint in the chain, and the handle is drawn automatically. You are ignoring the IK bone making up the metacarpal because you do not want it to move with the finger. It is mainly drawn to support the bone geometry. Select the IK handle and translate it in the side view. Check to make sure the joints rotate like your own finger. You will notice as the IK handle moves closer to the root, it tends to rotate in the X-axis. This is normal for IK and can easily be adjusted in other views. If the joints do not bend properly, press T on the keyboard to open the IK handle's manipulator tool. This displays the handle's rotation disc and joint chain plane. By translating the manipulator, you can rotate the rotation disc to change the plane in which the joint rotates.

Step 5: Create the rest of the fingers in the same manner. Align the index finger with the forearm. Eventually this will contain the wrist control. Pay close attention to the rotation of the thumb and the fact that it only requires four joints. The thumb is a saddle joint; therefore, it is necessary to rotate the rotation handle so the joints of the thumb rotate into the palm as shown in Figure 13.9.

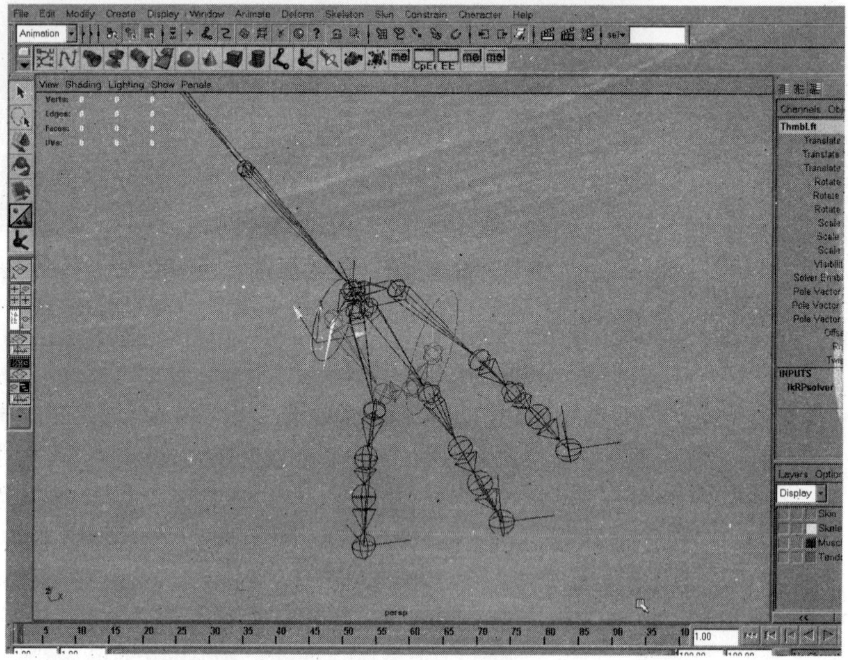

FIGURE 13.9 Rotate the IK handle's rotation disc to create the action of the opposable thumb.

Step 6: Select the root joint to all of the fingers and make them children of the last joint of the arm. By doing this, IK bones are automatically generated, connecting all the IK systems to the wrist joint as shown in Figure 13.10.

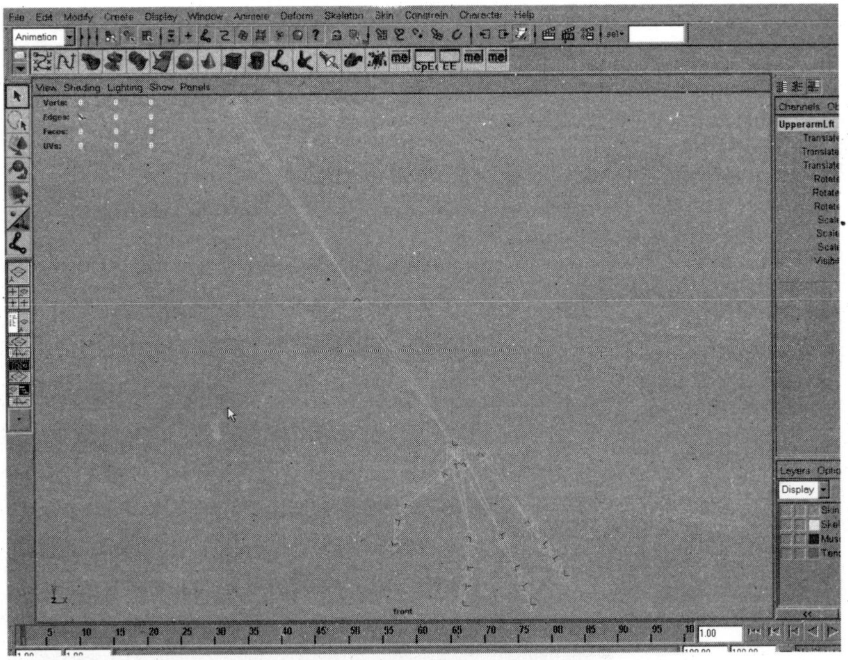

FIGURE 13.10 All of the bones are connected to the wrist.

Step 7: Create an IK handle from the root of the arm to the wrist. Draw another from the wrist to the base of the middle finger metacarpal. Add any remaining handles and check the rotations of all of the joints.

Step 8: Save this scene as "IK_Arm." It is used in the next tutorial.

Supination and Pronation

The action of the muscles and bones of the forearm is a complex action to achieve. In order to maintain realism and proper deformations, it is necessary to duplicate this motion. As with everything, you must understand the action before you can recreate it. When the arm is extended and the palm is facing up, the movement is called supination. The opposite of this is pronation, when the palm is facing down. The action occurs by the ends of the radius and ulna trading places, in turn causing the wrist to rotate. To accomplish this in Maya, you need to create a pivot joint. The following tutorial explains the procedure.

TUTORIAL

PRONATION

Step 1: Load the scene file called IK_Arm from the previous tutorial. Draw a separate IK system for each bone as shown in Figure 13.11, and give each one an IK handle.

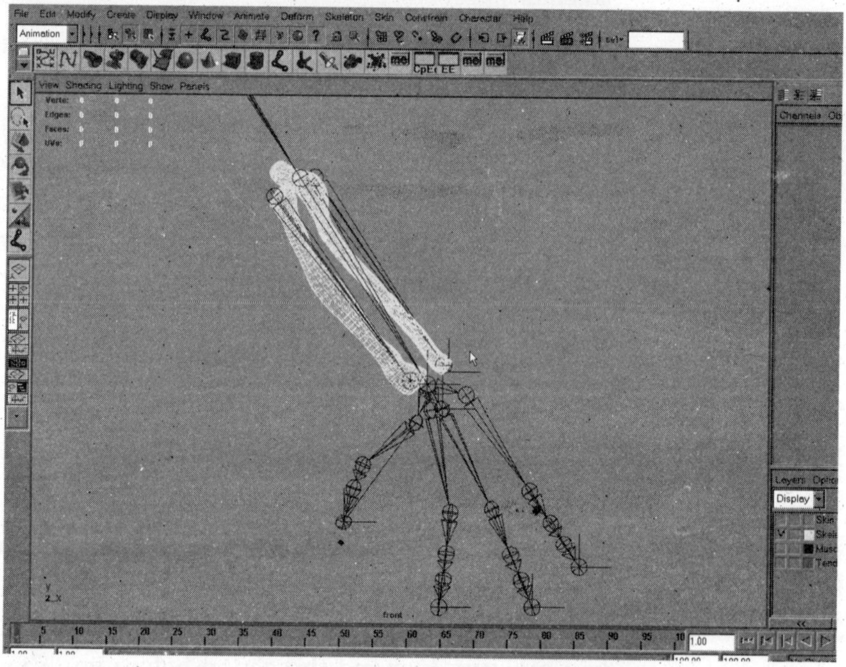

FIGURE 13.11 Create two separate IK systems, one for the radius and one for the ulna.

Step 2: Create two locators by selecting Locator from the Create pull-down menu. Snap both of these locators to the root of the arm, and freeze their transformations. Make one locator a child of the other. Select the IK systems of the radius and ulna and make them children of the parented locator. Figure 13.12 shows the setup.

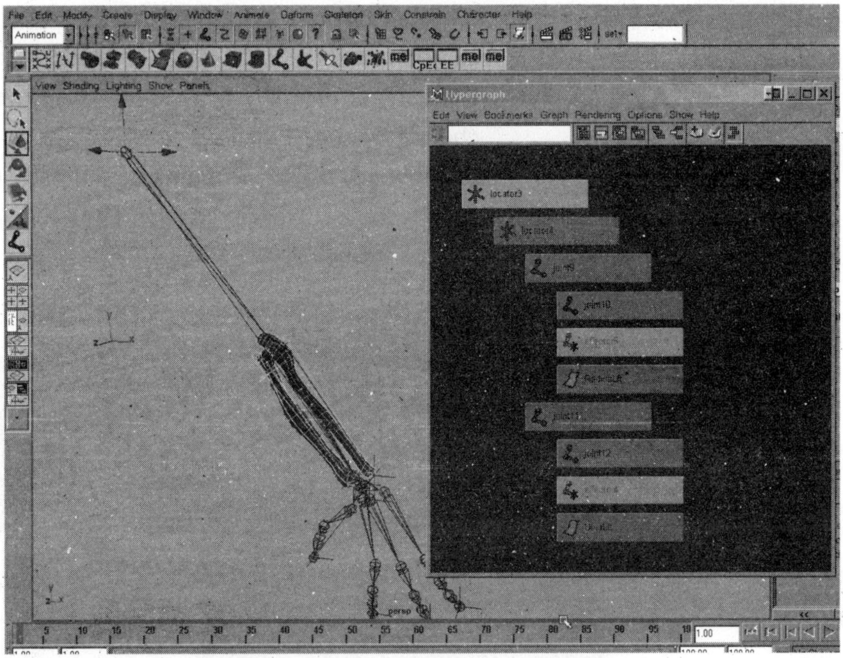

FIGURE 13.12 Create two locators and parent one to the other. Make the radius and ulna IK systems a child of the bottom locator.

Step 3: Make the top locator a child of the upper arm root. By creating two dummy objects (locators) in this manner, you keep the two IK systems separate from the arm skeleton. This way Maya does not automatically connect the joints.

Step 4: Generate another locator and snap it to the IK handle of the ulna. Freeze the transforms. Point constrain the IK handle to the new locator by selecting the locator first, then the handle, and choose point from the Constrain menu. Parent the ulna locator to the wrist joint.

Step 5: Select the radius IK handle and make it a child of the wrist joint. Draw another IK handle from the elbow to the wrist. There are now three IK handles controlling the arm. Rename the handle from the arm root to the wrist "ArmLft," rename the handle from the elbow to the wrist "PronateLft," and call the last handle "WristLft." Make PronateLft a child of ArmLft, and then select PronateLft. Under the Window pull-down menu choose General Editors, Channel Control, which brings up the channel controller. Move all of the attributes to Non-Keyable except for Twist and Visibility. Figure 13.13 shows this action.

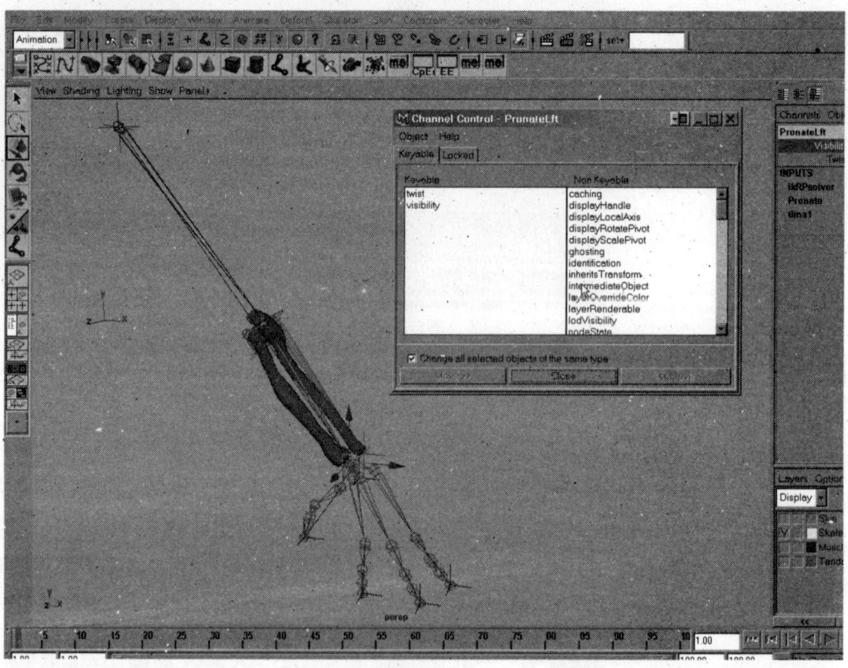

FIGURE 13.13 Move all of the attributes to Non-Keyable except for Twist and Visibility.

Step 6: With PronateLft still selected, open up the expression editor from the Window pull-down menu under Animation editors, and click on twist. From the Selected Obj & Attr dialog box double-click on the text and with the middle mouse button drag it down into the expression window. Finish the expression with the following:

```
PronateLft.twist=WristLft.twist/2;
```

This expression tells the twist control of the PronateLft IK handle to rotate at half the speed of the WristLft twist handle.

Step 7: This setup allows the radius to roll over the ulna in the wrist. To see this action, select the WristLft IK handle. In the channel box select twist. Move the mouse into the viewport and

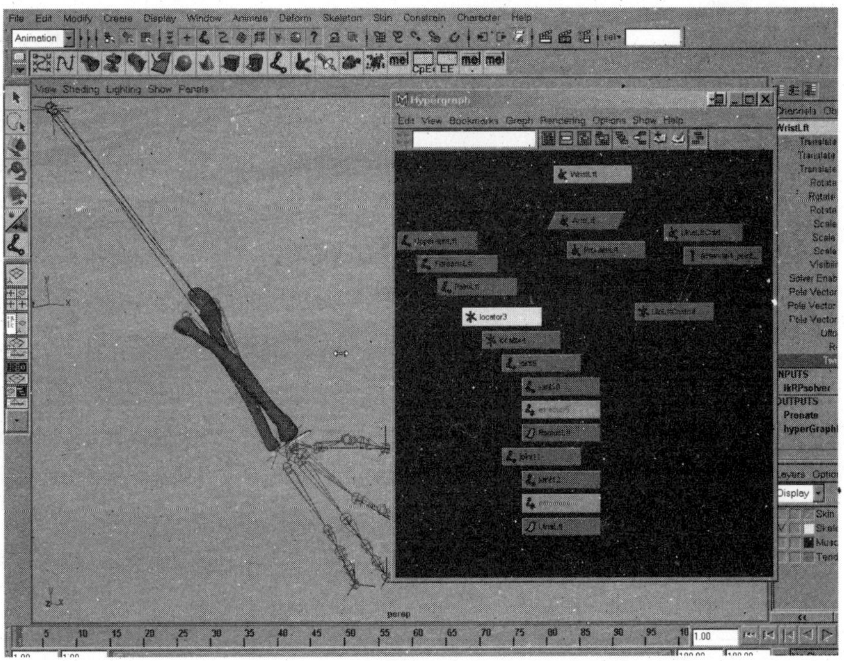

FIGURE 13.14 This is the hierarchy for supination and pronation of the wrist.

with the middle mouse button scroll from left to right. If you have built your character with the back of his hand facing out, pronation will be from 0 to −180 degrees. Figure 13.14 shows the action and the hierarchy.

Connecting Bones

Once the IK is functioning properly, you can attach the bones. After attaching them, make them into rigid bodies. This allows them to collide with the character's skin. The following tutorial explains the procedure.

TUTORIAL

Rigid-Body Bones

Step 1: Check the bones and make sure all of the geometry is uniformly spaced. If you have sharp edges, smooth them out. Check the normals as well and make sure they are facing out. Freeze the transforms on every bone and delete all history.

Step 2: One by one, make each bone a child of its corresponding IK joint. After the bone is parented, freeze the transformations again. This keeps the bone from flying off its parent after it has been made into a rigid body.

Step 3: Switch to the Dynamics module. Either one by one or as an entire group, select all of the bones and make them passive rigid bodies with the default settings. This is located under the Soft/Rigid Bodies pull-down menu. Passive rigid bodies allow the object's translate and scale parameters to be keyable.

CONCLUSION

The bones are ready for action. Using the methods described for the arm, you can build the entire character. Remember, the bones do not deform the skin very much. The main purpose is to define joint placement, and proper articulation. The next chapter focuses on building muscles and tendons.

CHAPTER 14 MUSCLES AND TENDONS

In a living organism, it is the brain that causes the muscles to expand and contract, which move bones and joints. In a digital character, you have to do things in reverse. By moving IK joints, you move bones, which in turn drives the muscles. The order is different, but the results are the same.

In the previous chapter, you set up a skeleton for your creature. Now you will add muscles over the bones and under the skin. Just like the skeleton, the muscles will never be rendered. In addition, tendons are connected to a few of the muscles. Like all systems of the human body, myology, the study of muscles, is an immense topic. To fully understand these actions, it is best to consult articles or books dedicated to the subject.

Muscle and Tendon Motion

There are three basic parts to a muscle: the origin, the belly, and the insertion. The origin is the root of the muscle. It is from here that the muscle pulls. The belly is the body of the muscle. This is the part doing the contracting. It contracts, or pulls, toward the origin. The insertion, or end, of the muscle pulls on the bone or tendon.

A contracting muscle also expands. When a muscle tightens, its fibrous tissue accumulates in the belly causing the surrounding tissue to expand. This is the muscle bulge. Tendons attached to the muscle, in turn, are pulled, activating bone rotation at the joint. The length of the tendon only changes nominally if at all.

Bones are acted upon by more than one muscle. A bone is loosely connected to other bones by joint tissue, but tissue alone is not enough to support the weight of the bone. In order to stabilize a bone or keep it straight, many muscles act upon it. This same action occurs to return a bone to its original position. For instance, when the bicep contracts, the tricep and brachii muscles return it.

MODELING MUSCLES AND TENDONS

When modeling muscles, we follow the same rules as modeling bones. They too are transformed into rigid bodies and act as a collision object against the skin. However, they have one additional dimension, they deform. This means the muscles must have enough geometry to support proper motion.

The most challenging aspect of muscle creation is that they work best when they conform to the skin. The following tutorial outlines an effective way to accomplish this.

TUTORIAL

BUILDING MUSCLES

Step 1: Load the "Building_Muscles" scene file from the CD-ROM or the skeleton you created. Create a primitive NURBS sphere with eight spans in the U and the V. Delete the last hull from the top and the bottom. This leaves a large hole at both poles.

ON THE CD

Step 2: Select the last hull at the top and bottom of the sphere. Scale these out in the Y-axis to give the sphere an origin point at the top and an insertion point at the bottom as shown in Figure 14.1.

Step 3: In the side view, flatten the back of the sphere. This gives the muscle a flat surface so it can lie on top of a bone; it also helps in deformation. The muscle can now be scaled from this flat base outward without it scaling in both directions. Figure 14.2 shows the finished shape.

Step 4: In shaded mode, there is a thick, green line running down the length of the muscle. This is the seam. Move the seam to the middle of the back of the surface, the side that lies against the bone. To do this, enter component mode and

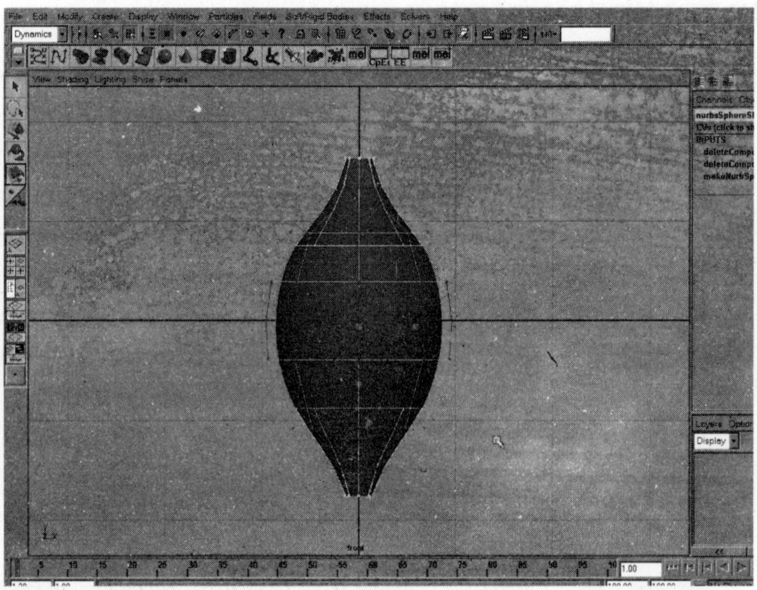

FIGURE 14.1 Pull the top and bottom of the sphere out.

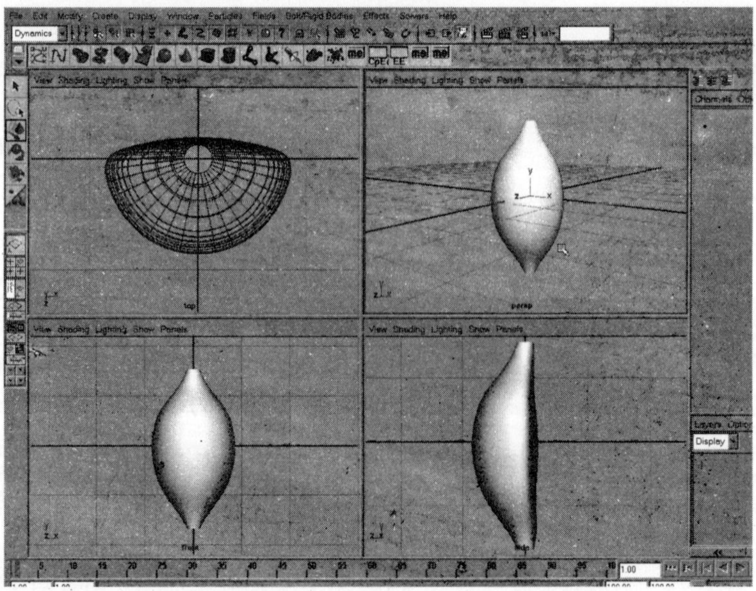

FIGURE 14.2 This is the look of a finished muscle.

choose isoparms for a selection mask from the Status Line. Highlight the middle isoparm by clicking on it in the viewport. From the Edit NURBS pull-down menu choose Move Seam as shown in Figure 14.3.

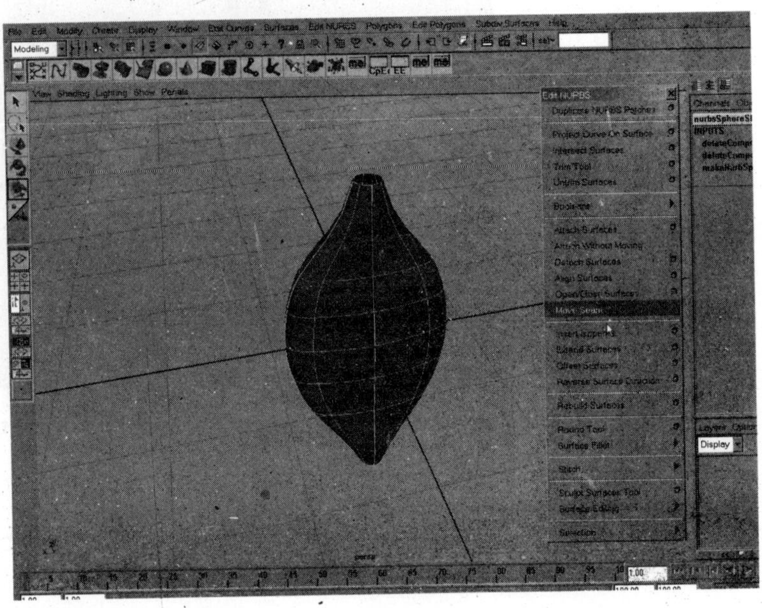

FIGURE 14.3 Move the seam of the muscle to the back of the surface.

Step 5: From the Edit NURBS pull-down menu open the Rebuild Surfaces options box, and choose Uniform for the rebuild type. Set the parameter range to 0 to # Spans and change the number of spans to 10 in the U and 10 in the V as shown in Figure 14.4.

Step 6: Delete the history and freeze the transformations. From the Modify pull-down menu choose Center Pivot. This places the pivot point directly in the center of the model. From the side view, press the Insert key on the keyboard, and move the centered pivot to the base of the muscle. Press Insert again.

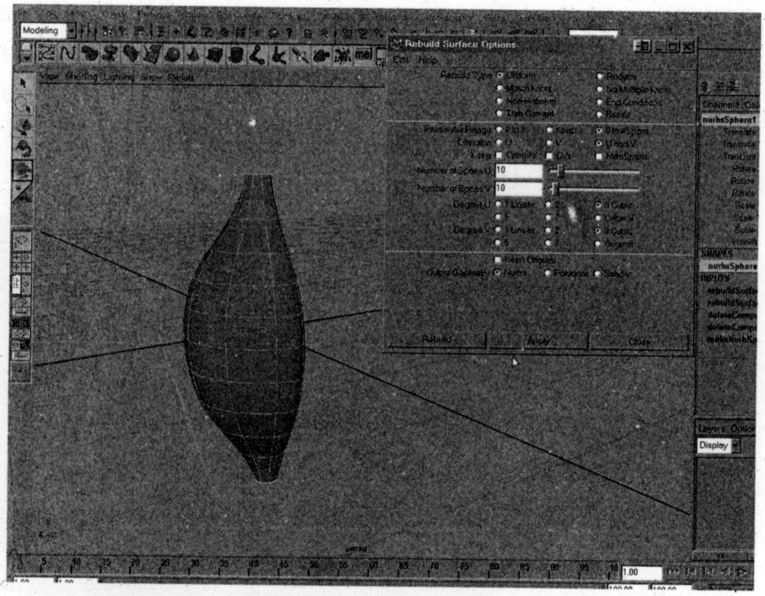

FIGURE 14.4 This is the rebuilt muscle and the settings used.

You are now able to scale the muscle in the Z-axis with minimal movement to its base.

Step 7: Freeze the transforms, and reposition the muscle to a place in the character. We will make this muscle the bicep. Translate it over the humerus. Scale, rotate, and translate the muscle into the appropriate position as shown in Figure 14.5.

Step 8: Turn the skin and shaded mode on. Most likely the muscle is penetrating the skin. First determine if its position is proper. Examine the skin surface closely. If the shape of the bicep is modeled into the skin, the muscle needs to fit inside that pocket. If the skin hasn't been modeled for the bicep, you have a little more leeway. Reposition the muscle with the transform tools. Do not worry about it penetrating the skin just yet. At this point, you want the belly of the muscle to stick out of the skin slightly.

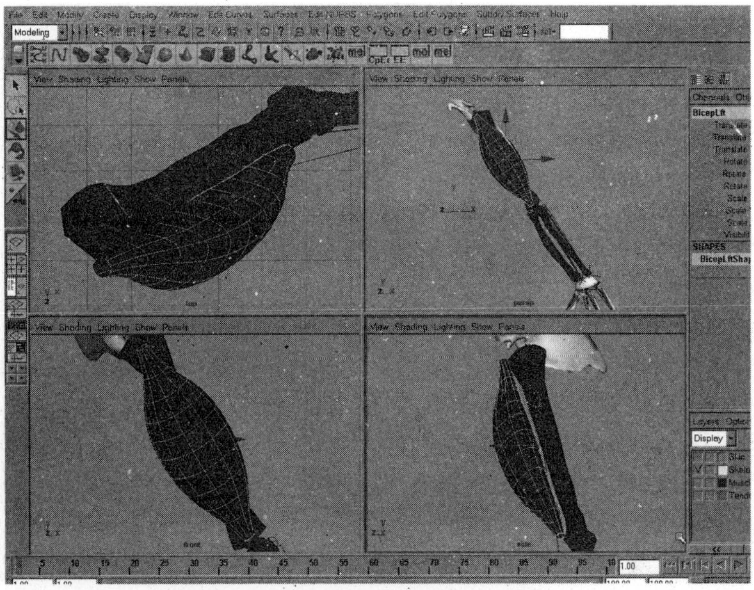

FIGURE 14.5 Reposition the muscle to be the bicep.

Step 9: Enter component mode and choose CV from the selection mask. Push each CV just under the skin. You might be able to select groups of CVs, which is fine, just as long as you leave the base of the muscle flat against the bone. For easier manipulation, use the arrow keys on the keyboard to walk up and down the CV selection. Figure 14.6 shows the form-fitted muscle.

This is the basic shape and method used to build the majority of the muscles. There are three key points to remember when building a muscle. The first is to have uniform geometry. Although this implies the rebuild type, it mainly refers to the isoparms or vertices being evenly spaced. Second, the surface is well rounded with a large surface area. This improves collision detection, ultimately improving deformations. Third, the back of the belly of the muscle

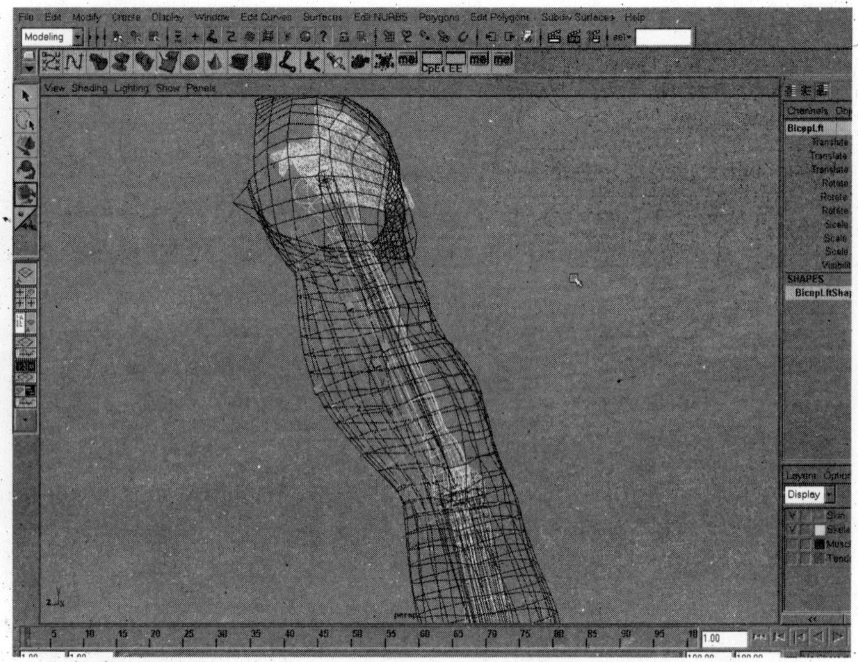

FIGURE 14.6 This is the bicep muscle placed just under the surface of the skin.

lies flat against the bone. It doesn't have to touch it and it doesn't matter if it penetrates it, it just needs to be parallel to it.

Tendons can be trickier in both modeling and animating. Due to the overall width of a tendon, it might not be possible to include these in the model. The skin must be dense enough to support this fine deformation effect. To help offset this, it is a good idea to make the width of the tendon larger than it normally is.

TUTORIAL

BUILDING TENDONS

Step 1: Draw a spline curve in the top view with the CV curve tool under the Create pull-down menu. Use about eight CVs to create a circle. Do not try to close the curve with the last CV.

Use Open/Close Curves from the Edit Curves pull-down menu instead, and choose blend from the tool options.

Step 2: Reshape the curve into a nice-looking circle. Open the options box for the Rebuild Curve tool located under the Edit Curves pull-down menu. Choose Uniform for the rebuild type and change the number of spans to 8.

Step 3: Go to the location on the skin where the tendon needs to be placed and make the skin surface live by selecting it and clicking on the magnet in the status line.

Step 4: With the CV curve tool, draw a spline on the surface where the tendon should go. Add a little extra to the beginning and end of the curve and complete it. If need be, while still in live mode, modify the curve to fit the surface better. Click on the magnet again to exit live mode.

Step 5: Select the circle and then the path curve on the surface. Open the Extrude options from the Surfaces pull-down menu. Reset the settings and use Tube, At Path, Component, and Profile Normal, and then apply the settings. The results are shown in Figure 14.7. In order for the resulting surface to be created properly, the circle or profile curve must be rotated in the direction you want it to extrude. For instance, the character's arm basically runs up and down in the Y-axis. The curve on the surface travels in the same direction. Therefore, the circular curve needs to be on the XZ-plane. Think of it as a ring toss; the ring must be able to fall on top of the post and slide down.

Step 6: Chances are the extruded curve is not the right width. Modify the profile curve to get the desired shape and size. With history on, the extruded surface updates automatically. As a side note, for more complex extrusions and extrusions of varying thickness, you can use multiple profile curves.

Step 7: Translate the path curve so it sits under the skin as shown in Figure 14.8.

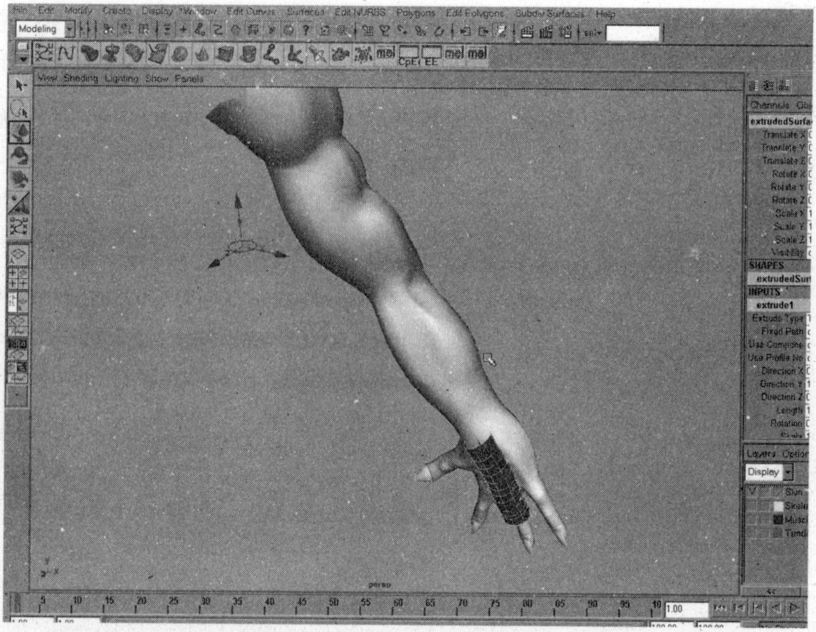

FIGURE 14.7 These are the results of extruding a curve along a path.

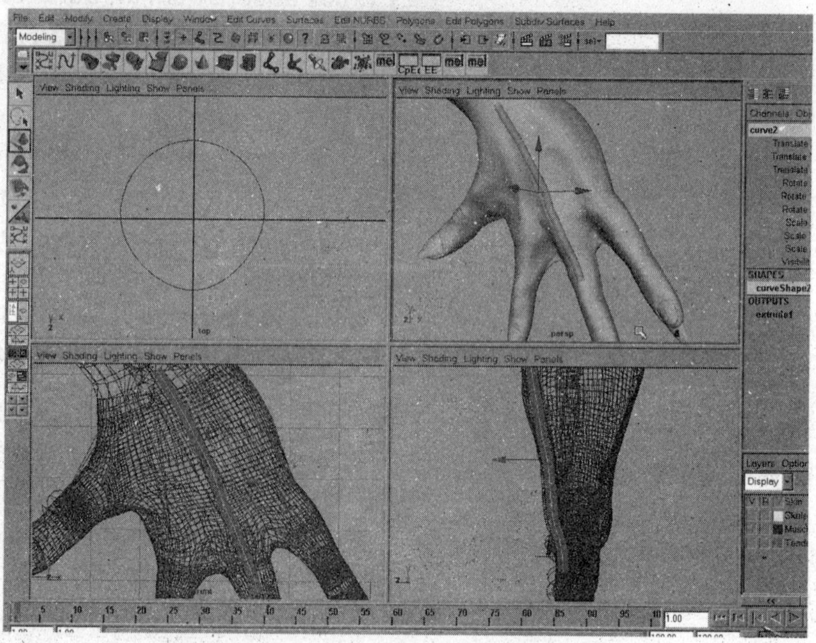

FIGURE 14.8. This is the extruded tendon under the skin.

Step 8: Once the tendon is positioned and shaped properly, delete the history and freeze the transformations. The curves can be deleted, too. Depending on the quality of the surface extruded, you might or might not need to rebuild it.

Step 9: Throughout the body, tendons connect to muscle. To achieve a suitable connection between two models, rebuild the surfaces to the same number of spans in the connecting direction. Check the number of spans in the surfaces by opening up their Attribute editors and looking at Spans UV under the NURBS Surface History tab. In Figure 14.9 the bicep has ten spans in the U while the tendon has only eight. Rebuild the tendon to ten spans only in the U using Uniform for the rebuild type.

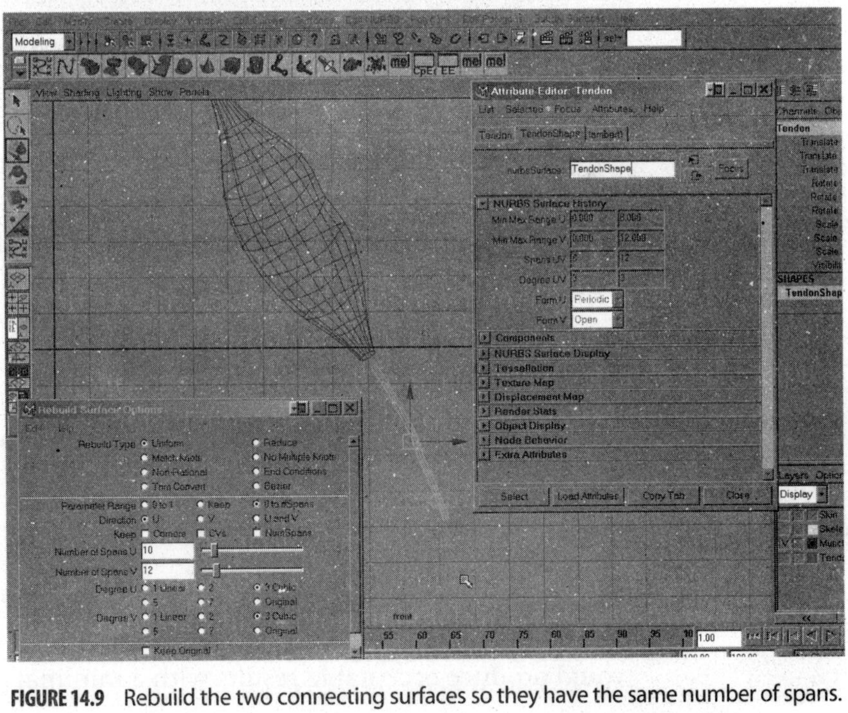

FIGURE 14.9 Rebuild the two connecting surfaces so they have the same number of spans.

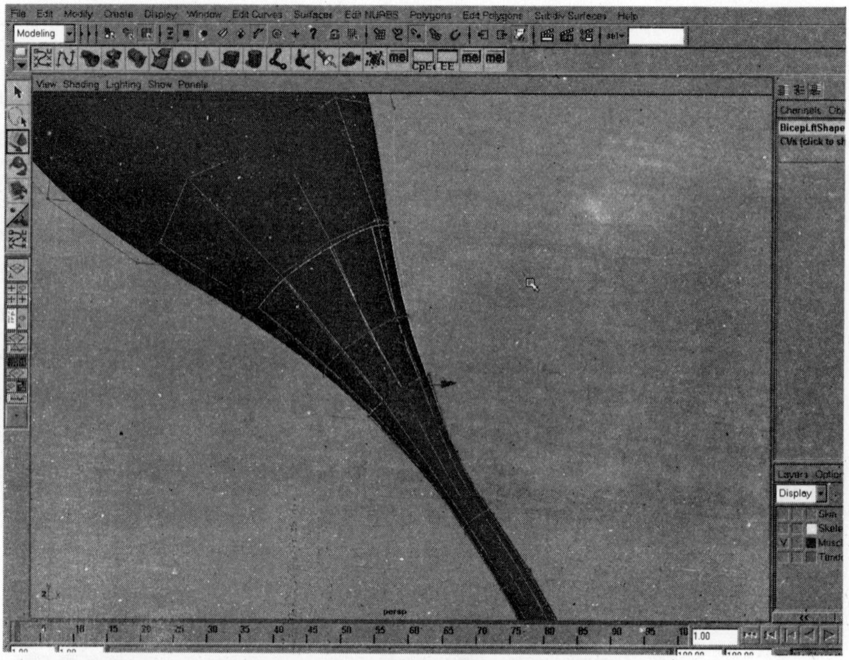

FIGURE 14.10 The bicep and the tendon have been attached by snapping to point.

Step 10: Move the seam on the tendon to match the bicep muscle. Starting at the seam, snap the endpoints of the tendon to the endpoints of the bicep (Figure 14.10). Use the arrow keys on the keyboard to walk up and down the CV selection. The two surfaces will be kept together during muscle setup.

SIMULATING MUSCLE MOTION

It is possible to setup the muscles with a varying degree of complexity. You could simply scale a muscle in the desired axis, which would produce acceptable results with a minimal amount of setup.

The motion of the muscle would not be true to life, but this would only be noticeable under close scrutiny. Another, more extreme, option is to set the muscle up to mimic real muscle motion, which entails connecting the muscle across multiple joints. This means the muscle and tendons have to deform with the rotations of the bones and expand and contract as they would normally. The following tutorials outline three different muscle setups using the bicep muscle as an example. These techniques are described in order of complexity, starting with the most basic.

TUTORIAL

BICEP MUSCLE 1

Step 1: Load the "Bicep_Muscle" scene file from the CD-ROM.

ON THE CD

Step 2: Select the bicep muscle and freeze all of the transformations.

Step 3: Make the muscle a child of the humerus bone, and freeze the transforms again. Freezing the transforms now allows the bicep to inherit the transforms of the humerus. The humerus is inheriting the transforms of the IK bone, which are in proper alignment for scaling the bicep muscle outward.

Step 4: Switch to Dynamics and make the bicep a passive rigid body.

Step 5: With the bicep selected, open the Expression Editor. Type the following expression and rename it Bicep:

```
BicepLft.scaleZ=ForearmLft.rotateZ/100+1;
BicepLft.scaleX=ForearmLft.rotateZ/–300+1;
BicepLft.scaleY=ForearmLft.rotateZ/200+1;
```

This expression connects the scale values of the bicep to those of the rotating joint of the forearm. In dividing the values, the influence of the rotation is minimized. Adding one returns the scale values back to their default settings.

Step 6: Test the expression by moving the arm's IK handle. The results are shown in Figure 14.11.

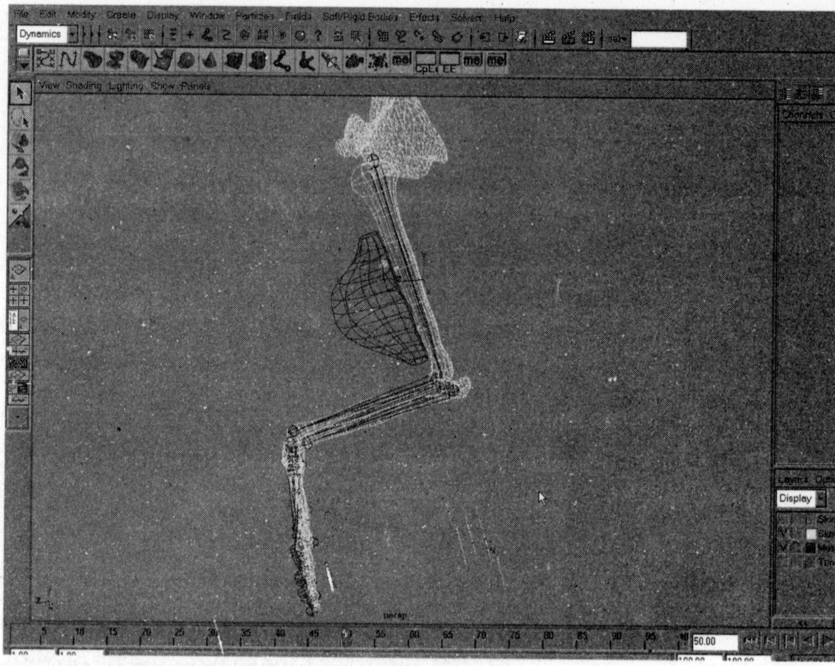

FIGURE 14.11 The bicep muscle flexes based upon the rotation of the rotating forearm.

The bicep is ready to be applied to the skin.

TUTORIAL

BICEP MUSCLE 2

With this setup, the muscle mimics the contraction and expansion effects of a real muscle.

Step 1: Load the "Bicep_Muscle2" scene file from the CD-ROM.

ON THE CD

Step 2: Select the bicep muscle and freeze the transforms.

Step 3: Draw an IK chain the length of the muscle consisting of three joints in the front view. Place one joint at the start of the muscle, another in the middle of the belly, and the last at the end. In the side view, translate and rotate the joints so they run parallel to the bicep muscle.

Step 4: Create another bone in the side view. Draw it from the middle joint to just outside of the belly as shown in Figure 14.12. Move this bone in the front view so it sits on top of the first chain drawn.

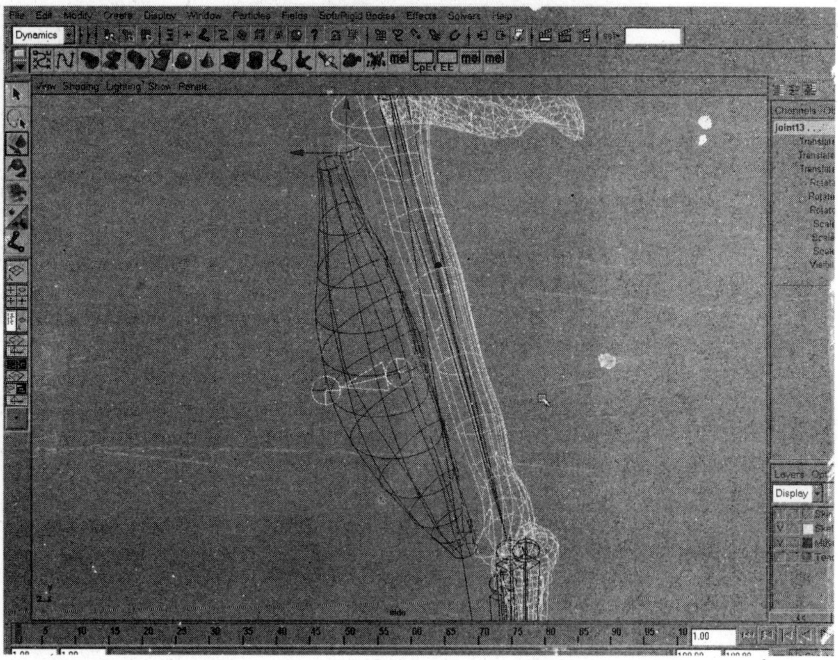

FIGURE 14.12 Draw a third bone from inside the muscle out.

Step 5: Select the root of the new chain and make it a child of the middle joint. This automatically creates another bone between the two. This is necessary to allow the protruding bone to be scaled independently. Select the root of the entire chain. Freeze the transforms and reorient the axes with the joint mel script.

Step 6: Switch to Dynamics and make the bicep a passive rigid body.

Step 7: Select the parent of the chains and the bicep muscle and switch to the Animation module. Open the Smooth Bind options box from the Skin/Bind Skin pull-down menu. Bind to the complete skeleton with the closest distance method. Change the Max Influences to 3 with a dropoff rate of 2. These values depend on distance. You might have to modify them to fit the scale of your joints and geometry.

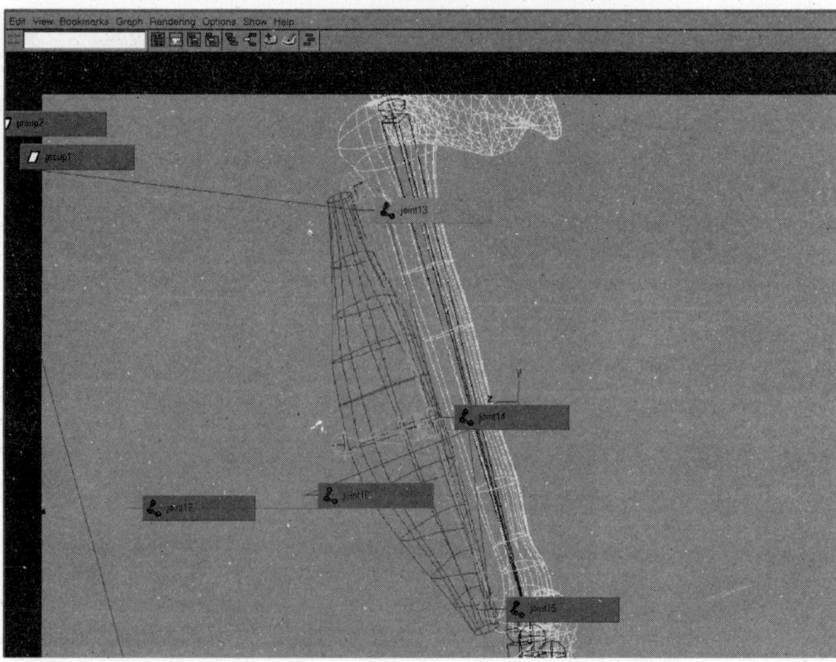

FIGURE 14.13 This is the hierarchy for attaching the bicep to the humerus.

Step 8: Select the chain root and group it to itself two times. Group is under the Edit pull-down menu. Select the top of the group and make it a child of the humerus. Figure 14.13 shows what the hierarchy should resemble.

Step 9: Open the expression editor and type the following expression. Use Figure 14.13 for reference to the joint names. Figure 14.14 shows the muscle fully contracted.

```
joint13.scaleX=ForearmLft.rotateZ/-300+1;
joint16.scaleX=ForearmLft.rotateZ/100+1;
joint16.scaleZ=ForearmLft.rotateZ/200+1;
```

FIGURE 14.14 This is the bicep muscle fully contracted.

The bicep is ready to be applied to the skin.

TUTORIAL

BICEP MUSCLE 3

This muscle setup deforms the muscle and tendons across two joints and is the closest to simulating the action of a real muscle.

Step 1: Load the "Bicep_Muscle3" scene file from the CD-ROM.

ON THE CD

Step 2: Draw IK joints from the scapula to the inside edge of the radius. Create a total of four joints or four bones: an IK bone for the connecting origin of the muscle, two bones in the belly with a centered joint, and another bone for the insertion at the radius. Rename the joints, starting at the scapula, "BicepJnt1" through "BicepJnt5." Use Figure 14.15 as reference.

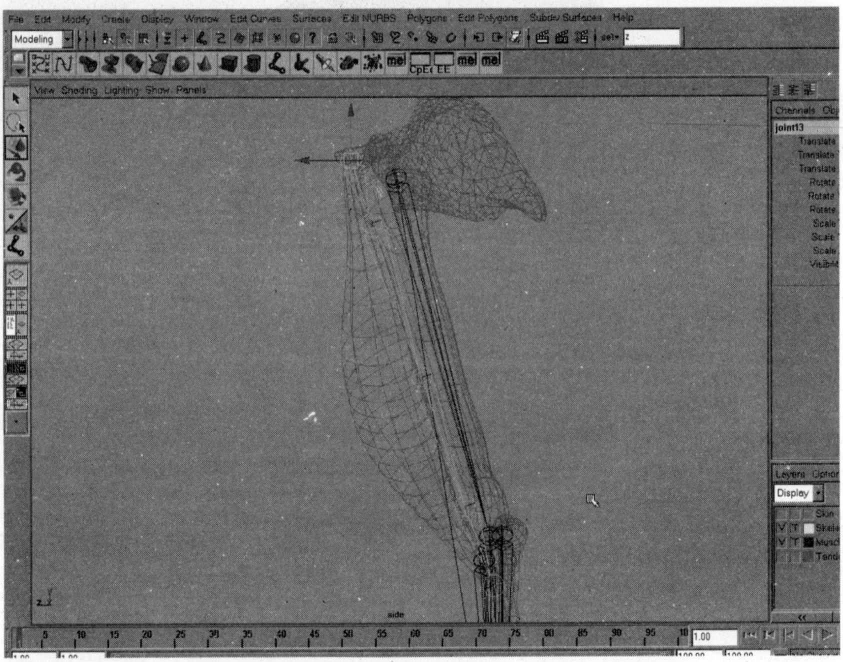

FIGURE 14.15 Draw four bones inside the bicep.

Step 3: Draw another bone in the side view from the middle joint inside the belly of the muscle out. Move the IK-skeleton to the center of the belly. Parent the root of the new IK system to the middle joint or BicepJnt3 as shown in Figure 14.16. Freeze the transformations and reorient the joints.

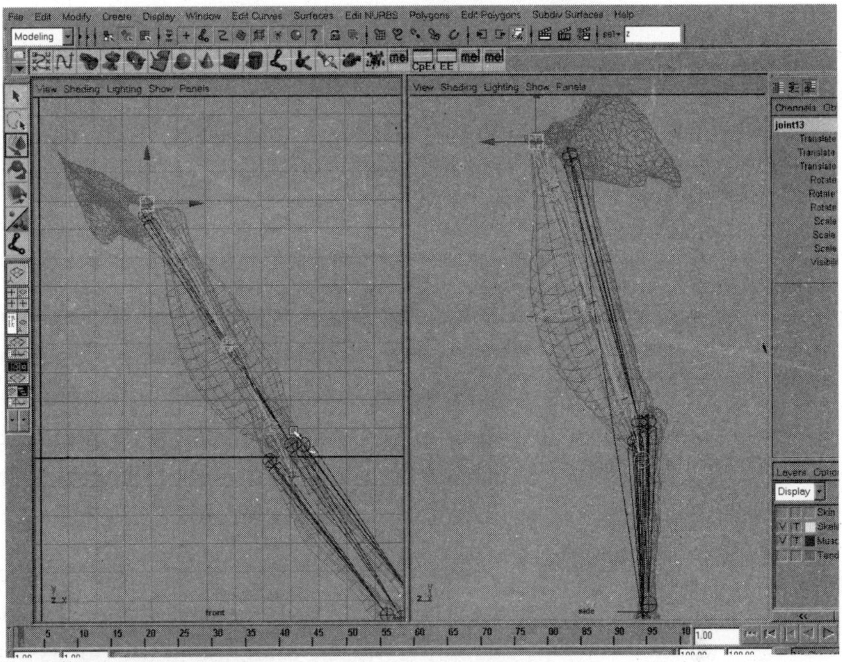

FIGURE 14.16 Parent another joint to the middle joint on the existing IK system.

Step 4: Freeze the transforms and delete the history of the muscle. Check the surface normals to confirm they are facing out, and make the muscle a passive rigid body.

Step 5: Select the IK skeleton and the muscle, and open the smooth bind options. Change the settings to Complete Skeleton and Closest Distance. Change the Max Influences to 3 with a dropoff rate of 1 and bind the muscle.

Step 6: Under the Skeleton pull-down menu, choose the IK Spline Handle Tool. Using the default settings, pick the root, then the joint connecting to the radius. The handle generates a curve to manipulate the joints. The handle itself does not cause the joints to rotate except if you use the twist and roll options.

Step 7: Using the Outliner or Hypergraph, select the curve created by the IK Spline Handle Tool. Switch to the component editor. If you used the default settings, the curve has four CVs. Select the first CV at the scapula. Open the Create Cluster Tool options box under the Deform pull-down menu. Use the default settings and create a cluster handle for the first CV. Parent the handle to the scapula.

Step 8: Select the next CV and assign a cluster handle to it. Parent the handle to the humerus bone. This automatically creates a group node for the handle to preserve the handle's position. This could be done manually by grouping or parenting the cluster handle prior to making it a child of the humerus bone. Repeat this process for the third CV.

Step 9: Select the last CV and assign a cluster handle to it. Parent the cluster handle to the radius bone. The four cluster handles keep the muscle attached to the bones in four locations. The muscle now moves and deforms with the actions of three bones: the scapula, humerus, and radius.

Step 10: In real life, the bicep muscle contracts, causing the forearm to rotate. In order to accomplish this digitally, you need to do the reverse. As the forearm rotates in the Z-axis, the bicep muscle needs to contract and expand to preserve its volume, giving it realism. Open the expression editor and type the following expression:

```
BicepJnt6.scaleX=ForearmLft.rotateZ/100+1;
BicepJnt3.scaleY=ForearmLft.rotateZ/150+1;
```

```
BicepJnt2.scaleX=ForearmLft.rotateZ/-500+1;
BicepJnt4.scaleX=ForearmLft.rotateZ/300+1;
BicepJnt4.scaleZ=ForearmLft.rotateZ/150+1;
```

The scalings of BicepJnt2 and BicepJnt4 in the X-axis mathematically cancel each other out. BicepJnt2 pulls the muscle up, while BicepJnt4 pushes the tendon back down, keeping it locked to the radius bone.

Step 11: For heightened realism, add a twist to the end of the bicep muscle. Select the IK spline handle and rename it "BicepTwist." Add the following line to the existing expression:

```
BicepTwist.twist=WristLft.twist/2;
```

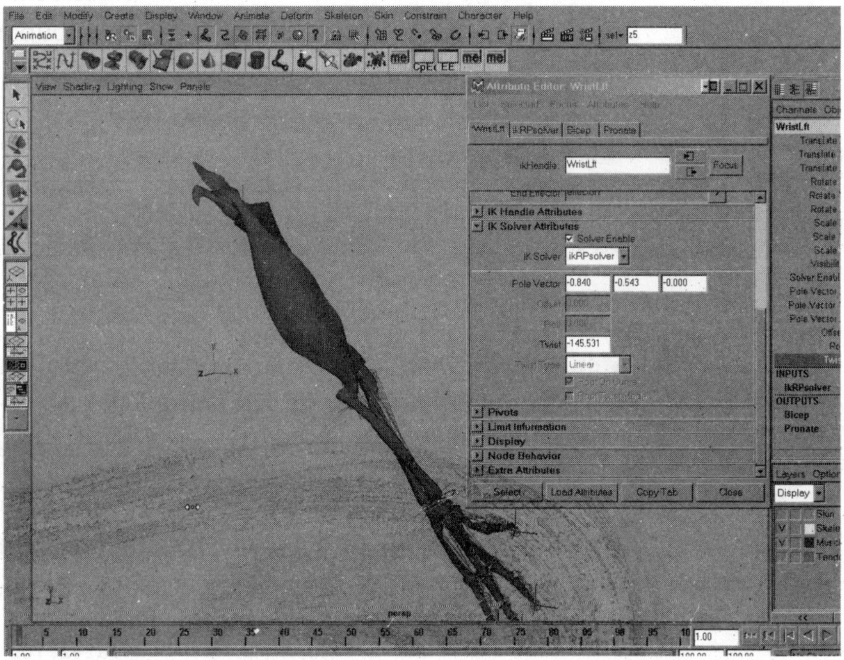

FIGURE 14.17 The bicep muscle now twists with the rotation of the radius.

Open up the attribute editor for BicepTwist, and click on the IK Solver Attributes tab. Change the twist type to ease in. Select the WristLft handle, and in the channel box select the twist attribute. Move the mouse into the view and with the middle button pressed slide the mouse from left to right. Use Figure 14.17 for reference.

SIMULATING TENDON MOTION

Tendon setup is similar to the extreme muscle setup, except tendons do not expand or contract. They act as levers between muscles and bones. They do, however, deform with the bones as the bone rotates. For the majority of the tendons in the body, a simple setup is not enough. The majority of visible tendons cross joints and move in a way that can only be accomplished by attachments to multiple bones. The following tutorial explains this method.

TUTORIAL

HAND TENDON

Step 1: Load the "Hand_Tendon1" scene file from the CD-ROM.

ON THE CD

Step 2: Draw an IK system in the side view by placing a joint at every bend in the hand. Position the IK skeleton in the tendon as shown in Figure 14.18. Remember to freeze the transforms and reorient the joint if you reposition it.

Step 3: Make a Spline IK handle from the root to the tip of the joint.

Step 4: Select the resulting curve and open the tool options for Rebuild Curve found under the Edit Curves pull-down menu.

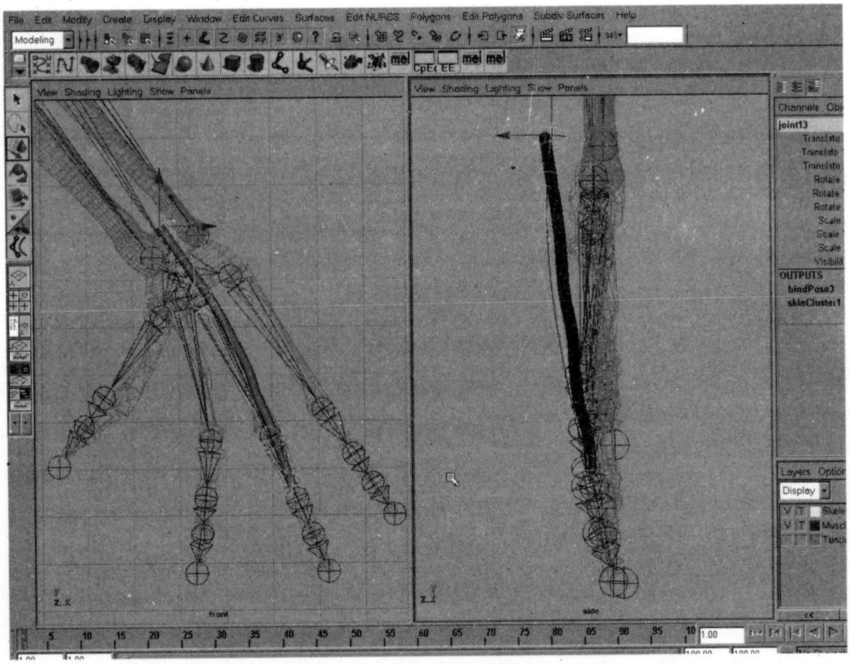

FIGURE 14.18 Place the IK skeleton inside the tendon.

Use the default settings and change the Number of Spans to 2. This gives the curve a total of five CVs.

Step 5: Select the tendon. Freeze the transforms and make the tendon a passive rigid body.

Step 6: Smooth bind the tendon to the chain using three influences and a dropoff rate of 2.

Step 7: Create a cluster handle for each CV in the curve of the spline handle.

Step 8: Parent the first two handles to the radius. The third handle is parented to the wrist or the carpal bones. Cluster handles 4 or 5 get parented to the first bone of the ring finger.

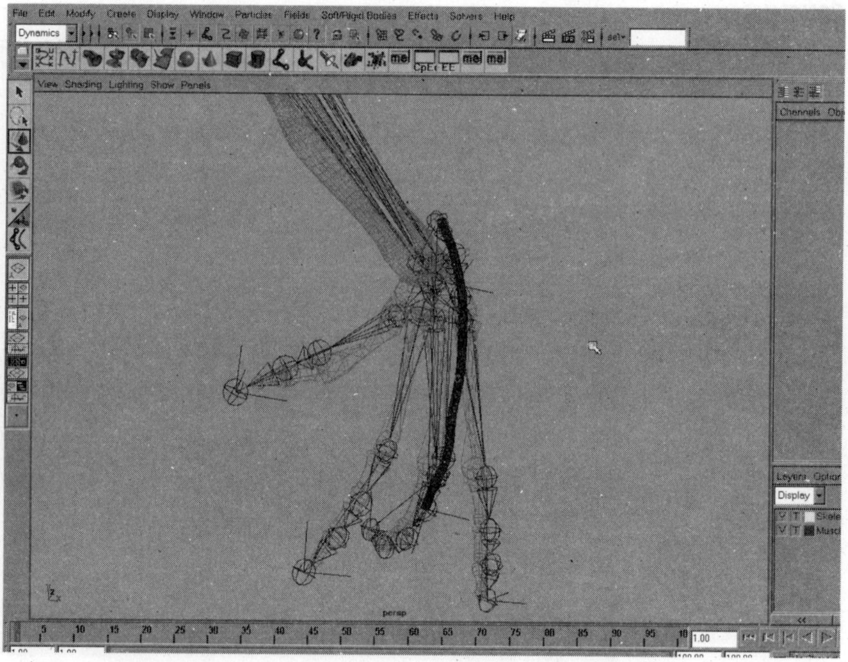

FIGURE 14.19 The fully rigged tendon and its resulting deformation.

Step 9: Open the expression editor and add the following expression to the fourth cluster handle:

```
cluster4Handle.translateZ=RngLft2.rotateZ/80;
```

The expression pushes the tendon out slightly when the finger bends. With the cluster handles, it is easier to vary the degree of protrusion through some simple expressions.

Step 10: Test the deformations by moving the wrist IK handle. You can achieve different effects by resampling the number of spans in the spline handle's curve. The fewer CVs in the curve, the more play the chain has, which might be more desirable. Figure 14.19 shows the deformation effects in the tendon.

CONCLUSION

Any one of the three setups described above can be used for muscle control. It is important to remember that if you are binding a muscle to IK, you should make the muscle a passive rigid body prior to binding. If you are simply parenting the muscle, then make it a passive rigid body after the parent-child relationship has been established. Muscle motion can be animated through a variety of expressions. The ones used in the above tutorials are basic expressions to get the muscle up and running. They can be replaced easily with more complex math for smoother deformations and action.

Muscles are the most prominent deforming objects under your creature's skin. The process of creating a working muscle can get confusing. The following checklist helps bring it into perspective.

1. Shape the muscle based upon the skin's surface.
2. Rebuild the muscle to make the geometry uniform.
3. Move the seam to the back of the muscle.
4. Delete the history.
5. Freeze the transforms.
6. Orient the direction of the surface normals.
7. Make the muscle a passive rigid body.
8. Skin with a smooth bind.

Up to this point, you have only set the stage for skin deformation. In the next chapter, you will apply the rigid-body anatomy to the skin and give the skin properties.

CHAPTER

15 THE DYNAMICS OF LIFE

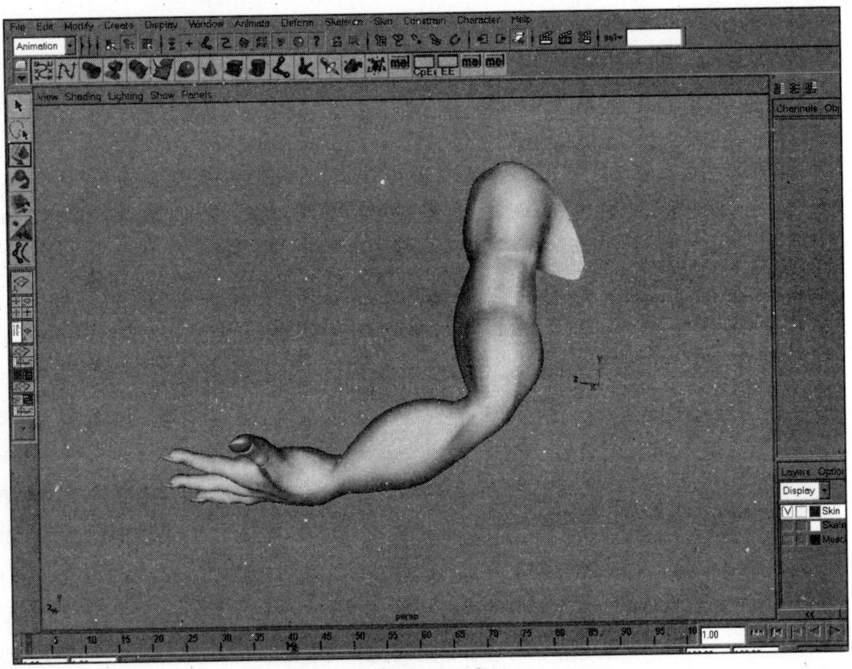

In the past two chapters, you built bones, muscles, and tendons. These parts were given the default properties of a passive rigid body, which allows geometry to collide with other rigid bodies or with particles. Other rigid bodies are merely obstacles to be set in motion; however, they do not deform. To create skin, you must make your character's model a soft body. This adds a particle to every vertex or CV on the assigned geometry. The particle drives the vertex or CV based upon dynamic simulation in Maya.

THE SKIN

Digital skin is dependent on several factors working together and is very similar to modifying normalized weights. When you add a value to a vertex, values are subtracted from the other weighted vertices. In a sense, you cannot modify one without affecting the other. With digital skin, in order to define a type of skin, you must find the proper balance between attributes.

The first part in the creation of digital skin is to make the geometry a soft body. In doing so, a copy is created that serves as a goal object. The goal object retains the original shape of the skin and, in a sense, always gives the particles a place to go. Since each particle is assigned to a vertex, the geometry moves in response to a collision or field acted upon the particles. The particle shape then returns to its original position described by the goal object. To drive the skin, you bind the goal object to the IK. Animating the skeleton moves the goal object, which in turn moves the particle object. The bound skin requires little setup because all of its deformations come from the rigid-body anatomy.

At this point, you have skin that jiggles. However, it jiggles as a whole and not in individual locations, making it look like a large Jell-O sculpture. To give it form and function, link the muscles, bones, and tendons to the particles to serve as collision objects. When these objects hit the particles, the particles react, giving us the illusion of a muscle bulging under the surface of the skin. Collision detection is a very sensitive thing that works best if the geometry of the colliding object (muscles, bones, and tendons) is greater than that of the surface skin. If the skin geometry is too high, every little detail shows through. Although this sounds perfect, it tends to reveal too much, usually in the form of popping triangles or collapsing geometry.

The following tutorial takes you through the creation of skin. Add the attributes to your character or practice with the Fire Monster's arm.

TUTORIAL

MAKING SKIN

Step 1: Load "ArmSkin1" from the CD-ROM. The scene file contains the Fire Monster's arm geometry and the bicep muscle from the Bicep Muscle 3 tutorial. All of the geometry, except for the arm, consists of passive rigid bodies. Turn the skeleton and muscle layers off.

ON THE CD

Step 2: Select the arm and switch to Dynamics. From the Soft/Rigid Bodies pull-down menu open the tool options for Create Soft Body. Change Create Options to Duplicate, make original soft. Check Hide non-soft object and Make non-soft a goal. Apply the settings.

Step 3: Hide the original geometry. In the Hypergraph or Outliner, select the copy and unhide it.

Step 4: Select all of the joints except those in the bicep, the last joint of every chain, and the joints of the radius and ulna. This is a total of eighteen joints. Shift-select the arm geometry and switch to Animation. Open the Smooth Bind options under the Skin/Bind Skin pull-down menu. Change the Bind To setting to Selected Joints and the Bind Method to Closest Distance. Then use 5 for the Max Influences and Dropoff Rate. Apply the settings.

Step 5: Test the deformations to make sure they are smooth. This bind is supposed to be generic. You want the detailed deformations to come from under the skin. Raise the arm and rotate the wrist. The deformations don't have to be perfect, just relatively smooth; any imperfections can be fixed later. Before addressing binding problems, you first want to attach the muscles and bones. These collision objects shape the skin for you. By trying to correct any deformation issues now, you could destroy the natural effects of the skin. Figure 15.1 shows an example.

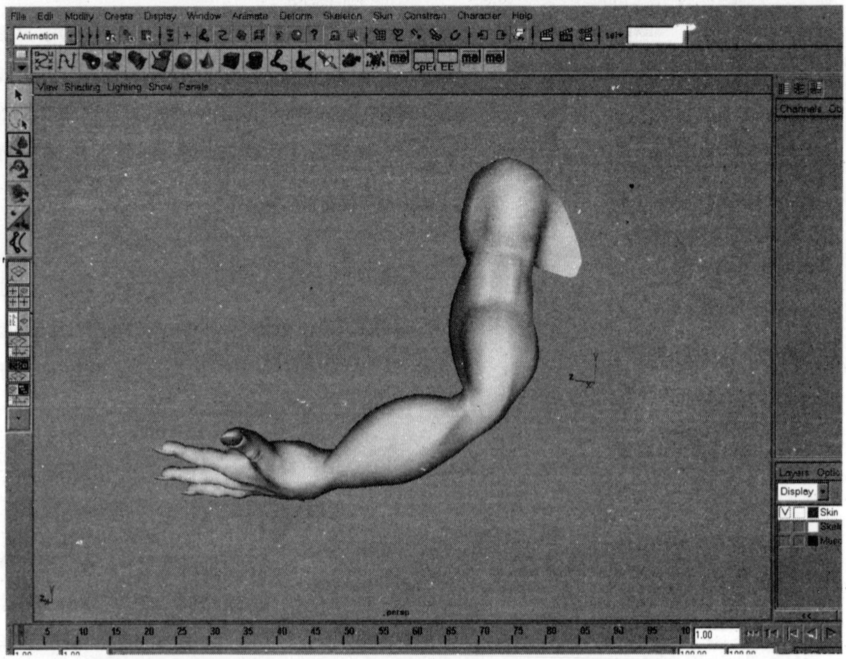

FIGURE 15.1 Test the generic bind by moving the arm and wrist IK handles.

Step 6: Hide the copy and unhide the original. In the Hypergraph or Outliner, select the particle node of the arm. In the channel box change the Goal Smoothness to .1 and the Goal Weight to 1.

Goal Weight—Determines how fast the skin returns to its original position. This is basically the elasticity of the skin. A value of 0 tells the skin not to follow the original geometry or goal. A value of 1 tells it to follow it exactly. Anything in between causes the skin to jiggle as it moves.

Goal Smoothness—Determines how soft the transition is from skin position to goal position. With a goal weight of .5, the skin lags behind the current position of the goal. Instead of moving linearly toward the goal, the smoothness causes the skin to speed up and slow down based upon its proximity to the goal.

These two might sound identical; however, if the Goal Weight is set to 1, the Goal Smoothness has no effect. This is because the skin is already in its final position. Another way to think of these two attributes is to say the Goal Weight controls the elasticity and the Goal Smoothness controls the strength of the elastic; the stronger the elastic, the greater the bounce.

It is possible to apply per-particle skin weights. This allows you to paint weights for the skin, adding jiggle only in certain areas. Painting weights allows you to define the skin's attributes at every location, heightening realism. This effect can be used for loose skin. It could also be used for fat; however, this takes away some of the reality of our creature. Fat deposits are actually collected masses of cells under the skin and take on their own properties. This is discussed fully in the next chapter.

Step 7: The Fire Monster has little to no loose skin. However, if your character does, add it at this point before any muscles or bones have been attached. To practice, add some loose skin to the back of the Fire Monster's arm. This effect won't look natural on this creature because his geometry wasn't modeled to incorporate any loose skin. To add weight on a per-particle basis, select the geometry and choose the Paint Soft Body Weights Tool options from the Soft/Rigid Bodies pull-down menu. The geometry turns solid white. If you do not see any change in the color, open the Display tab in the tool settings window. Check the Color Feedback. Under the Paint Attributes tab change the value to .3. In the perspective window, orbit the camera to the back of the arm. Hold down B on the keyboard to scale the size of the brush stroke. Paint a line on the surface as shown in Figure 15.2. After you paint a stroke, click Smooth under the Paint Attributes tab and smooth out the edges of the stroke. This gives the area a nice falloff, preventing hard-edged deformations.

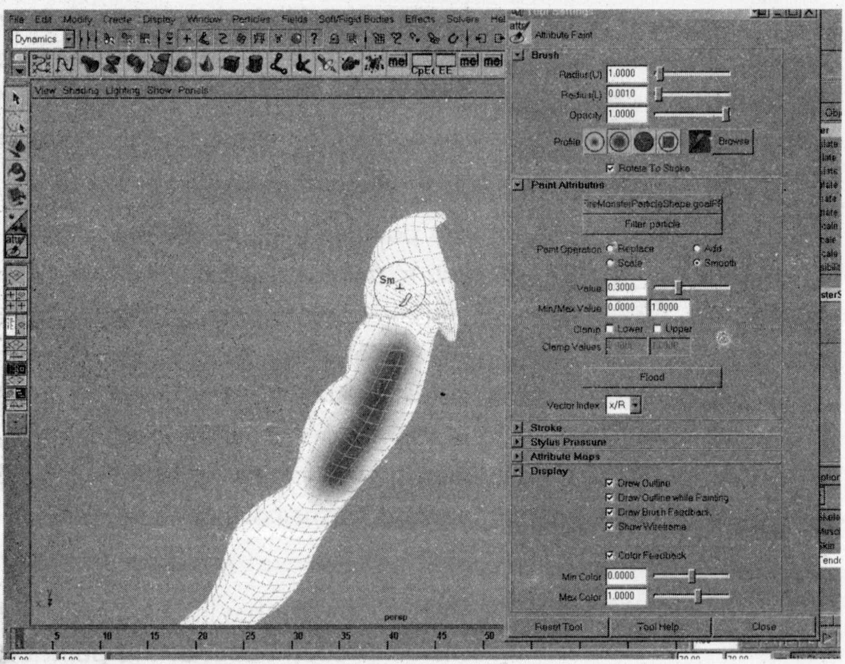

FIGURE 15.2 With the Paint Soft Body Weights Tool, you can alter the thickness of the skin or sagginess of the skin.

ON THE CD

Step 8: In Step 7, it was stated that the Fire Monster has no loose skin. This is true; however, there are areas in most creatures containing more blood, tissue, and minimal fat deposits or, simply put, softer skin. In addition, when muscles are at rest, they bounce slightly against the skin, causing some surface jiggle. These areas could be defined with a skin weight texture map. Figure 15.3 shows the painted weights over the muscle areas. These weights were painted with a value of .8 and smoothed with a value of 1. This provides a slight jiggle to the skin when the arm's motion stops abruptly. You could import this map from the CD-ROM by opening the Attribute Maps tab in the tool options of the paint tool. Choose the Import tab and then click the Import button.

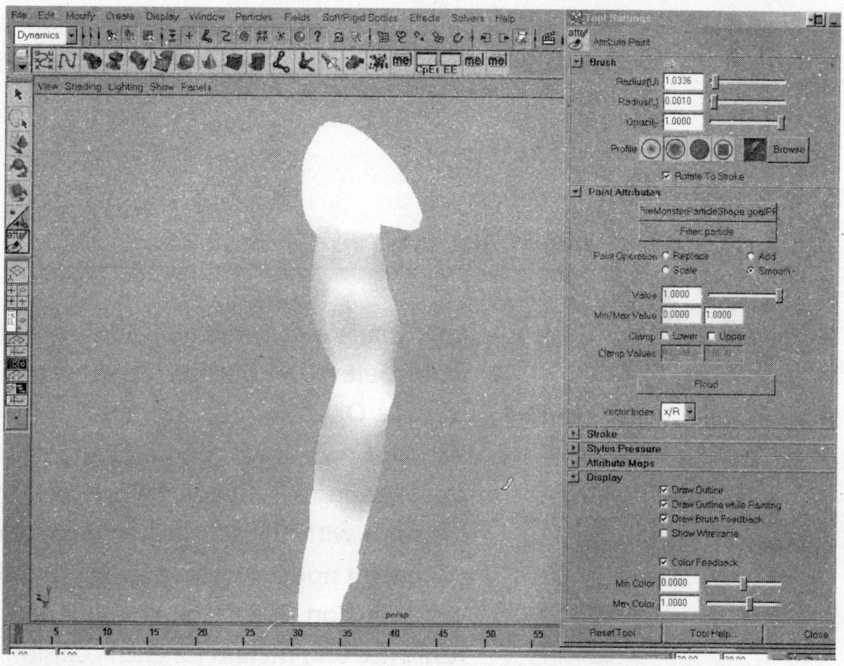

FIGURE 15.3 Values have been painted in certain areas of the arm for a slight skin jiggle.

Step 9: Select the particle node of the soft body. Change the Goal Smoothness to 1 and the Goal Weight to .8. This gives the skin a subtle bounce only in the area painted. Playblast the animation.

It is important to remember that your creature's skin is a dynamic simulation, and it must adhere to all of the procedures and properties of running a simulation. If you are unfamiliar with the inner workings of dynamic simulations, take some time to learn their functionality.

DEFORMING THE SKIN WITH ANATOMY

The elasticity and thickness of the skin is established; it's now time to add the anatomy. Muscles drive the majority of the skin deformations. Practice on the Fire Monster by adding the bicep muscle in the following tutorial.

TUTORIAL

ADDING ANATOMY

Step 1: Load the Maya scene file "Adding_Anatomy" from the CD-ROM. Select the particle object and Shift-select the bicep muscle. Open the tool options for Make Collide under the Particles pull-down menu. Change the Resilience to 0 and the Friction to 1. Apply the options. The bicep muscle now interacts with the skin. When you create a collision, a geoconnector node is created as an input to the soft-body particles. Click on this in the channel box. You can modify the resilience and friction for each collision.

ON THE CD

Tessellation Factor—Increases or decreases the amount of triangles used to collide with the skin. Adding a high value increases simulation time and collision accuracy. If your collision objects are basic shapes, reduce this number or leave it at about 200 for better performance.

Resilience—Describes how the skin will rebound off the muscle. A value of 0 allows collision without the particles of the skin bouncing off it. Chances are this will always be 0. Skin really doesn't bounce off of muscle or bone.

Friction—Describes the velocity and direction of the reflecting skin particle. A value of 1 bounces the particle straight off of the collision object. However, with a resilience of 0, the particle doesn't bounce, but rather continues in the direction of the colliding object. If you lower the Friction to .2 and have a Resilience of 0, the skin will appear to slip off of the muscle or colliding object. Muscular characters should have a high amount of friction to keep the shape of the skin in the shape of the muscle. The tighter the creature's skin, the higher the friction.

Step 2: Test the deformation effects by animating the arm with keyframes. Make sure to hide the arm geometry or turn its layer off before setting any frames. Collision detection is done as a simulation; therefore, it must be solved at every frame. If it isn't allowed to do this, the model might blow apart. This can be corrected by returning to the first frame on the time slider. Animate the arm as if it were curling a weight, and then turn off the muscle and skeleton layers and turn on the skin layer. Play through the time slider or render as a playblast. Figure 15.4 shows the final frame of the arm.

Step 3: Select the bones one by one and assign them as collision objects to the particles. It is possible to add all of the bones at once under a single geoconnector node; however, doing this eliminates the ability to modify the collision attributes for each bone.

Step 4: Turn on the tendon layer, and select the particle node and the tendon geometry. From the Particle pull-down menu

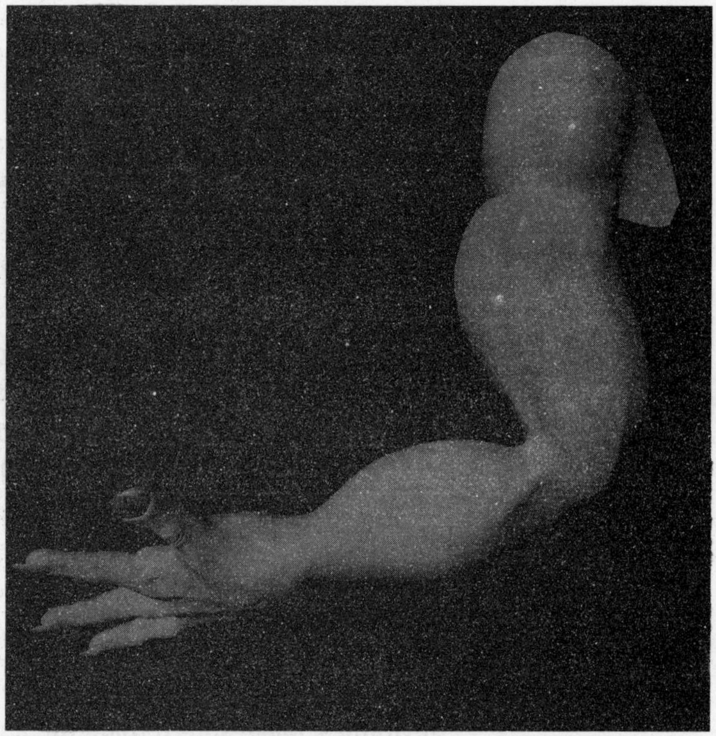

FIGURE 15.4 The arm has been animated into this final pose.

choose Make Collide. Set the attributes to a Resilience of 0 and a Friction of 1.

Step 5: Return to the first frame of animation. Select the ArmLft IK handle, and break all of the connections in the channel box to remove the animation. Select the WristLft IK handle, and break its connections as well.

Step 6: Animate the ring finger folding into the palm and a little movement to the wrist in order to get the tendon to move. Turn the skin layer off for better performance.

Step 7: Frame the tendon in the perspective view. Hide all of the layers except for the skin. Playblast the animation.

NURBS surfaces work best for the underlying anatomy, but they are not necessary. Regardless of the type of geometry, the probability is high for it to penetrate the skin. This is of no concern as long as the skin is deforming. When you render or test the skin deformations, simply hide the anatomy.

It is important to remember that the skin can only deform based upon its geometry. This is good and bad. If the skin only has a few faces, the deformation might look blocky. At the same time, if you increase the amount of faces, the skin can actually pick up too much detail and deform perfectly. This sounds good, but it is actually bad. What happens is that the skin wraps tightly around the muscle, eliminating all interpolation between surrounding vertices and giving the appearance that the skin has no elasticity. The vertices on either side of the muscle can also slip underneath it. By having less geometry, the skin is forced to taper the effects of anatomy deformations, making for a more realistic form.

Add muscles to your character's skin one at a time, and test each one as you go. The muscles often need to be tweaked to deform the skin properly. After you add a new muscle, test it with the effects of the old muscle to make sure they work together.

Wrinkles

Regardless of age, skin exhibits wrinkles. These defining lines can be modeled directly into the creature or painted in the texture map. However, wrinkles are not always visible. Sometimes the skin has to move before a wrinkle is exposed. In order to achieve this digitally, springs are used as connective tissue. The tissue runs between the skin and the underlying anatomy. When the skin folds, the connective tissues hold or pull the skin. By connecting springs from the soft-body particles to locations on the modeled muscle or bone, the same effect can be achieved.

Springs can be tricky. If the values of a spring are set too high, they can bounce themselves out of Cartesian space. You must find the proper balance between the number of springs and their individual strength. The attribute to control this delicate balance is the Stiffness, which determines how rigid a spring is. The more springs created, the less stiffness needed. However, it is not a one-to-one comparison. It is not true to say that one spring is equivalent to five springs with respective stiffness. Five springs will always have a greater influence than one. Springs are created between points. Each point can radiate a spring to every adjacent point causing a greater force in multiple directions, whereas one spring can only apply force in a single direction. Figure 15.5 shows spring disbursement on a simple object.

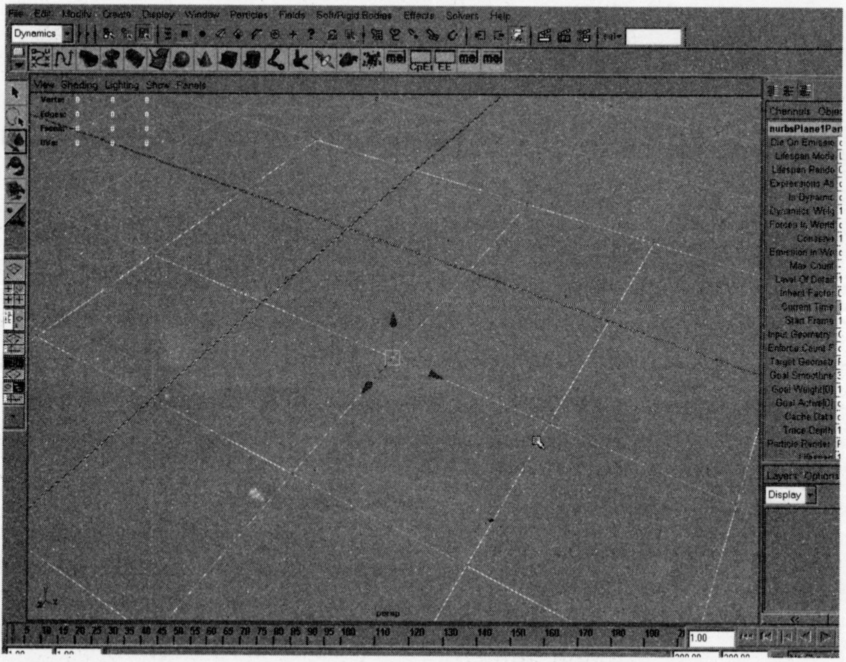

FIGURE 15.5 This shows multiple springs being connected to all of the vertices.

TUTORIAL

WRINKLES

Step 1: ON THE CD Load the scene file "Wrinkles.mb" from the CD-ROM. Select a row of vertices where the wrinkle is to be placed, and then select vertices on an object underneath the wrinkle to attach the connective tissue or springs. It is best to try to select as many vertices as possible within a suitable range of the wrinkle. The more vertices you can include, the stronger the connection will be.

Step 2: From the Soft/Rigid Bodies pull-down menu open the options for Create Springs. Use the default settings, but change the Creation Method to All. This setting draws a spring between all pairs of selected points. Apply the settings.

Step 3: In the Channel box change the Stiffness value based on the amount of springs. Start with a value of 300. Hide the Dynamics in the current window by unchecking them from the Show pull-down menu. Play through the time slider beginning at frame 1, and watch the wrinkle area closely. As soon as you see the springs begin to bounce uncontrollably, stop the animation. Return to frame 1 and lower the Stiffness by one hundred units. If the springs don't bounce, raise the attribute. Continue this process until you find a workable value. Figure 15.6 shows a single wrinkle added to the Fire Monster's wrist.

ON THE CD Wrinkles are a subtle effect and can get lost easily in bad or flat lighting. If you are having a problem seeing the effect, relocate the camera or change the lighting setup to increase the contrast before adjusting any of the spring attributes. Located on the CD-ROM in the folder for Chapter 15 is an animation and corresponding scene file of an existing wrinkle. Play the animation to see the wrinkle effect on the Fire Monster's wrist.

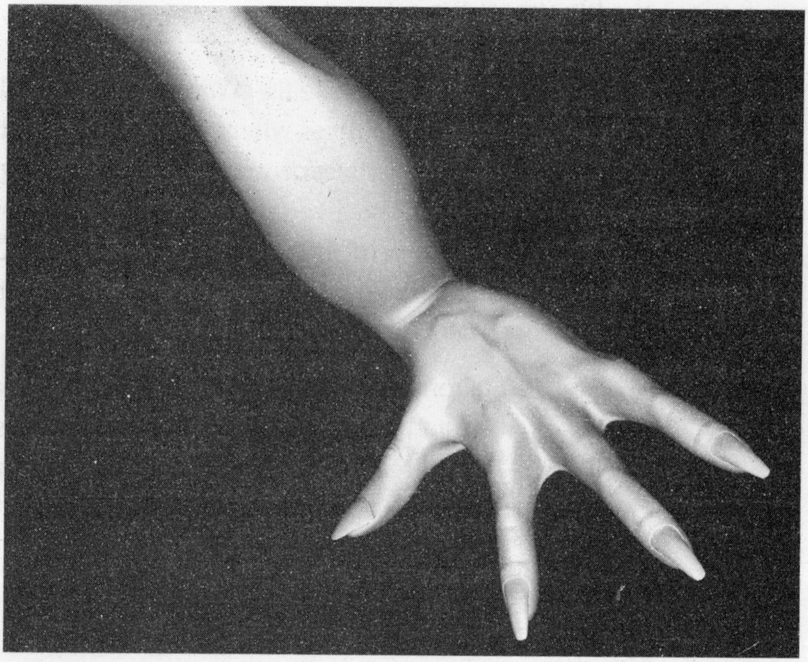

FIGURE 15.6 This is an example of one wrinkle added to the Fire Monster's wrist.

Springs can add amazing detail to your character's skin. They are costly, however, and should be used sparingly. Multiple wrinkles in the same area can be achieved as long as you leave enough space between them. Leave three or four rows of vertices unconnected to allow them to push against the spring-attached area. Without unattached vertices separating two wrinkles, the effect gets lost. Figure 15.7 shows an example of poor wrinkle spacing. This would produce little to no results.

Try to keep wrinkle setup as simplistic as possible. There are very few attributes to modify in the spring that affect the wrinkle positively. Adding per-spring values overcomplicates the effect with little benefit. It would also take forever to modify the hundreds of springs generated. To support the final look of the wrinkle, paint a defining line in the color map.

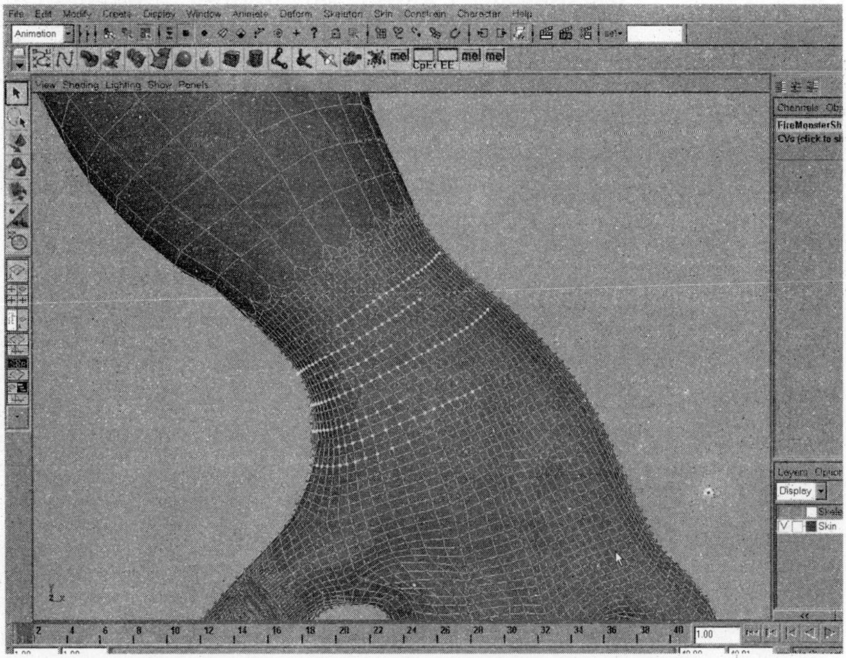

FIGURE 15.7 Adding springs to the vertices selected has no effect because of the lack of space between each desired wrinkle.

Conclusion

Understanding the attributes of the individual Maya tools and how they correlate to skin is key to successfully setting up your creature. Experiment with one attribute at a time to grasp its effect. The following chart offers a quick reference to the Maya attributes and the effect they give in relation to skin. The attributes are listed in application order.

Soft Object—The deforming skin

Goal Object—Smooth-bound original shaped skin; causes the skin to return to its original position

Goal Weight—Skin elasticity or thickness

Goal Smoothness—Elastic strength

Resilience—Controls the amount of rebound or bounce; best set to 0
Friction--Roughness of the underlying anatomy
Stiffness—Connective tissue rigidity

In the next chapter, yo.. will add the last element of the anatomy to your creature—fat deposits.

CHAPTER

16 FAT

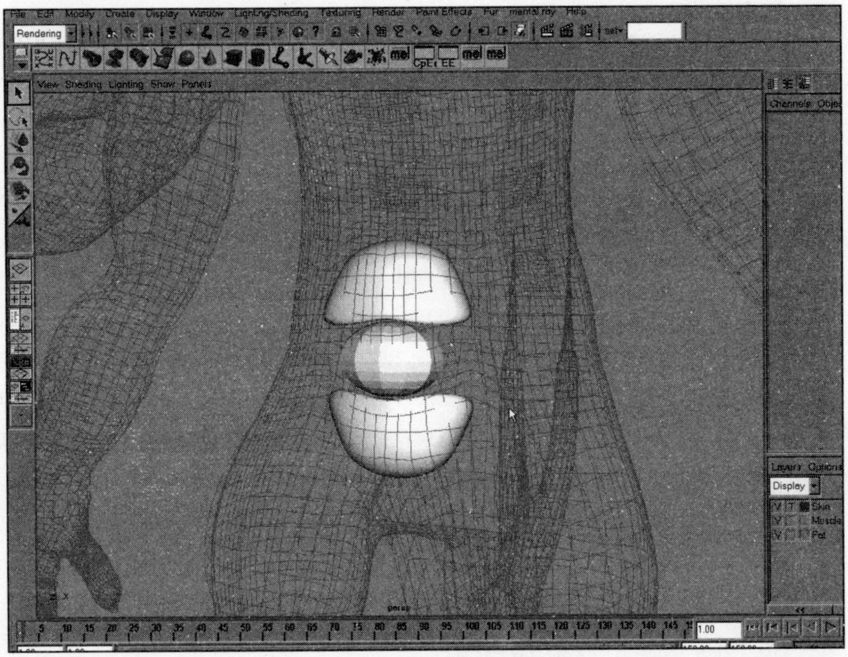

Your creature is close to completion, but one thing remains—fat. All creatures, great and small, have fat deposits. However, these only need to be modeled or added to the character if they are of a certain size because minor jiggle is picked up in the skin. What you want to focus on is the large, blubbery type of fat. These are highly visible and should have already been shaped into your creature's skin.

Creating Fat Deposits

Fat should be smooth and rolling; the model itself should appear soft. Real fat, or subcutaneous fat, sits directly under the skin and doesn't move independently of it. Instead it is connected to the skin and directly influences it.

When the fat model is finished, it becomes a soft body just like the skin. However, instead of standing on its own, it is bound to the skin's goal object. This creates a solid connection and causes the hidden goal object to jiggle. This motion is then translated to the soft-body skin during simulation. The Goal Weight and Goal Smoothness of the fat soft body control the motion of the fat. The motion is then assisted by the addition of springs. As an example, the following tutorial goes through the process of building a fat body in the belly of the Fire Monster.

TUTORIAL

Fat Deposit

Step 1: Load the scene file called "Fat_Deposit.mb" from the Chapter 16 directory on the CD-ROM. The scene file contains the soft-body Fire Monster rigged with a generic smooth bind. The current geometry is the goal object, or copy. There is also a muscle layer that contains two rigid-body objects. Create a primitive polygon sphere with twelve subdivisions

ON THE CD

around the axis and along the height. Scale it proportionately to fit inside the creature's belly (Figure 16.1). Since it is going to be bound to the goal object through a smooth bind, the fat can sit outside of the geometry. It does not need to fit perfectly. Rename the sphere "FatBody," and delete the history and freeze the transforms.

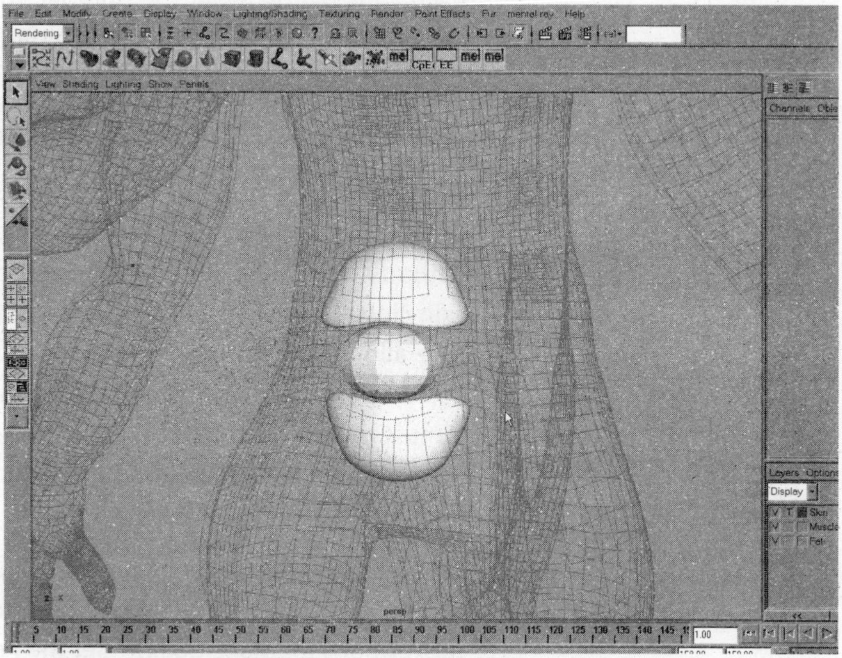

FIGURE 16.1 A primitive polygon sphere is placed in the belly of the Fire Monster.

Step 2: Select FatBody and make it a soft body. Use the Duplicate Make Original Soft setting. In the Channel box change the Goal Smoothness to 3 and the Goal Weight to .6. These operate just as they do with skin.

Step 3: Select the copy of the Fire Monster, which is the goal object to the Fire Monster's skin, and then select the original FatBody node. Go into the Animation module. Under the Skin pull-down menu select Edit Smooth Skin and open the tool settings for Add Influence. Change the Dropoff rate to 10. The Dropoff controls how quickly the influencing object's power decreases. The higher the number, the faster the numbers fall based upon their distance from the influence object. Set the Polygon Smoothness to 1. This affects the amount of weight applied to each vertex—the lower the number, the greater the weight. These values work together just as NURBS surfaces do.

Step 4: Select the copy of FatBody or goal object and make it a child of joint25.

Step 5: Turn on Use Components under the Skin Cluster tab. This can be found on any object that has been bound, such as the FatBody or joint30. All of the bound objects use the same skin cluster node, so you only need to modify one. This feature allows the components, or in this case the individual control vertices of the fat belly, to influence the bound skin. It must be turned on because soft bodies affect geometry at a component level. If it is not turned on, the fat deposits have no effect.

Step 6: Select the Particle node of the FatBody, and Shift-select the top muscle. From the Particles pull-down menu open the tool options for Make Collide. Set the Friction to .7 and apply the settings. Repeat this procedure for the other muscle.

Step 7: Hide everything in the scene except for the muscles and fat. Play through the time slider to see the results. The fat bounces in between the two rigid-body muscles.

Step 8: The deformation effects on the FatBody are acceptable, but they lack a weighted jiggle. Real fat hangs off the body and displaces its own weight. To achieve this effect, add springs to the FatBody. Select the FatBody node and open the tool options for Create Springs from the Soft/Rigid Bodies pull-down menu. Change the creation method to wireframe and the wire walk length to 3. The walk length expands the amount of springs created based on the value entered. The higher the value, the more springs are created between each vertex. This creates a stronger fat body.

Step 9: In the Attribute editor change the Stiffness to 150 and the damping to 0.

Step 10: Hide all of the objects except for the Fire Monster's original skin. Play the animation to test the results.

As demonstrated in the tutorial, to further the effects of the fat body, place rigid bodies above and below it to restrict its motion. The rigid bodies do not have to be muscle groups. They could be justified as folds in the skin or restrictive clothing, such as a belt. Adding springs adds jelly-like properties to the fat. Change the wire walk length with the wireframe creation method to alter the density of the fat. The rigid bodies and springs drastically alter the shape of the fat body, simulating a fat roll as seen in Figure 16.2.

Another advantage to the rigid bodies is that they can act as a constraint to the top and bottom of the fat body. Scale or move vertices from the ends of the fat body inside each of the rigid bodies as shown in Figure 16.3.

The particles of the fat body collide with the interior of the rigid body holding them in place. This allows you to increase the Goal Smoothness to 4. Figure 16.4 shows the results.

CONCLUSION

Play with the number of springs added to the fat body and the stiffness of the springs to achieve different looks. If you increase the number of springs, you need to decrease the stiffness. Test the

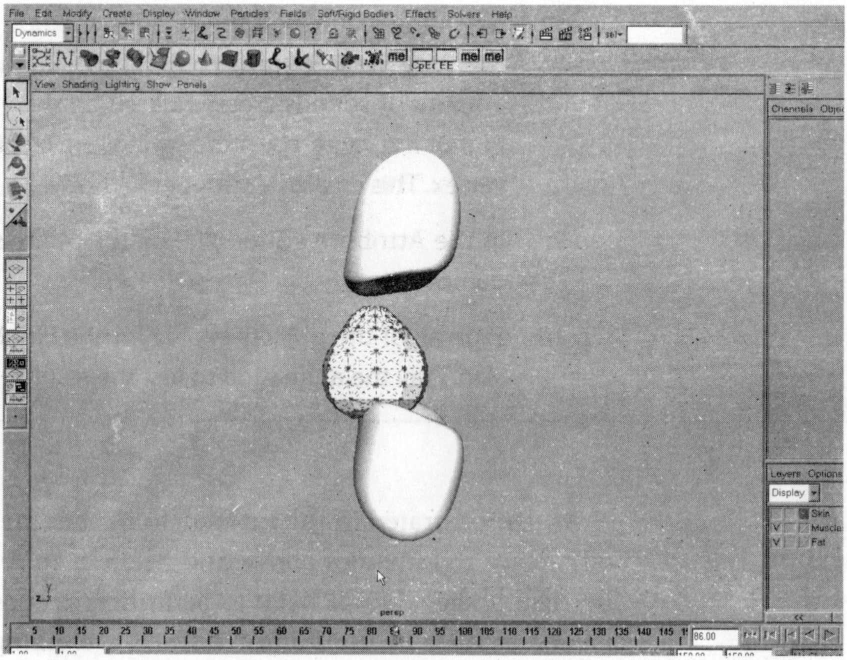

FIGURE 16.2 Using rigid bodies and springs, you can create the effect of a fat roll.

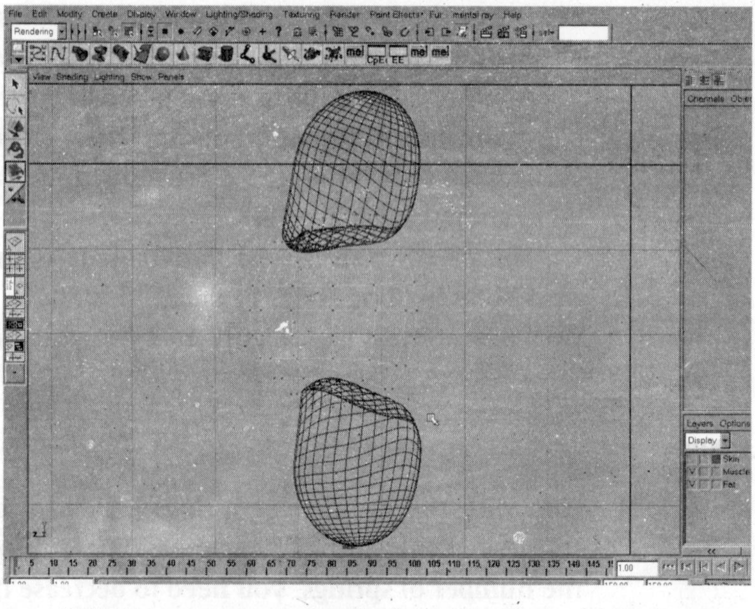

FIGURE 16.3 Move the ends of the fat body inside the rigid bodies.

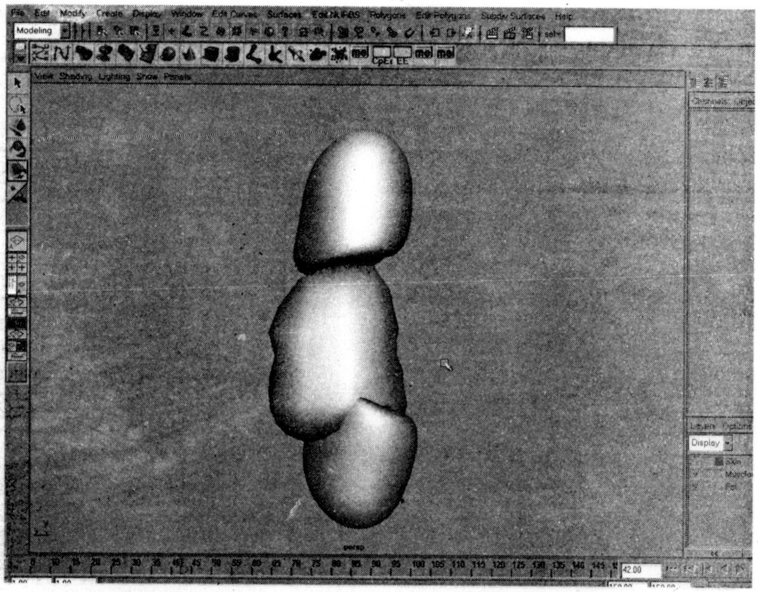

FIGURE 16.4 This is the result of a Goal Smoothness of 4.

simulation after every change to make sure you have valid numbers. Springs make it quite obvious when you enter a value they do not like. This might be indicated by your creature's bouncing out of control or off of the screen.

There are other tools in Maya to add fat or jiggle to your creature. The difference is that by assigning it to the goal object, you get a layered realistic effect. The fat retains its own properties and can be modified separately from the skin. In addition, the properties of the skin influence the jiggle of the fat. Therefore you could have thick, heavy skin with a layer of fat underneath it.

Fat should be used sparingly in most creatures. Not because it is expensive, but because most creatures don't have large deposits of fat. Some characters may not require any at all; for small areas of jiggle, just paint soft-body weights as discussed in Chapter 15.

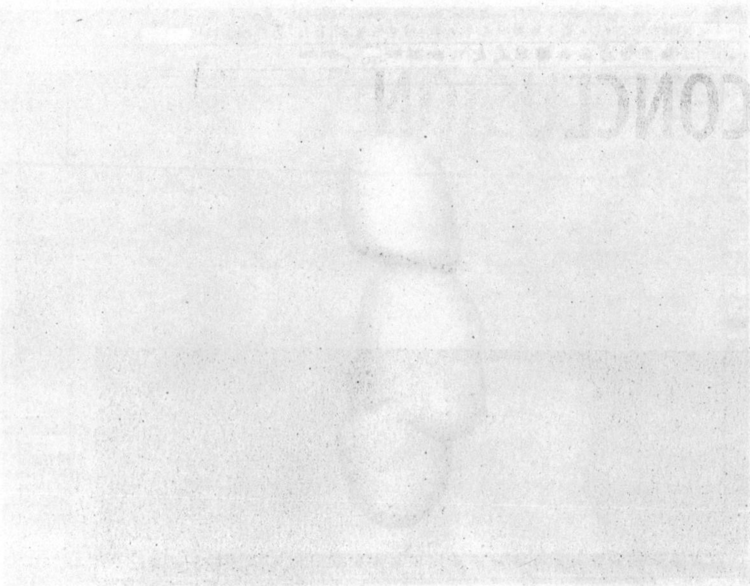

PART

VI CONCLUSION

CHAPTER

17 WRAPPING IT UP

This concludes the creation of a feature creature. The procedures and results outlined in this book can be difficult, challenging, and at times seem incomprehensible. Stick with it; the results are well worth it.

These techniques and tools are still in their infancy. The possibilities are endless. The procedures and explanations in this book are just a foundation. They can easily be expanded upon to create stunning effects based upon real physics.

Think in terms of reality. When in doubt, search it out. Reproduce reality and don't let the tools dictate your methods. These tools are not like a hammer and nail; you need to predict the result in order to use them properly.

TROUBLESHOOTING

With any complex system, problems do arise. Adding one muscle to the skin is relatively trouble free. Most creatures are going to have a hundred or more muscles. This makes managing the character difficult, and getting feedback becomes daunting and slow. The following is a list of common problems and fixes.

Problem: The skin is jagged and rough when it deforms as shown in Figure 17.1.

Solution: Smooth the geometry of the underlying anatomy. Patches and faces should all be quadrangular and uniform.

Problem: The skin only reacts to part of the rigid-body anatomy. Figure 17.2 shows an example of the bicep muscle affecting only part of the skin.

Solution: This problem is typical with NURBS surfaces. Rebuild the surface to change the parameterization to uniform and add more isoparms. Check to make sure they are evenly spaced. It might be necessary to reloft the muscle.

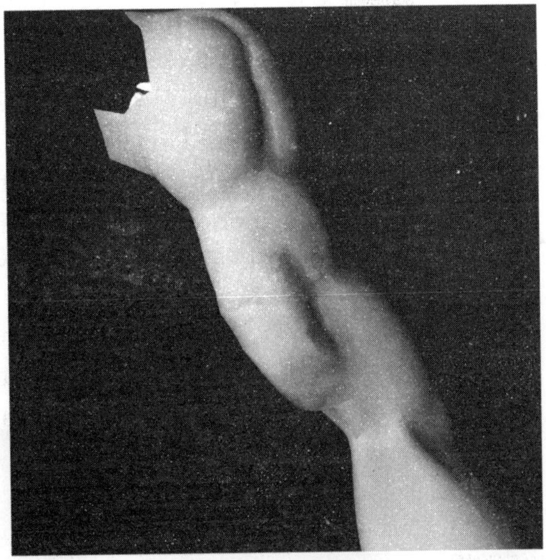

FIGURE 17.1 This is the result of bad muscle geometry.

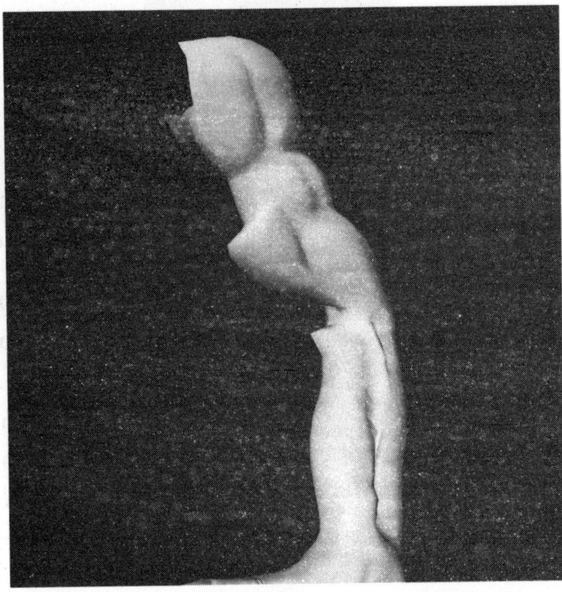

FIGURE 17.2 Collision detection can fail with a NURBS surface if it is poorly parameterized.

Problem: The skin slips under a muscle, bone, or tendon as shown in Figure 17.3.

Solution: This can happen for several reasons. The edge of the rigid body could be too sharp, catching a row of vertices. Simply smooth or round the surface. Another reason is the rigid body may be scaling or animating out too far, blocking a row of vertices. To fix this, reduce the amount of scale or limit its flexing in the problem axis.

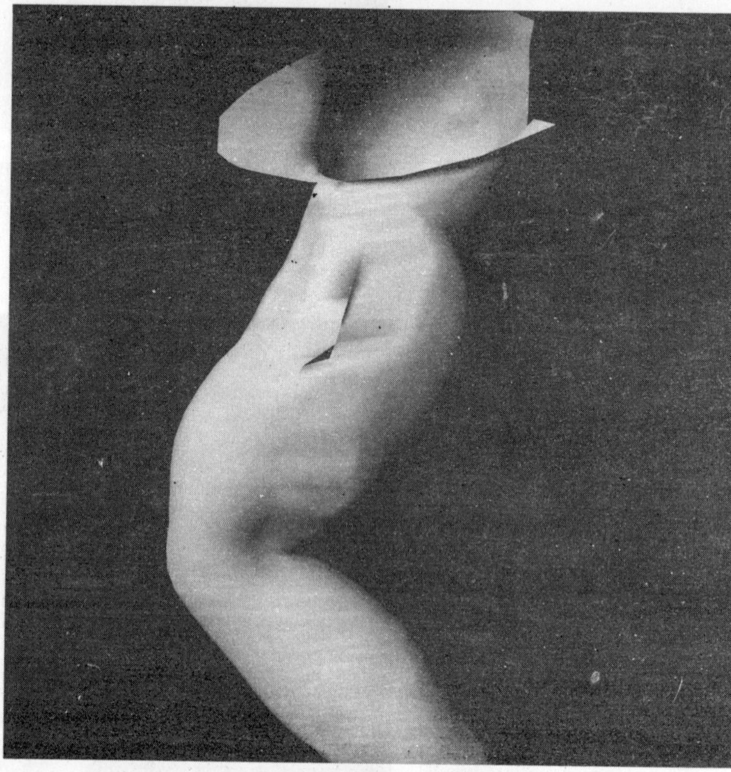

FIGURE 17.3 The skin geometry is caught on the edge of the bicep muscle.

Problem: Rigid-body anatomy flies out of the skin or away from its assigned hierarchy as shown in Figure 17.4.

Solution: This occurs from the transforms not being frozen properly. Remove the rigid body and unparent the object, then reposition it. Freeze the transforms and assign it as a child to the appropriate group. Freeze the transforms again and then make it a rigid body.

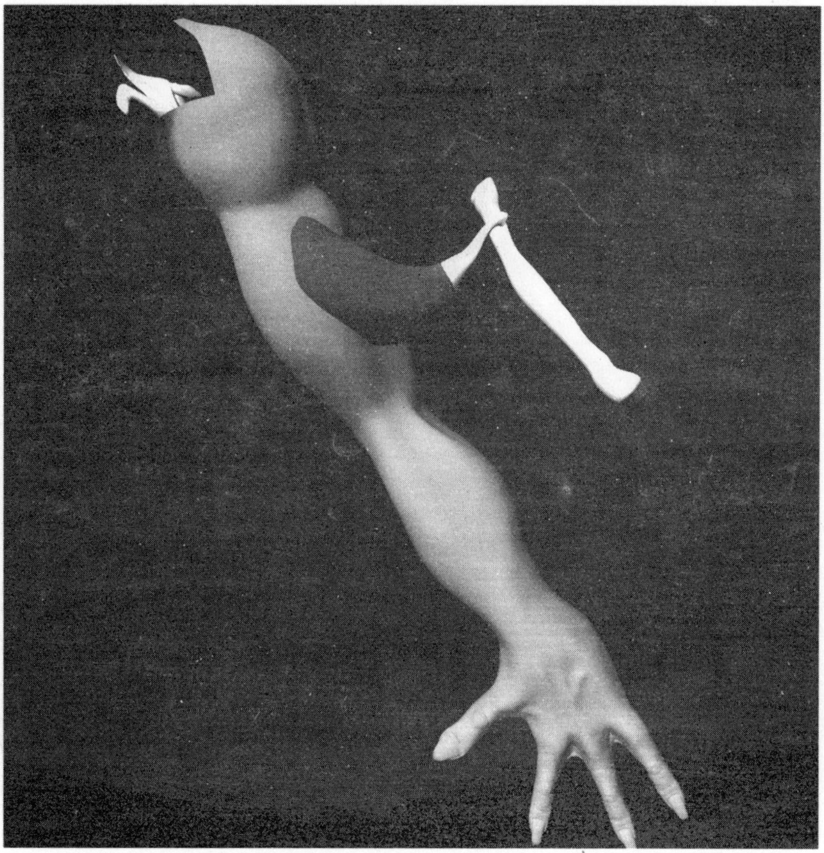

FIGURE 17.4 This shows a bone automatically positioned outside of the skin as a result of the transforms not being frozen.

Problem: The skin suddenly reacts at the beginning of an animation or motion as shown in Figure 17.5.

Solution: This is basically surface shock. It happens because the skin is a simulation and it needs time to ramp up. To correct this, add a few frames in the beginning to give the simulation a chance to settle in. Also make sure none of the rigid bodies are being animated without a little bit of ease in or slow initial ramping values. Even fast motion in the real world has a slight ramp up. The problem is that the computer is much faster.

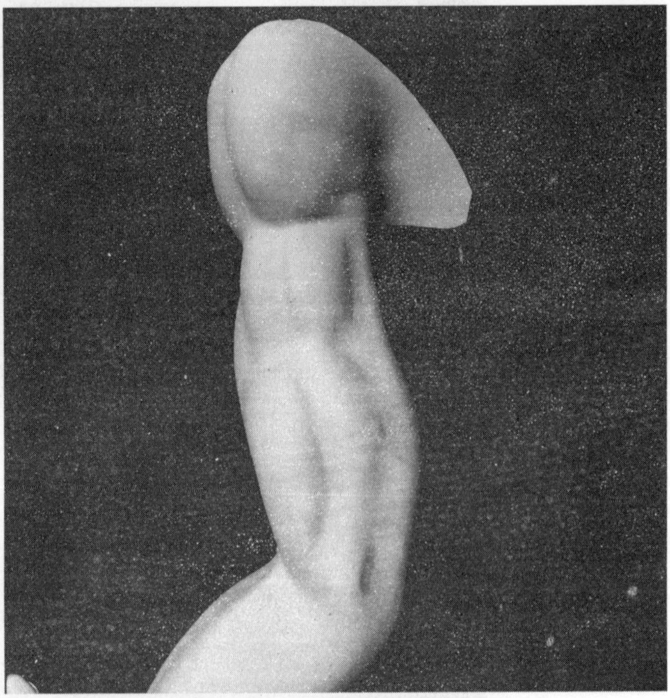

FIGURE 17.5 This shows an example of surface shock at the first couple of frames of animation.

Problem: When adding fat, the skin of the creature flies off the screen or bounces uncontrollably. Figure 17.6 shows an example.

Solution: This happens because the fat body is influencing too many vertices on the skin. Reduce the amount of influence when adding the fat body to the skin by modifying the Dropoff and Polygon smoothness values.

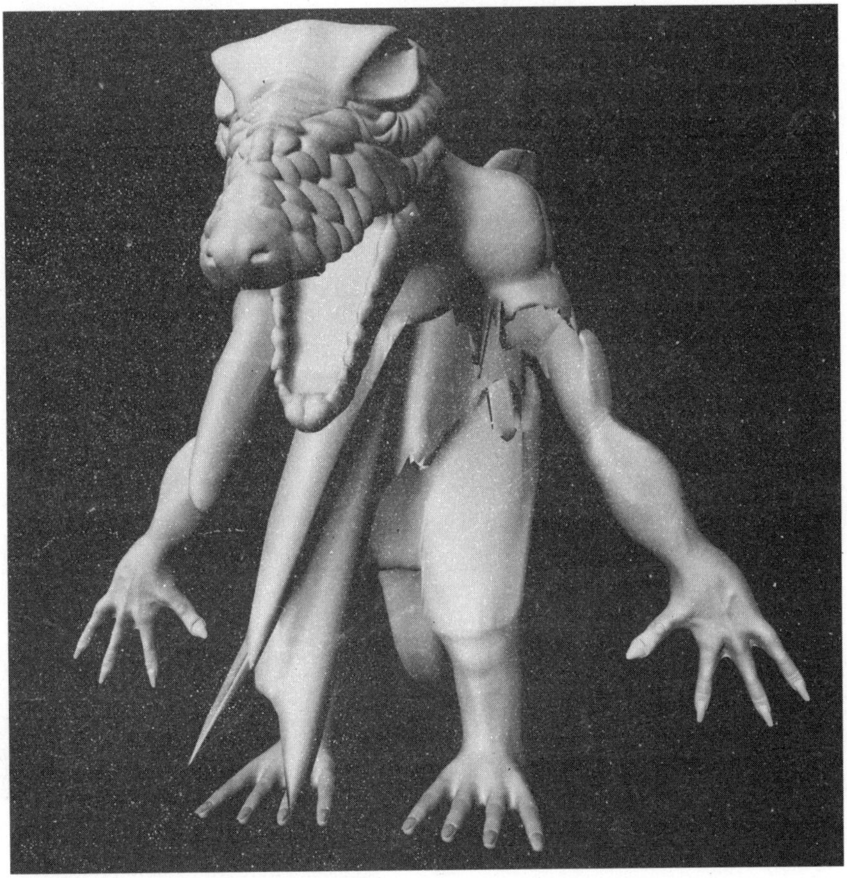

FIGURE 17.6 This shows the skin bouncing uncontrollably, a result of too large an influence.

Future Endeavors

Like any good feature, there is always a sequel. Technology moves fast; for the latest updates and to see the Fire Monster in action, visit *http://www.speffects.com.*

APPENDIX

ABOUT THE CD-ROM

This CD-ROM contains files to help you build a feature creature. The CD-ROM is broken up into chapters, and each folder contains files relevant to the chapter. Some of these folders, which are listed below, include before-and-after Maya scene files while others contain raw data. Be sure to check the system requirements contained in this document.

- CHAPTERS: Each chapter folder on the CD-ROM corresponds to a chapter in the book. The folders contain tutorials, images, and animations. Many have Maya scene files to allow you to work along with the tutorials. Most of these scene files come in two parts; the first part is named after the tutorial and is set up based on Step 1 of the lesson, and the second part is the completed tutorial and the appropriate results.

System Requirements

- Intel Pentium III, Intel Pentium 4, or AMD Athlon 1 GHz processor or better is recommended.
- Windows 2000 or Windows NT 4.0 or later (256 MB RAM)
- 100 MB+ of available hard disk space
- 24-bit or better video display card
- Maya 4.0 or higher
- Windows Media Player
- Adobe Photoshop
- Please visit *http://www.aw.sgi.com* for specific requirements and specifications for Maya.

INDEX

A

Age
eyes and, 216
fat deposits and, 44–45
physical attribute changes and, 52–53
Anatomy, 35–45
bones and joints, 288–290
connective tissue, 45–46
eyes, 216
fat, 43–45
female *vs.* male, 44–45, 52–54
muscles and tendons, 40–43
skeletons, 38–40
skin layer, 36–38
veins, sculpting tutorial, 111–112
Armatures
mounting on platforms, 86–89
tools required to build, 68–69
tutorial on building, 69–96
wire to build, 67
Assets
names and naming conventions, 25–27
organization and management of, 24–31
Attach Surfaces options of Edit NURBS menu, 149–150
Attribute editor, 280–281
Attributes
Friction attribute, 346
Goal Object attribute, 345
Goal Smoothness attribute, 335, 345
Goal Weight attribute, 335, 345
Resilience attribute, 346
skin, effects of attributes on, 345
Soft Object attribute, 345
Stiffness attribute, 346

B

Ball-and-socket joints, 289
Bi-axial joints, 39
Bicep motion tutorials, 317–326
Bind poses, 31–32
Biology
common features and evolution of life, 34–35
physical design and evolutionary forces, 52–54
see also Anatomy
Birail tool, 144–147, 198, 201
Blend method of Attach Surfaces, 149–150
Bones
arm bone tutorial, 193–198
connecting, 302
leverage and, 39
rigid-body bones tutorial, 302
size of, 192
skeleton model of, 192
skull modeling tutorial, 198–205
see also Skeletons
Brainstorming sessions, 20–21
Brushes, 65
saving, 261–262
Budget, 22
Bump maps, 271–275

C

Calipers, 65–66
CD-ROM, contents, 366
Characters, development of, 20–21
Chord-length parameterization, 167
Claws, modeling and skinning, 226–231
Clays

cracking during drying, 130–132
oil-based clay, 60
oil- *vs.* water-based clays, 94
polymer clay, 61–62
for sculpting, 58–61, 102–103
Cleanup tool, Polygons menu, 184, 189–190
Clone tools and cloning, 266
Collision detection, 195
bone size and, 192
jagged points and, 40
muscle motion and, 311
Collisions, creating, 338–339
Color maps, 252–260
Component mode, entering, 175
Computers
"housekeeping" and organization, 23, 28–29
system requirements, 366
Control vertices, 139–143
CV control tool, 139–143
Coordinates, models and symmetry, 28
Creases. *See* Wrinkles
Crease tools, 213–214
Create Cluster tool, Deform menu, 324
Cut UVs option of Polygon menu, 187
CV control tool, 139–143
CV curve tool, Create menu, 193–194

D

Default poses, 31–32
Defenses, skeletal structure and, 38–39
Deformations
anatomy and deformation of digital skin, 338–342
Deform menu, 324
testing with animation, 339–340
Deform menu, 324
Dental tools, 62–63
Detach Surfaces option of Edit NURBS menu, 148–149
Diffuse maps, 267–268
Directories, absolute and relative paths, 31
Displacement height tutorial, 276–281
Displacement maps, 275–284
Distortion of textures, 162–163
checker pattern to reveal, 237–238
UV placement and, 163
Duplicate tool for mirroring, 201–202

E

Edges
converting to, 239
removing hard edges, 281
Edit Curves menu, 201
Edit NURBS menu options
Attach Surfaces option, 149–150
Detach Surfaces option, 148–149
Rebuild Surfaces option, 150–151
Edit points, 167
displaying, 141
Edit Polygon menu, 177
Environment, physical attributes and, 52–54
EP Curve tool, 144
Evolution, 34–35
Exoskeleton, modeling, 209
Extruding, 176
Eyes
modeling tutorial, 216–222
size and environment, 53

Eye sockets
  modeling, 201–204
  skinning, 218–220

F

Fat, 43–45
  anatomical information, 348
  fat deposit tutorial, 348–352
  jiggles, 45, 351–353
  simulating motion of, 351–353
  troubleshooting tips, 363
Feet
  sculpting in clay, 126–129
  SubD modeling of, 179–181
Fingernails, modeling and skinning, 226–231
Fingers, modeling bones for, 198
Friction attribute, 346
Friction for collisions, 338–339

G

Gender
  fat deposits and, 44–45
  physical attributes and, 52–54
Global Stitch tool, 147
Goal Object attribute, 345
Goal Smoothness attribute, 335, 345
Goal Weight attribute, 335, 345
Guide maps, 254

H

Hair
  hairy skin, 37
  UV placement and, 236
Handles, 324
Hands
  anatomy of, 222
  sculpting in clay, 126–129
  skinning tutorial, 222–231
  SubD modeling of, 176–178
  tendon motion tutorial, 326–328
Heads, detail in models of, 208
Highlights, 269–271
Hinge joints, 288
History option, 194
Hypershader, 253

I

Inverse kinematics (IK)
  arm construction tutorial, 292–297
  connecting bones, 302
  IK joints, 40
  IK skeletons, 42
  locators, creating, 299
  skeletal systems described, 290–292
  and transform inheritance, 317, 320
Isoparms, cleaning up after SubD, 148–151

J

Jiggles, life-like, 332–333, 337
  fat and, 45, 351–353
Joints
  ball-and-socket joints, 289
  defined, 39
  hinge joints, 288
  IK and FK joints, 40
  labeling of, 38
  pivot joints, 289

saddle joints, 289–290
Junctions, adding, 182

K

Keyboard characters, 26

L

Layers. *See* Levels (subdivision layers)
Levels (subdivision layers), 168–168, 170
detail and, 201
Lights and lighting
diffuse maps and, 267–268
for sculpting, 98
specular maps, 269–271
wrinkles and, 343
Live tool tutorial, 138–147
Birail tool, 144–147
control vertices, 139–143
CV control tool, 139–143
edit points, displaying, 141
EP Curve tool, 144
Square tool, 146
Stitch tools, 147
Loft tool, Surface menu, 193–194

M

Magnets, Snapping Magnets, 177
Maps
bump maps, 271–275
color maps, 252–260
diffuse maps, 267–268
displacement maps, 275–284
guide maps, 254
specular maps, 269–270
Maquettes
painting of, 133
steps in construction, 54–58
see also Armatures; Sculpting
Mirroring, Duplicate tool, 201–202
Modeling tools, 62–63
Models, reference sources for, 34–35
Modify, Transformation Tools menu, 217
Mold, preventing, 103
Motion
anatomy of muscles and tendons, 306
bicep motion tutorials, 317–326
simulation, 316–317, 326
skeletons and, 288–303
tendon motion tutorial, 326–328
Move and Sew UVs tool, 187–188
Multi-axial joints, 39
Multiple displacement map tutorial, 283–284
Muscles and tendons
anatomical information, 40–41
bicep motion tutorials, 317–326
digital muscles and tendons, 41–42
modeling of, 307, 329
motion and anatomy of, 306
motion simulation, 316–317, 326, 329
muscle building tutorial, 307–312
tendon building tutorial, 312–316

N

Names and naming conventions, 25–27
for directories, 31
for elements, 28–29

maximum length of, 27
special characters used in, 26–27
Unix names, 26
Non-manifold geometry, 158–161
texture mapping and, 164
Nonplanar polygons, 157, 159
Non Uniform Rational B-Splines (NURBS). *See* NURBS (Non Uniform Rational B-Splines)
Normalize UVs, 248–249
Nose, skinning tutorial, 209–216
Nostrils, skinning, 214–216
NURBS (Non Uniform Rational B-Splines)
as bones, 192, 195
compared with polygon object, 166
defined and described, 165–167
edit points, 167
Live tool tutorial, 138–147
parameterization, 167
patches, creating, 137–151
SubD tutorial, 138–147

O

Occupation, physical attributes and, 52–54
Oil-based clay, 60
Open / Close Curves, Edit Curves menu, 201
Organization methods, 22–31
CG project management, 24–31
computer housekeeping, 23
names and naming conventions, 25–27
project directories, 31
scale of projects and, 28
three-ring binders, 23–24

P

PaintFX tutorial, 260–265
Painting, maquettes, 133
Paint Soft Body Weights tool, Soft / Rigid Bodies menu, 336
Parameterization, 167
Partial Crease Edge / Vertex, Subdiv Surfaces menu, 209
Particles menu, 338
Patches, NURBS
Live tool tutorial, 138–147
SubD tutorial, 138–147
Photoshop, working with in Maya, 254–257
Physical design development, 52–54
Physics-driven skin, 15
Pivot joints, 289
Pivot points, placing, 309
Planar polygons, 157–158
Planning. *See* Pre-production
Plastic wrap, 65
Polygon menu, 184, 187, 189–190
Polygon objects
as bones, 192
defined and described, 157–158
non-manifold geometry of, 158–159
vs. NURBS surfaces, 166
vertices of, 157, 161–162
Polymer clay, 61–62
Poses, bind poses, 31–32
Pre-production
brainstorming, 20–21
budget, 22
organization methods, 22–31
sketches, 54
story development, 21

Project directories, 31
Pronation of arm, 297–302
Proxies, polygon proxies (SubD level 0), 170, 208
  described, 174
  tutorial for, 175–185

Q

Quills
  sculpting in clay, 123–124, 129–130
  SubD modeling and, 185

R

Reflectivity, diffuse maps, 267–268
Relax UVs tool, 240
Render time, excessive geometry and, 156
Resilience attribute, 346
Resilience for collisions, 338–339
Resolution
  output resolution of textures, 243–245
  tutorial on determining resolution, 245–249
  UV placement and, 236
Rigid Body tool, 205, 329
Rubber stamps, 64
  making your own, 109–111
  tutorial for maquette textures, 109–111
Rulers and calipers, 65

S

Saddle joints, 289–290
Scale, 28, 30
Scanning
  converting raw data to NURBS, 136–137
  described, 136
  laser-scanning, 136–137
  point-to-point scanning, 137, 138
Scripts, 21
Sculpting
  armatures for, 67–96
  biomechanical vein tutorial, 111–112
  "build-up" method tutorial, 103–109
  clays for, 58–61, 102–103
  cracks, preventing and repairing, 130–132
  phases in, 103
  rubber stamps for texturing, 109–111
  sockets for teeth and quills, 123–124
  step-by-step tutorial, 113–130
  steps in maquette construction, 54–58
  tools for, 61–66, 114
  working environments, 96–99
  wrinkles or creases, 117–118
Seams
  locations of, 151
  NURBS modeling and, 167
  painting out, 265–267
  UV placement and, 187–188
Sgraffito tools, 62
Shunt muscles, 41, 43
Skeleton menu, 324
Skeletons
  anatomical information, 38–39
  digital skeletons, 39–40
  endoskeletons and exoskeletons, 38–39

Inverse Kinematics (IK), 42, 290–292, 292–297
joints described, 289–290
motion and, 288–303
muscularity and strength of, 39
see also Bones
Sketching, 54
Skin
anatomical information, 36–38
anatomy and deformation of digital skin, 338–342
attributes, effects on skin, 345
digital skin, 37–38, 332–333
as dynamic simulation, 338
hairy skin, 37
on hands, 222–231
latex rubber stamps for texture, 109–111
making skin tutorial, 333–338
modeling of, 208
muscle motion and, 310
nose, skinning tutorial, 209–216
painting (per-particle) weights, 335–336
physics-driven skin, 15
springs and, 341–342, 344
troubleshooting tips, 358–363
see also Wrinkles
Skulls, modeling tutorial, 198–205
Smooth-bound objects, tutorial, 6–14
Snapping Magnets, 177
Snouts, skinning tutorial, 209–216
Soft-body objects, 38
Soft Object attribute, 345
Soft / Rigid Bodies menu, 336
Spans UV, 150–151
Specular maps, 269–270
Spines
sculpting in clay, 123–124, 129–130
SubD modeling and, 185
Spin muscles, 41, 43
Spline Handle tool, Skeleton menu, 324
Split Polygon tool, Edit Polygon menu, 177
Sponges, used in sculpting, 63–64, 115–116, 121–122
Springs
as connective tissue, 45–46
fat and, 351–353
and skin, 342
Spurt muscles, 41–42
Square tool, 146
Stiffness attribute, 346
Stitch tools, 147
Storyboards, 21
Story phase of pre-production, 21
SubD. *See* Subdivision surfaces (SubD)
Subdivision surfaces (SubD)
bone construction and, 192
converting to, 188–189
defined and described, 168–170
layers and, 170
limitations of, 170
polygon proxies (SubD level 0), 170, 174, 175–185
SubD to NURBS tutorial, 138–147
SubD tutorial, 147–151
texturing and, 236
UV placement, 170–171
Subdiv Surfaces menu, 209
Supination of arm, 297–298
Surface History Tab, 150–151
Surface menu, 193–194
System requirements, 366

T

Teeth
  sculpting in clay, 123–124, 129–130
  SubD modeling and, 185
Tendons. *See* Muscles and tendons
Tessellation Factor for collisions, 338–339
Textures and texturing
  Attribute editor and, 280–281
  bump maps, 271–275
  checker patterns to reveal distortion, 237–238
  for clay sculptures, 64
  color maps, 252–260
  diffuse maps, 267–268
  displacement maps, 275–284
  guide maps, 254
  NURBS UVs and, 168
  output resolution of, 243–245
  Paint FX tutorial, 260–265
  resolution and, 236–249
  rubber stamps to create, 109–111
  scaling of, 254
  seams, painting out, 265–267
  specular maps, 269–270
  sponges and sculpting textures, 115–117, 121–122
  stretching of warping of, 162
  Texturing menu, 253–254
  UVs and, 161–162
  UV Texture Editor, 253
Texturing menu, 253–254
3D Paint tool, Texturing pull-down menu, 253–254
Three-ring binders, 23–24
Toes, SubD modeling of, 179–181
Tools
  for armature building, 68–69
  for sculpting clay, 61–66
  see also Specific Maya tools
Transformation Tools menu, 217
Troubleshooting
  "locked" objects, 26
  tips, 358–363

U

Uni-axial joints, 39
Uniform parameterization, 167
Unix, naming conventions, 26
UVs, polygon, 161–165
  automatic mapping procedure and, 188
  Cut UVs option of Polygon menu, 187
  distorted textures and placement of, 162–163
  grouping, 164, 185, 248
  mapping tutorial, 237–243
  Move and Sew UVs tool, 187–188
  NURBS UVs, 168
  overlapping, 240
  placement of, 162–164, 185
  resolution and UV placement, 236
  roughing UVs tutorial, 186–189
  subdivision surfaces and placement of, 170–171

V

Vertices, Snapping Magnets and, 177

W

Water-based clay, 59–60, 102–103
Web addresses
  Maya specifications, 366
  updates and Fire Monster, 364
Weights
  Goal Weight attribute, 335, 345
  painting (per-particle) weights, 335–336
  Paint Soft Body Weights tool, 336
Work habits, working environments, 96–99
Wrinkles
  lighting and, 343
  modeling of, 209–214
  sculpting in clay, 117–119
  springs and, 344
  tutorial on digital skin wrinkles, 343
Wrists, modeling bones of, 196–198

Z

0 Level. *See* Proxies, polygon proxies (SubD level 0)

FIREWALL MEDIA

(An imprint of Laxmi Publications Pvt. Ltd.)

Computer Books *for School, BCA, MCA, IGNOU, DOEACC and Engineering Students and Professionals*

ISBN	TITLE	AUTHOR	PRICE	PAGES
	.NET			
8170087155	**Building Business Intelligence Applications with .Net**	Robert Ericsson	Rs. 295.00	404
8170083567	**Learning VB.Net Through Applications**	Clayton Crooks	Rs. 295.00	450
8131800865	**Magic of C# with .Net Frame Work**	Shibi Panikkar, Kumar Sanjeev	Rs. 495.00	950
8170082471	**Magic of ASP.Net with C#**	Shibi Panikkar, Kumar Sanjeev	Rs. 395.00	828
8170089662	**ASP.Net Interview Questions and Answers**	J. Rajaram	Rs. 95.00	175
	A TO Z SERIES			
8170083214	**Access 2002 from A to Z**	Julia Kelly, Stephen L. Nelson	Rs. 75.00	185
8170083222	**Excel 2002 from A to Z**	Stephen L. Nelson	Rs. 75.00	193
8170083230	**Front Page 2002 from A to Z**	Heather Williamson	Rs. 85.00	219
8170083249	**Outlook 2002 from A to Z**	Stephen L. Nelson	Rs. 75.00	202
8170083257	**Page Maker 7 from A to Z**	Marc Campbell	Rs. 75.00	202
8170083265	**PowerPoint 2002 from A to Z**	Stephen L. Nelson	Rs. 75.00	202
8170083273	**Windows XP from A to Z**	Pat Coleman	Rs. 95.00	249
8170083281	**Word 2002 from A to Z**	Stephen L. Nelson	Rs. 75.00	199
817008329X	**XML from A to Z**	Heather Williamson	Rs. 75.00	200
8170083303	**Dreamweaver 4 from A to Z**	Heather Williamson	Rs. 85.00	215
	BEGINNERS & GENERAL INTEREST			
817008248X	**Shortcuts to Success in Computing**	Dheeraj Mehrotra	Rs. 55.00	110
8170083311	**Pictorial Computer Dictionary**	Dheeraj Mehrotra	Rs. 45.00	156
8170083486	**Pocket Net Browser**	Dheeraj Mehrotra	Rs. 95.00	302
8170084261	**1000 IT Quizzes**	Dheeraj Mehrotra	Rs. 75.00	120
8131800679	**Information Technology Bible**	Remesh Bangia	Rs. 295.00	567
8131800377	**Fundamentals of Information Technology Including MS Office**	Dinesh Maidasani, Jai Narayan Yadav	Rs. 175.00	356
813180089X	**Fundamentals of Information Technology Including MS Office (Hindi Medium)**	Dinesh Maidasani, Jai Narayan Yadav	Rs. 175.00	425
8170089719	**Foundations of Computer Science**	Ashok Arora	Rs. 250.00	386

Please write for a free color Firewall Media Catalog for details on the above books.

ISBN	TITLE	AUTHOR	PRICE	PAGES
	CALL CENTERS			
8170082196	**Call Centers Made Easy**	Stephen Medcroft	Rs. 195.00	310
	CISCO			
8170087481	**Enabling IP Routing with Cisco Routers**	R. Das, K. Chakrabarty	Rs. 295.00	486
817008749X	**Designing Networks with Cisco**	H. Pasricha, D. Jagu	Rs. 195.00	316
8170087503	**Cisco IP Routing Protocols: Troubleshooting Techniques**	V. Anand, K. Chakrabarty	Rs. 295.00	409
	DATABASES			
8170089530	**DBMS—Complete Practical Approach**	Sharad Maheshwari, Ruchin Jain	Rs. 350.00	656
8170082404	**Learn to Program Visual Basic-Examples**	John Smiley	Rs. 295.00	482
8170082412	**Learn to Program Visual Basic-Databases**	John Smiley	Rs. 325.00	653
8170082420	**Learn to Program Visual Basic-Objects**	John Smiley	Rs. 325.00	670
817008475X	**IT Resources-Access 2002 VBA Programming Access**	Michele Amelot	Rs. 195.00	424
8170084512	**The Power of Oracle 9i**	Rajiv Parida, Vinod Sharma	Rs. 475.00	1035
8170088518	**Principles and Implementation of Data Warehousing**	Rajiv A. Parida	Rs. 295.00	487
817008864X	**DBA Study Guide OCP Prep Guide**	Nazar Abdul	Rs. 295.00	474
8170088658	**Oracle 11i—The Complete Reference**	Rashmi Anandi	Rs. 495.00	975
8131800067	**Toxonomy of Database Management System**	Aditya Kumar Gupta	Rs. 75.00	146
8131800385	**Introduction to SQL and PL/SQL**	Sharad Maheshwari, Ruchin Jain	Rs. 200.00	389
	DOEACC 'O' LEVEL			
8170088089	**DOEACC 'O' Level Model Test Papers**	Ramesh Bangia	Rs. 175.00	296
8170089115	**DOEACC 'O' & 'A' Level Programming & Problem Solving Through 'C' Language (Model Test Paper with Solutions)**	Mukesh Sharma	Rs. 95.00	213
8170089069	**DOEACC 'O' & 'A' Level Business Systems (Model Test Paper with Solutions)**	Mukesh Sharma	Rs. 100.00	252
8170085640	**Programming and Problem Solving Through "C" Language**	Harsha Priya, R. Ranjeet	Rs. 95.00	306

Please write for a free color Firewall Media Catalog for details on the above books.

ISBN	TITLE	AUTHOR	PRICE	PAGES
8170084474	**IT Tools and Applications**	Ramesh Bangia	Rs. 145.00	370
8170085594	**Business Systems**	Ramesh Bangia	Rs. 175.00	452
8170089514	**Internet & Web Design**	Ramesh Bangia	Rs. 150.00	300

ELECTRONIC COMMERCE

8170085497	**Electronic Commerce**	Pete Loshin, John Vacca	Rs. 295.00	472
817008119X	**E-Commerce**	Mamta Bhusry	Rs. 95.00	215
8170083524	**Marketing in the Cyber Age**	Kurt Rohner	Rs. 295.00	223

HARDWARE/EMBEDDED SYSTEMS

8170087473	**Essential Electronics for PC Technicians**	John W. Farber	Rs. 295.00	546
8170086264	**Grid Computing: A Practical Guide to Technology and Applications**	Ahmar Abbas	Rs. 295.00	408
8170088186	**CD Cracking Uncovered Protection Against Unsanctioned CD Copy**	Kris Kaspersky	Rs. 295.00	422
8170083435	**Practical Linux Programming: Device Drivers, Embedded Systems and the Internet**	Ashfaq A. Khan	Rs. 295.00	420
8170083575	**TCP/IP Application Layer Protocols for Embedded Systems**	M. Tim Jones	Rs. 295.00	460
8131800520	**PC Repair and Maintenance : A Practical Guide**	Joel Rosenthal, Kevin Irwin	Rs. 195.00	362
8131800768	**The A+ Certification and PC Repair Handbook**	Christopher A Crayton, Joel Z. Rosenthal	Rs. 495.00	888

INTERNET & WEB TECHNOLOGY

8170083206	**The Internet Handbook for Writers, Students and Teachers**	Mary McGuire, Linda Stilborne	Rs. 195.00	276
8170084776	**Way in-Internet Getting Started**	Elizabeth Bramire	Rs. 95.00	165
8170088976	**Web Technology**	Ramesh Bangia	Rs. 250.00	560
8170087163	**Web Design with Macromedia Studio MX 2004**	Eric Hunley	Rs. 295.00	558
8170083400	**Professional Web Design (Techniques and Templates)**	Clint Eccher	Rs. 295.00	425
8170088046	**HTML, XHTML, CSS and XML**	Teodoru Gugoiu	Rs. 195.00	355
8170083583	**FrontPage 2000 for Visual Learners**	Chris Charuhas	Rs. 95.00	200
8170083591	**HTML & Java Script for Visual Learners**	Chris Charuhas	Rs. 95.00	200

ISBN	TITLE	AUTHOR	PRICE	PAGES
8170083605	**The Visual Learners Guide to Managing Web Projects**	Chris Charuhas	Rs. 95.00	130
8170083613	**Dreamweaver 4 for Visual Learners**	Chris Charuhas	Rs. 95.00	200
8170084768	**IT Resource-Implementing XML: Managing and Formatting Data**	Johhny Brochard	Rs. 125.00	279
8170089476	**Design Your Web World**	Sunil Jalota	Rs. 75.00	146

KEEPING AHEAD SERIES

ISBN	TITLE	AUTHOR	PRICE	PAGES
8170084652	**Keeping Ahead-Exchange 2000 Server**	Philippe Levesque	Rs. 145.00	285
8170084660	**Keeping Ahead-Windows 2000 Professional**	Jose Dardoigne	Rs. 175.00	388
8170084679	**Keeping Ahead-Windows 2000 Server**	Philippe Mathon	Rs. 175.00	360
8170084687	**Keeping Ahead-Linux Administration Kernel Version 2.0 to 2.2**	Bruno Guèrin	Rs. 125.00	240
8170084695	**Keeping Ahead-Using Linux Kernel Version 2.0 to 2.2**	Bruno Guèrin	Rs. 125.00	258
8170084709	**Keeping Ahead-Java 2**	Benjamin Aumaille	Rs. 145.00	284
8170084717	**Keeping Ahead-SQL Server 7**	Joelle Mosset	Rs. 145.00	329
8170084725	**Keeping Ahead-JavaScript and VBScript**	Benjamin Aumaille	Rs. 145.00	313
8170084733	**Keeping Ahead-C++ Programming Language**	Bruno Dubois	Rs. 125.00	234
8170084741	**Keeping Ahead-TCP/IP in the NT Environment**	Bruno Ferec	Rs. 125.00	230

MCSE

ISBN	TITLE	AUTHOR	PRICE	PAGES
817008489X	**MCSE-Administering SQL Server 7.0**	Jerome Gabillaud	Rs. 295.00	580
8170084903	**MCSE-Networking Essentials**	Jose Dordoigne	Rs. 245.00	453
8170084911	**MCSE-Windows 2000 Professional**	Jose Dordoigne	Rs. 325.00	665
817008492X	**MCSE-Windows 2000 Server**	Phillippe Mathon	Rs. 345.00	712

MULTIMEDIA AND ANIMATION

ISBN	TITLE	AUTHOR	PRICE	PAGES
8170088208	**3DS Max 6 Animation with Character Studio 4 and Plug-Ins**	Boris Kulagin, Dmitry Morozov	Rs. 175.00	216

ISBN	TITLE	AUTHOR	PRICE	PAGES
8170088216	**Adobe Audition: Soundtracks for Digital Video**	Roman Petelin, Yury Petelin	Rs. 195.00	278
8170086205	**Building A Digital Human**	Ken Brilliant	Rs. 295.00	380
8170086213	**Making Digital Videos**	Ben Long	Rs. 295.00	284
8170087171	**Illustrating with Macromedia Flash ™ MX2004**	Robert Firbaugh	Rs. 245.00	366
8170082439	**Multimedia Basics-Technology (Vol. I)**	Andreas Holzinger	Rs. 195.00	312
8170082447	**Multimedia Basics-Learning (Vol. II)**	Andreas Holzinger	Rs. 195.00	326
8170082455	**Multimedia Basics-Design (Vol. III)**	Andreas Holzinger	Rs. 195.00	280
8170083532	**Maya Feature Creature Creations**	Todd Palamar	Rs. 295.00	376
8170083540	**Sound Forge Power**	Scott R. Garrigus	Rs. 195.00	344
8131800288	**Multimedia and Web Technology**	Ramesh Bangia	Rs. 395.00	878
813180044X	**Photoshop CS**	Shruti Lal	Rs. 195.00	434

NETWORKING

ISBN	TITLE	AUTHOR	PRICE	PAGES
817008721X	**Networking Essentials**	Jose Dordoigne	Rs. 195.00	453
8170089328	**TCP/IP Distributed System**	Vivek Acharya	Rs. 250.00	474
8170087023	**Computer Networks**	Ajit Kumar Singh	Rs. 95.00	181
8131800148	**The Real—world Network Troubleshooting Manual**	Alan Sugano	Rs. 295.00	396
817008203X	**Telecom & Networking Glossary**	Robert Mastin	Rs. 300.00	250
8170082048	**Data Networking Made Easy**	Karen Patten	Rs. 360.00	350
8170082056	**Digital Convergence**	Andy Covell	Rs. 300.00	234

OFFICE AUTOMATION

ISBN	TITLE	AUTHOR	PRICE	PAGES
8170089891	**Desk Top Publishing**	Dinesh Maidasani	Rs. 150.00	311
8170087805	**Learning Computer Fundamentals, MS Office and Internet & Web Technology**	Dinesh Maidasani	Rs. 95.00	301
8170087686	**MS-Word 2000 Thumb-Rules and Details**	Snigdha Banerjee	Rs. 175.00	390
8170089239	**Computer Accounting with Tally 7.2**	Firewall Media	Rs. 195.00	330

ON YOUR SIDE SERIES

ISBN	TITLE	AUTHOR	PRICE	PAGES
8170084830	**On your Side-Powerpoint 2002**	Andrew Blackburn	Rs. 145.00	282
8170084849	**On your Side-Excel 2002**	Adrienne Tommy	Rs. 125.00	275

Please write for a free color Firewall Media Catalog for details on the above books.

ISBN	TITLE	AUTHOR	PRICE	PAGES
8170084857	**On your Side-Word 2002**	Adrienne Tommy	Rs. 125.00	289
8170084865	**On your Side-Access 2002**	Adrienne Tommy	Rs. 125.00	303
8170084873	**On your Side-Frontpage 2002**	Andrew Blackburn	Rs. 95.00	245
8170084881	**On your Side-Windows XP**	Adrienne Tommy	Rs. 125.00	310

OPERATING SYSTEMS

ISBN	TITLE	AUTHOR	PRICE	PAGES
8170087236	**Linux—A Practical Approach**	B. Mohamed Ibrahim	Rs. 95.00	187
8170088623	**Red Hat Linux Study Guide**	Vijay Shekhar	Rs. 350.00	635
8170088631	**Red Hat Linux-The Complete Bible**	Vijay Shekhar	Rs. 545.00	1176
8170089581	**Unix and Shell Programming**	Archana Verma	Rs. 80.00	137
8170089131	**Operating System Concepts**	P.S. Gill	Rs. 95.00	181
8170083427	**The MS-Windows XP Professional Handbook**	Louis Columbus	Rs. 295.00	330
8170084784	**Way in-Windows XP Home Edition**	Andrew Blackburn	Rs. 95.00	183
8170086221	**Cyber Rookies—Operating System Fundamentals**	D. Irtegov	Rs. 295.00	498

PROGRAMMING

ISBN	TITLE	AUTHOR	PRICE	PAGES
8170087791	**The Art of Programming Through Flowcharts & Algorithms**	Anil Bikas Chaudhuri	Rs. 95.00	160
8170086248	**Preventative Programming Techniques: Avoid and Correct Common Mistakes**	Brian Hawkins	Rs. 295.00	322
8170083443	**Learning Computer Programming : It's not about Languages**	Mary Farrell	Rs. 295.00	375
8170086256	**Object-Oriented Programming: From Problem Solving to Java**	José M. Garrido	Rs. 295.00	360
817008931X	**Object-Oriented Programming-Concept and Implementation**	A. Rajesh	Rs. 95.00	182
8170089107	**Java: J2SE-5 A Practical Approach**	B. Mohammad Ibrahim	Rs. 175.00	332
8170089409	**Advance Java**	Gajendra Gupta	Rs. 175.00	305
8170088038	**Assembly Language Programming for Intel Processors Family**	Vasile Lungu	Rs. 295.00	577
8170088178	**The Assembly Programming Master Book**	Vlad Pirogov	Rs. 395.00	726
813180075X	**Java Messaging**	Eric Bruno	Rs. 295.00	480

ISBN	TITLE	AUTHOR	PRICE	PAGES
	PROGRAMMING - C#, C, C++			
8170083702	**The Power of C#**	Rajiv Parida	Rs. 295.00	576
8170085632	**Mastering Graphics Programming in 'C'**	Sudhir Dawra	Rs. 145.00	286
8170088879	**Programming in C and Numerical Analysis**	J.B. Dixit	Rs. 350.00	355
8170087074	**Mastering C Programs**	J.B. Dixit	Rs. 195.00	434
8170081262	**Programming in C**	J.B. Dixit	Rs. 295.00	506
8170087619	**Unix and C Programming**	Ashok Arora, Shefali Bansal	Rs. 295.00	606
817008878X	**C Interview Questions and Answers**	J. Rajaram	Rs. 75.00	139
8170089034	**Pragmatic C**	R.K. Jangda	Rs. 150.00	258
8170086140	**Data Structure for 'C' Programming**	Ajay Kumar	Rs. 145.00	290
8170081270	**Programming in C++**	J.B. Dixit	Rs. 260.00	602
8170088194	**Hackish C++ Pranks & Tricks**	Michael Flenov	Rs. 245.00	326
8170082889	**Basics of C++ Programming**	Nishant Kundalia	Rs. 95.00	168
8170083648	**Mastering C++ Programs**	J.B. Dixit	Rs. 295.00	598
817008623X	**Cyber Rookies—C++ Programming Fundamentals**	Chuck Easttom	Rs. 295.00	417
8131800202	**Data Structure using C++**	N. Jayalakshmi	Rs. 65.00	126
8170089123	**C++ Made Easy**	T.D. Malhotra	Rs. 250.00	449
8131800393	**C++ & Introduction to C#**	T.D. Malhotra, Rajeev A. Parida, A. Rajesh	Rs. 200.00	440
8131800350	**OOPS with C++**	M. Jaya Prasad	Rs. 150.00	317
	SECURITY			
8170083419	**Computer Forensics : Computer Crime Scene Investigation**	John Vacca	Rs. 445.00	731
8131800156	**Computer Evidence (Collection and Preservation)**	Christopher L.T. Brown	Rs. 295.00	394
8170083494	**Firewall Architecture for the Enterprise**	Norbert Fohlmann, Tim Crothers	Rs. 295.00	480
8170086272	**Net Spies**	Andrew Gauntlett	Rs. 195.00	210
3826607546	**Firewall Systems**	Norbert Pohlmann	Rs. 1630.00	544
8131800504	**Homeland Security Techniques and Technologies**	Jesus Mena	Rs. 295.00	346

ISBN	TITLE	AUTHOR	PRICE	PAGES

ENGINEERING AND TECHNOLOGY

ISBN	TITLE	AUTHOR	PRICE	PAGES
817008718X	**Human Aspects of Software Engineering**	James E. Tomayko, Orit Hazzan	Rs. 195.00	338
8131800032	**Management Information Systems**	Avdhesh Gupta, Anurag Malik	Rs. 195.00	400
8170087953	**Human Computer Interaction**	Rajendra Ranjan Kumar	Rs. 95.00	210
8170088097	**Structured System Analysis and Design**	Preeti Gupta	Rs. 125.00	192
817008802X	**Autocad 2005 for Engineers**	Ionel Simion	Rs. 175.00	271
8170088054	**Digital Signal Processing Fundamentals**	Ashfaq A. Khan	Rs. 295.00	391
8131800164	**Digital Communication System Using System VUE**	Dennis Silage	Rs. 295.00	365
8170089719	**Foundations of Computer Science**	Ashok Arora	Rs. 250.00	386
817008363X	**Practical Project Management**	Ivan Bayross	Rs. 195.00	342
8131800806	**Digital Signal Processing using MATLAB and Wavelets**	Michael Weeks	Rs. 350.00	452
8131800792	**Classical Electrodynamics**	Hans C. Dhanian	Rs. 395.00	620
8131800512	**The Software Vulnerability Guide**	Herbert H. Thompson, Scott G. Chase	Rs. 195.00	368
8131800776	**Robot Modelling and Kinematics**	Rachid Manseur	Rs. 295.00	380
8131800369	**System Software**	M. Joseph	Rs. 95.00	185

STRAIGHT TO THE POINT SERIES

ISBN	TITLE	AUTHOR	PRICE	PAGES
8170084601	**STTP : Word 2002**	Corinne Hervo	Rs. 45.00	154
817008461X	**STTP : Excel 2002**	Corinne Hervo	Rs. 45.00	153
8170084628	**STTP : Dreamweaver 4**	Corinne Hervo	Rs. 45.00	135
8170084636	**STTP : Flash 5**	Corinne Hervo	Rs. 45.00	183
8170084644	**STTP : Photoshop 6**	Corinne Hervo	Rs. 45.00	152
817008881X	**STTP : MS Office 2000**	Dinesh Maidasani	Rs. 125.00	290
8170086100	**STTP : MS Office 2003**	Dinesh Maidasani	Rs. 145.00	288
8170087651	**STTP : MS Word 2003**	Firewall Media	Rs. 60.00	150
8170088011	**STTP : Photoshop CS**	Firewall Media	Rs. 60.00	150
8170088143	**STTP : MS Excel 2003**	Firewall Media	Rs. 60.00	150
8170088151	**STTP : CorelDraw 12**	Firewall Media	Rs. 60.00	150
8131800105	**STTP : 3ds MAX 7**	Dinesh Maidasani	Rs. 95.00	182
8131800083	**STTP : Auto CAD 2006**	Dinesh Maidasani	Rs. 95.00	190
8131800245	**STTP : CorelDraw X3**	Dinesh Maidasani	Rs. 75.00	188

Please write for a free color Firewall Media Catalog for details on the above books.

ISBN	TITLE	AUTHOR	PRICE	PAGES
8131800253	**STTP : Dreamweaver 8**	Dinesh Maidasani	Rs. 75.00	148
8131800237	**STTP : Photoshop CS2**	Dinesh Maidasani	Rs. 75.00	172
8170088380	**STTP : Tally 7.2**	Firewall Media	Rs. 175.00	322
8131800091	**STTP : Flash 8**	Dinesh Maidasani	Rs. 95.00	180
8131800407	**STTP : My SQL 5.0**	Dinesh Maidasani	Rs. 85.00	166
8131800458	**STTP : Microsoft Power Point 2003**	Dinesh Maidasani	Rs. 75.00	142

STUDIO FACTORY

8170084792	**Studio Factory—Photoshop 6**	Christophe Aubry	Rs. 175.00	364
8170084806	**Studio Factory—Flash 5**	Sami Ben Yahiya	Rs. 145.00	314
8170084814	**Studio Factory—Dreamweaver Ultradev 4**	Phillippe Chatellier	Rs. 95.00	240
8170084822	**Studio Factory—Dreamweaver 4**	Christophe Aubry	Rs. 175.00	373
8170087643	**Studio Factory—Dreamweaver MX**	Christophe Aubry	Rs. 195.00	407
8170087627	**Studio Factory—Flash MX**	Arnaud Blanche	Rs. 145.00	337
817008766X	**Studio Factory—Photoshop 7**	Cyril Guerin	Rs. 195.00	420

LAXMI PUBLICATIONS (P) LTD

113, Golden House, Daryaganj, New Delhi-110002

Phone : **011 - 43 53 25 00**

Fax : **011 - 43 53 25 28**

EMAIL : info@laxmipublications.com

Website : www.laxmipublications.com

BRANCHES

- 129/1, IIIrd Main Road, IX Cross, Chamrajpet, **Bangalore** (*Phone* : 080-26 61 15 61)
- 26, Damodaran Street, T. Nagar, **Chennai** (*Phone* : 044-24 34 47 26)
- 43/1394D, St. Benedict's Road, Ernakulam North, **Cochin** (*Phone* : 0484-239 70 04)
- Pan Bazar, Rani Bari, **Guwahati** (*Phones* : 0361-254 36 69, 251 38 81)
- 4-2-453, Ist Floor, Ramkote, **Hyderabad** (*Phone* : 040-24 75 02 47)
- Adda Tanda Chowk, N.D. 365, **Jalandhar City** (*Phone* : 0181-222 12 72)
- 106/A, Ist Floor, S.N. Banerjee Road, **Kolkata** (*Phones* : 033-22 27 37 73, 22 27 52 47)
- 18, Madan Mohan Malviya Marg, **Lucknow** (*Phone* : 0522-220 95 78)
- 142-C, Victor House, Ground Floor, N.M. Joshi Marg, Lower Parel (W), **Mumbai** (*Phones* : 022-24 91 54 15, 24 92 78 69)
- Radha Govind Street, Tharpagna, **Ranchi** (*Phone* : 0651-230 77 64)